T0094066

Absolute Beginners Guide to Computing

Wallace Wang

Apress®

Absolute Beginners Guide to Computing

Wallace Wang
San Diego, California
USA

ISBN-13 (pbk): 978-1-4842-2288-1
DOI 10.1007/978-1-4842-2289-8

ISBN-13 (electronic): 978-1-4842-2289-8

Library of Congress Control Number: 2016960208

Managing Director: Welmoed Spahr
Acquisitions Editor: Louise Corrigan
Technical Reviewer: Fabio Ferracchiati
Editorial Board: Steve Anglin, Pramila Balan, Laura Berendson, Aaron Black, Louise Corrigan, Jonathan Gennick, Todd Green, Robert Hutchinson, Celestin Suresh John, Nikhil Karkal, James Markham, Susan McDermott, Matthew Moodie, Natalie Pao, Gwenan Spearing
Coordinating Editor: Nancy Chen
Copy Editor: Mary Bearden
Compositor: SPi Global
Indexer: SPi Global
Artist: SPi Global, Image courtesy of Freepik

Distributed to the book trade worldwide by Springer Science+Business Media New York, 233 Spring Street, 6th Floor, New York, NY 10013. Phone 1-800-SPRINGER, fax (201) 348-4505, e-mail orders-ny@springer-sbm.com, or visit www.springer.com. Apress Media, LLC is a California LLC and the sole member (owner) is Springer Science + Business Media Finance Inc (SSBM Finance Inc). SSBM Finance Inc is a Delaware corporation.

For information on translations, please e-mail rights@apress.com, or visit www.apress.com.

Apress and friends of ED books may be purchased in bulk for academic, corporate, or promotional use. eBook versions and licenses are also available for most titles. For more information, reference our Special Bulk Sales–eBook Licensing web page at www.apress.com/bulk-sales.

Any source code or other supplementary materials referenced by the author in this text are available to readers at www.apress.com. For detailed information about how to locate your book's source code, go to www.apress.com/source-code/. Readers can also access source code at SpringerLink in the Supplementary Material section for each chapter.

Printed on acid-free paper

This is book is dedicated to everyone who has suffered through the complexity, confusion, and chaos of trying to use a computer. The problem is rarely due to the user not knowing how to use a computer. The problem most often lies with the horrible, confusing, and unnecessarily complicated way most computers have been designed. So this book is dedicated to everyone who has longed for a better way to learn how to use and actually enjoy their computer. Welcome to the future where computers actually work to make the lives of people easier and more enjoyable.

Contents at a Glance

Contents

About the Author

Wallace Wang has written dozens of computer books over the years beginning with ancient MS-DOS programs like WordPerfect and Turbo Pascal, and graduating up to writing books on Windows programs like Visual Basic and Microsoft Office.

When he's not helping people discover the joys of personal computing with a computer that's actually fun to use, he performs stand-up comedy and appears on two radio shows on KNSJ in San Diego (http://knsj.org) called "Notes From the Underground" and "Laugh In Your Face Radio" (http://www.laughinyourfaceradio.com).

He also writes a screenwriting blog called "The 15 Minute Movie Method" (http://15minutemoviemethod.com), a blog about the latest cat news on the Internet called "Cat Daily News" (*http://catdailynews.com*), and a blog about the latest trends in technology called "Top Bananas" (http://www.topbananas.com).

About the Technical Reviewer

Fabio Claudio Ferracchiati is a senior consultant and a senior analyst/developer using Microsoft technologies. He works at BluArancio S.p.A (www.bluarancio.com) as Senior Analyst/Developer and Microsoft Dynamics CRM Specialist. He is a Microsoft Certified Solution Developer for .NET, a Microsoft Certified Application Developer for .NET, a Microsoft Certified Professional, and a prolific author and technical reviewer. Over the past ten years, he's written articles for Italian and international magazines and co-authored more than ten books on a variety of computer topics.

Acknowledgments

Thanks go to all the wonderful people at Apress for giving me a chance to write about the wonderfully bizarre, yet fascinating world of personal computing.

Additional thanks go to Dane Henderson and Elizabeth Lee (`www.echoludo.com`), who share the airwaves with me on our radio show called "Notes From the Underground" on KNSJ.org. More thanks go to Chris Clobber, Diane Jean, and Ikaika Patria for letting me share their friendship and lunacy every week on another KNSJ radio show called "Laugh In Your Face Radio" (`http://www.laughinyourfaceradio.com`) where we combine comedy with political activism and commentary.

A special mention goes to Michael Montijo and his indomitable spirit that has him driving from Phoenix to Los Angeles at least once a month for the past 15 years to meet with Hollywood executives. One day when you hear about his cartoon series "Life of Mikey" and "Pachuko Boy," you'll know how they finally appeared on television because he never gave up on his dream despite all the obstacles in his way.

Thanks also go to my wife, Cassandra, and my son, Jordan, for putting up with a house filled with more gadgets than actual living people. Final thanks go to my cats, Oscar and Mayer, for walking over the keyboard, stepping on the trackpad and mouse, and chewing on power cords at the most inconvenient times of the day.

Introduction

Most people don't buy a computer because they want to learn how to decipher file name extensions or understand how the hierarchy of folders works on a hard drive. Instead, most people buy a computer because they want to accomplish a specific task that's important to their own lives such as saving and viewing photographs, playing music, or typing and printing a letter. That's why thick books explaining how to use the Windows 10 operating system can be so intimidating. These thick books assume readers want to become computer experts by learning how Windows 10 works.

That's why far too many computer books exhaustively explain every possible feature of Windows 10 without telling you why you might want to use that particular feature. That's like forcing you to learn how a six-cylinder internal combustion engine works before you can learn how to drive to the supermarket.

This book is different because it teaches you the most common tasks you'll need to be productive on a computer. You won't learn every possible feature of Windows 10. Instead, you'll just learn enough so you can feel comfortable using your computer.

A computer is nothing more than a tool. What you do with that tool is entirely up to you.

A paintbrush is also a tool, but if you give a paintbrush to the average person, they might be able to scribble some blobs of pretty colors on a canvas. Yet if you give a paintbrush to an artist like Michelangelo, you'll get a work of art painted on the ceiling of the Sistine Chapel.

So this book won't waste your time teaching you what different tools can do. Instead, this book focuses on teaching you how to use different tools so you can create useful results on your computer.

Whether you need to write a letter, jot down some notes, edit a picture, or play music, this book will show you the fastest, simplest, and easiest way to achieve a given task so your computer gets the job done.

Understanding How Windows 10 Works

Whether you have a PC that sits on a desk or a laptop that you can take with you, every computer is nothing more than a chunk of hardware. What makes that chunk of hardware work is a special program called an operating system.

Windows 10 is the operating system that controls a PC. Don't worry. You don't have to become an expert on Windows 10 to use a computer. All you need to know is how to find and use the right program to accomplish a specific task such as:

- Play music

- Write letters

- Edit video

- Browse web pages on the Internet

- Send and receive e-mail

- And many other tasks

While Windows 10 makes a PC work, individual programs stored on your PC let you perform specific tasks. For example, your PC might have a word processor so you can type and print letters, an e-book viewer so you can read e-books, and a game program so you can play Solitaire.

Each time you install a new program, you make your PC more versatile and capable of performing different tasks. With the right program, your PC can do almost anything. However, this book focuses solely on using the various features of Windows 10.

So whether you've used a computer before or you're a complete novice to computers, don't worry. This book won't bog you down with technical details. Instead, you'll learn what to do, how to do it, and more importantly, why to do it.

When you want to work or play, you want to find the quickest way to get what you want without the nuisance of technical jargon or complicated procedures getting in your way. So get ready to learn shortcuts, tips, and basic instructions for getting the most out of your PC today.

What to Expect From This Book

Don't expect to learn every possible feature available about Windows 10. Also don't expect dense explanations that show how to do something without telling you why you might want to do it in the first place.

What you can expect from this book is a chance to learn how to use Windows 10 on your PC as quickly, easily, and painlessly as possible.

This book won't have all the answers to using Windows 10, but it will have lots of tips and tricks for helping you work faster and more efficiently than ever before.

Once you learn just enough to get started, you'll feel more comfortable until you'll be able to figure out how to use your PC all by yourself. Fair enough? If so, then turn the page and let's get started.

PART I

Basic Training

One of the biggest problems with learning anything new is knowing where to get started. In this part of the book, you'll learn the most common commands for using Windows 10 no matter what program you might need to use.

You'll learn how to give commands using a mouse, trackpad, and keyboard, how to start and stop programs, how to write and edit text, and how to save your data in files that you can organize in different ways.

By the time you've read this part of the book, you should feel confident that you can use your computer all by yourself.

CHAPTER 1

■ ■ ■

Understanding Computers

Most computers tend to work in similar ways. A monitor displays information, a processor calculates new results, and input devices such as a keyboard, mouse, or trackpad (sometimes called the touchpad) allow someone to control the computer.

The monitor can show useful information such as stock quotes or news stories displayed on a web page.

The keyboard, mouse, or trackpad lets you control the computer by typing text or manipulating items on the screen, such as editing a photograph or choosing commands.

Once you give commands to the computer, the processor calculates a new result and displays those changed results on the screen.

Using a computer is essentially a back-and-forth conversation where the computer shows information on the monitor and then waits for you to do something about it. You can use the keyboard, mouse, or trackpad to manipulate data on the screen, such as editing text, viewing a different web page, or modifying a picture. Once you've given a command to the computer, it changes the data on the screen and shows the results so you can do something else.

The software is what makes every computer do something useful. By installing different programs, you can literally make the computer do practically anything you want.

Some people use a computer to write letters, play games, draw cartoons, plot stock market prices, or edit movies. Software turns your computer into a versatile tool customized for your particular needs.

However, the most important software every computer needs is called an operating system because it literally controls how the entire computer works. On a PC, the most recent operating system is called Windows 10.

Windows 10 controls the physical parts of a PC such as sending data to a printer or accepting characters typed from the keyboard. To use a PC, you need to learn the basics for using Windows 10.

Don't worry. You don't need to learn every possible technical detail about Windows 10. All you really need to know are the basics for using Windows 10 so you can do something useful with your computer.

■ **Note**   The whole purpose of an operating system is to act as an intermediary between the hardware of a computer and a program such as a word processor or game. Programs don't communicate directly with hardware so they communicate with the operating system, which takes care of making the hardware work. Every computer needs an operating system. PCs use Microsoft Windows or Linux, a Macintosh uses macOS, an iPhone uses iOS, and most other smartphones and tablets use Android. That's why when you buy software, it can only run on a specific operating system.

© Wallace Wang 2016
W. Wang, *Absolute Beginners Guide to Computing*, DOI 10.1007/978-1-4842-2289-8_1

Why Computers Are So Difficult to Understand

In the early days of computers, you had to be a computer expert just to turn on a computer, let alone use it. Fortunately, computers have gotten much easier to use, but in case you still feel computers are too hard to use, the reason is because computer programmers and engineers created and designed computers for themselves.

Think about how every field has its own jargon and way of thinking. Accountants know the meaning of terms like balance sheets, cash flow, and equity, while plumbers can easily understand terms like auger, closet bend, and dip tube. If you're not an accountant, you won't understand common accounting terms. Likewise, if you're not a plumber, you won't understand common plumbing terms.

If you're not a computer expert, you won't understand common computer terms, and that's why computers have always seemed so confusing and difficult to use. Most computer manuals are written by programmers for other programmers, using terms that they already understand. If you don't understand common computer terms, you probably won't understand most computer manuals, help files, or other types of documentation that are supposed to help you but often tend to confuse and frustrate you even more.

Even worse, programmers already know how to use a computer, so they readily skip over steps, assume too much, and gloss over explanations. The actual steps for using a computer are often based on earlier, more primitive ways of using a computer. If you aren't familiar with these, you probably won't completely understand why today's computers work the way they do.

For example, the first IBM PC came with a keyboard that combined a numeric keypad with cursor keys, as shown in Figure 1-1. If you wanted to use the numeric keypad, you had to press a special Num Lock key. If you wanted to move the cursor on the screen, you had to press the Num Lock key a second time to turn off the numeric keypad so you could use the cursor keys.

Figure 1-1. *The keyboard of the original IBM PC combined cursor keys with a numeric keypad*

How could you tell if the Num Lock key was on or off on the original IBM PC keyboard? You couldn't. You had to press a key on the numeric keypad and if it typed a number, then you knew the Num Lock key was turned on. If it moved the cursor, then you knew the Num Lock key was turned off.

IBM later redesigned the keyboard to offer separate cursor keys and numeric keys. Inexplicably, the separate numeric keypad still retained the Num Lock key so it could double up as a cursor keypad. This meant you now had one dedicated cursor keypad and a second cursor/numeric keypad, as shown in Figure 1-2.

Figure 1-2. *IBM modified the keyboard to include a separate cursor keypad along with a second cursor/ numeric keypad*

Why would anyone ever turn off the Num Lock key so they could have two separate cursor keypads? They wouldn't, yet you can still see this horrible design in many PC keyboards even today.

Computer manufacturers often retain old features out of inertia and familiarity. Rather than question why certain features exist and eliminate outdated ones, computer people tend to keep old features and pile on new ones to create a confusing mess that only they can understand.

Just as computer people have retained obsolete hardware designs, so too have they retained obsolete software designs.

In the old days, people used floppy disks, which were circular disks coated with magnetic material. These early floppy disks were 8 inches in size but later shrank down to 5.25 inches and eventually to 3.5 inches in size, as shown in Figure 1-3. They were called floppy disks because they were plastic disks that would flop up and down if they weren't enclosed in a protective plastic case.

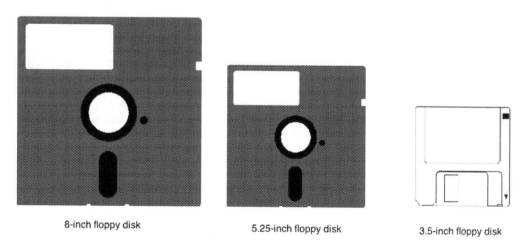

8-inch floppy disk   5.25-inch floppy disk   3.5-inch floppy disk

Figure 1-3. *Early computers stored data on 8-, 5.25-, and 3.5-inch floppy disks*

A 3.5-inch floppy disk could only hold a maximum of 1.44 megabytes of data. Today, a single audio file of a popular song takes up more than 3 megabytes. Since floppy disks weren't able to store today's larger files, they quickly fell out of popularity. That's why you never see floppy disk drives on any modern computer today.

Yet if you look at the user interface of many programs such as Microsoft WordPad, you can still see that Microsoft uses a floppy disk icon to represent the Save command, as shown in Figure 1-4.

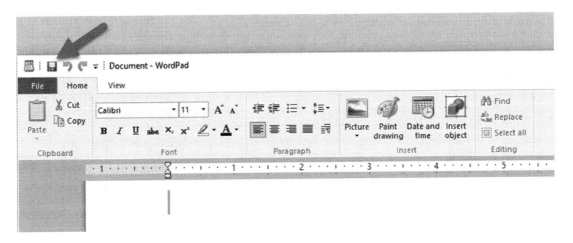

Figure 1-4. Microsoft WordPad uses a floppy disk icon to represent the Save command

Even though people haven't used a floppy disk in over a decade and many newer computer users have never seen a floppy disk in their life, Microsoft and many other companies still use the floppy disk icon to represent the Save command.

None of this makes sense unless you understand the historical origins. Even when you do understand the historical origins, it still doesn't make any sense to cling to antiquated features and icons that no longer have any meaning today.

Another curious relic from the past involves naming disk drives. When computers first appeared, they had only one floppy disk drive that was called the A: drive. To make it easy to copy files from one floppy disk to another, newer computers offered two floppy disk drives where the second floppy disk drive was called the B: drive.

When hard disks became popular, they were called the C: drive. Soon computers started dropping the second floppy disk drive (the B: drive) so computers only had an A: drive (a floppy disk drive) and a C: drive (the hard disk). Eventually people stopped using floppy disks altogether so computers eliminated all floppy disk drives. That left the hard drive, which is still referred to as the C: drive.

Once you understand that computers once had two floppy disk drives labeled the A: drive and B: drive, you can understand why the hard drive had to be called the C: drive. Without this knowledge, you may wonder why the hard drive is called the C: drive and no other drives are called the A: or B: drive.

Despite the fact that many computer users have never seen a floppy disk or floppy disk drive, the File Explorer program on Windows 10 still refers to the hard disk as the C: drive, as shown in Figure 1-5.

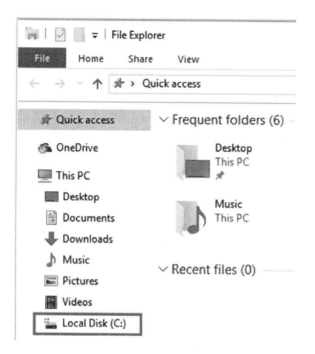

Figure 1-5. *The Windows File Explorer program still identifies the hard disk of every computer as the C: drive*

Labeling the hard drive as the C: drive no longer makes sense, yet computers continue using letter designations to identify different drives such as the CD/DVD drive, external hard disks, or USB flash drives connected to a computer.

Computers are so hard to understand because they force people to decipher obsolete ideas based on the past that few people know about any more.

The next time you have trouble using a computer, don't blame yourself. Chances are good you're simply being confused by antiquated and obsolete ideas that are no longer necessary but still exist.

Computers Are Designed for Experts, Not Beginners

Programmers create and design computers, so to better understand how any computer works, you need to understand how programmers think. Programmers tend to create multiple ways to perform the exact same command because they like having different ways to do the exact same task.

For example, to save a file in almost any program, you typically have three ways to choose the exact same Save command:

- Click the File menu and choose Save

- Click the Save icon

- Press Control + S (abbreviated as Ctrl+S)

Why do computers offer so many ways to perform the exact same command? It's because programmers like shortcuts. Clicking the File menu and choosing Save takes two steps, but clicking the Save icon only takes one and pressing Ctrl+S can be even faster.

The drawback of so many options is that they tend to confuse beginners. Car manufacturers never give you three different ways to signal a left turn because that would just confuse drivers. Instead, car manufacturers give you one simple way to signal a left turn. Once you learn this one, simple way, you never again have to relearn anything different or new to signal left turns.

Rather than simplifying computers, multiple options get in the way by making computers harder to use. Computer novices just want to learn one way to perform a task. Only computer experts care about using multiple shortcuts to perform the same task, so ultimately computers are designed to satisfy experts, not beginners.

Keep in mind that whenever you learn anything for the first time, you'll always feel clumsy and awkward. With a little practice, you'll become more proficient until one day you'll find yourself performing tasks without thinking.

Using a computer is a skill that anyone can learn and develop. The more you use Windows 10, the more comfortable you'll get with it. The more comfortable you get, the more adventurous you'll get and start exploring on your own.

Best of all, once you run into problems and learn how to fix them yourself, your confidence level will start increasing until one day you won't have any problems at all using Windows 10.

Understanding the Windows 10 Desktop

Windows 10 is an operating system that acts as an interpreter between you and your computer. First, Windows 10 gets data from the computer and displays this information on the screen. If you select a command to manipulate the data on the screen, Windows 10 obeys and displays new information on the screen. Based on this new information, you can choose more commands.

When Windows 10 displays information on the screen and shows a list of commands you can choose from, that's called a user interface. The main Windows 10 user interface is called the Desktop, which consists of three parts, as shown in Figure 1-6:

- *Start menu*: Displays menus and tiles on the left side of the screen

- *Desktop*: Displays an image to fill the screen

- *Taskbar*: Displays icons at the bottom of the screen

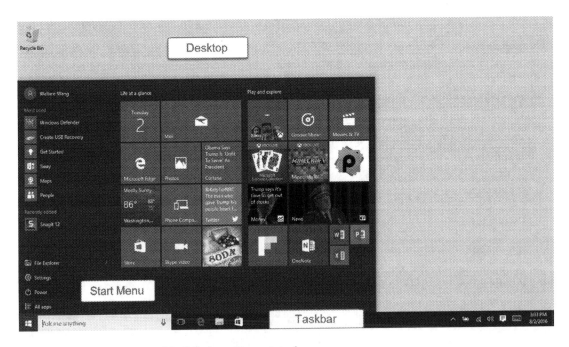

Figure 1-6. *The three parts of the Windows 10 user interface*

The Start menu lets you access all the programs installed on your computer. You can open the Start menu in one of two ways:

- Click the Windows icon in the lower left corner of the screen (it looks like four squares tilted at an angle)

- Press the Windows icon on your keyboard (it looks like four squares tilted at an angle)

Once the Start menu appears, you can click the program or feature you want to use. To make the Start menu go away, you have three options:

- Click the Windows icon in the lower left corner of the screen (it looks like four squares tilted at an angle)

- Press the Windows icon on your keyboard (it looks like four squares tilted at an angle)

- Press the ESC key in the upper left corner of your keyboard

The Desktop fills the screen and can display any image you like to customize the appearance of your screen. The Desktop is also a place to store icons that represent data or programs. By putting icons on the Desktop, you can find them easily. When you open a program, it will open and display one or more windows that appear on the Desktop as well.

At the bottom of the screen is the Taskbar, which displays icons that represent your currently running programs such as a word processor or browser, or icons that represent functions of your computer such as volume control or battery life.

Every time you use your computer, you'll see the Start menu icon and the Taskbar at the bottom of the screen and the Desktop filling the rest of the screen.

Using a Keyboard

By itself, the Desktop does nothing but display information on the screen and wait for you to choose a command. To choose a command, you have to use the keyboard and a mouse or trackpad.

The keyboard contains letters, numbers, and symbols (such as $, &, @, and #) that you can type. Besides these character keys, keyboards also contain additional sets of keys, as shown in Figure 1-7:

- Function keys at the top of the keyboard.

- Cursor keys.

- Modifier keys.

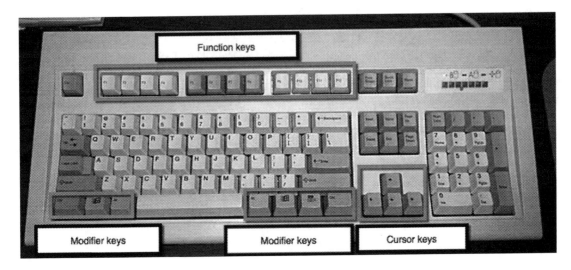

Figure 1-7. *The different types of keys on a keyboard*

Function keys are another throwback to earlier computers. In the old days, many programs allowed you to give a command by pressing a function key. Pressing the F1 function key might display help while pressing F10 might print data.

Nowadays, hardly any programs let you give commands by pressing a function key. That's why most computers now assign hardware controls to the function keys such as screen brightness, rewind/fast forward, volume control, and mute.

■ **Note**   In the rare event that you need a function key, you'll need to hold down the Fn key (normally located in the bottom left corner of the keyboard) and then press a function key. The Fn key tells your computer to ignore any hardware controls assigned to a function key.

Why do function keys still exist even though most programs completely ignore them? It's because function keys can be used to create custom shortcuts as well as maintain compatibility with the handful of older programs that may still use function keys.

In general, most people will never use function keys but they exist for more advanced users. Because most people aren't advanced users, function keys simply clutter up the keyboard and add to the confusion of using a computer.

The cursor keys consist of four arrows, one each pointing up, down, left, and right. Cursor keys are most often used when typing and editing text. The cursor appears on the screen as a vertical line that blinks on and off to make it easy to find on the screen.

Whenever you type any characters on the keyboard, they'll appear wherever the cursor currently appears, as shown in Figure 1-8.

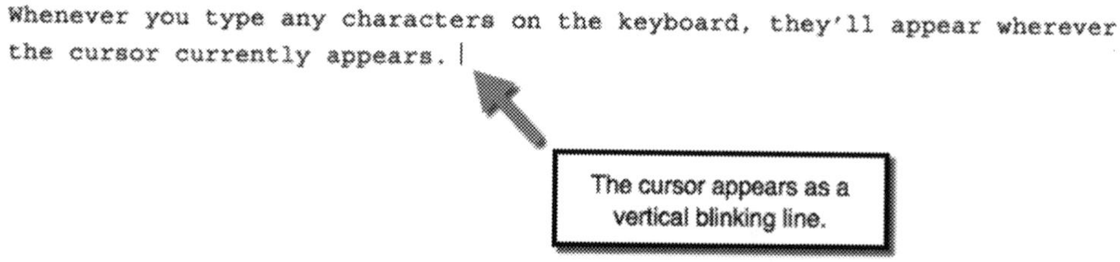

```
Whenever you type any characters on the keyboard, they'll appear wherever
the cursor currently appears. |
```

The cursor appears as a
vertical blinking line.

Figure 1-8. *The cursor lets you point where you want to edit text*

Modifier keys allow you to use ordinary keys in different ways. The most obvious modifier key is the Shift key. Holding down the Shift key while pressing a letter key creates an uppercase letter. Holding down the Shift key while pressing a number key on the top row creates a symbol, such as $ or #.

Three other modifier keys include Control, Windows, and Alt. Like the Shift key, the Control, Windows, and Alt keys work with other keys, such as Ctrl+A or Alt+F7.

Modifier keys change the behavior of other keys. In most programs, you can hold down the Control key, tap the S key, and let go of both to choose the Save command, which is often abbreviated as Ctrl+S.

You can also use two modifier keys along with a third key to choose a command such as holding down the Control key, holding down the Shift key, and tapping the N key, which is abbreviated as Ctrl+Shift+N.

Modifier keys let you choose commands through the keyboard. For typing different characters, the most commonly used modifier key is the Shift key. The Control key is most often used to run common commands such as the Save command (Ctrl+S) or the Print command (Ctrl+P). The Alt key is less commonly used.

Using a Mouse or Trackpad

Back in the early days of computers, all you could create on a computer was text, so a keyboard worked just fine. To give commands to a computer, engineers had to modify the standard keyboard with function keys, modifier keys, and cursor keys.

When Microsoft introduced Windows, people could create and edit graphics as well as text. How can you edit and manipulate graphics using a keyboard? You can't.

That's why PCs use a mouse so you can point on the screen. The screen always displays a pointer that lets you point and click on commands or manipulate objects. By moving the mouse, you can move the pointer on the screen.

A trackpad works as an alternative to a mouse. A trackpad lets you move the pointer on the screen by sliding your finger across the surface of the trackpad.

Laptops use a trackpad to save space while desktop computers typically use a mouse. However, you can always add a trackpad to a desktop computer or a mouse to a laptop. Some people prefer a mouse, others prefer a trackpad, and some people even use both.

On a mouse, you'll often have three types of controls, as shown in Figure 1-9:

- A left button

- A scroll wheel in the middle of the mouse

- A right button

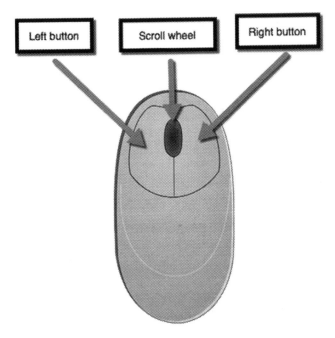

Figure 1-9. *The left button, scroll wheel, and right button on a typical mouse*

Pressing the left button on a mouse once and letting go is known as a click or left-click. Most of the time when you use a mouse, you'll use the left mouse button.

Pressing the right button is known as a right-click. This often displays a menu of options that pops up wherever the pointer happens to be, as shown in Figure 1-10.

Figure 1-10. *Right-clicking often displays a pop-up menu of commands*

Since right-clicking is a shortcut, it's possible to use a computer and never press the right button.

The scroll wheel (which may not be available on all computer mice) offers another shortcut for scrolling through long documents on the screen, such as in a word processor or web browser. By rolling the scroll wheel up or down, you can scroll information on the screen up or down rather than using the vertical scroll bars on the right side of a window or constantly pressing the Page Down or Page Up keys.

In addition, some programs also recognize when you press down on the scroll wheel, allowing it to act like a third mouse button. Pressing the scroll wheel like a button acts as a shortcut in certain programs that support this feature.

Because a trackpad works just like a mouse, trackpads also offer a left and a right button, which work exactly like the left and right buttons on a mouse.

As a shortcut, many trackpads let you press one fingertip down anywhere on the surface of the trackpad to perform a left-click command. If you press two fingertips down on the trackpad surface, you can perform a right-click command.

On many trackpads, sliding two fingers up or down on the trackpad surface scrolls information up or down on the screen like the scroll wheel of a mouse. Essentially anything you can do with a mouse you can do with a trackpad and vice versa.

To help you learn how to point and click using a mouse or trackpad, try the following exercise:

1. Turn on your PC by pressing its On button.

2. Move the pointer over the Windows Start menu icon (the four squares icon tilted at an angle in the bottom left corner of the screen) and press the left button to click. The Start menu appears (see Figure 1-6).

3. Point to and click Settings. The Settings window appears, as shown in Figure 1-11.

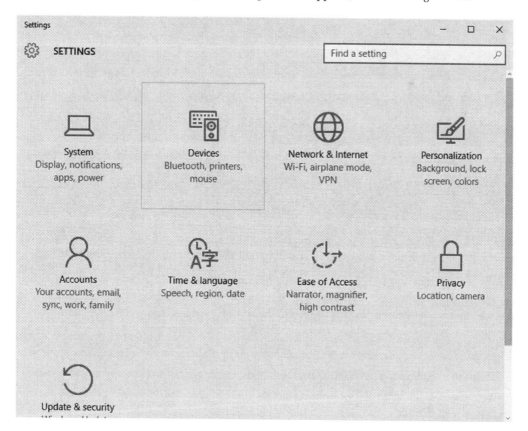

Figure 1-11. *The Settings window*

4. Point to and click the Devices icon. A Devices window appears.

5. Point to and click the Mouse & touchpad option in the left pane to display settings you can modify for your mouse or trackpad, as shown in Figure 1-12.

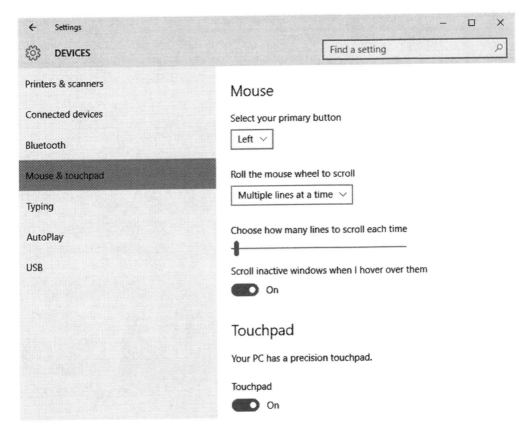

Figure 1-12. The Mouse & touchpad options let you modify how your mouse or touchpad behaves

6. Point and click the big X icon in the upper right corner of the Settings window. This big X icon represents the Close window command.

Congratulations! By using the mouse or trackpad in the above exercise, you've learned where to find settings so you can customize your mouse or trackpad.

You also learned how to use the Start menu icon in the bottom left corner of the screen and how to close an open window on the screen.

To use Windows 10, you must learn how to point and click using a mouse/trackpad. Pointing and clicking (often just referred to as just clicking) is a crucial part in using Windows 10.

▓ **Note**   Be careful when pointing and clicking. If the pointer is slightly off, clicking can display completely different options than you might expect. This huge, commonly made mistake can make Windows 10 seem unpredictable and difficult to use.

After you point at any item, be especially careful when clicking. There's a huge difference between clicking the left mouse button once, double-clicking (clicking the left mouse button twice in rapid succession), and right-clicking (clicking the right mouse button once).

To see the difference between left- and right-clicking, try the following exercise:

1. Move the pointer over the Windows Start menu icon (four squares tilted at an angle).

2. Press the left mouse button to click. The Start menu appears (see Figure 1-6).

3. Press the ESC key to make the Start menu disappear. Make sure the pointer still appears over the Windows Start menu icon in the lower left corner of the screen.

4. Now right-click. Notice that instead of the Start menu appearing, an entirely different menu appears, as shown in Figure 1-13.

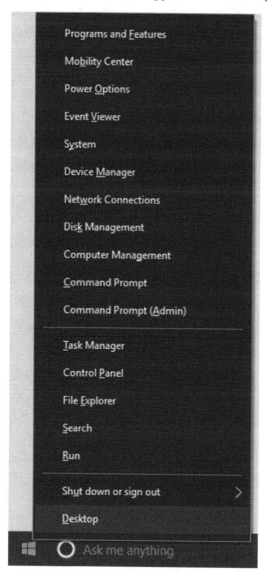

Figure 1-13. *Right-clicking on the Start menu icon displays a different menu*

5.   Press the ESC key to make the Start menu disappear.

How to Turn a PC Off

The most crucial lesson to learn is how to turn a PC on and off. One reason why computers seem so confusing is that they don't work the way you'd expect them to. When you have a blender, you turn it on by flicking a switch to the On position. Then to turn it off, you flick that same switch to the Off position. The same switch turns a blender on and off.

That's not how computers work, and that's part of the reason why computers can be so frustrating and confusing. To turn a PC on, you press the On button on the PC unit.

To turn off a PC, you have two choices:

- Hold down the power button (which is the On button on the PC unit itself)

- Choose the Shut Down command from the Start menu

If you want to use the power button to turn off your PC, hold the power button for a few seconds until your PC shuts down. One problem with using the power button to turn off your PC is that if you have any files that you haven't saved, you'll lose all unsaved data when your PC turns off.

A safer way to turn a PC off is to shut down Windows 10. When you shut Windows 10 down, the operating system first checks if you have any unsaved data. If so, Windows 10 displays a message on the screen asking if you want to save your data. Regardless of how you answer, Windows 10 then makes sure all files on your computer are closed before shutting off your PC. This helps to avoid your data getting lost or scrambled.

To shut down Windows 10, follow these steps:

1.   Click the Windows Start menu icon in the lower left corner of the screen.

2.   Click Power. A pop-up menu of options appears, as shown in Figure 1-14.

Figure 1-14. Clicking the Power option on the Start menu displays various options

3.   Click Shut down. If you have any unsaved data, Windows 10 will ask if you want to save it.

▓ **Note** The Sleep command turns off your screen to reduce its power consumption, but keeps your PC on. The Restart command turns your PC off and then back on again, which can be a handy command to use when (not if) your PC freezes or acts erratically.

To give you yet a third option for shutting down a PC, you can also right-click the Windows Start menu icon to display a menu. From this menu, you can choose the Shut down or sign out option to display another menu that lets you choose the Shut down command, as shown in Figure 1-15.

Figure 1-15. *Right-clicking the Windows Start menu icon gives you another way to shut down Windows 10*

Always (yes, always) turn off your PC using the Shut down command. If you fail to use the Shut down command, you could lose data.

Summary

Computers display information on the screen and wait for the user to choose a command to modify the screen information somehow. To give commands to a computer, you have to use the keyboard and the mouse. Instead of a mouse, you may have a trackpad that mimics a mouse.

By moving the mouse or sliding your finger on the surface of a trackpad, you can move a pointer on the screen. Left-clicking (pressing down and letting go of the top left corner of a mouse or pressing one finger down on a trackpad surface and letting go) selects something on the screen such as a pull-down menu command.

Most importantly, always (yes, always) turn your PC off by shutting down Windows 10 through the Windows Start menu icon and then choosing the Shut down command. The Shut down command can help you avoid losing data such as important business reports.

Remember, using a computer is a skill that you can always improve through practice. Don't be afraid to experiment and play around with your PC. The best way to learn anything is through constant practice and experimentation until you feel more and more comfortable using your PC.

CHAPTER 2

▦ ▦ ▦

Giving Commands with the Mouse, Trackpad, and Keyboard

In Chapter 1, you learned the basics of using a mouse/trackpad to point and click to choose commands. Besides knowing how to use a mouse/trackpad, you also need to know how to type and edit text using a keyboard.

In general, the mouse/trackpad is the main way to give commands or manipulate items on the screen. The keyboard is the main way to create text or offer shortcuts to commonly used commands.

Once you understand how to move the pointer on the screen by moving the mouse (or sliding your finger across the trackpad surface), you need to know how to give commands to Windows 10.

The most common types of commands you can give with a mouse or trackpad include:

- Pointing and clicking

- Hovering

- Dragging

- Double-clicking

Pointing and clicking means moving the pointer over an item on the screen and then clicking the left mouse button. This selects an item such as a menu command, an icon that represents a command, or a picture. You can also point and click the mouse/trackpad when you want to move the cursor to a different location in a document.

Hovering means moving the pointer over an icon on the screen and leaving it there for a few seconds. This often displays a helpful description of what command that icon represents.

Dragging means placing the pointer over an object, holding down the left mouse button, and moving the pointer again. Dragging can be used to move items from one place to another or to select a range of items.

Double-clicking means moving the pointer over an item and clicking the left mouse button twice in rapid succession. Double-clicking is often a shortcut to select an item.

Out of all the mouse/trackpad commands, the most common command is point and click, often abbreviated as just the click command, or clicking.

© Wallace Wang 2016
W. Wang, *Absolute Beginners Guide to Computing*, DOI 10.1007/978-1-4842-2289-8_2

Pointing and Clicking

The most common use for clicking is to choose a command. For example, if you move the pointer over the Start menu icon and then click, you're telling Windows 10, "Open the Start menu now."

When the Start menu appears, you can move the pointer over another option such as Settings and click again, which tells Windows 10, "Open the Settings window."

When you move the pointer over the Devices icon in the Settings window and click, you tell Windows 10, "Open the Devices window."

When you move the pointer over the Mouse & trackpad option in the Devices window and click, you tell Windows 10, "Show me all the options for modifying the behavior of the mouse and trackpad."

When you finish changing options for the mouse or trackpad, you can then point at the big X icon (the close button) in the upper right corner of the Devices window and click to close and remove it.

This point-and-click procedure is something you'll use every time you use Windows 10. The most common use for point-and-click is to choose a command from a menu or to choose an option in a window such as clicking on a button or a check box.

▨ **Note**　Always make sure you point at the right item you want to choose before clicking the mouse or trackpad. If you point at the wrong item and click, you won't get the expected result, which will likely confuse and frustrate you.

Pointing at something on the screen and then clicking is the most common task you'll do with a mouse/trackpad. To give you practice pointing and clicking, try the following exercise to see what kind of PC you have and which version of Windows 10 you might be using:

1. Click the Start menu icon to open the Start menu.

2. Point and click on Settings. A Settings window appears.

3. Click the System icon. The System window now lists different options in the left pane.

4. Click About. The System window now lists information about the PC, as shown in Figure 2-1 (your specific information will vary).

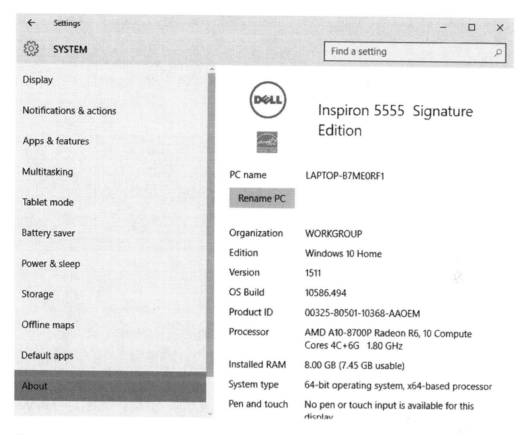

Figure 2-1. *Viewing the details of the PC*

5.   Click on the X icon (the close button in the upper right corner of the window) to close the System window.

Notice that by pointing and clicking with the mouse or trackpad, you can perform common tasks like choosing menu commands, opening and closing a window, and choosing options inside that window. In this case you learned how to identify the different features of your PC.

Hovering

Hovering means moving the pointer over something that appears on the screen. The most common use for hovering is to place the pointer over an icon and then wait a few seconds until a brief explanation of that icon's purpose pops up.

By hovering the pointer over different parts of any program's user interface, you can often learn what command each icon represents.

Hovering lets you tell Windows 10, "Do you see where the pointer is? Show me a brief description of what appears underneath the pointer."

Move the pointer over any icon on the Taskbar that appears at the bottom of the screen and you'll see a brief description of what that icon represents. For example, if you move the pointer over the "e" icon on the Taskbar, you'll see a tiny window appear that shows that the icon represents the Microsoft Edge browser program, as shown in Figure 2-2.

Figure 2-2. *Hovering lets you view brief descriptions of icons that appear on the screen*

Dragging

Pointing and clicking is the most common use for the mouse and trackpad to select commands and options. Another common use for the mouse and trackpad is called dragging.

Dragging involves three steps:

- Move the pointer over the object you want to manipulate

- Hold down the left mouse/trackpad button

- Move the mouse (or slide your finger across the trackpad surface)

Dragging is most often used to move something on the screen such as a window, a picture, or a chunk of text. For novices, dragging might initially feel awkward since you need to hold down the left mouse button while moving the mouse (or keeping your finger pressed down while moving your fingertip across the trackpad surface), so here's a simple exercise to let you practice dragging.

▓ **Note**   To move anything on the screen with the mouse or trackpad, make sure you select it first. That means positioning the pointer exactly over the object you want to move. If the pointer isn't over the object you want to move, then dragging won't appear to do anything but move the pointer.

---

1. Click the Start menu icon to display the Start menu.

2. Choose (point and click on) File Explorer. The File Explorer window appears.

3. Move the pointer over the blank area (called the Title Bar) to the right of the File Explorer name at the top of the window, as shown in Figure 2-3.

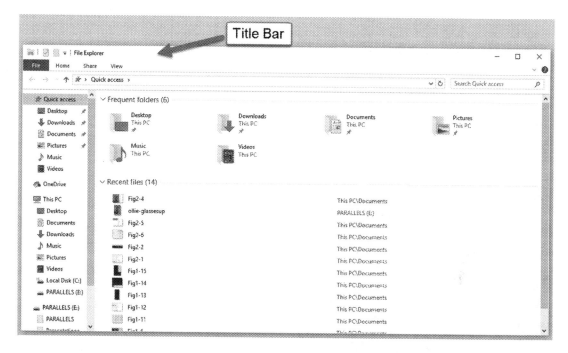

Figure 2-3. *The Title Bar of a window appears at the top of the window*

4. Hold down the left mouse button and move the mouse (or press down on the trackpad surface and move your finger). Holding down the left mouse button or pressing down on the trackpad surface while moving the mouse or your finger at the same time is called dragging. Notice that the window moves wherever you move the pointer.

5. Release the left mouse button or lift your finger off the trackpad when you're happy with the position of the File Explorer window.

6. Click the X icon (close button) in the upper right corner of the File Explorer window to make it disappear.

Remember, when dragging the mouse (or trackpad), keep the left mouse button down or finger pressed down on the trackpad. If you lift your finger up too soon, Windows 10 will stop moving your selected object on the screen.

Right-Clicking

Right-clicking is used far less often because it represents a shortcut to accessing commands. The main idea behind right-clicking is that you point to an item and then right-click to view only those commands you're most likely to need right now.

It's possible to use Windows 10 without ever using the right-click. However, right-clicking offers shortcuts to common commands. To right-click, first move the pointer over the object you want to manipulate. Then press the right mouse button.

When you right-click over an item, a pop-up menu appears, showing you a list of commands for manipulating the object the pointer currently appears on. So if you right-click on a picture, you'll only see a pop-up menu of commands for manipulating pictures, as shown in Figure 2-4.

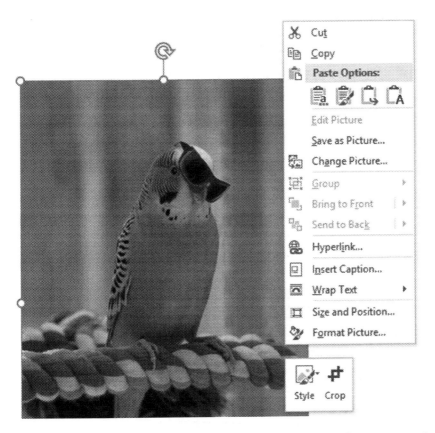

Figure 2-4. Right-clicking over an image displays a pop-up menu of image manipulation commands

If you right-click over selected text, you'll only see a pop-up menu of commands for manipulating text, as shown in Figure 2-5.

Figure 2-5. *Right-clicking over selected text displays a pop-up menu of text manipulation commands*

To see how right-clicking can display a pop-up menu of commands, try the following exercise:

1. Move the pointer anywhere over the Desktop.

2. Click the right button (and lift your fingers up). A pop-up menu appears, as shown in Figure 2-6.

Figure 2-6. *Right-clicking over the Desktop displays a pop-up menu of commands for manipulating the Desktop*

3. Click the Personalize command. The Personalization window appears.

4. Click the X icon (the close button) in the upper right corner of the Personalization window to make it disappear.

Let's see how to find the Personalize command without right-clicking. It takes the same number of steps, but notice how you need to hunt around to finally find it:

1. Click the Start menu icon to open the Start menu.

2. Click Settings. The Settings window appears.

3. Click the Personalization icon. The Personalization window appears.

4. Click the X icon (the close button) in the upper right corner of the Personalization window to make it disappear.

Both methods work, but right-clicking saves you the time of hunting around the screen, looking for the right commands to choose. Just remember that right-clicking may not always display a pop-up menu of commands for everything the pointer appears over.

Using the Keyboard

The keyboard is mostly used to create and edit text. Beyond the normal character keys that let you type letters, numbers, and symbols, the two other types of keys on the keyboard are the cursor keys and the modifier keys.

The cursor keys let you move the cursor up, down, left, or right within text. Occasionally you can also use the cursor keys to move objects on the screen after you have selected them.

The modifier keys are used to change the behavior of another key such as the S or O key. By pressing a modifier key with another key, you can access keystroke shortcuts for common commands.

The most common modifier key is the Control key and the most common keystroke shortcuts that work in nearly every Windows program are:

- Control + N: The New command

- Control + O: The Open command

- Control + P: The Print command

- Control + C: The Copy command

- Control + X: The Cut command

- Control + V: The Paste command

- Control + S: The Save command

The advantage of keystroke shortcuts is that they let you choose a command quickly without wasting time looking for that command in a menu. The disadvantage is that you must memorize the keystrokes to choose your favorite commands.

To help you find keystroke shortcuts for common commands, hover the pointer over an icon. If a keystroke shortcut exists, it will appear along with the command name, as shown in Figure 2-7.

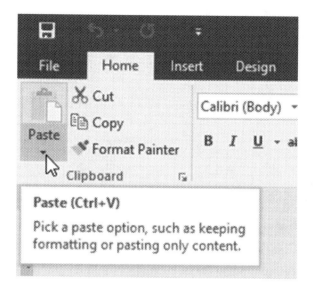

Figure 2-7. *Hovering the pointer over an icon can display the icon name and keystroke shortcut*

Common keystroke shortcuts only use two keys such as Ctrl+S. Less common keystroke shortcuts use three or more keys, such as Ctrl+Shift+Command+T.

To see how keystroke shortcuts work, try the following exercise:

1. Press Windows + E. The File Explorer window appears.

2. Press Windows + D. Notice that although the File Explorer window was open, the Windows + D keystroke shortcut temporarily hides all open windows so you can see the Desktop. (The D in the Windows + D command stands for Desktop.)

3. Press Windows + D. The first time you pressed the Windows + D shortcut, Windows 10 hides all open windows so you can see the Desktop. If you press Windows + D a second time, it reopens all previously open windows.

4. Press Windows + I. The Settings window appears. This is a shortcut so you don't have to open the Start menu and choose Settings.

5. Press Windows + X. A pop-up menu appears. Notice this is the same pop-up menu that appears if you right-click the Windows icon.

The Windows keystroke shortcuts you just practiced are:

- Windows + D: Show Desktop

- Windows + E: Open the File Explorer

- Windows + I: Open the Settings window

- Windows + X: Show the Start menu pop-up menu (equivalent to right-clicking)

For commonly used commands, it's much faster to memorize and use keystroke shortcuts. For less commonly used commands, it's easier just to use menus and icons rather than trying to memorize obscure keystroke combinations.

Commonly used keystrokes often use the first letter of a command to make it memorable, such as Ctrl+S for the Save command and Windows+D for the Show Desktop command.

Remember, to use keystroke shortcuts you must hold down all keys at the same time. The simplest way to do this is to press each key one at a time, and when you've held all the keys down, release them at the same time.

Summary

The three ways to control your computer involve the mouse, trackpad, and keyboard. Most desktop computers use the mouse, while most laptops use the trackpad, but it's possible to use both.

The four commands for using a mouse or trackpad are click, hover, drag, and right-click.

Clicking means pressing the left mouse button once and letting go, or pressing one finger on the trackpad surface and letting go.

Hover means moving the pointer over part of the screen such as an icon. This usually displays a brief explanation of what command the icon represents.

Dragging means holding down the left mouse button while moving the mouse, or pressing one finger down on the trackpad while sliding your fingertip across the trackpad surface.

Right-clicking means pressing the right mouse button once and letting go, or pressing two fingers down on the trackpad surface and letting go. Right-clicking displays a pop-up menu of common commands for manipulating the object that the pointer currently appears on.

The keyboard offers modifier keys to choose shortcuts. The most common modifier key is the Control key.

Make sure you feel comfortable using the mouse to click and drag. Right-clicking is optional but can make using Windows 10 much easier.

To find common keystroke shortcuts, hover the pointer over different program icons to see if there's an equivalent keystroke shortcut. Just remember that not all commands have keystroke shortcuts.

Once you get comfortable giving commands to your PC through the mouse/trackpad and keyboard, you'll be ready to start exploring and customizing the different features of Windows 10.

CHAPTER 3

■ ■ ■

Running Programs

The main reason to use Windows 10 is to run programs (also called applications) on your PC. Some common types of applications include word processors, games, browsers, spreadsheets, databases, and painting or drawing programs. By installing different applications, you can make your PC perform a variety of different tasks.

To run a program, your computer needs memory, often referred to as RAM (random access memory). Some programs need a small amount of memory, while others need a larger amount of memory. If a program needs a certain amount of memory but your computer has less memory, you won't be able to run that program.

You can run one or more programs at the same time, depending on how much memory your PC has. The more memory your PC has, the more programs you can run simultaneously.

The main reason to have two or more programs open at the same time is so you can view and share data between them or quickly switch between programs. For example, you can copy text from a browser and paste it into a word processor document.

Generally, you'll want to run a program as long as you need it and then shut it down when you're finished with it. So the main steps when using any program are:

- Launching or starting a program

- Using a program

- Quitting a program

Remember that there are almost always multiple ways of doing anything with a computer. So when you learn two or more ways to perform the exact same task, just choose the method you like best and feel free to ignore the other methods.

Finding a Program

Before you can use any program, you will first have to find it. Almost every program gets stored in a special location called the Program Files folder. To help you identify different programs, each program appears as a colorful icon along with a descriptive name.

To find and launch a program, you have several options:

- Look for the program on the Start menu

- Look for the program on the Taskbar

- Look for the program displayed as a tile

- Double-click a file created by the program you want to launch

- Search for the program by name

© Wallace Wang 2016

W. Wang, *Absolute Beginners Guide to Computing*, DOI 10.1007/978-1-4842-2289-8_3

Using the Start Menu

Looking for a program on the Start menu is the easiest and most intuitive way to find and launch a program. The top of the Start menu lists the programs you've used most often.

In case you want to launch a program that isn't listed in the top of the Start menu, you can browse through the entire list of programs installed on your computer by following these steps:

1. Click the Windows icon in the bottom left corner of the screen to open the Start menu.

2. Click All apps near the bottom of the Start menu. A list of installed programs appears, as shown in Figure 3-1. (You may need to scroll up and down to view the entire contents of this list.)

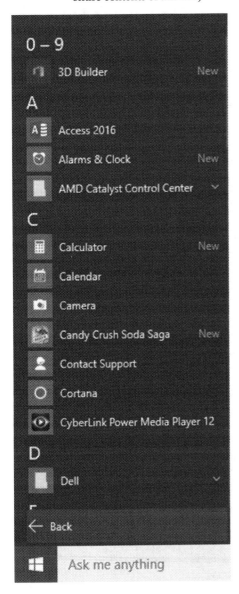

Figure 3-1. *The All apps option displays a list of installed programs*

3. Click the name of the program you want to launch, such as Calculator or Alarms
    & Clock.

Notice that when you launch a program, its program icon appears on the Taskbar at the bottom of the screen. The Taskbar displays a line underneath each icon that represents the currently running programs, as shown in Figure 3-2.

Figure 3-2. Lines appear underneath icons of currently running programs

Pinning Program Icons on the Taskbar

The more programs you install on your computer, the longer and more crowded the Start menu's list of programs will get. As a shortcut, you can pin your favorite program icons to the Taskbar. Then you will be able to just click your favorite program's icon on the Taskbar to load that particular program.

Windows 10 already places several icons on the Taskbar, such as the File Explorer and Edge icons, but you can always add to or remove program icons from the Taskbar so it only displays icons of the programs you use most often.

To pin a program icon to the Taskbar, follow these steps:

1. Launch the program you want to pin to the Taskbar. When you launch a program,
    its icon automatically appears on the Taskbar with a line underneath it.

2. Right-click the program icon displayed on the Taskbar. A pop-up menu appears,
    as shown in Figure 3-3.

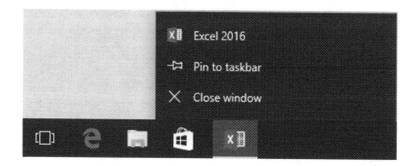

Figure 3-3. Right-clicking a program icon displays a pop-up menu

3. Choose Pin to taskbar. From now on, your chosen program icon will always
    appear on the Taskbar whether or not that program is running.

To remove a program icon from the Taskbar after you've pinned it, repeat the above steps except in step 3, choose Unpin from taskbar.

Pinning Program Icons as Tiles

Each time you open the Start menu, the right side of the Start menu displays tiles. Some of these tiles represent constantly changing information such as sports scores or weather information, but some of these tiles can also represent program icons. By pinning your favorite programs as tiles, you can get quick access to your commonly used programs.

To pin a program icon to the Start menu as a tile, follow these steps:

1. Click the Windows icon in the bottom left corner of the screen to open the Start menu.

2. Click All apps to display a list of all the programs installed on your computer.

3. Right-click the program you want to pin to the Start menu as a tile. A pop-up menu appears, as shown in Figure 3-4.

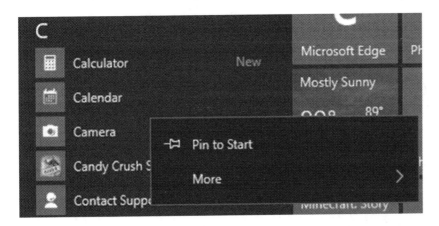

Figure 3-4. *Right-clicking a program name displays a pop-up menu*

4. Choose Pin to Start. Windows 10 now displays your chosen program as a tile on the Start menu.

Once you've pinned a program icon to the Start menu, you may want to resize and move that icon. Resizing a tile can make it bigger or smaller. Moving a tile can place it in a location that you like.

To resize a tile icon, follow these steps:

1. Click the Windows icon in the bottom left corner of the screen to open the Start menu.

2. Right-click the tile you want to resize. A pop-up menu appears.

3. Choose Resize. Another menu appears, as shown in Figure 3-5.

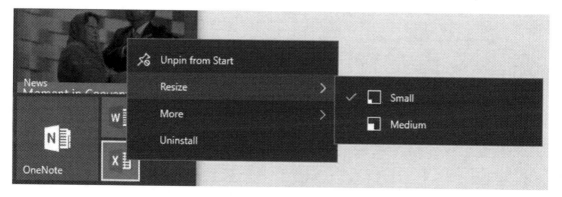

Figure 3-5. *You can resize a tile*

4. Choose a size such as Small or Medium.

To move a tile, follow these steps:

1. Click the Windows icon in the bottom left corner of the screen to open the Start menu.

2. Place the pointer over the tile you want to move.

3. Hold down the left mouse button and move (drag) the mouse to move the tile to a new location.

4. Release the left mouse button when the tile appears in the location you want.

Double-Clicking to Load a File and Launch a Program

The Start menu is the most straightforward way to find and launch a program, although clicking an icon on the Taskbar can be much faster. No matter how you launch a program, you can then open an existing file to edit that file's contents.

Opening a file takes two steps (launch a program and then open a file). As a shortcut, you can also double-click directly on any file to launch the program that created that file.

For example, if you double-click an Excel file, you can launch Microsoft Excel. (If you don't have Microsoft Excel installed on your computer, Windows 10 will try to open the file with a similar program.) Double-clicking a file loads that file and the program that created it in a single step.

To double-click a file to load that file and the program that created it (assuming that program is installed on your computer), follow these steps:

1. Click the Windows icon in the bottom left corner of the screen to open the Start menu.

2. Click File Explorer (or just click the File Explorer icon on the Taskbar if it's visible). The File Explorer window appears.

3. Double-click a file. If Windows 10 isn't sure which program to open, you'll see a dialog box listing currently installed programs you can use, as shown in Figure 3-6.

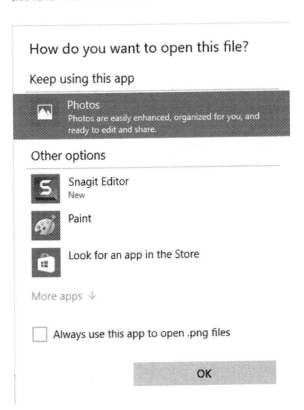

Figure 3-6. *Windows 10 may ask which program to use to open a file*

Searching a Program by Name

The Start menu lets you browse through the programs installed on your computer, but sometimes the Start menu doesn't display all available programs. If you know a program exists on your computer but can't find it on the Start menu, you can search for that program by name.

To search for a program by name, follow these steps:

1. Click the Windows icon in the bottom left corner of the screen to open the Start menu.

2. Click in the Search text box and type all or part of the program name. A list of matching programs appears, as shown in Figure 3-7.

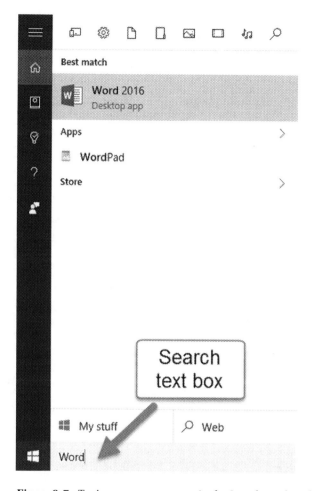

Figure 3-7. Typing a program name in the Search text box displays matching programs

3. Click the program name you want to launch, such as Word 2016.

Using a Program

Each time you launch a program, three things happen:

- The program icon appears on the Taskbar

- A line appears underneath the program icon on the Taskbar to let you know that program is running

- The program's window appears on the screen

Most programs display a window on the screen that contains information. A word processor window might contain text, a game might contain animation, and a drawing program might contain lines and shapes. When you have multiple programs running, you'll often have multiple windows on the Windows 10 Desktop, as shown in Figure 3-8.

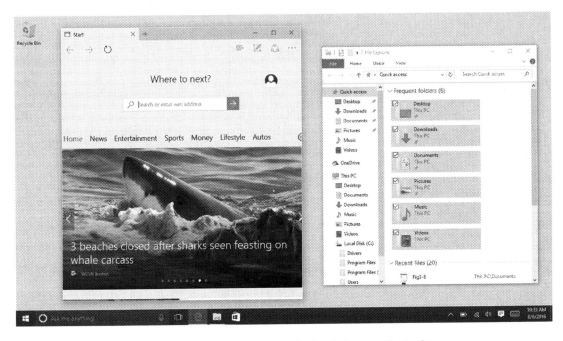

Figure 3-8. *A typical Windows 10 screen may display multiple windows on the Desktop*

Moving Windows

Program windows can either fill the entire screen or just part of the screen. When program windows only fill part of the screen, you can easily view data in multiple windows side by side.

For example, you could have a word processor window open so you could type and have a browser window open so you can look up and reference information as you type.

Many programs also let you open up two or more windows. For example, you could open two windows in a word processor. That way you could edit two documents at the same time, such as two chapters in a book.

When program windows fill only part of the screen, you can move them around by following these steps:

1. Move the pointer over the title bar of the window you want to move. The title bar appears at the top of the window.

2. Hold down the left mouse button (or press a finger on the trackpad surface). Keep the left mouse button or trackpad pressed down.

3. Move the mouse or slide your fingertip across the trackpad surface. Steps 2 and 3 are known as *dragging*. As you drag the mouse or trackpad, the window moves with the pointer.

4. Release the left mouse button (or lift your finger off the trackpad) when you're happy with the new position of the window, as shown in Figure 3-9.

Figure 3-9. *Dragging the title bar of a window moves it to a new location on the screen*

When you only have a few windows on the screen, it can be easy to see what each window contains. However, once you have multiple windows on the screen, so many windows can make everything look cluttered and confusing. To avoid getting overwhelmed by seeing so many program windows on the screen, you have two options. First, you can resize a window to make it fill most of the screen. Second, you can hide windows so you can focus only on the windows of one program.

By filling most of the screen or hiding the other windows, you can focus on the contents of the windows you want to see without distraction.

Resizing Windows

Windows 10 provides several ways to resize a window:

- Click the Maximize button in the upper right corner of the window, as shown in Figure 3-10

- Drag the sides or corners of a window to enlarge or shrink it

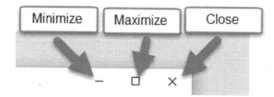

Figure 3-10. *The Minimize, Maximize, and Close buttons on a window*

In the upper right corner of every window you'll see three buttons:

- *Minimize*: Minimizes the window

- *Maximize*: Displays the window to fill the entire screen

- *Close*: Closes the window

The Minimize button temporarily hides the window out of sight. This can be useful when you want to view other windows without closing the current window.

The Maximize button expands a window to full screen. This can help you focus on a single task without the distraction of other open windows on the screen.

Once a window completely fills a screen, the Maximize button turns into a Restore button in the same location. By clicking the Restore button, you can shrink that window back to its original size before you clicked the Maximize button.

The Close button closes the window. If you haven't saved the contents of the window, Windows 10 will ask if you want to save the data.

To see how the Maximize/Restore button works, follow these steps:

1. Click the Windows icon in the bottom left corner of the screen to open the Start menu.

2. Click File Explorer (or just click the File Explorer icon on the Taskbar if it's visible). The File Explorer window appears.

3. Click the Maximize button in the upper right corner. Notice the File Explorer window now fills the entire screen and the Maximize button has been replaced with the Restore button.

4. Click the Restore button. Notice that now the Maximize button appears again and the File Explorer window shrinks.

Maximizing a window to full screen and back to normal size works with almost every window. When you want to avoid distractions, maximize a window to full size.

A second way to resize a window is to drag a corner or edge of the window with the mouse or trackpad. To resize a window with the mouse or trackpad, follow these steps:

1. Move the pointer over the edge or corner of any window until the pointer turns into a two-way pointing arrow, as shown in Figure 3-11.

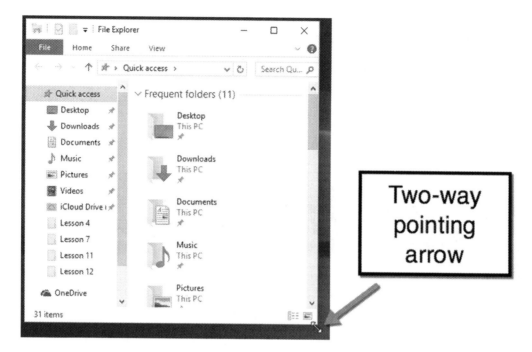

Figure 3-11. *When the two-way pointing arrow appears, you can drag to resize the window*

2. Hold down the left mouse button (or press a finger on the trackpad).

3. Drag the mouse (or slide your finger across the trackpad surface) to shrink or enlarge the window.

The combination of moving and manually resizing a window with the mouse or trackpad can be convenient for aligning two or more windows next to each other.

Switching Windows

When you have multiple programs open, you can switch from working in one program to another. If a single program displays two or more windows (such as a word processor displaying two or more documents), you can switch to different windows within the same program.

To switch windows, you can do one of the following:

- Click in another window visible on the screen

- Click another program icon, one that has a line underneath it, on the Taskbar

- Press Alt+Tab to display thumbnail images of all currently open windows, then click the window you want to view

If you have multiple windows open for the same program, you can switch to a different window from that same program by following these steps:

1. Move the pointer over the program icon on the Taskbar. Thumbnail images of all open windows for that program appear, as shown in Figure 3-12.

Figure 3-12. *Thumbnail images shows all open windows for that program*

2. Click the thumbnail image of the window you want to view.

Minimizing Windows

Minimizing windows lets you temporary hide that window from view. To minimize a window, click its Minimize button.

Once you've minimized a window, you can open it again by clicking its program icon on the Taskbar and then clicking the thumbnail image of that window. To see how this works, try the following:

1. Click the Windows icon in the bottom left corner of the screen to open the Start menu.

2. Click File Explorer (or just click the File Explorer icon on the Taskbar if it's visible). The File Explorer window appears.

3. Click the Minimize button in the upper right corner. Notice the File Explorer window disappears.

4. Click the File Explorer icon on the Taskbar. A thumbnail image of the window appears.

5. Click the thumbnail image of the window. The File Explorer window appears on the screen again.

Minimizing windows can be handy for temporarily tucking one or two windows out of sight, but if you minimize too many windows, you may lose track of how many minimized windows you have open.

Closing Windows

Minimizing windows tucks them out of sight but keeps them ready to view again. However, if you don't need a window anymore, it's better just to close it completely. The fewer open windows you have, the less cluttered your screen will be and the more memory your other open windows can use to make your entire computer run faster.

To close a window, you have several options:

- Click the Close button of that window

- Move the pointer over the program icon on the Taskbar and when the thumbnail image of the window appears, click its Close button

- Right-click the program icon on the Taskbar and when a pop-up menu appears, choose Close window (or Close all windows), as shown in Figure 3-13.

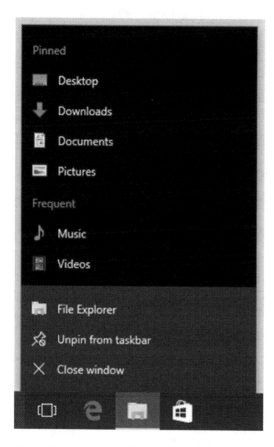

Figure 3-13. *Right-clicking a program icon on the Taskbar displays a pop-up menu*

Using Task View

If you have multiple programs running at the same time, you'll likely have numerous windows open on the Desktop. Unfortunately, opening too many windows will likely bury some open windows underneath other open windows. Even though a window may be open, you may not see it on the screen.

To solve this problem, Windows 10 offers a feature called Task View, which can help display open windows as thumbnail images.

To use Task View, follow these steps:

1. Press Alt+Tab. Task View displays all currently open windows as thumbnail images, as shown in Figure 3-14.

Figure 3-14. Task View can show you all currently open windows at once

2.   Click the thumbnail image of the window you want to display on the screen.

▓ **Note**   Some trackpads let you swipe three fingers up on the trackpad surface to open Task View.

Quitting a Program

When you close a window, the program that opened it continues running. That gives you the option of opening other windows in that same program. If a program only displays one file, closing its last open window also exits or quits that program.

▓ **Note**   **Save any data before quitting a program.** If you try to close a window that contains data you haven't yet saved, a dialog box appears asking if you want to save your data.

Summary

Windows 10 runs all the time and waits for you to choose other programs to launch such as a spreadsheet or a game. Using the Start menu is the simplest way to find a program to run, but you can also create shortcuts for a program on the Taskbar or as a tile on the Start menu.

You can open as many programs as you wish. Each time you open a program, it displays a window with data that you can manipulate. A single program can open multiple windows.

You can manually move and resize windows or choose various commands to make a window fill the screen. Minimizing windows makes it easy to keep too many windows from cluttering the screen.

If you're done with certain data, you can close the window displaying that data. If you haven't saved your data, a dialog box appears asking if you want to save the data.

When you have multiple windows open, you can switch between multiple programs by clicking a window belonging to another program, or by clicking a program icon displayed on the Dock. Any program icon that has a line underneath it on the Taskbar is currently running.

By pressing Alt+Tab, you can use Task View to view and select any currently open window.

By allowing you to run multiple programs at the same time and display multiple windows from each program, Windows 10 lets you share data between programs or view data from two or more different programs so you can work more effectively no matter what you need to do with your computer.

CHAPTER 4

Typing and Editing Text

Most people use a computer to type text for writing letters, e-mail messages, blog posts, social media messages, or even numbers for creating budgets. Since typing text (letters, numbers, and symbols) is so common, you need to know how to type and edit text no matter what type of program you may be using.

The basics of typing and editing text include knowing:

- How to type text including unusual symbols such as foreign language characters

- How to select text

- How to copy, move, and delete text

Before you can type text, you need to move the cursor where you want that text to appear. The cursor shows exactly where text will appear the moment you start typing.

To move the cursor to a new location, you can press the up, down, left, or right arrow cursor keys on the keyboard, or you can move the pointer and click the mouse or tap the trackpad.

Typing creates text such as letters, numbers, or symbols. Once you've typed text, you can also modify it. To modify text, you must first select the text you want to modify using either the keyboard or mouse/trackpad. Once you've selected the text to modify, you can then choose a way to modify that text, such as deleting that text or moving that text to a new location.

Moving the Cursor

The fastest way to move the cursor is to use the mouse/trackpad by pointing and clicking. The problem with using the mouse/trackpad is that it's not always precise. Trying to position the pointer in the exact spot where you want the cursor to appear can be difficult, so that's why you may also want to use the keyboard.

The keyboard's cursor keys move the cursor slowly one character to the left or right, or one line up or down. Although the cursor keys move the cursor slowly, it does move it more precisely.

It's often faster to move the cursor using the mouse/trackpad to place the cursor near the area where you want to start typing. Once you place the cursor near the area where you want to type, you can use the cursor keys on the keyboard to move the cursor more precisely to the exact position.

© Wallace Wang 2016
W. Wang, *Absolute Beginners Guide to Computing*, DOI 10.1007/978-1-4842-2289-8_4

To make the keyboard faster at moving the cursor, Windows 10 offers several keystroke shortcuts:

- *Home*: Moves the cursor to the beginning of a line

- *End*: Moves the cursor to the end of a line

- *Ctrl+Left arrow*: Moves the cursor one word to the left

- *Ctrl+Right arrow*: Moves the cursor one word to the right

- *Ctrl+Up arrow*: Moves the cursor up to the beginning of the previous paragraph

- *Ctrl+Down arrow*: Moves the cursor down to the beginning of the next paragraph

▓ **Note**   Not all programs will accept these keystroke shortcuts for moving the cursor.

Selecting Text

After you've created text, you can manipulate it in several ways, such as:

- Deleting text

- Changing the text size

- Changing the text font

- Changing the text color

- Copying text to paste in another location

- Moving text to another location

Before you can manipulate text, you must first select the text you want to modify. To select text, you can use the mouse, the keyboard, or a combination of both.

Selecting Text with the Mouse/Trackpad

The mouse/trackpad offers two different ways to select text. If you click the mouse/trackpad anywhere in text, you move the cursor where you clicked. However, if you double-click within a word, you can select just that word. If you triple-click, you can select an entire paragraph. Remember:

- Click places the cursor in text

- Double-click inside a word selects that word

- Triple-click inside a paragraph selects that entire paragraph

▓ **Note**   Just remember that double-clicking and triple-clicking mean clicking in rapid succession. If you allow too much time to pass between clicks, Windows 10 will interpret them as multiple single clicks.

If you want to select text within a paragraph or spanning across multiple paragraphs, double- or triple-clicking won't work. That's when you need to drag the mouse/trackpad over the text you want to select.

To select text by dragging, follow these steps:

1. Move the pointer to the beginning of the text you want to select.

2. Hold down the left mouse button (or press down on the trackpad with one finger).

3. Move the mouse (or slide your fingertip across the trackpad while pressing down). As you move the mouse or slide your finger across the trackpad, you'll select text.

4. Release the left mouse button (or lift your finger off the trackpad) when you're done selecting text, as shown in Figure 4-1.

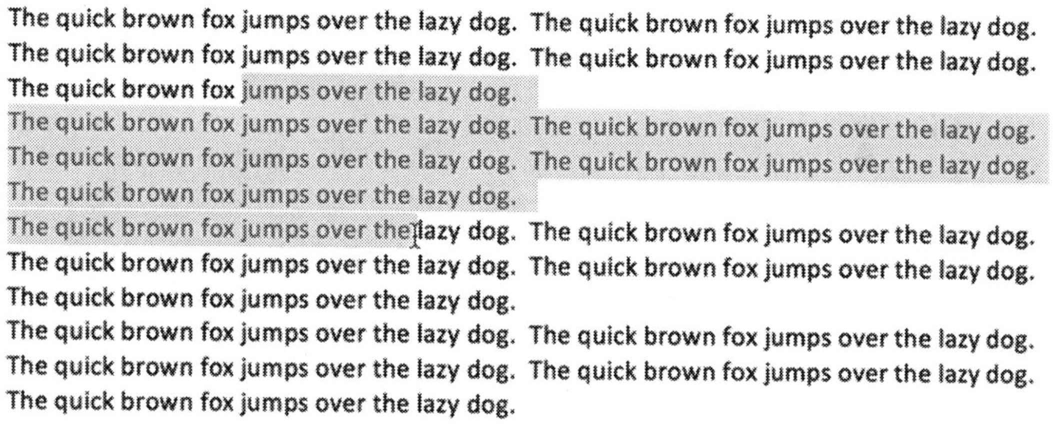

The quick brown fox jumps over the lazy dog. The quick brown fox jumps over the lazy dog.

Figure 4-1. *Dragging the mouse or on the trackpad selects text*

A double- or triple-click is one way to select entire words or paragraphs. Dragging is a second way to select multiple lines of text. A third way to select text is using a combination of the Shift key and the mouse/trackpad:

1. Move the cursor to the beginning of the text you want to select.

2. Move the pointer to the end of the text you want to select.

3. Hold down the Shift key and click the left mouse button (or press and let go of the trackpad surface) to select the text.

Selecting Text with the Keyboard

Using the mouse to select text can often be imprecise because you need to click exactly where you want to define the beginning or end of the text you want to select. If you're a single letter off, then your selected text won't be exactly what you wanted.

For more accuracy in selecting text, you can use the keyboard. To select text with the keyboard, follow these steps.

1. Move the cursor to the beginning of the text you want to select.

2. Hold down the Shift key and press the up/down, left/right cursor keys. Each time you press a cursor key, you'll select text in the direction you moved the cursor.

3. Release the Shift key when you're done selecting text.

▓ **Note**   Don't forget that in addition to using the cursor keys, you can also use the shortcut keys for moving the cursor to the beginning of a line (Home) or the end of a line (End).

If you ever select text and then change your mind, you can de-select text in one of two ways:

- Tap any of the cursor keys

- Click anywhere

Deleting Text

One of the simplest ways to modify selected text is to delete it. After you've selected text, just tap the Delete or Backspace key on the keyboard.

▓ **Note**   Any time you modify text, such as deleting text, and suddenly change your mind, you can press Ctrl+Z to choose the Undo command. The Undo command reverses the last command you chose. If you keep choosing the Undo command, you'll keep reversing the last commands you chose.

Copying Text

Another common way to manipulate text is to copy it from one file and place another copy of that same text somewhere else. You can copy text and paste it in another location within the same document or copy and paste text from one program to a completely different program. For example, you might want to copy text from a browser (Edge) window and paste it in a word processor (Microsoft Word) window.

To copy text, you must:

1. Select the text you want to copy.

2. Choose the Copy command.

3. Move the cursor to the new location where you want to place a second copy of the selected text.

4. Choose the Paste command.

To choose the Copy command, you have three options:

- Click the Copy icon (if one exists)

- Press Ctrl+C

- Right-click over the selected text and when a pop-up menu appears, choose Copy, as shown in Figure 4-2

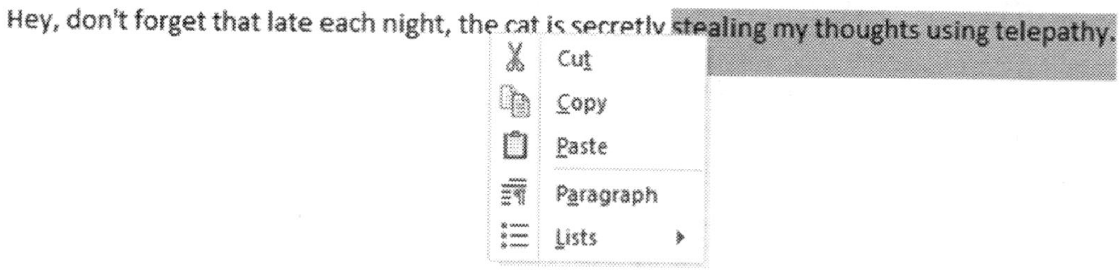

Hey, don't forget that late each night, the cat is secretly stealing my thoughts using telepathy.

✂	Cut
📋	Copy
📋	Paste
☰	Paragraph
☲	Lists ▸

Figure 4-2. *Right-clicking the selected text displays a pop-up menu*

Whenever you copy anything, Windows 10 stores that selected item temporarily. If you select and copy something else, Windows 10 forgets any previously copied item. That means if you select and copy a paragraph, then select and copy a second paragraph, Windows 10 will only remember the last paragraph you selected and copied.

After you've selected and copied text, you'll eventually need to use the Paste command to place a copy of that text somewhere else. You have three ways to choose the Paste command:

- Click the Paste icon (if one exists)

- Press Ctrl+V

- Right-click over the selected text and when a pop-up menu appears, choose Paste (see Figure 4-2)

Moving Text

When you copy text, you create a duplicate of any text you selected. However, if you want to move text from one location to another, you need to use the Cut command as follows:

1. Select the text you want to move.

2. Choose the Cut command (your selected text will disappear).

3. Move the cursor to the new location where you want to move the selected text.

4. Choose the Paste command.

To choose the Cut command, you have three options:

- Click the Cut icon (if one exists)

- Press Ctrl+X

- Right-click over the selected text and when a pop-up menu appears, choose Cut (see Figure 4-2)

▓ **Note**　Remember, when you select text and choose the Cut command, make sure you move the cursor to a new location and choose the Paste command as soon as possible. If you select text, choose the Cut command, and then choose either the Cut or Copy command on different selected text, Windows 10 will lose your previously cut text.

Copying and Moving Text by Dragging

If you find copying and cutting too slow, many programs (but not all of them) allow you to copy and cut text by using the mouse or trackpad instead. To copy or move text using the mouse or trackpad, you need to follow these steps:

1. Select the text you want to move.

2. Move the pointer over the selected text using the mouse or trackpad.

3. Hold down the left mouse button (or press a finger on the trackpad surface).

4. Drag the mouse (or slide your finger on the trackpad surface). As you drag the mouse or slide your finger on the trackpad surface, the cursor moves to show where the text will appear when you let go of the mouse or trackpad.

5. Release the mouse or trackpad to move your text at the current cursor location.

These steps let you move selected text by dragging it to a new location. This is equivalent to choosing the Cut and Paste command.

If you only want to copy text, hold down the Control key in step 3 before holding down the left mouse button or pressing a finger on the trackpad surface. Then in step 5, release the Control key along with the mouse or trackpad. When you copy text by holding down the Control key, you'll see a plus sign in a box, as shown in Figure 4-3.

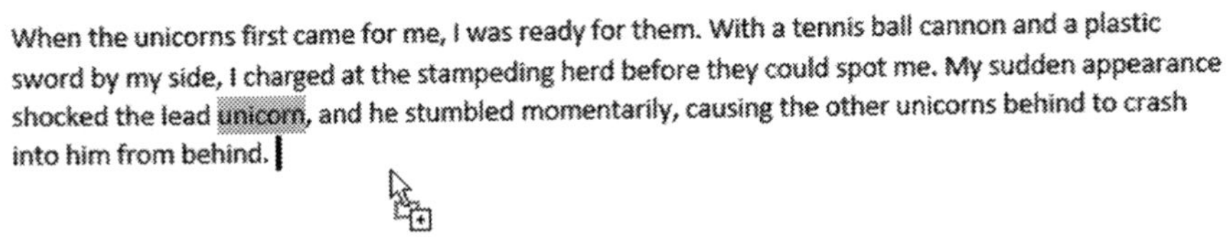

When the unicorns first came for me, I was ready for them. With a tennis ball cannon and a plastic sword by my side, I charged at the stampeding herd before they could spot me. My sudden appearance shocked the lead unicorn, and he stumbled momentarily, causing the other unicorns behind to crash into him from behind. |

Figure 4-3. Holding down the Control key while dragging displays a plus sign in a box to identify the Copy command

Formatting Text

The most visually interesting way to modify text is to format it. Formatting can mean one or more of the following:

- Changing the text size (known as the font size)

- Changing the text font

- Changing the text color and/or background color

- Changing the text style (bold, underline, or italics)

The font size defines how big or small text might appear, measured in points, as shown in Figure 4-4.

This text appears in 12 point.

This text appears in 18 point.

This text appears in
36 point.

This text
appears in 48
point.

This text
appears in
72 point.

Figure 4-4. *The different appearance of text displayed in various font sizes*

Fonts determine the appearance of each character. For example, fonts can make your text look like Old English, calligraphy, or even handwriting, as shown in Figure 4-5.

This text appears in Courier font.

This text appears in Brush Script font.

THIS TEXT APPEARS IN GOUDY STOUT FONT.

THIS TEXT APPEARS IN STENCIL FONT.

Figure 4-5. *The different appearance of text displayed in various font styles*

▒ **Note**   Not all computers have the same fonts installed and not all programs support text formatting. If you need to share files with others, make sure they have the same fonts installed or else your text will look different on another computer.

Text color defines the color of each character. In this book, every character is colored black. The text background defines the color that appears behind each character. In this book, the background color is white.

Changing the text background is like using a highlighting marker to emphasize text such as making the text background yellow or orange. When working with text colors and background colors, always make sure they contrast.

For example, you don't want to choose a light text color and a light background color because then it will be hard to read. Instead, you either want a darker text color and a lighter background color, or a lighter text color and a darker background color, as shown in Figure 4-6.

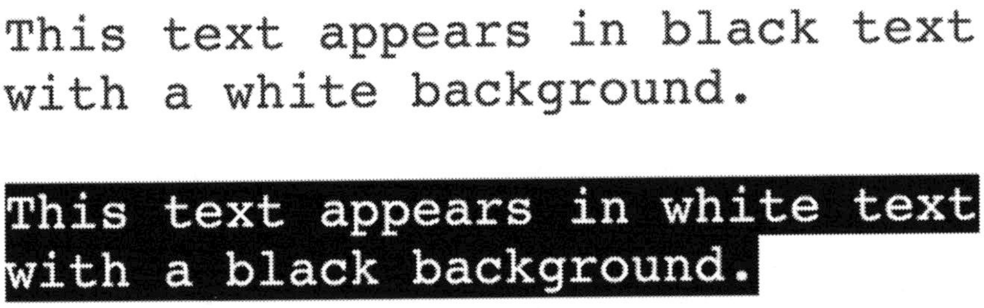

```
This text appears in black text
with a white background.
```

```
This text appears in white text
with a black background.
```

Figure 4-6. *Changing the text color and background color can make text stand out*

Yet another way to format text is to modify its style. The three most common styles are Underline, Bold, and Italics, which you can also combine, as show in Figure 4-7.

This text appears in underline.

This text appears in bold.

This text appears in italics.

This text appears in italics and underline.

Figure 4-7. *Three common formatting styles for text*

To choose different styles for text, you can use keyboard shortcuts as follows:

- Ctrl+U to underline text

- Ctrl+B to bold text

- Ctrl+I to italicize text

To turn off a text style, simply select the text again and choose the same command. So if you formatted text with underlining, you could select that underlined text and choose the underline command again (Ctrl+U) to remove the underlining.

Typing Unusual Characters

Most keyboards display letters, numbers, and symbols, such as #, *, and @, that you can type just by pressing a key or holding down the Shift key and pressing a key.

However, what happens if you need to type characters that don't appear on a keyboard? For example, many keyboards don't have keys for typing foreign language characters that use accent marks.

Fortunately, Windows 10 offers two ways for typing foreign language characters:

- Use the Character Map program

- Type a numeric code while holding down the Alt key

The Character Map program displays different types of unusual characters, as shown in Figure 4-8.

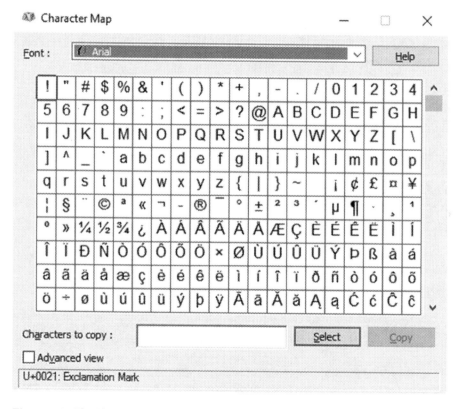

Figure 4-8. *The Character Map program lets you click an unusual character to insert*

To use the Character Map program to insert unusual characters, follow these steps:

1. Click in the Search text box that appears to the right of the Windows icon on the Taskbar.

2. Type Character map until you see Character Map listed in the Start menu, as shown in Figure 4-9.

51

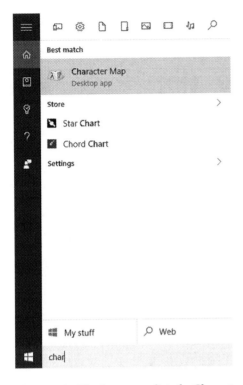

Figure 4-9. *The Start menu lists the Character Map program*

3. Click Character Map to launch the Character Map program.

4. Click a character you want to use and click the Select button.

5. Click in the window where you want to insert the character you chose in step 4.

6. Choose the Paste command (Ctrl+V) to paste the unusual character. You may need to format this unusual character to match the rest of the surrounding text.

Another way to insert unusual characters is to hold down the Alt key and type a numeric code that represents the unusual character you want to type. These shortcuts are listed in Table 4-1.

■ **Note**   When typing the numeric code, you must use the numbers on the numeric keypad. If your computer lacks a numeric keypad, such as on laptops, you won't be able to use this method to type foreign language characters.

Table 4-1

Accent	A	E	I	O	U
Grave	À 0192	È 0200	Ì 0204	Ò 0210	Ù 0217
	à 0224	è 0232	ì 0236	ò 0242	ù 0249
Acute	Á 0193	É 0201	Í 0205	Ó 0211	Ú 0218
	á 0225	é 0233	í 0237	ó 0243	ú 0250
Circumflex	Â 0194	Ê 0202	Î 0206	Ô 0212	Û 0219
	â 0226	ê 0234	î 0238	ô 0244	û 0251
Tilde	Ã 0195		Ñ 0209	Õ 0213	
	ã 0227		ñ 0241	õ 0245	
Umlaut	Ä 0196	Ë 0203	Ï 0207	Ö 0214	Ü 0220
	ä 0228	ë 0235	ï 0239	ö 0246	ü 0252

To type one of these foreign language characters, you need to hold down the Alt key and then type the numeric code on the numeric keypad, such as Alt+0239. Remember, you must type the zero (0) in front of these codes.

Summary

As you can see, there are multiple ways to modify the appearance of text in any program. With most programs, you can find different ways to emphasize and spice up the appearance of anything you write.

Just remember that you can use the mouse and/or keyboard to select text. The mouse can be faster, but the keyboard can be more precise.

Once you've selected text, you can then modify it by changing its size, font, or style. One common way to manipulate text is to copy or move it. To copy selected text, use the Ctrl+C command. To cut selected text, use the Ctrl+X command.

After you've copied or cut text, you can paste it using the Ctrl+V command. Just make sure that after you cut or copy selected text, you choose the Paste command as soon as possible because if you choose the Cut or Copy command again, the Paste command will only work with the last text selected.

Finally, if you don't see a character on the keyboard that you need to use, you can type foreign language characters by either using the Character Map program or by typing a numeric code while holding down the Alt key.

With so many ways to create and manipulate text, you'll be able to make your text look good no matter which program you use most often.

CHAPTER 5

■ ■ ■

Understanding Files and Folders

When you use most programs such as a word processor or a spreadsheet, you'll need to save data. That way the next time you need that data, you can use or modify it without having to retype everything all over again.

For example, if you're writing a letter or a report in a word processor, you'll want to save that letter or report so you won't have to retype the entire letter or report. Whenever you save data from a program, that program saves it in a file.

A file acts like a box that holds your stuff. If you write a letter in a word processor, that file contains your letter. If you type a list of names and addresses in a database, that file contains your names and addresses. If you draw a picture in a graphics program, that file contains your picture.

Almost every program can save data in a file. When you save data in a file, you need to give the file a name. This file name can be anything you want, although it's best to choose a descriptive name that helps you remember what type of data the file contains.

For example, you might give one file a name like "Tax Returns 2018" and another file a name like "Birthday Picture in Hawaii." File names typically consist of letters, numbers, and spaces. Descriptive file names are for your benefit only. Windows 10 only cares that each file, in the same folder, has a different name. It's actually possible to use identical file names multiple times as long as you store each identically named file in a different folder, but this can easily confuse people and is not recommended.

How Windows 10 Organizes Files

Every PC stores files on a disk that holds everything needed to make your computer work including the Windows 10 operating system and programs such as a word processor or browser.

One problem with storing everything on a single disk is that it's like tossing all your clothes in one big pile in a closet. This would make finding anything slow, confusing, and time-consuming.

Just as you would organize a closet to store shoes on a shelf and hang different clothes on hangars, so too you can organize your computer's disk into separate sections to hold different items. When you divide a computer's disk into parts, you use something called folders.

A folder on your PC lets you organize related files together. Some common folders that Windows 10 has already created for storing similar types of files are shown in Figure 5-1:

- *Documents*: Contains files you create

- *Downloads*: Contains files downloaded from the Internet

- *Videos*: Contains video files

- *Music*: Contains audio files such as songs

- *Pictures*: Contains graphic images such as digital photographs

© Wallace Wang 2016
W. Wang, *Absolute Beginners Guide to Computing*, DOI 10.1007/978-1-4842-2289-8_5

▦ **Note**   You can actually store any type of file in any folder. However, it's best to store related files in the right folders such as storing all videos in the Videos folder and all audio files in the Music folder so you can easily find them again.

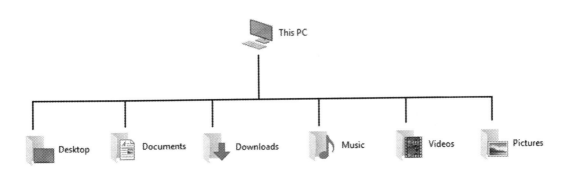

Figure 5-1. *Every computer divides its disk into folders for organizing related files*

Folders help keep all your files organized. To avoid any single folder from getting too cluttered, you can create folders within folders (often called subfolders).

The Documents folder stores most of your files. Most likely you'll need to create additional folders within the Documents folder to keep everything organized.

For example, you might divide the Documents folder so it contains a folder for your personal files and a second folder for your work files. Within your work folder, you might create additional folders related to budgets, another folder related to travel expenses, and a third folder related to sales. By creating multiple folders within folders, you can keep your files organized.

The main program for viewing files and folders stored on your computer is the File Explorer program, which you can open either through the Start menu or by clicking the File Explorer icon (if it exists) on the Taskbar.

▦ **Note**   A file contains data such as text or pictures. A folder does nothing more than hold files or other folders in one place.

Navigating Through Folders

Once you open the File Explorer window, you can view the contents of a folder in one of two ways, as shown in Figure 5-2:

- Double-click any folder displayed in the File Explorer window
- Click a folder name displayed in the left pane (sidebar) of the File Explorer window

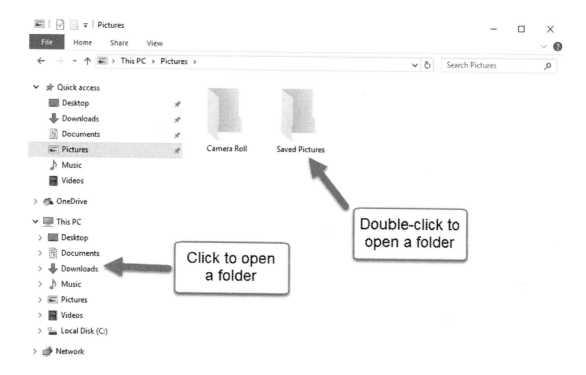

Figure 5-2. *Two ways to open and view the contents of a folder*

Your hard disk is divided into multiple folders and each folder may also be further divided into multiple folders. So the biggest problem is navigating from one folder to another.

To help you navigate through your folders, File Explorer offers three navigation arrows, as shown in Figure 5-3:

- Back (Alt+Left arrow)

- Forward (Alt+Right arrow)

- Up (Alt+Up arrow)

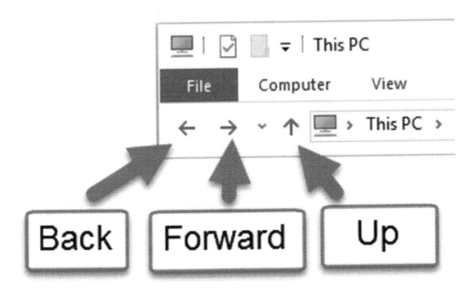

Figure 5-3. *The Back, Forward, and Up buttons let you navigate through folders*

The Back button takes you to the previous folder you viewed. As an alternative to clicking the Back button, you can press Alt+Left arrow.

The Forward button normally appears dimmed until you click the Back button at least once. Then if you click the Forward button, you can move forward to the folder you had viewed prior to hitting the Back button. As an alternative to clicking the Forward button, you can press Alt+Right arrow.

The Up button takes you to the folder that encloses the currently displayed contents. As an alternative to clicking the Up button, you can press Alt+Up arrow.

To see how the Back, Forward, and Up buttons work, follow these steps:

1. Click the Windows icon on the Dock to open the Start menu.

2. Click the Documents folder in the left pane of the File Explorer window. Notice that the Forward arrow button appears dimmed.

3. Click the Downloads folder in the left pane of the File Explorer window.

4. Click the Back button. The File Explorer window now takes you back to the Documents folder because that was the folder you viewed before viewing the Downloads folder. Notice that now the Forward arrow button no longer appears dimmed.

5. Click the Forward button. The File Explorer window now takes you forward to the Documents folder because that was the folder you viewed before clicking the Back button.

6. Click the Up button. The File Explorer window now shows the folder that holds the Documents folder.

If you click the Back button multiple times, you'll view the folders you had previously viewed. The Forward button simply reverses the order of the folders you viewed using the Back button.

Viewing the Contents of a Folder

Once you find a folder to view, you can view the contents of that folder in the following ways:

- Icons (Extra large, Large, Medium, or Small)
- List
- Details
- Tiles
- Content

On the View tab, icons display the file or folder as an image with its name underneath. Using the larger size icons makes it easier to see, but the smaller icon sizes can display more items at once, as shown in Figure 5-4.

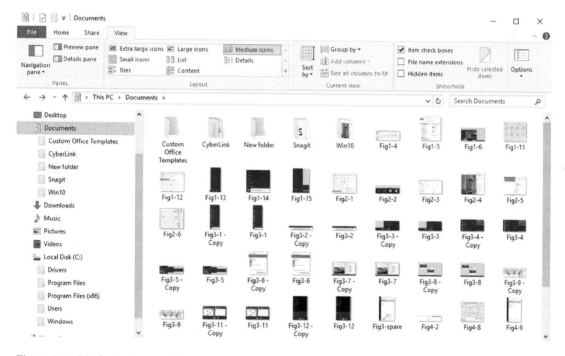

Figure 5-4. *Displaying items as icons*

▥ **Note** If you have graphics or pictures stored in a file, the Extra large, Large, and Medium icon views can display thumbnail images of the images stored in each file.

Selecting List displays files or folders in columns, which can make it easier to browse through a large number of items at once, as shown in Figure 5-5.

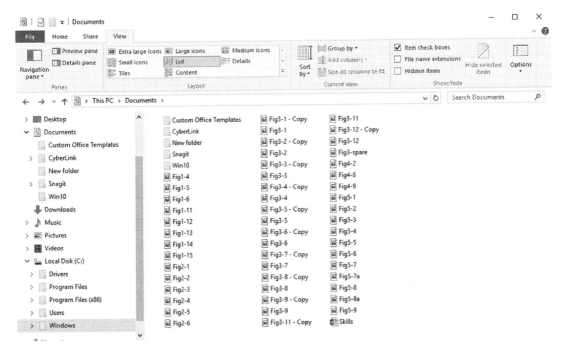

Figure 5-5. *Displaying items in a list*

Selecting Details displays files or folders in rows where each row contains the time and date the file was created or last modified, the type of file it may be, and its size, as shown in Figure 5-6.

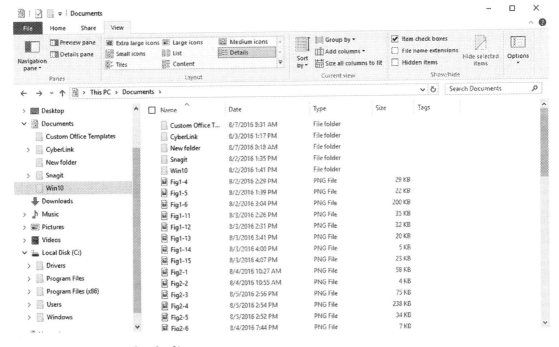

Figure 5-6. *Displaying details of items*

Selecting Tiles displays items as icons but also includes the file type and file size, as shown in Figure 5-7.

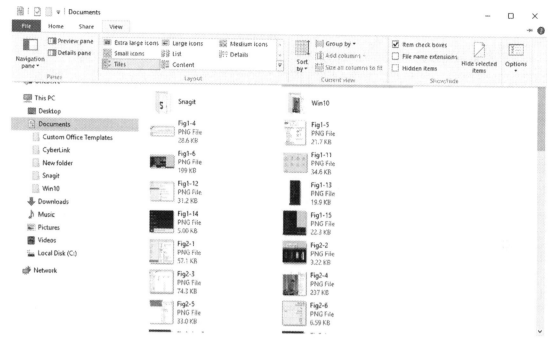

Figure 5-7. *Tiles displays items as icons along with the file type and size*

Selecting Content displays items in rows and also lists the file type and file size, as shown in Figure 5-8.

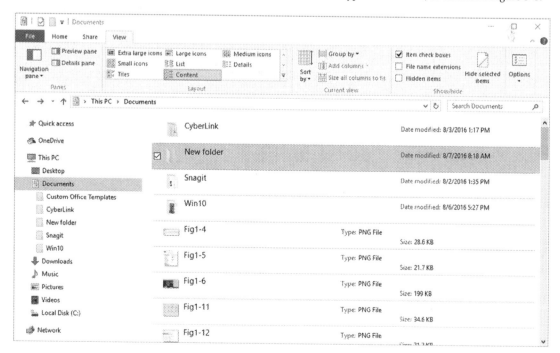

Figure 5-8. *Content view displays items as icons along with the file type and size in rows*

To see how to change the way a folder's content appears in the File Explorer window, follow these steps:

1. Click the Windows icon on the Dock to open the Start menu.

2. Click File Explorer. The File Explorer window appears.

3. Click a folder in the left pane such as the Documents folder. The File Explorer window displays the contents of the Documents folder.

4. Click the View tab. The View tab displays different options such as Small icons or Details, as shown in Figure 5-9.

Figure 5-9. *The View tab lets you changing how to display the contents of a folder*

5. Click different options such as Medium icons or List to see how it changes the appearance of your folder contents.

Creating Folders

Although Windows 10 includes some folders for storing different types of files, at some point you'll likely need to create your own folder for your documents. You can create a folder in the File Explorer window by doing one of the following:

- Click the Home tab and click New Folder

- Press Ctrl+Shift+N

When you first create a folder, that folder gets the generic folder name of "New folder," as shown in Figure 5-10.

Figure 5-10. *A new folder has a generic folder name*

To rename a folder, follow these steps:

1. Right-click the folder you want to rename. A pop-up menu appears, as shown in Figure 5-11.

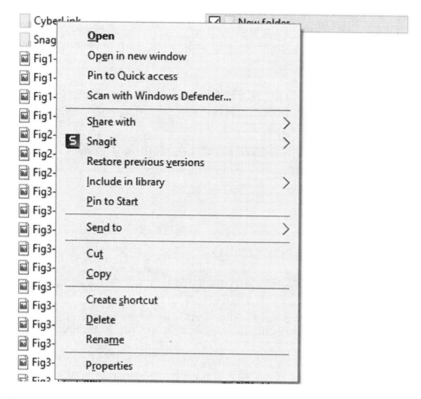

Figure 5-11. *Right-clicking a folder displays a pop-up menu*

2. Choose Rename. The current folder name now appears selected.

▨ **Note** Another way to rename a folder is to select it and then press the F2 function key to highlight the current folder name. (On some keyboards you may need to hold down the Fn key before pressing F2.)

---

3. Type a new name for your folder, or edit the existing name, and press Enter when you're done.

Remember, every folder needs a descriptive name, but two folders stored inside the same folder cannot have the same folder name.

While it's possible to give two or more folders identical names as long as they're stored in different folders, it's best to always give every folder a distinctive name. That way you'll avoid confusion when trying to find a specific folder.

Summary

Every computer has a disk for storing everything. To organize your files, your disk is divided into multiple folders where each folder stores related files. Some common folders that Windows 10 has already created for you include Documents (for storing your files), Music (for storing your songs), and Pictures (for storing your digital photographs).

Folders often contain other folders. The File Explorer helps you find your way through these multiple hierarchies of folders within folders. You can view a folder's contents by doing one of the following:

- Double-click a folder

- Click a folder in the left pane of the File Explorer window

- Click the Back, Forward, or Up buttons in the upper left corner of the File Explorer window

Once you've selected a folder to open, you can view that folder's contents in several ways:

- Icons (Extra large, Large, Medium, or Small)

- List

- Details

- Tiles

- Content

The Icons views let you determine how many items to display at once. The larger icons make each item easier to see, but the smaller icons can show more items at the same time.

The List and Details views are better for viewing large number of items stored in a folder. The Tiles and Content views are best for seeing both the item and details (file type and size) about each item at the same time.

You can also create your own folders by choosing the New Folder command. When you create a new folder, it will have the generic name of "New folder" so you'll need to change its name to something more descriptive.

Ultimately, folders exist to help you stay organized. By giving your folders descriptive names, you'll easily be able to find the files stored in each folder.

CHAPTER 6

Manipulating Files

Files typically contain either text or graphics. Once you save data in a file, you can always copy, modify, move, or delete that file. Since files can contain personal or work data that are likely important to you, you need to know how to manipulate any files stored on your computer.

You can manipulate a file by modifying the contents of that file or by changing the characteristics of that file.

To modify the contents of a file, you'll need to open that file with a program. If you have a word processor file, you'll need a word processor program to edit the text stored in that file. If you have a graphics file, you'll need to use a graphics editor to change the pictures stored in that file.

Beyond changing the contents of a file, you may also need to change the characteristics of that file such as:

- Renaming a file

- Copying a file

- Moving a file to a new location

- Deleting a file

Think of files as boxes containing stuff. You can modify the stuff inside the box or you can mark up the outside of the box, move the box to a new location, or throw away the whole box (and everything inside it) altogether.

Opening a File

To open a file, you have two options. First, you can start the program that created that file. If you want to open a file that you created using Microsoft Word, you'll need to start Microsoft Word. (If you don't remember which program created the file you want to open, choose the second way to open a file as explained later.)

Once you start the program that created the file, choose the Open command in that program to display an Open dialog box and then select the file you want to open, as shown in Figure 6-1.

© Wallace Wang 2016
W. Wang, *Absolute Beginners Guide to Computing*, DOI 10.1007/978-1-4842-2289-8_6

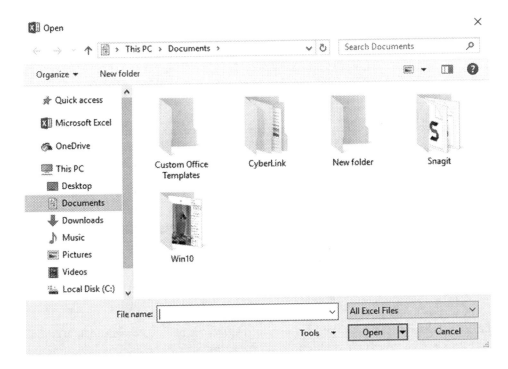

Figure 6-1. *A typical Open dialog box lets you open a file within a program*

A second way to open a file is to open File Explorer and then do one of the following:

- Double-click the file

- Right-click the file and when a pop-up menu appears, click Open

Both of these methods open the file and load the program that created it at the same time. If you're ever in doubt about which program created a file, just double-click that file (or right-click and choose Open) and Windows 10 will suggest a program to open it.

If a specific program is already running, a third way to open a file is to right-click that program's icon on the Taskbar to display a pop-up menu of your most recently opened files for that program.

Sometimes you might have a file that had been created by a program that you don't have on your computer, or you might want to edit a file using a different program. For example, you might have a file created by Microsoft Word but you may want to edit that file using a different word processor instead. When you want to edit a file using a different program than the one that originally created it, follow these steps:

1. Click the Windows icon to open the Start menu.

2. Choose File Explorer.

3. Right-click the file you want to open and choose Open with. A submenu appears, listing all the programs Windows 10 thinks can open your chosen file, as shown in Figure 6-2.

▓ **Note**   Even though the Open with submenu may display a program name, there's no guarantee that the listed program can actually open your chosen file.

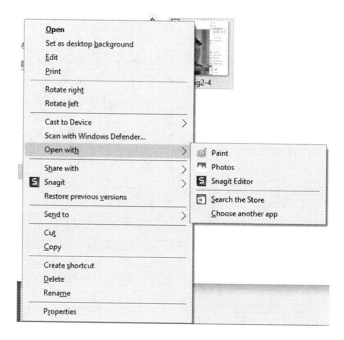

Figure 6-2. *The Open with command lets you choose which program to use to edit a file*

4. Click the program name that you want to open your chosen file. If possible, Windows 10 opens your file within the program you chose.

Although every file contains data, every program can potentially store data in a file differently. The way a program saves data in a file is called the *file format*. If you type the exact same letter in two different word processors, the first word processor would save the data in one file format and the second word processor would save that same data in an entirely different file format.

Fortunately, most programs can save files in multiple formats so you can use the file format most convenient for you. For example, Microsoft Word can save files in its own Word format or in another format such as Rich Text Format that other word processors can open. By saving files in different formats, you can share documents with someone who might be using a different program.

To help identify the file format, programs typically add an identifying extension to that file name. This file extension helps identify which programs created the file and how those data might be stored.

Some common file formats are:

- *Graphic files*: .png, .jpg, .tiff, .gif, .psd

- *Word processor files*: .doc, .docx, .rtf, .txt

- *Spreadsheet files*: .xls, .xlsx, .csv

- *Slide show presentation files*: .ppt, .pptx

The file extension appears after the file's name. So if you named a file "Letters to Grandma" it might have a file extension that makes the whole file name look like "Letters to Grandma.docx" or "Letters to Grandma.rtf".

In general, all graphics programs, such as Photoshop, are able to open a variety of different graphic file formats. Even though the .psd format is specific to Adobe Photoshop, almost all graphics programs can open, edit, and save files in the .psd format as well.

While most word processors can open, edit, and save files in the Microsoft Word (.doc and .docx) file formats, not all word processors can. To guarantee compatibility between word processors, you can save word processor documents in either the .rtf or .txt formats.

The .rtf (Rich Text Format) format saves both text and formatting. The .txt (Text or ASCII) format only saves text. If you share files in either the .rtf or .txt format, you'll be able to open the file in practically any word processor on any computer.

For sharing spreadsheet or database files, the universal file format is .csv (Comma-Separated Values). This format separates data with a unique character, typically a comma.

Like the .txt format, the .csv does not save any formatting but just saves the data. If you need to share data between different spreadsheets or databases, you can always use the .csv format.

While file extensions can help you identify a file format, file extensions can be hidden. If a file extension isn't visible, you can still view the file extension by following these steps:

1. Click the Windows icon to open the Start menu.

2. Choose File Explorer.

3. Right-click the file you want to examine. A pop-up menu appears, as shown in Figure 6-3.

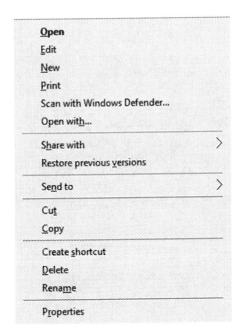

Figure 6-3. The Properties command is available when you right-click a filec

4.   Click Properties. A Properties window appears, as shown in Figure 6-4.

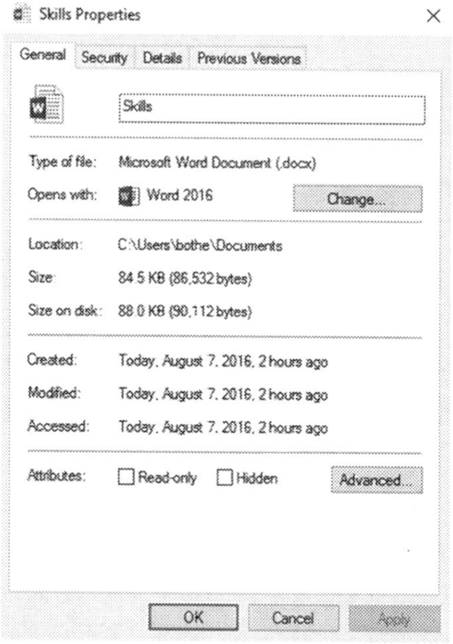

Figure 6-4. *The Properties windows displays additional information about a file*

The Properties window identifies the file extension and the program that created that file in multiple places:

- The icon of the program that created the file appears in the upper left corner of the Properties window and also next to the Open with: label, as shown in Figure 6-5.

- The Type of file label identifies the file format along with its file extension that identifies the program that created the file such as Microsoft Word (.docx).

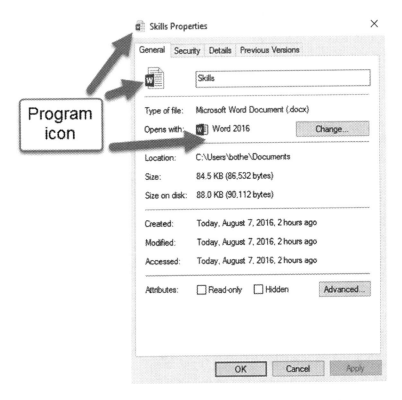

Figure 6-5. *The Properties window displays the file format and the program that created the file in multiple places*

Creating and Saving a File

All files are created by different programs. A word processor lets you type text, a paint program lets you draw pictures, a game lets you store high scores, and a video editor lets you modify video. Windows 10 even creates files to store data for its own use, although you may never know they exist.

With most programs, you'll have the option to create a new file. Two common ways to create a new file in any program is to:

- Click the File tab and click New

- Press Ctrl+N

When you create a new file within a program, you'll see an empty window. Within this window you can create your data such as typing a business report or drawing a picture.

Once you create a new file, you'll eventually want to save it. Two common ways to save a file is to:

- Click the File tab and click Save

- Press Ctrl+S

When you save a new file, you'll need to define the following:

- The file name

- The location where you want to save the file

The file name can contain up to 255 characters but should be descriptive of the file's contents. For example, naming a file "Tax Returns" can help you find which file contains your tax return data.

The location of a file can be any folder, but most people usually save their files in the Documents folder. Of course, to further organize their files, they often create multiple folders inside the Documents folder.

The first time you save a file, you'll always need to define a file name and location of the folder to save the file in. From that point on, saving that file simply saves the contents of that file so you never need to worry about the file name or location again.

Renaming a File

When you first save a file, you must give it a descriptive and unique name. That means you can't give two files in the same folder the exact same name, but you could give two files the same name if they're stored in separate folders. However, this isn't recommended since it will likely cause confusion at some point.

At any time, you can always rename a file by either editing its existing name or giving it an entirely different name altogether.

To rename a file, follow these steps:

1. Click the Windows icon to open the Start menu.

2. Choose File Explorer.

3. Click the file you want to rename.

4. Right-click the file and when a pop-up menu appears, choose Rename.

5. Use the cursor keys to edit this existing name or type an entirely new name.

▨ **Note** Another way to rename a file is to select it and then press the F2 function key to highlight the current folder name. (On some keyboards you may need to hold down the Fn key before pressing F2.)

Copying a File

Copying a file makes a duplicate of that file. When you copy a file, you can store the copy of that file anywhere else such as in a different folder on your computer or on a separate device like a USB flash drive or an external hard drive.

Copying a file involves three steps. First, click to select the file you want to copy in the File Explorer window.

To select only one file, just click that one file to highlight it.

To select two or more files, hold down the Control key and click each file you want to select. This method lets you select two or more files that aren't necessarily next to each other.

To select a range of files that are next to each other, follow these steps:

1. Click the Windows icon to open the Start menu.

2. Choose File Explorer.

3. Click the first file you want to select.

4. Hold down the Shift key and click the last file you want to select. The File Explorer selects the range of files, as shown in Figure 6-6.

☐ Name ^	Date	Type	Size	Tags
🖼 Fig3-12 - Copy	8/6/2016 11:39 AM	PNG File	14 KB	
🖼 Fig3-12	8/6/2016 11:38 AM	PNG File	14 KB	
🖼 Fig3-spare	8/6/2016 11:52 AM	PNG File	22 KB	
🖼 Fig4-2	8/6/2016 2:07 PM	PNG File	8 KB	
🖼 Fig4-8	8/6/2016 3:13 PM	PNG File	26 KB	
☑ 🖼 Fig4-9	8/6/2016 3:40 PM	PNG File	18 KB	
☑ 🖼 Fig5-1	8/6/2016 5:00 PM	PNG File	6 KB	
☑ 🖼 Fig5-2	8/6/2016 5:28 PM	PNG File	47 KB	
☑ 🖼 Fig5-3	8/6/2016 6:00 PM	PNG File	17 KB	
☑ 🖼 Fig5-4	8/7/2016 8:45 AM	PNG File	107 KB	
☑ 🖼 Fig5-5	8/7/2016 8:45 AM	PNG File	73 KB	
☑ 🖼 Fig5-6	8/7/2016 8:46 AM	PNG File	90 KB	
☑ 🖼 Fig5-7	8/6/2016 6:26 PM	PNG File	82 KB	
☑ 🖼 Fig5-8	8/7/2016 8:41 AM	PNG File	73 KB	
🖼 Fig5-9	8/6/2016 6:26 PM	PNG File	19 KB	
🖼 Fig5-10	8/7/2016 8:19 AM	PNG File	4 KB	
🖼 Fig5-11	8/7/2016 8:22 AM	PNG File	30 KB	
🖼 Fig6-1	8/7/2016 10:01 AM	PNG File	47 KB	
🖼 Fig6-2	8/7/2016 10:06 AM	PNG File	31 KB	
📃 Skills	8/7/2016 8:31 AM	Microsoft Word D...	85 KB	
🖼 Fig6-3	8/7/2016 10:47 AM	PNG File	9 KB	
🖼 Fig6-4	8/7/2016 10:47 AM	PNG File	22 KB	
🖼 Fig6-5	8/7/2016 10:47 AM	PNG File	35 KB	

Figure 6-6. *Clicking once, holding down the Shift key, and clicking a second time selects the range of files*

Second, after you have selected one or more files, choose the Copy command in one of three ways:

- Click the Home tab and click Copy

- Press Ctrl+C

- Right-click the selected file and when a pop-up menu appears, choose Copy

Third, open the folder where you want to store the copied file and choose the Paste command in one of three ways:

- Click the Home tab and click Paste

- Press Ctrl+V

- Right-click the selected file and when a pop-up menu appears, choose Paste

Copying a File with the Copy to: Command

To make copying files easier, the Home tab of the File Explorer window offers a special Copy to: command. This command gives you another way to specify the folder to place a copy of a file.

To use the Copy to: command, follow these steps:

1. Click the Windows icon to open the Start menu.

2. Choose File Explorer.

3. Click the file (or select the files) you want to copy.

4. Click the Home tab and click the Copy to: icon to display a pull-down menu, as shown in Figure 6-7.

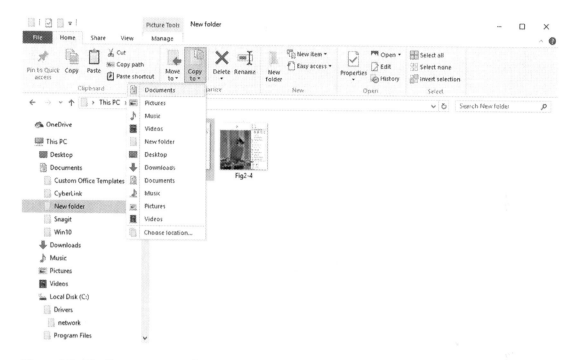

Figure 6-7. *The Copy to: command icon appears on the Home tab*

5. Click Choose location (or click a folder listed in the pull-down menu such as Documents or Pictures). If you chose Choose location, a Copy Items dialog box appears, as shown in Figure 6-8.

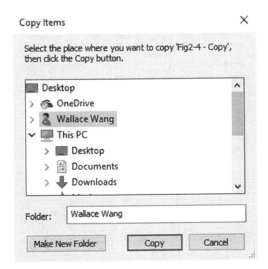

Figure 6-8. *The Copy Items dialog box lets you choose a folder*

6. Click a folder to store the copied file and click the Copy button.

Copying a File with the Mouse/Trackpad

You can also use the mouse/trackpad to copy a file from one folder to another. Dragging means holding down the left button while moving the mouse or sliding a finger on a trackpad.

To copy a file by dragging, follow these steps:

1. Click the Windows icon to open the Start menu.

2. Choose File Explorer. A File Explorer window appears.

3. Make sure you can see the folder in the File Explorer window where you want to store the copied file (or files).

4. Click the file (or select the files) you want to copy.

5. Hold down the Control key and keep it held down.

6. Drag the selected file (or files) over the folder that you want to place it in. Notice that as you drag the file, a + Copy to label appears underneath the file icon to show that you are copying a file to another folder, as shown in Figure 6-9.

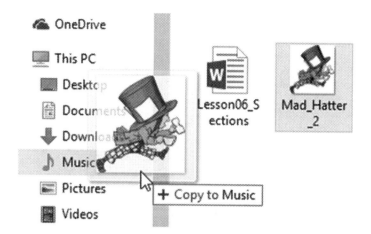

Figure 6-9. *The + Copy to label appears when you drag a file while holding down the Control key*

7. Point to a folder where you want to store the copy of the file.

8. Release the Control key and the mouse/trackpad button.

Moving a File

Unlike copying a file, moving a file physically moves that file to a new location. To move a file, you must use the Cut command in addition to the Paste command.

First, select one or more files to move.

Second, after you have selected one or more files, choose the Cut command in one of three ways:

- Click the Home tab and click Cut

- Press Ctrl+X

- Right-click the selected file and when a pop-up menu appears, choose Cut

Third, open the folder where you want to store the copied file and choose the Paste command in one of three ways:

- Click the Home tab and click Paste

- Press Ctrl+V

- Right-click the selected file and when a pop-up menu appears, choose Paste

Moving a File with the Move to: Command

To make copying files easier, the Home tab of the File Explorer window offers a special Move to: command. This command gives you another way to specify the folder to place a copy of a file.

To use the Move to: command, follow these steps:

1. Click the Windows icon to open the Start menu.

2. Choose File Explorer.

3. Click the file (or select the files) you want to copy.

4. Click the Home tab and click the Move to: icon to display a pull-down menu, as shown in Figure 6-10.

Figure 6-10. The Move to: command icon appears on the Home tab

5. Click Choose location (or click a folder listed in the pull-down menu such as Documents or Pictures). If you chose Choose location, a Move Items dialog box appears.

6. Click a folder to store the copied file and click the Move button.

Moving a File with the Mouse/Trackpad

You can also use the mouse/trackpad to move a file from one folder to another. Dragging means holding down the left button while moving the mouse or sliding a finger on a trackpad.

To move a file by dragging, follow these steps:

1. Click the Windows icon to open the Start menu.

2. Choose File Explorer. A File Explorer window appears.

3. Make sure you can see the folder in the File Explorer window where you want to store the copied file (or files).

4. Click the file (or select the files) you want to copy.

5. Drag the selected file (or files) over the folder that you want to place it in.

6. Point to a folder where you want to store the copy of the file.

7. Release the mouse/trackpad button.

▓ **Note** To copy a file with the mouse/trackpad, hold down the Control key. To move a file with the mouse/trackpad, you do not need to hold down any keys on the keyboard.

Deleting a File

No matter how important a file might be, you may eventually want to delete it. To delete a file, you need to move it to the Recycle Bin folder. There are several ways to delete a file:

- Drag the file to the Recycle Bin icon on the Desktop (usually in the upper left corner of the screen, as shown in Figure 6-11)

Figure 6-11. *The Recycle Bin icon appears on the Desktop*

- Right-click the selected file and when a pop-up menu appears, choose Delete
- Click the selected file, click the Home tab, and click the Delete icon

Remember, once you delete a file, you can still retrieve that file from the Recycle Bin in case you change your mind. To retrieve a file from the Recycle Bin, follow these steps:

1. Right-click the Recycle Bin icon on the Desktop. A pop-up menu appears, as shown in Figure 6-12.

Figure 6-12. *Right-clicking the Recycle Bin displays a pop-up menu*

2. Choose Open. A Recycle Bin window appears, as shown in Figure 6-13.

Figure 6-13. *The Recycle Bin window*

3. Select a file (or multiple files) that you want to retrieve.

4. Click the Restore the selected items (or Restore all items) icon on the Manage tab.

When you retrieve one or more items, Windows 10 puts those files back in the original folders before you deleted them. So if you had a file stored in the Documents folder and then deleted it, the Restore command would take that file out of the Recycle Bin and place it back in the Documents folder.

If you're sure you want to delete all the files stored in the Recycle Bin, you can permanently delete these by emptying the Recycle Bin.

To empty the Recycle Bin, right-click the Recycle Bin icon on the Desktop and when a pop-up menu appears, choose Empty Recycle Bin.

After you choose the Empty Recycle Bin command, Windows 10 deletes all files in it permanently, so always make sure there aren't any files in the Recycle Bin that you might need later.

■ **Note**   Using special forensic software, it's always possible to retrieve some, if not all, previously deleted files. The longer a file has been deleted, the harder it will be to retrieve that file.

Searching for a File

Perhaps the biggest problem with files is trying to find them again. Storing files in folders with descriptive names is only part of the solution. No matter how carefully you may name folders and store files in the most appropriately named folder, chances are good you'll forget where you saved a particular file.

When you want to find a file or folder without navigating through multiple folders, you have several ways to search:

- By name
- By date modified
- By kind (file type)
- By size

Searching by Name

To search for a file (or folder) by name, follow these steps:

1. Click the Windows icon to open the Start menu.

2. Choose File Explorer. A File Explorer window appears.

3. Click in the Search text box that appears in the upper right corner of the File Explorer window. The Search Documents text box appears, as shown in Figure 6-14.

Figure 6-14. *The Search Documents text box*

4. Click This PC, Current folder, or All subfolders in the upper left corner of the File Explorer window. This option lets you limit whether to search your entire computer or just a specific folder.

5. Type all or part of the name of a file you want to find. As you type, File Explorer displays file and folder names that match what you've typed, as shown in Figure 6-15.

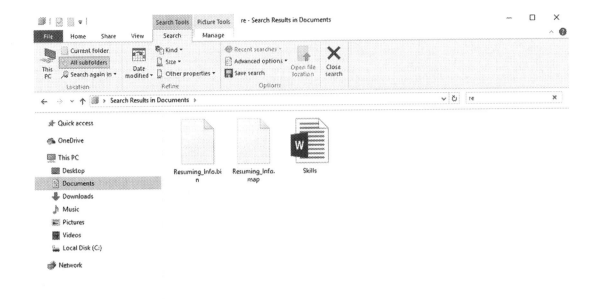

Figure 6-15. *As you type, File Explorer displays matching files*

6. Click the Close search icon when you're done searching.

Searching by Date Modified

If you want to find a file you recently created or edited, it can be much faster to search for files based on the date they were modified, such as viewing only files modified today or last week.

To search for files (or folders) by their modified date, follow these steps:

1. Click the Windows icon to open the Start menu.

2. Choose File Explorer. A File Explorer window appears.

3. Click in the Search text box that appears in the upper right corner of the File Explorer window. The Search tab appears.

4. Click the Date modified icon on the Search tab, as shown in Figure 6-16.

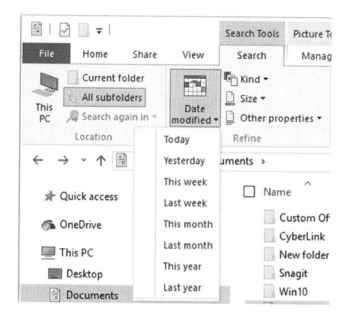

Figure 6-16. *The Date modified icon displays a pull-down menu of different options*

5. Click an option such as Today, Last Month, or Yesterday. The File Explorer displays only those files matching your chosen criteria.

6. Click the Close search icon when you're done.

Searching by Kind

Many times you know the type of file you want to find such as an audio, video, or picture file. To help you search just for specific types of files, you can search by different kinds of files.

To search for files (or folders) by kind, follow these steps:

1. Click the Windows icon to open the Start menu.

2. Choose File Explorer. A File Explorer window appears.

3. Click in the Search text box that appears in the upper right corner of the File Explorer window. The Search tab appears.

4. Click the Kind icon on the Search tab, as shown in Figure 6-17.

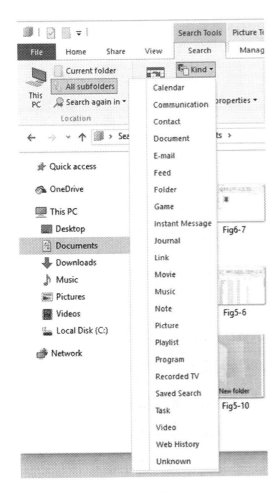

Figure 6-17. *The Kind icon displays a pull-down menu of different options*

5. Click an option such as Document, Movie, or Note. File Explorer displays only those files matching your chosen criteria.

6. Click the Close search icon when you're done.

Searching by Size

If you start running out of space, you can start deleting files to make more room. One way to do that easily is to search for the largest files on your computer and see which ones you no longer need.

To search for files (or folders) by their size, follow these steps:

1. Click the Windows icon to open the Start menu.

2. Choose File Explorer. A File Explorer window appears.

3. Click in the Search text box that appears in the upper right corner of the File Explorer window. The Search tab appears.

4. Click the Size icon on the Search tab, as shown in Figure 6-18.

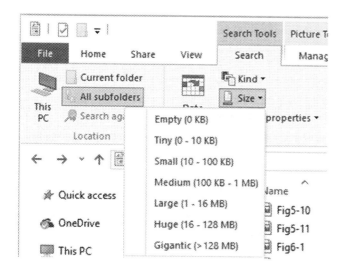

Figure 6-18. *The Size icon displays a pull-down menu of different options*

5. Click an option such as Small, Medium, or Large. File Explorer displays only those files matching your chosen criteria.

6. Click the Close search icon when you're done.

Using OneDrive

Every computer has a limited amount of built-in storage. If you need more storage, one option is to use an external hard disk. However, if you're using a laptop, lugging an external hard disk around isn't practical. That's why Microsoft offers another option, called OneDrive, that only relies on an Internet connection.

Think of OneDrive as an external hard disk accessible over the Internet. The main advantage of storing files on OneDrive is that if your computer gets stolen, fails, or destroyed, all of your files are still safely stored on OneDrive. The disadvantage of OneDrive is that you always need an Internet connection to access OneDrive.

Another drawback of OneDrive is that Microsoft only gives you a limited amount of storage for free, such as 5GB. If you want more storage space, you'll need to pay for it. From a privacy point of view, any files stored on OneDrive are physically out of your control so there's always a small chance others could access those files without your knowledge or permission.

Before you can use OneDrive, you need to create an account that uniquely identifies you. To create a OneDrive account for free, visit Microsoft's web site at https://onedrive.live.com/about/en-us/.

OneDrive can be handy for accessing files from different computers. For example, you might create a file on a desktop computer and store that file on OneDrive. Now if you travel with a laptop, you can access that file on OneDrive (as long as you have an Internet connection).

Each time you modify a file on OneDrive, you're only modifying one file so you'll never have multiple copies of the same file. OneDrive basically gives you a safe place to store files (unless you accidentally delete the files off OneDrive).

Think of OneDrive as a second disk on the Internet. Just as you can divide the disk in your computer into folders, so too you can divide OneDrive into folders to organize your files and view the contents of iCloud in the File Explorer.

To view your OneDrive storage, make sure you have an Internet connection and have set up an OneDrive account. Then follow these steps:

1. Click the Windows icon to open the Start menu.

2. Choose File Explorer. A File Explorer window appears.

3. Click on OneDrive in the left pane of the File Explorer window, as shown in Figure 6-19. The File Explorer window displays the contents of your OneDrive store.

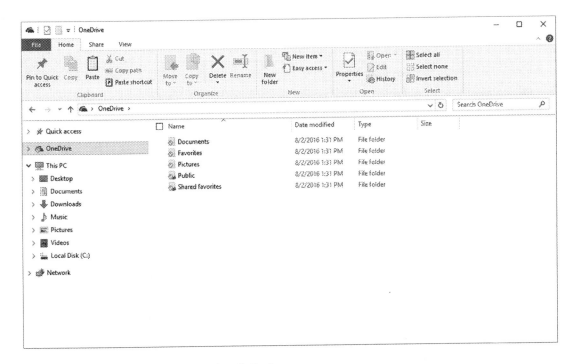

Figure 6-19. *Accessing OneDrive from the File Explorer*

Once you open your OneDrive store, you can store files on OneDrive, create folders, and copy or move files between OneDrive and your computer.

Summary

File management is one of the most critical, yet confusing, parts about using any computer. Before creating files, it's best to develop a plan to keep all your files organized.

Typically, you can store all your critical files inside the Documents folder, but make sure you create additional folders to keep your various files organized so you can find them again.

No matter how carefully you may organize files, you'll probably find it faster to search for files rather than look for a folder manually. You can search for files by size, kind, date modified, or name.

You can rename, copy, move, and delete any file. Just remember that if you delete a file, you can always retrieve it later from the Recycle Bin. However, once you empty the Recycle Bin, then all files will be gone for good.

Files contain your important data so make sure you know how to create files, save them, and find them again. Managing files might feel as exciting as organizing a closet, but when you take the time to do it, you'll be glad you did.

CHAPTER 7

Sharing Files

Most of the time you'll create and modify files for your own use. However, you may need to share files with other people. Sometimes you may want to let them see what you've created, but other times you may need to let them edit your file and send it back to you. Since sharing files is often necessary, you need to know how to share files easily.

In a perfect world, you should be able to share files as easily as you can share a newspaper or magazine. In reality, sharing files isn't as simple as you might expect.

Remember, programs store data in a specific file format. That means a file created by Microsoft Word can't be opened with Adobe Photoshop and a video edited by Adobe Premiere can't be opened by Microsoft Excel.

To share files successfully, one or more of the following criteria must be met:

- Each person must have the same program that created the file

- The receiver must have a program that can import the file

- The sender must have a program that can export the file into another file format that the receiver can open

Files can contain the exact same data but if they're stored in different file formats, not everyone will be able to access that data.

To simplify this problem of file formats, a company called Adobe created a universal file format called a Portable Document File (PDF). Files stored in this Portable Document File format have the .pdf file extension.

The advantage of .pdf files is that they preserve all text formatting as well as displaying graphics. Even better, you can share .pdf files with all types of computers including Windows, Linux, OS X, and even iOS and Android devices.

The disadvantage of .pdf files is that they can be viewed but can only be partially edited and modified. Many government agencies and companies create .pdf files of forms that you can either edit by typing new text or that you can print and fill out by hand.

Creating a PDF File

With Windows 10, you can turn any file into a .pdf file just by using the Print command. Instead of printing the contents of a file to paper, you print your file to a .pdf file that displays your data exactly as if it were printed on a piece of paper. Since almost every program can print data, every program can create a .pdf file that you can share with others.

© Wallace Wang 2016
W. Wang, *Absolute Beginners Guide to Computing*, DOI 10.1007/978-1-4842-2289-8_7

To create a .pdf file from most programs that can display text or graphics, follow these steps:

1. Open a file that you want to save as a .pdf file such as a word processor document, spreadsheet, or slide show presentation.

2. Choose the Print command by clicking the File tab and choose Print. A Print window opens.

3. Click the Printer pop-up menu. A pop-up menu appears, as shown in Figure 7-1.

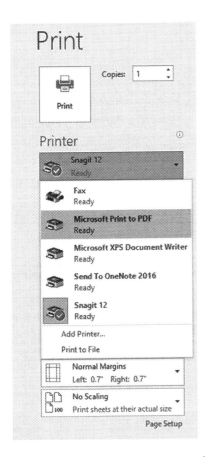

Figure 7-1. *The Printer pop-up menu displays a list of printer options*

4. Choose Microsoft Print to PDF.

5. Click the Print button. A Save Print Output As dialog box appears, as shown in Figure 7-2.

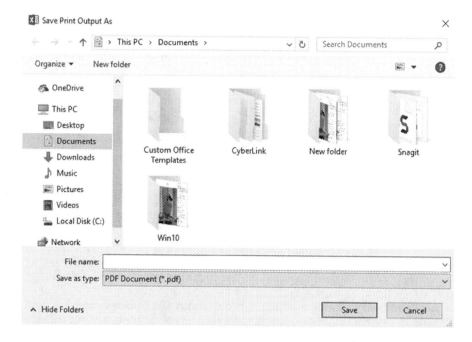

Figure 7-2. The Save Print Output As dialog box lets you define where to save the PDF file

6. Click the folder where you want to save your .pdf file.

7. Type a descriptive file name for your .pdf file.

8. Click the Save button. Your .pdf file gets saved in the folder and file name that you chose.

Opening a PDF File

To open and view the contents of a .pdf file on any computer, you would normally use a special PDF viewing program such as Adobe Reader. However, if you don't have the free Adobe Reader program installed, Windows 10 will open a .pdf file in the Edge browser program so you don't need to download and install Adobe Reader on your computer.

To open a .pdf file on a PC, you can just double-click a .pdf file in the File Explorer window.

Importing a File

If you want to share a file with another person, it's always easiest if that other person has the exact same program as you do on their computer. That way you can share your files without any problems.

Unfortunately, not everyone uses the exact same programs all the time. Even different versions of the same program might save files in slightly different formats. When someone sends you a file created by another program, you need to know which type of program might be able to open that file. When a program can open a file created by another program, that's called importing. Some common types of file formats are shown in Table 7-1.

Table 7-1. *Commonly Shared File Formats*

File Type	Common File Extensions	Created by This Program	Can Be Imported by This Windows 10 Program
Word processor document	.doc, .docx	Microsoft Word	WordPad
Graphics	.jpg, .png, .gif	Any graphics program	Photos
Spreadsheets	.xls, xlsx	Microsoft Excel	Most spreadsheets
Presentation slide shows	.ppt, .pptx	Microsoft PowerPoint	Most presentation programs
Audio	.mp3, .wav, .aiff, .aac	Any audio player or editor	Groove Music
Video	.avi, .mov, .mpg, .mpeg, .mp4, .wmv	Any video player or editor	Movies & TV

Once you can identify the type of program that created the file, you can use a similar program to import and open that file. For example, if you wanted to import and open a .docx file, you know it's a word processor file so you should be able to import and open that file using almost any word processor such as WordPad.

Likewise, if you wanted to import and open a .xlsx file, you could use any spreadsheet program such as the free LibreOffice. If you wanted to import and open a .pptx file, you could use the presentation program in LibreOffice.

▨ **Note**   When you import a file, you may lose the original formatting of that data.

Exporting a File

Because so many people use Microsoft Office either with Windows or on Macintosh, many people share word processor documents saved in Microsoft Word format, spreadsheets in Microsoft Excel format, and presentations in Microsoft PowerPoint format. Most modern programs can import Word, Excel, and PowerPoint files.

So if you need to share a file with someone who doesn't have the same program as you, save that file as a .pdf file if the receiver won't need to edit that data. If others need to edit the data, then you should export the file as a Microsoft Word, Excel, or PowerPoint file.

All Word, Excel, and PowerPoint files come in two file formats. First, there's the old file format used in earlier versions of Word (.doc), Excel (.xls), and PowerPoint (.ppt).

Second, there's the new file format used in more recent versions of Word (.docx), Excel (.xlsx), and PowerPoint (.pptx).

For maximum compatibility, export files into the new file format of Word (.docx), Excel (.xlsx), or PowerPoint (.pptx). If you need to share files with someone using an older computer running any version of Word 2003, Excel 2003, or PowerPoint 2003 or earlier versions, you may need to share files using the older file format of Word (.doc), Excel (.xls), and PowerPoint (.ppt).

To export a file from most programs, click the File menu and choose Export or Save As. Then choose the file format you want to use such as Word or Excel.

If you need to share files with programs that won't accept a Word, Excel, or PowerPoint format, you may need to export your files in one of the following types of file formats that practically all programs and computers can import:

- Text (for word processor documents)

- Rich Text Format (for word processor documents)

- CSV (Comma-Separated Value) (for spreadsheets)

Text files contain nothing but text such as letters, punctuation marks, and symbols. Unlike a word processor file format, text files don't contain any formatting.

Rich Text Format (.rtf) files contain text and formatting. If you need to retain the formatting of text, try saving a file in the .rtf format first.

CSV files contain nothing but numbers and text separated by commas, tabs, or other symbols. Like text files, CSV files contain only data but no formatting or formulas. Spreadsheets and databases can often exchange data through CSV files.

Remember, when you export data to text or CSV file formats, you'll lose all formatting such as bold, fonts, or font sizes. To retain formatting, share your files as Microsoft Word, Excel, or PowerPoint files if possible.

▓ **Note**   You can purchase special file conversion programs that are especially useful for converting files trapped in formats that are no longer popular such as dBASE, Lotus 1-2-3, WordStar, or WordPerfect files.

Compressing Files

If a file is small, it will be easy and fast to copy a file from one computer to another. Unfortunately, many graphics and video files can be extremely large. Even worse, if you want to share multiple files, you don't want to copy each file individually.

To solve both of these problems, you can compress files. Compressing a file offers two huge benefits:

- It can often shrink a file size up to half its original size

- It can combine multiple files into a single file

Compressing saves space and stuffs multiple files into a single compressed file called a ZIP file. ZIP files can be opened or unzipped by Windows, Linux, and Macintosh computers, so compressing is a way to make file sharing easier for everyone.

To compress one or more files, follow these steps:

1. Click the Windows icon to open the Start menu.

2. Choose File Explorer.

3. Choose one of the following:

    a. Click a file to compress.

    b. Hold down the Control key and click two or more files.

    c. Click the first file to compress, hold down the Shift key, and click the last file to compress to select a range of files.

> ■ **Note**   Rather than select two or more files to compress, you can also select one or more folders, which will compress all files within that folder.

4. Choose one of the following:

    a. Click the Share tab and choose Zip.

    b. Right-click the selected file or files and when a pop-up menu appears, choose Send to. When a submenu appears, choose Compressed (zipped) folder, as shown in Figure 7-3.

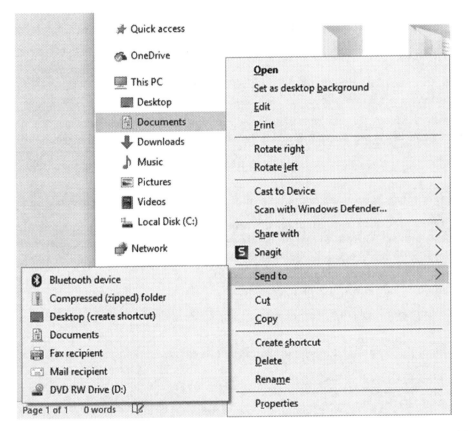

Figure 7-3. *Right-clicking a file (or files) displays a pop-up menu for creating a compressed (zipped) folder*

Compressed files appear in the same folder as the file (or files) you chose to compress. Compressed (ZIP) files appear as a folder icon with a zipper on it, as shown in Figure 7-4.

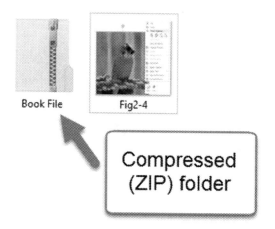

Figure 7-4. *You can identify a ZIP file by its icon*

Once you've compressed a file, you can share that file with others. If someone sends you a ZIP compressed file, you can unzip that file by following these steps:

1. Click the Windows icon to open the Start menu.

2. Choose File Explorer.

3. Click the ZIP file you want to unzip. An Extract tab appears, as shown in Figure 7-5.

Figure 7-5. *The Extract tab appears whenever you select a compressed (ZIP) folder*

4. Click the Extract all icon. A dialog box appears, asking where you want to store the extracted (unzipped) files, as shown in Figure 7-6.

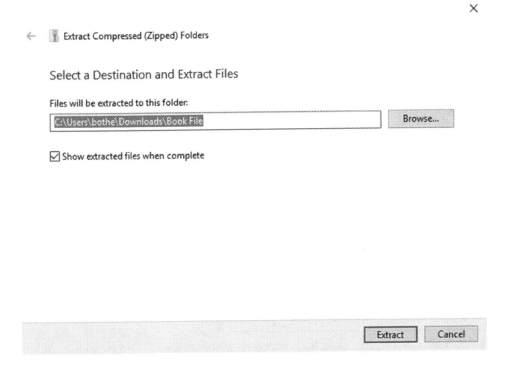

Figure 7-6. *A dialog box lets you choose a new location to save the uncompressed (unzipped) files*

5.   Click the Browse button and click a folder to hold the files extracted from the compressed (ZIP) folder.

6.   Click the Extract button. Your extracted files appear in a folder stored in the location you specified in step 5.

Using a USB Flash Drive

Almost every computer has a USB drive, which means nearly every computer can use a USB flash drive. A flash drive looks like a rectangular stick, as shown in Figure 7-7, where one end plugs into the USB port of a computer.

Figure 7-7. *The appearance of a typical USB flash drive*

By plugging a flash drive into one computer, you can copy (or move files) to that flash drive. Then unplug the flash drive and plug it into another computer so you can copy (or move) files on to this second computer.

To use a flash drive for copying (or moving) files from one computer to another, follow these steps:

1. Plug the flash drive into the computer that contains the files you want to copy or move.

2. Click the Windows icon to open the Start menu.

3. Choose File Explorer.

4. Copy (or move) files to the flash drive.

5. Right-click the flash drive icon in the left pane of the File Explorer window. A pop-up menu appears, as shown in Figure 7-8.

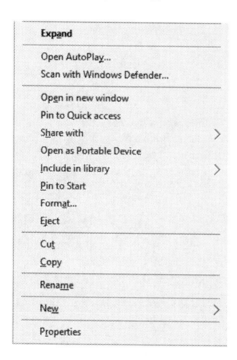

Figure 7-8. Right-clicking a flash drive icon displays a pop-up menu

6. Choose Eject.

7. Remove the flash drive and plug it into a different computer.

At this point you can copy (or move) files from the flash drive to the other computer. Remember, make sure you right-click the flash drive icon in the File Explorer window and choose the Eject command. If you fail to use the Eject command before removing a flash drive, you could lose or corrupt data on the flash drive. Always (yes, always) use the Eject command before removing a flash drive from any computer.

Using File Attachments with E-mail

If you want to share files with someone in another location (such as another city), you can send them using e-mail. Instead of just sending a message as text, you can send one or more files, known as file attachments.

To send file attachments by e-mail, you need to set up an e-mail account on your computer (see Chapter 18) and know the e-mail address for the other person. Follow these steps to send an attachment in e-mail:

■ **Note**   You may want to compress a file first before sending it by e-mail to make it smaller or to send multiple files at once. Many e-mail accounts have a limit on the maximum file size you can send by e-mail.

---

1. Click the Windows icon to open the Start menu.

2. Choose File Explorer.

3. Click the file you want to send.

4. Choose one of the following:

    a. Click the Share tab and choose Email.

    b. Right-click the selected file or files and when a pop-up menu appears, choose Send to. When a submenu appears, choose Mail recipient, as shown in Figure 7-9.

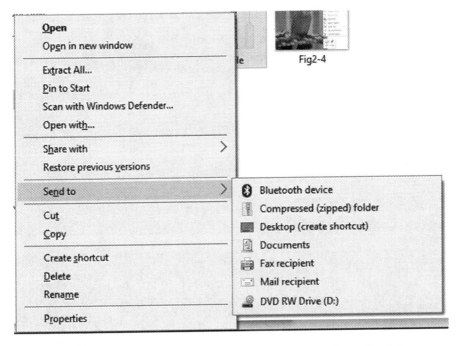

Figure 7-9. The Send to command on the pop-up menu displays the Mail recipient command

Summary

Before you share files with another computer, make sure that the other computer will be able to open your file. You may need to export your file into another file format or make sure the other computer can import your file in its current format.

If you just want to share a file for someone to view but not edit, then you can save the file in the .pdf file format, which practically every computer can open. If you want to share a file for someone else to edit, save it in a commonly used file format.

For graphics, that means saving files in .jpg, .png, or .psd files that nearly every graphics program can import. For word processor documents, save files in .doc or .docx format. For spreadsheets, save files in .xls or .xlsx format. For presentations, save files in .ppt or .pptx format.

To make it easy to share files, you can compress the files. Compressed files take up less space and also let you combine multiple files into a single file.

If you need to share files with a nearby computer, use a flash drive and make sure you use the Eject command before removing any flash drive from a computer.

If you need to share files with someone in another location, attach the file as an attachment to an e-mail message.

Files contain important data so make sure you know how to share files with others. After all, your data are only useful if someone else can view them.

PART II

Customizing Windows 10

When you first plug in a computer and turn it on, your monitor will look exactly like every other computer in the world running that same operating system. While this may be nice, you may want to spend a little time customizing the way your computer looks and works.

Such customization can make your computer reflect a unique expression of your own personality. For example, you might want to display personal pictures on your screen, or you may want to install certain types of programs such as games or specialized software such as programs that help you write novels or create animated cartoons.

By learning to customize your computer for personal reasons or productivity needs, you can turn your computer into a specialized machine that's uniquely suited to help make your life easier.

CHAPTER 8

■ ■ ■

Using the Start Menu and Taskbar

The simplest way to control your computer is through the Start menu. The Start menu provides quick access to all your installed programs so you can control your computer. In addition, the Start menu can display constantly changing information such as sports scores, stock quotes, or the latest world news. By knowing how to use and customize the Start menu, you can make the Start menu a shortcut to getting more done with your computer.

Three ways to open the Start menu include:

- Pressing the Windows key on the keyboard
- Clicking the Windows icon in the lower left corner of the screen
- Press Ctrl+Esc

When you open the Start menu, you'll see three parts, as shown in Figure 8-1:

- The left side displays a vertical row of icons representing commonly accessed items such as the File Explorer program and the Settings window.
- The middle section lists all the programs installed on your computer.
- The right side displays rows and columns of tiles that show information or provide quick access to programs.

© Wallace Wang 2016
W. Wang, *Absolute Beginners Guide to Computing*, DOI 10.1007/978-1-4842-2289-8_8

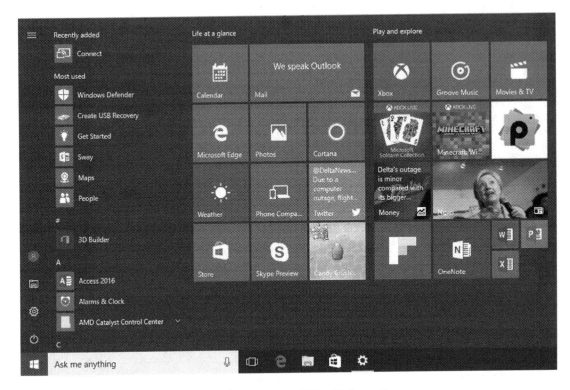

Figure 8-1. *The Start menu displays lists of programs and tiles of information*

Customizing the Left Pane

The far left pane of the Start menu normally displays a vertical column of icons, but it also displays an Expand/Collapse icon at the top. Clicking this Expand/Collapse icon lets you condense or expand this left pane. When condensed, the left pane displays only icons. When expanded, the left pane displays icons along with descriptive text, as shown in Figure 8-2.

Figure 8-2. *You can expand and collapse the left pane of the Start menu*

When collapsed, the left pane displays only icons. But if you hover the mouse pointer over an icon, a description of that icon appears.

When expanded, the left pane displays both icons and descriptive text, but at the expense of taking up more room on the screen. By default, the left pane always appears collapsed until you click the Expand / Collapse icon.

Initially, the left pane displays four icons:

- *Account*: Lets you change your account settings, lock the screen, or sign out of your account

- *File Explorer*: Loads the File Explorer program for creating, deleting, viewing, moving, or copying files or folders.

- *Settings*: Lets you change various settings to customize Windows 10.

- *Power*: Lets you choose between Sleep, Shut down, or Restart. Sleep conserves power while keeping your computer on and ready to wake when you touch a key. Shut down closes Windows 10 and turns off your computer. Restart shuts down your computer and turns it back on again.

The icons on the left pane of the Start menu give you one-click access to commonly used programs. If you want to change which icons appear on this left pane, follow these steps:

1. Click the Windows icon in the lower left corner of the Taskbar. The Start menu appears.

2. Click Settings. The Settings window appears.

3. Click Personalization. The Personalization window appears.

4. Click Start in the left pane.

5. Click Choose which folders appear on Start. (You may need to scroll down to find this option.) Another Settings window appears, listing different icons you can choose to hide or display on the left pane, as shown in Figure 8-3.

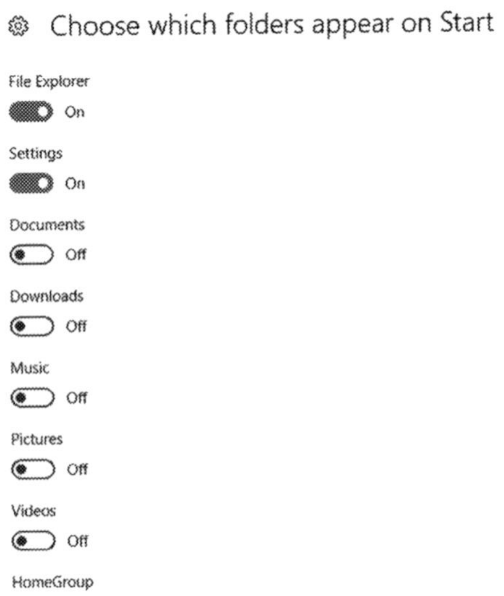

⚙ Choose which folders appear on Start

File Explorer

⬤▭ On

Settings

⬤▭ On

Documents

◯▭ Off

Downloads

◯▭ Off

Music

◯▭ Off

Pictures

◯▭ Off

Videos

◯▭ Off

HomeGroup

Figure 8-3. *Choosing which icons should appear on the left pane of the Start menu*

6. Choose the icons you want to hide or display on the Start menu such as Music or Downloads.

7. Click the close icon in the upper right corner of the Settings window.

Using the Program List

The middle section of the Start menu lists all programs installed on your computer. Use this program list every time you want to find a program installed on your computer. The Start menu's list of programs consists of two parts:

*   Most used (at the top)

*   An alphabetized list of all programs (at the bottom)

The Most used list displays the most recently used programs so you can quickly access them without hunting for them in the All apps menu at the bottom of the Start menu. As soon as you start using a different program often, this Most used list changes.

The alphabetized list of all programs lets you find programs installed on your computer but which you may not have accessed often enough to make the program name appear on the Most used list.

The program list may occasionally display suggested programs you might be interested in downloading from the Microsoft Store. If you find these sporadic suggestions annoying, you can turn them off.

Another option you can modify is whether to show a list of the most recently installed programs. This can be handy to verify whether or not a program properly installed on your computer or to spot programs that may have been installed on your computer without your knowledge.

A third option you can modify is called Show jump list, which displays an arrow to the right of a program that appears under the Most used category, as shown in Figure 8-4. Clicking this arrow displays a list of files you've most recently opened using that program.

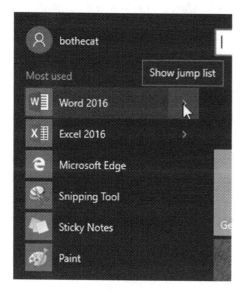

Figure 8-4. *A Jump List displays commonly accessed files in a submenu for Most used apps*

To customize the program list, follow these steps:

1. Click the Windows icon in the lower left corner of the Taskbar. The Start menu appears.

2. Click Settings. The Settings window appears.

3. Click Personalization. The Personalization window appears.

4. Click Start in the left pane.

5. Choose the different options you want turned on (or off) such as Show recently added apps or Show most used apps.

6. Click the close icon (X) in the upper right corner of the Settings window.

Customizing the Tiles

The tiles on the right side of the Start menu can offer you a handy way to view constantly changing information such as weather forecasts or sports scores. Another use for tiles is to create shortcuts to your favorite programs such as Microsoft Word or Excel. By putting tiles of your favorite programs on the Start menu, you can quickly find and access the programs you use most often.

Two different ways you can modify tiles on the Start menu include:

- *Show more tiles*: Lets you change whether to show more or less tiles on the right side of the Start menu

- *Use Start full screen*: Displays the tiles to fill the entire screen (similar to the old Windows 8 screen)

Whether or not to show tiles depends on your personal preference. Some people like seeing the tiles on the Start menu while others do not. If you use tiles often, or if you're using your PC as a tablet, then you might find displaying tiles on the full screen can make it easier to access your favorite programs.

To customize the appearance of tiles on the Start menu, follow these steps:

1. Click the Windows icon in the lower left corner of the Taskbar. The Start menu appears.

2. Click Settings. The Settings window appears.

3. Click Personalization. The Personalization window appears.

4. Click Start in the left pane of the Personalization window. A list of options appears, as shown in Figure 8-5.

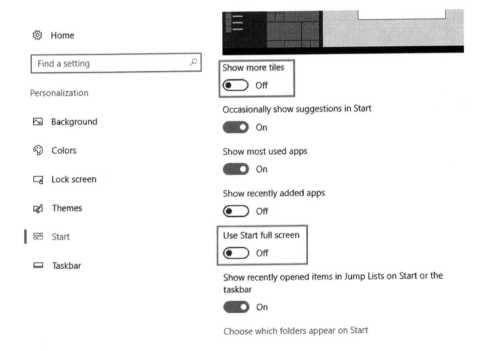

Figure 8-5. Changing the appearance of tiles on the Start menu

5. Choose one or more of the following options:

    a. Show more tiles.

    b. Use Start full screen.

6. Click the close button in the upper right corner to make the Personalization window disappear.

Rearranging and Resizing Tiles

Windows 10 automatically adds multiple tiles to the Start menu such as showing the weather forecast for your area or displaying common apps like the calendar or photos. If you don't like the arrangement of tiles, you can always move them to another location.

You may also notice that some tiles are larger than others. This lets you enlarge the tiles you use most often and shrink the tiles you use less often. By moving and resizing tiles, you can customize the appearance of the tiles on the Start menu.

To move tiles around, follow these steps:

1. Click the Windows icon in the lower left corner of the Taskbar. The Start menu appears.

2. Move the pointer over the tile you want to move.

3. Hold down the left button and drag the mouse (or slide your finger across the trackpad surface). As you drag the tile around, the other tiles will move out of the way.

4. Release the left button when you're happy with the location of the tile.

To resize a tile, follow these steps:

1. Click the Windows icon in the lower left corner of the Taskbar. The Start menu appears.

2. Right-click the tile you want to resize. A pop-up menu appears.

3. Choose Resize. A submenu appears listing different size options such as Small, Medium, Wide, and Large, as shown in Figure 8-6.

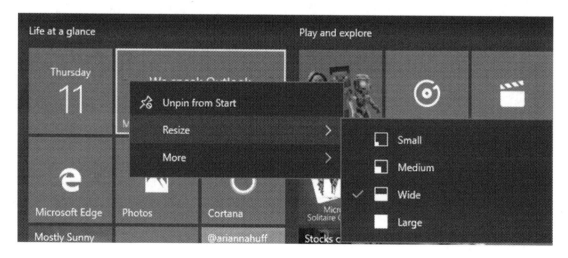

Figure 8-6. *Choosing a size for a tile*

■ **Note**   The Small tile size only displays an icon on the tile. The Medium, Wide, and Large tile sizes display both an icon and descriptive text.

Adding and Removing Tiles

Tiles represent a graphical way of displaying apps you can launch from the Start menu. If you wanted to launch Microsoft Word, you could click Microsoft Word in the program list, or you could click the Microsoft Word tile.

Since tiles always appear on the Start menu and tiles are easy to spot on the screen, you can add your favorite programs as a tile on the Start menu.

To add a tile to the Start menu, follow these steps:

1. Click the Windows icon in the lower left corner of the Taskbar. The Start menu appears.

2. Scroll through the program list until you find the program you want to display as a tile.

3. Right-click that program name. A pop-up menu appears, as shown in Figure 8-7.

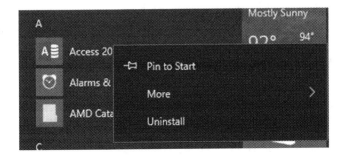

Figure 8-7. *Right-clicking a program name displays a pop-up menu*

4. Choose Pin to Start. Your chosen program now appears as a tile. You may want to resize the tile or move it to a new location.

Once you add programs as tiles to the Start menu, you may want to remove some tiles to avoid cluttering the screen with tiles you don't need that often. To remove a tile from the Start menu, follow these steps:

1. Click the Windows icon in the lower left corner of the Taskbar. The Start menu appears.

2. Right-click a tile that you want to remove. A pop-up menu appears, as shown in Figure 8-8.

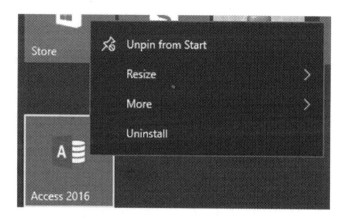

Figure 8-8. *Right-clicking a tile displays a pop-up menu*

3.   Choose Unpin from Start. Your chosen tile now disappears from the Start menu.

Turning On/Off Live Tiles

Tiles that represent programs such as Microsoft Excel or PowerPoint simply display an icon on the tile. However, some tiles (called live tiles) display changing information such as weather conditions or stock market quotes. While some people like seeing updated information displayed in a tile, others find this distracting. Fortunately, you can turn live tiles on or off.

To toggle live tiles on or off, follow these steps:

1.   Click the Windows icon in the lower left corner of the Taskbar. The Start menu appears.

2.   Right-click a live tile that you want to modify. A pop-up menu appears.

3.   Click More. A submenu appears, as shown in Figure 8-9.

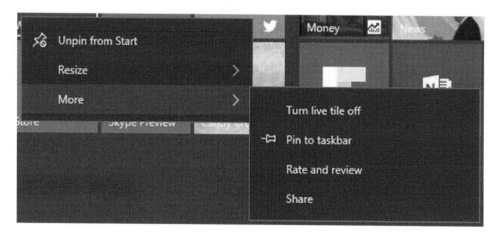

Figure 8-9. *Live tiles give you the option of turning them on or off*

4. Click Turn live tile off (or Turn live tile on).

▦ **Note** When live tiles are turned off, the tile displays a static icon on the tile.

Changing the Start Menu Color

If you don't like the color of the Start menu, you can choose a different color. This lets your Start menu stand out more or fade into the background so it's not so intrusive. It all depends on your personal preferences. Some of the different color options you can change include:

- *Accent color*: The color used for the background of most program icons if they don't have a specific color of their own.

- *Show color on Start, Taskbar, and Action Center*: The color used for the background for these three items.

- *Show color on title bar*: Uses the accent color to fill in the title bar of open windows.

- *App mode*: The two choices are Light (dark text against a light background) or Dark (light text against a dark background).

To change colors, follow these steps:

1. Click the Windows icon in the lower left corner of the Taskbar. The Start menu appears.

2. Click Settings. The Settings window appears.

3. Click Personalization. The Personalization window appears.

4. Click Colors in the left pane of the Personalization window. A list of options appears, as shown in Figure 8-10.

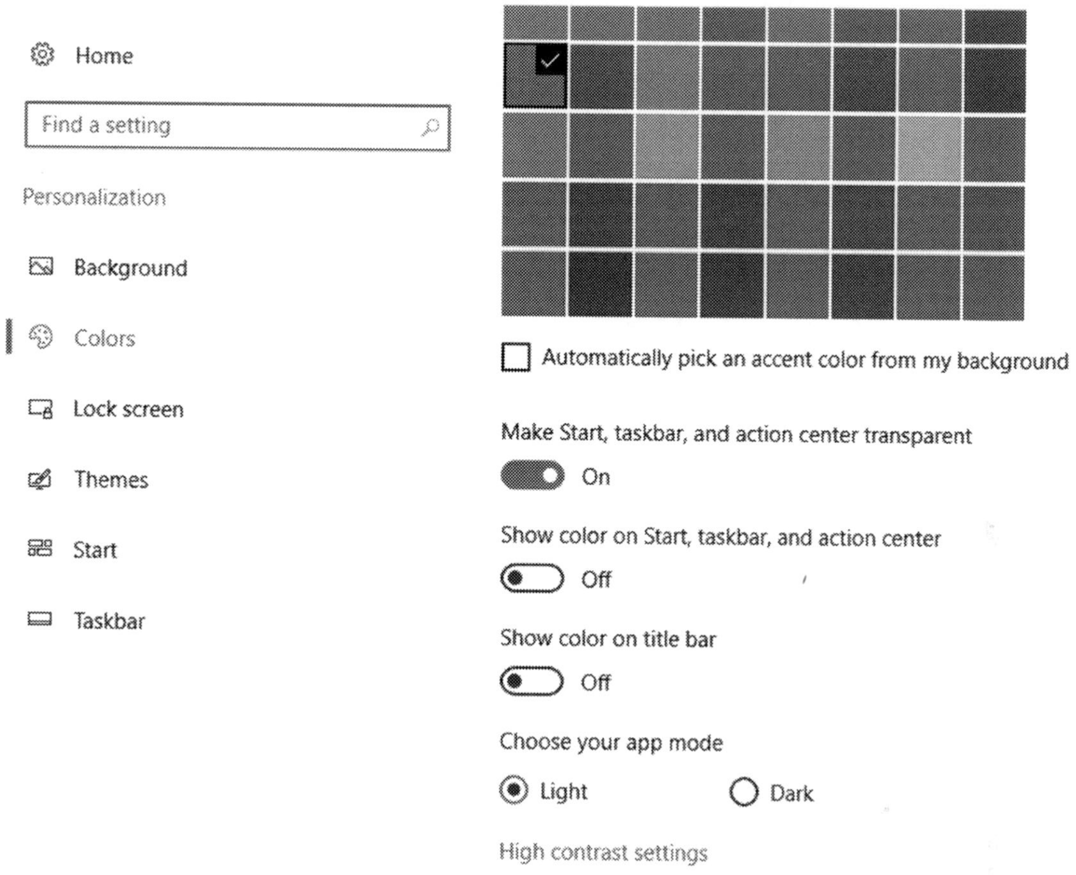

Home

Find a setting

Personalization

Background

Colors

Lock screen

Themes

Start

Taskbar

☐ Automatically pick an accent color from my background

Make Start, taskbar, and action center transparent

⬤ On

Show color on Start, taskbar, and action center

⬤ Off

Show color on title bar

⬤ Off

Choose your app mode

⦿ Light   ○ Dark

High contrast settings

Figure 8-10. *The Colors options in the Settings window*

5. Click the options you want to change such as Show color on title bar or Accent color.

6. Click the close button in the upper right corner to make the Colors window disappear.

Modifying the Taskbar

The Taskbar serves two purposes. First, it displays icons of all the currently running programs. By glancing at the Taskbar, you can quickly see which programs are running and then click an icon to switch to a particular program.

For example, you might be using Microsoft PowerPoint to create a presentation, so the PowerPoint icon would appear on the Taskbar. If you also have Microsoft Word open to create a document, the Microsoft Word icon will also appear on the Taskbar. By clicking the PowerPoint icon on the Taskbar, you can quickly switch to PowerPoint. By clicking the Word icon on the Taskbar, you can quickly switch to Word.

Second, the Taskbar acts as a shortcut. Rather than display program icons as tiles on the Start menu, you can place program icons on the Taskbar that stay visible whether or not you're actually running that program. This lets you place icons of your favorite programs on the Taskbar for one-click access to the programs you need most often.

Some common options you can choose for the Taskbar include:

- *Lock the Taskbar*: Keeps the Taskbar fixed in its current location. When unlocked, you can drag the Taskbar to the top, left, right, or bottom of the screen.

- *Automatically hide the Taskbar in desktop/tablet mode*: Hides the Taskbar and only displays it when you move the pointer toward the screen edge where the Taskbar is located (top, left, right, or bottom of the screen).

- *Use small Taskbar buttons*: Shrinks the size of icons that appear on the Taskbar.

- *Taskbar location on screen*: Lets you place the Taskbar on the top, left, right, or bottom of the screen.

- *Combine Taskbar buttons*: Displays icons with descriptive text, which means each icon takes up more room on the Taskbar.

To modify the Taskbar, follow these steps:

1. Click the Windows icon in the lower left corner of the Taskbar. The Start menu appears.

2. Click Settings. The Settings window appears.

3. Click Personalization. The Personalization window appears.

4. Click Taskbar in the left pane of the Personalization window. Scroll down to view the complete list of options appears, as shown in Figure 8-11.

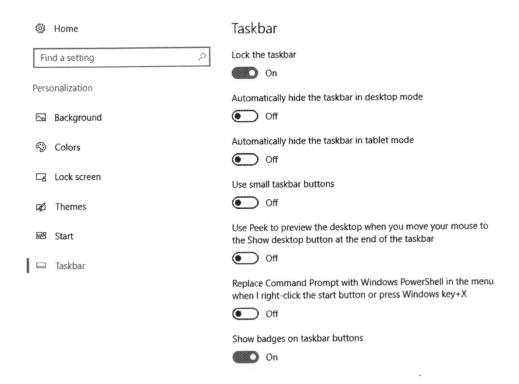

Figure 8-11. The Taskbar options in the Settings window

5. Choose the various options you want to modify.

6. Click the close button in the upper right corner to make the Personalization window disappear.

Defining Icons on the Taskbar

By default, the Taskbar displays various icons representing volume or Wi-Fi settings. If you don't want these options or want to make other options available on the Taskbar, you can always add or remove icons.
    To add or remove icons from the Taskbar, follow these steps:

1. Click the Windows icon in the lower left corner of the Taskbar. The Start menu appears.

2. Click Settings. The Settings window appears.

3. Click Personalization. The Personalization window appears.

4. Click Taskbar in the left pane of the Personalization window. Scroll down to the bottom of the list of options on the right side of the window until you see the Notification area category, as shown in Figure 8-12.

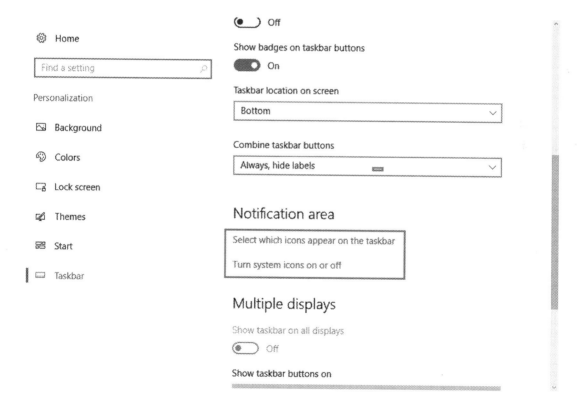

Figure 8-12. The two options for adding or removing icons from the Taskbar

5. Click one of the following to view a list of options:

    a. Select which icons appear on the taskbar (to view the options, as shown in Figure 8-13)

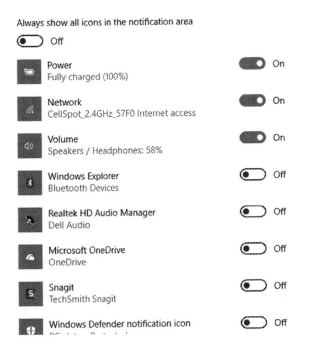

Figure 8-13. *The Select which icons appear on the taskbar list of options*

    b. Turn system icons on or off (to view the options, as shown in Figure 8-14)

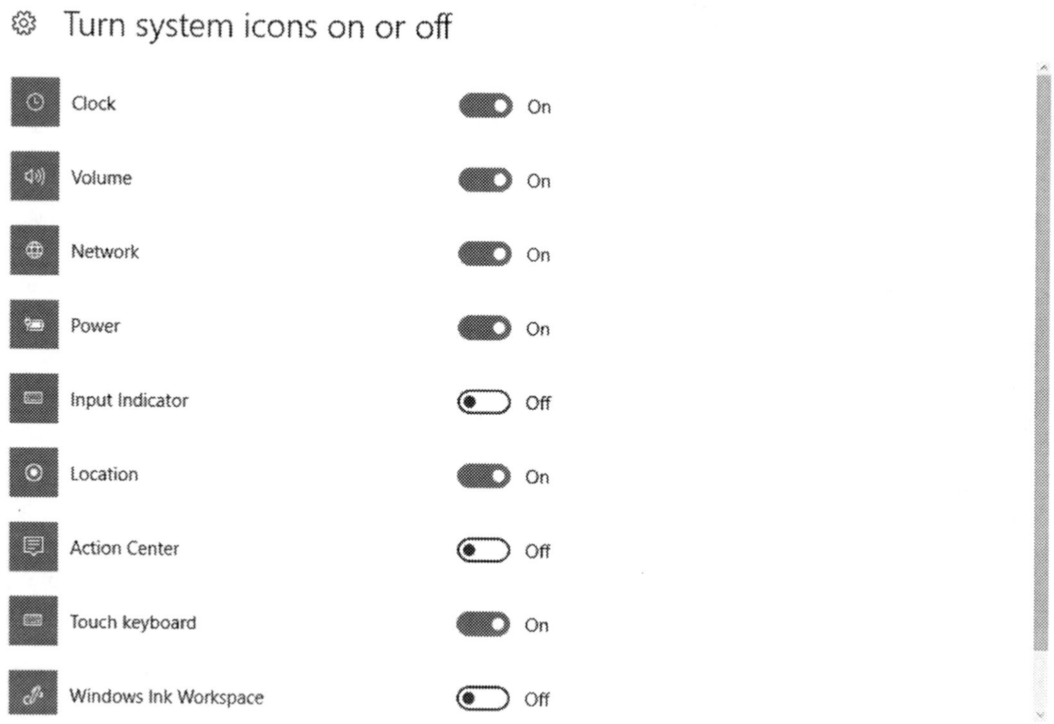

⚙ Turn system icons on or off

🕐	Clock	On
🔊	Volume	On
🌐	Network	On
🔋	Power	On
⌨	Input Indicator	Off
◉	Location	On
💬	Action Center	Off
⌨	Touch keyboard	On
🖊	Windows Ink Workspace	Off

Figure 8-14. *The Turn system icons on or off list of options*

6. Click the options you want to modify.

7. Click the close button in the upper right corner to make the Personalization window disappear.

Modifying the Taskbar by Right-Clicking

Opening the Settings window is one way to modify the Taskbar, but another way is to right-click somewhere on the Taskbar to display a pop-up menu, as shown in Figure 8-15. From this pop-up menu, you can lock/unlock the Taskbar or choose Settings to open the Settings window with the Taskbar option already selected in the left pane.

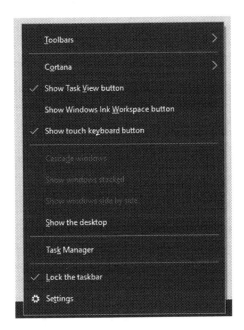

Figure 8-15. *Right-clicking somewhere on the Taskbar displays a pop-up menu*

■ **Note**   If you right-click somewhere on the Taskbar to display the pop-up menu, you can choose Show the desktop, which will automatically hide all open windows so you only see the Desktop. If you right-click the Taskbar a second time, the pop-up menu will display a Show open windows command, which will make all open windows visible on the Desktop again.

Adding Program Icons to the Taskbar

If you use a program often, such as Microsoft Word or Adobe Photoshop, you can pin that program's icon as a tile on the Start menu. This lets you open the Start menu and then click the program you want to use right away.

For another way to give you fast access to your favorite programs, you can pin a program icon to the Taskbar. Now even if you quit that program, its icon will remain on the Taskbar so you can launch it without opening the Start menu at all.

To pin a program icon to the Taskbar, follow these steps:

1. Open a program you plan to use often. Your chosen program's icon appears on the Taskbar.

2. Right-click the program icon on the Taskbar. A pop-up menu appears, as shown in Figure 8-16.

Figure 8-16. *Right-clicking a program icon lets you pin that program icon to the Taskbar*

3. Choose Pin this program to taskbar. Your chosen program icon now stays on the Taskbar even if you exit out of this program.

To add a program icon to the Taskbar, follow these steps:

1. Open a program you plan to use often. Your chosen program's icon appears on the Taskbar.

2. Right-click the program icon on the Taskbar. A pop-up menu appears, as shown in Figure 8-16.

3. Choose Pin this program to taskbar. Your chosen program icon now stays on the Taskbar even if you exit this program.

To remove a program icon to the Taskbar, follow these steps:

1. Right-click the program icon on the Taskbar. A pop-up menu appears.

2. Choose Unpin this program to taskbar.

Summary

The Start menu gives you access to all installed programs on your computer. The left side of the Start menu displays icons for commonly used features such as the File Explorer or the Power button to turn your computer off.

The middle part of the Start menu displays the list of all installed programs. Since scrolling through this list can get cumbersome, the Start menu displays a list of your most used programs at the top so you can find them quickly and easily.

The right side of the Start menu displays tiles. Some tiles represent programs and give you another way to place shortcuts to your favorite programs, but other tiles are "live," which means they display constantly changing information such as weather information or stock market quotes. You can customize the Start menu to make it look the way you want and organize information the way you like it best.

The Taskbar is another place to store program icons for fast access. You can customize the Taskbar to define which icons to display to give you one-click access to your favorite programs.

By customizing the Start menu and Taskbar, you can make Windows 10 easy for you to use with the programs you like best.

CHAPTER 9

Installing Software

By itself, Windows 10 simply makes your computer work. If you want to write a letter, balance a budget, play a game, or design an object such as an engine or a building, you need to use software. Windows 10 comes with plenty of free software, but it's likely you'll want to install additional programs to perform specific tasks. Installing software on a computer might seem straightforward, but you need to be aware of several issues.

Each time you install software on your computer, you risk infecting it with malware, which is short for malicious software. Common types of malware include viruses, trojans, spyware, and other types of programs whose sole purpose is either to keep you from using your computer or trick you into doing something such as giving someone money or access to your passwords. When installing software, you must always be aware of the threat of malware and understand the ways you can minimize your risk.

Of course, once you install software, you may want to remove that software later. In this chapter, you'll learn how to both install and remove software using Windows 10.

There are three ways to install software on a computer:

- By downloading a program off the Internet

- By installing a program off a DVD

- By installing a program off the Microsoft Store

Out of these three methods, installing a program off a DVD or from the Microsoft Store are the two safest methods. When you install software off the Internet, you must make sure you're not installing malware by mistake.

Finding Software on the Microsoft Store

The Microsoft Store contains a library of software that Microsoft has examined to make sure they're safe. The disadvantage of the Microsoft Store is that it doesn't contain all available Windows 10 software.

To access the Microsoft Store, you need a Microsoft Account, which is linked to a credit card. That allows you to purchase software securely without needing to retype a credit card number each time you want to buy another program from the Microsoft Store.

© Wallace Wang 2016
W. Wang, *Absolute Beginners Guide to Computing*, DOI 10.1007/978-1-4842-2289-8_9

■ **Note** To get a free Microsoft Account, visit `https://www.microsoft.com/en-us/account`.

To view the Microsoft Store, make sure you have an Internet connection and then choose one of the following, as shown in Figure 9-1:

- Click the Windows icon in the lower left corner of the screen to open the Start menu and then click the Microsoft Store icon

- Click the Microsoft Store icon on the Taskbar

Figure 9-1. *Finding the Microsoft Store icon on the Start menu and Taskbar*

The Microsoft Store window appears, as shown in Figure 9-2.

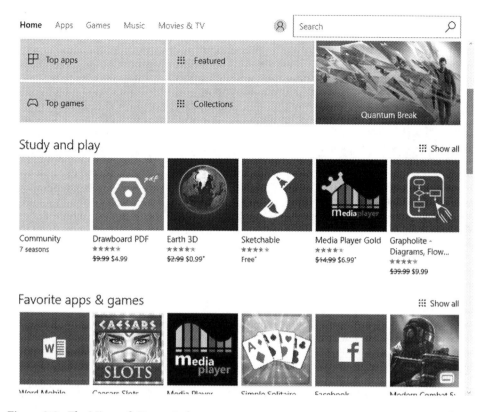

Figure 9-2. *The Microsoft Store window*

There are several ways to search for a program within the Microsoft Store. The Microsoft Store window organizes software into several different groups:

- Top apps

- Featured apps

- Favorite apps

The purpose of these different categories is to give you different ways to browse through the Microsoft Store. When you find an app that looks interesting, click it to read more detailed information about the app such as its price, what it does, and what it looks like, as shown in Figure 9-3.

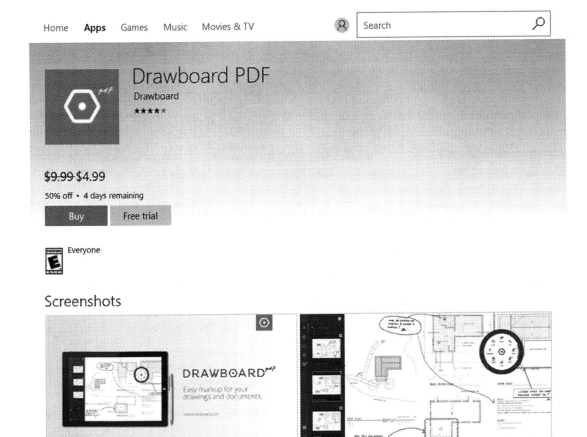

Figure 9-3. Clicking an app displays more information about that app

If you scroll down an app's description, you can view its system requirements, as shown in Figure 9-4.

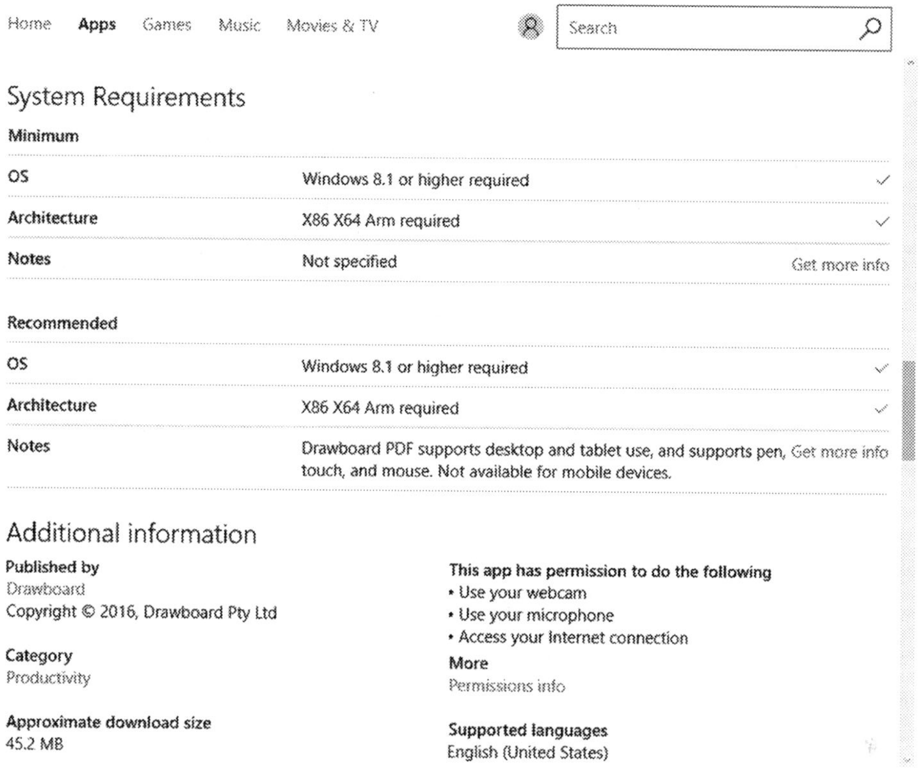

Figure 9-4. *Every app displays its system requirements near the bottom of its description*

Scroll even further and you can read reviews of each app by existing customers, as shown in Figure 9-5.

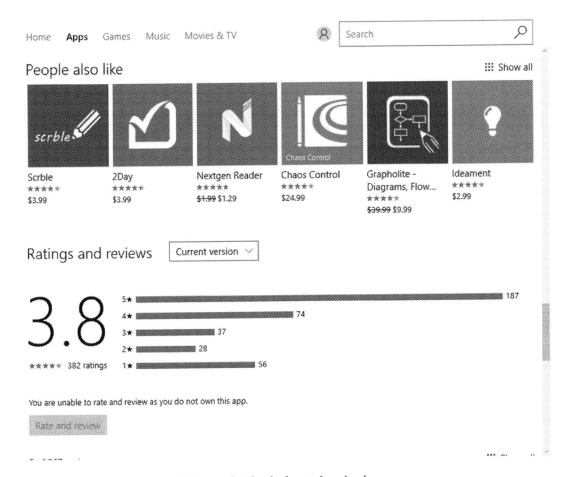

Figure 9-5. *Customer reviews can help you decide whether to download an app*

Another way to browse through the Microsoft Store is to search it. To search for a program by name or by function, follow these steps:

1. Click the Microsoft Store icon (either on the Start menu or the Taskbar). The Microsoft Store window appears (see Figure 9-2).

2. Click within the Search text box in the upper right corner of the Microsoft Store window.

3. Type all or part of a program name or category type (such as health or finance). As you type, a list of all programs that match your search criteria will appear, as shown in Figure 9-6.

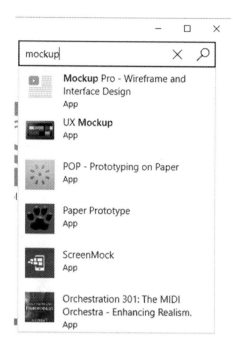

Figure 9-6. *Searching for a program in the Microsoft Store window*

Installing Software from the Microsoft Store

Once you find a program that you like, you can install it by clicking the price button or the button that says Free or Buy, as shown in Figure 9-7.

Figure 9-7. *Programs may be free or display a price*

If you click a Buy button, you'll need to access your Microsoft account to verify the purchase. If you have already purchased (whether the program cost money or was free) and downloaded a program from the Microsoft Store, its button will simply say Install to show that you have already installed the program on your computer.

Installing Software Off the Internet

Not all programs available for Windows 10 are available on the Microsoft Store. Because some developers prefer to distribute their software themselves, you can find plenty of programs available for downloading off the Internet.

Some of these programs are free but many cost money. The typical way to distribute software over the Internet is to bundle it in a special installation file.

You must first download the program to your computer. When you click a link to download a file, Windows 10 displays a message, asking if you want to save the file, as shown in Figure 9-8.

Figure 9-8. *Windows 10 asks if you want to save a file from the Internet*

Asking helps confirm that you really want to download a file in case a malicious web site is trying to install malware on your computer without your knowledge. The Save button saves the file in the Downloads folder. The Save As button lets you choose where to save the file and even gives the file a different name if you want.

As soon as the download is finished, Windows 10 will ask if you want to run the file, as shown in Figure 9-9.

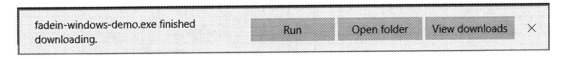

Figure 9-9. *After downloading a file, Windows 10 asks if you want to run it*

The Run button lets the downloaded program run. The Open folder lets you view the downloaded file in the File Explorer program. The View downloads button lets you view your most recent downloaded files, as shown in Figure 9-10.

Figure 9-10. *The Downloads window lists all your most recently downloaded files*

▓ **Note** To complete the installation process, you may need to type in a serial code when you first start the program. After you type in the serial code once, you won't have to type it again. However, keep the serial code in a safe place in case you need to install the software again at a later date.

Installing Programs from a DVD

If you buy software in a store, it will likely come on a DVD. To install software from a DVD, you must have a DVD drive. To install software from a DVD, follow these steps:

1. Insert the software DVD into the DVD drive of your computer.

2. Open the File Explorer program through the Start menu or the Taskbar. The File Explorer window appears.

3. Click the CD/DVD drive in the left pane of the File Explorer window to display the contents of the DVD.

4. Double-click a file called autorun or install, which will run the installation program that will guide you into installing the program on your computer, as shown in Figure 9-11.

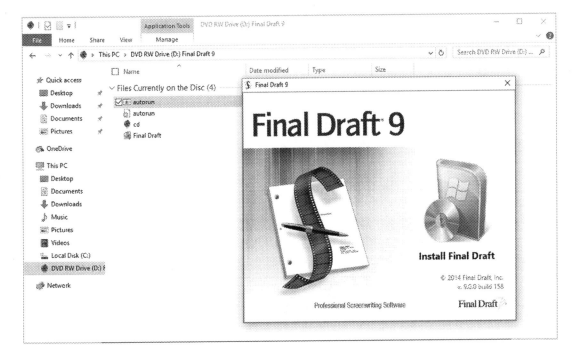

Figure 9-11. *Software on a DVD typically contains its own installation program*

■ **Note** After you install software from a DVD, store the DVD and any serial codes in a safe place in case you need to reinstall the software later.

Uninstalling Programs

Once you have installed a program, you may later want to remove it from your computer. To remove or uninstall a program, follow these steps:

1. Click the Windows icon in the lower left corner of the screen to open the Start menu.

2. Click the Settings icon. The Settings window appears.

3. Click the System icon. A list of System options appears.

4. Click Apps & features. A list of installed programs appears, as shown in Figure 9-12.

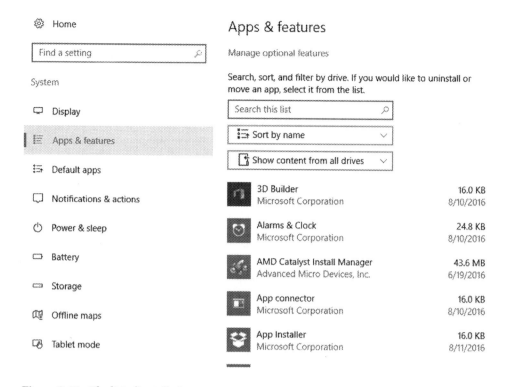

Figure 9-12. *The list of installed programs on a computer*

5. Click a program you want to uninstall. An Uninstall button appears underneath your chosen program, as shown in Figure 9-13.

Figure 9-13. *The Uninstall button lets you safely remove a program from your computer*

6. Click the Uninstall button if you're sure you want to remove the program from your computer.

7. Click the close button (the X icon in the upper right corner) to close the Settings window.

Updating Windows

Perhaps the most important program on your computer is Windows 10. Periodically, Microsoft improves Windows 10 by making it more stable and reliable while adding new features. To keep your copy of Windows 10 up to date, Microsoft will automatically update Windows 10.

One problem with this update process is that it can occur at a time when you need to use the computer and the update process makes you wait several minutes. To avoid this inconvenience, you can manually update Windows 10 or define settings so Windows 10 updates at a time when it won't interrupt you such as early in the morning or late at night. (Just remember to keep your computer turned on with an Internet connection during those times.)

To modify the Windows 10 update settings, follow these steps:

1. Click the Windows icon in the lower left corner of the screen to open the Start menu.

2. Click Settings. The Settings window appears.

3. Click the Update & security icon.

4. Click Windows Update in the left pane. The update settings appear, as shown in Figure 9-14.

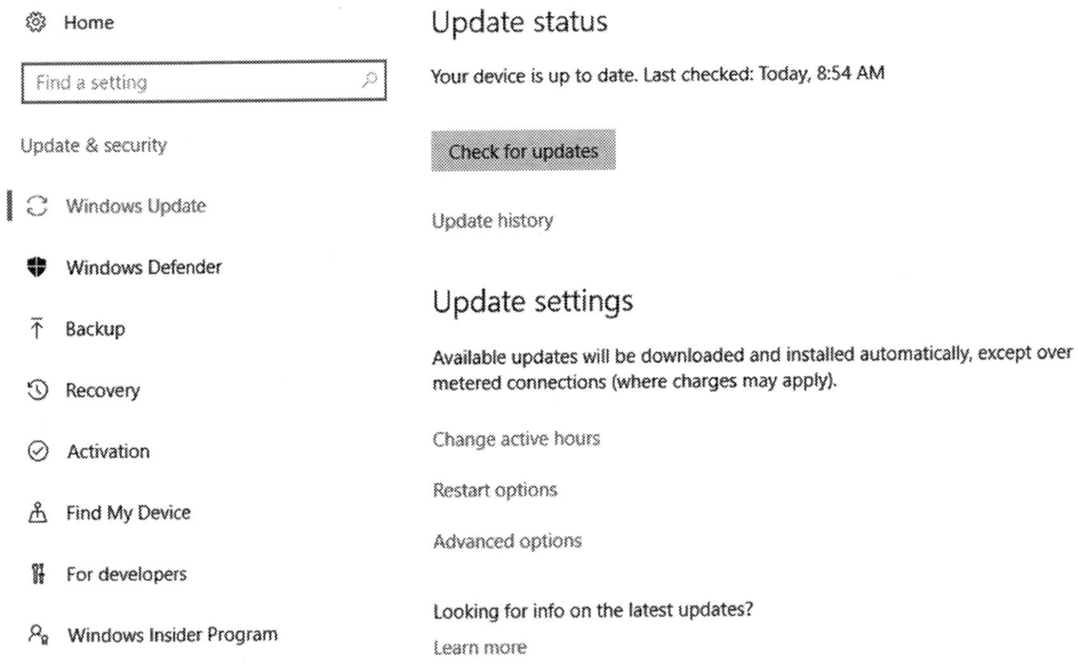

⚙ Home	**Update status**
Find a setting 🔍	Your device is up to date. Last checked: Today, 8:54 AM
Update & security	
	Check for updates
↻ Windows Update	
	Update history
🛡 Windows Defender	
	Update settings
↑ Backup	
	Available updates will be downloaded and installed automatically, except over
↺ Recovery	metered connections (where charges may apply).
⊘ Activation	Change active hours
	Restart options
🗚 Find My Device	
	Advanced options
🗏 For developers	
	Looking for info on the latest updates?
🗝 Windows Insider Program	Learn more

Figure 9-14. *The Update settings let you define how Windows 10 updates itself*

5. (Optional) Click the Check for updates button if you want to update Windows 10 right away.

6. (Optional) Click Change active hours. This displays a dialog box, as shown in Figure 9-15, that lets you define which hours you'll be using the computer so the update process won't restart your computer within this defined time period.

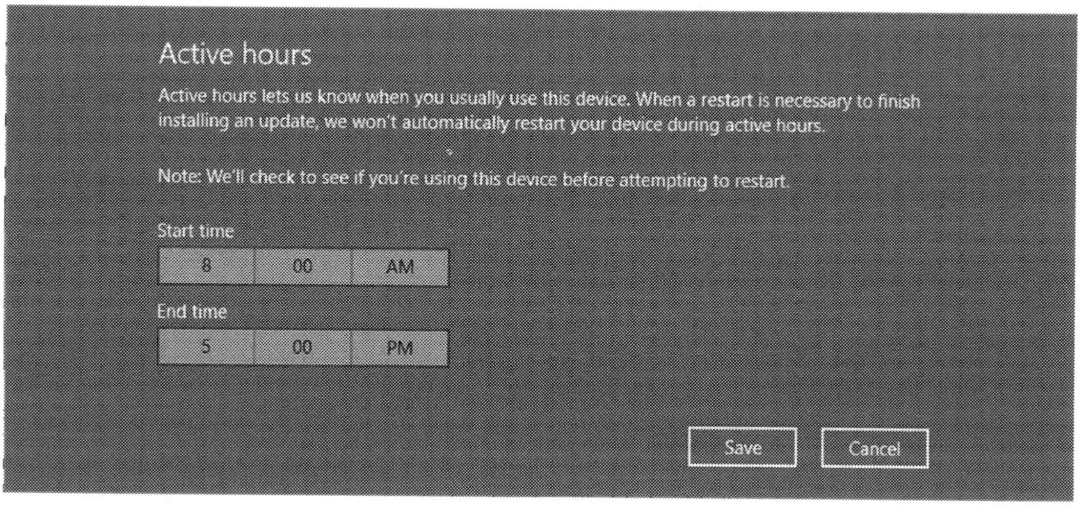

Active hours

Active hours lets us know when you usually use this device. When a restart is necessary to finish installing an update, we won't automatically restart your device during active hours.

Note: We'll check to see if you're using this device before attempting to restart.

Start time

| 8 | 00 | AM |

End time

| 5 | 00 | PM |

Save   Cancel

Figure 9-15. Defining the active hours when you'll be using the computer

7.   Click the close button (the X icon in the upper right corner) to close the Settings window.

Summary

Installing software is the most common way to customize your computer so it can perform the tasks you need. You can buy software through the Microsoft Store, from a retail store, or directly from a software publisher's web site.

The safest way to get software is either from the Microsoft Store or from the software publisher's official DVD installation disc.

When downloading and installing software over the Internet, make sure you trust the source to avoid infecting your computer with malware by mistake.

If you no longer want a particular program on your computer, you can uninstall it. This frees up space to store other programs.

The more you use a computer, the more likely you'll need to install programs and occasionally uninstall some programs you may no longer use. With the right software, you can customize your computer to perform nearly any task.

CHAPTER 10

▓ ▓ ▓

Customizing the Screen

You're going to spend most of your time looking at your computer screen so why not customize its appearance to make your computer uniquely yours? Customization can be for fun such as displaying pictures of your family or pets on the screen, or practical such as creating shortcuts to make your tasks easier and faster.

Some different ways to customize your screen include:

- Changing the wallpaper of the Desktop

- Defining a screensaver to appear after a period of inactivity

- Modifying the appearance of the mouse/trackpad pointer

▓ **Note** When you customize the way your computer looks and behaves, it won't look or behave like another computer. If you use multiple computers, you may want to customize all of them identically.

Changing the Desktop Wallpaper

The Desktop fills the entire screen so it will be the first image you see when you turn on your computer. In the old days, computer screens displayed a solid black or white background. While you could still use a solid color, you now have the option to display pictures, called the *wallpaper*.

Like real wallpaper, the wallpaper on your Desktop simply provides decoration on the screen. You can place any picture you want on the Desktop such as pictures captured from a digital camera or downloaded off the Internet.

If you get tired of looking at the same picture all the time, you can even have different pictures appear at random intervals. Wallpaper doesn't do anything useful, but it does make using a computer a little more fun.

The three different ways to change the Desktop wallpaper are:

- A single picture

- A solid background color

- A slideshow using pictures stored in a folder

If you choose a single picture, you can use one of the pictures that Windows 10 provides or use a picture of your own.

If you choose a slideshow, you'll need to select a folder containing two or more pictures.

© Wallace Wang 2016

W. Wang, *Absolute Beginners Guide to Computing*, DOI 10.1007/978-1-4842-2289-8_10

▨ **Note**   Make sure you don't choose a folder that may contain embarrassing or inappropriate images.

To change your Desktop wallpaper, follow these steps:

1. Click the Windows icon in the lower left corner of the screen to open the Start menu.

2. Click the Settings icon. The Settings window appears.

3. Click the Personalization icon. A list of options appears.

4. Click Background in the left pane to display different wallpaper options, as shown in Figure 10-1.

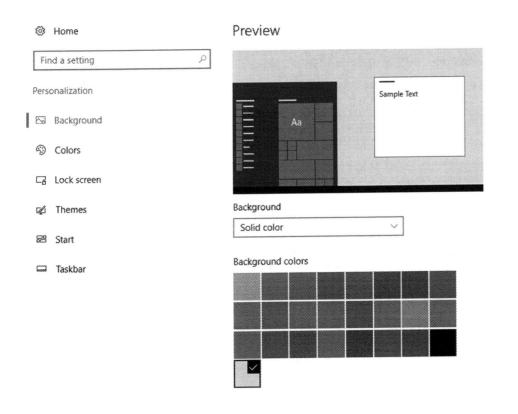

Figure 10-1. Options for changing the background image of the Desktop wallpaper

5. (Optional) Choose Solid color in the Background list box and click a color.

6. (Optional) Choose Picture in the Background list box, as shown in Figure 10-2, and click a picture or choose Browse to choose your own picture stored in a folder.

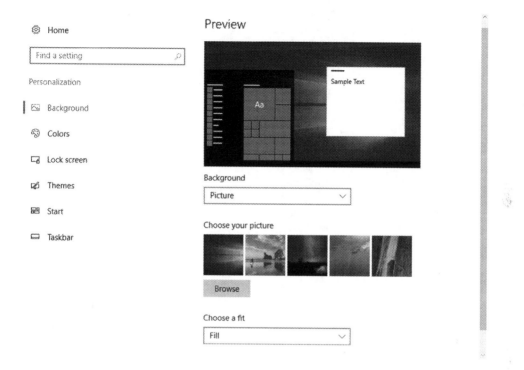

Figure 10-2. *Choosing a picture to appear as the Desktop wallpaper*

7. (Optional) Choose Slideshow under the Background list box, as shown in Figure 10-3, and click Browse to choose pictures stored in a folder.

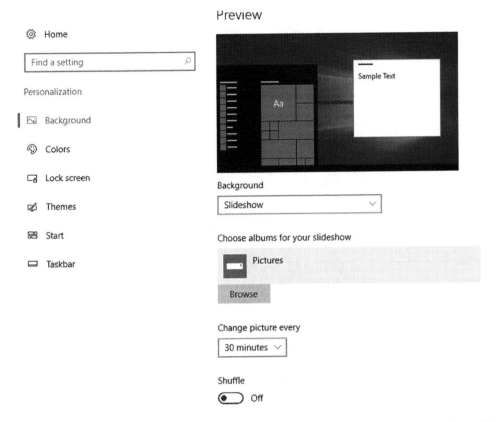

Figure 10-3. *Choosing a folder containing multiple pictures to appear as a slideshow as the Desktop wallpaper*

8. Click the close button (the big X) in the upper right corner of the Personalization window to close it.

Defining a Screensaver

Back in the days when computers used cathode-ray tube (CRT) monitors, leaving the same image on the screen for long periods could literally burn that image into the glass screen. If you look at old arcade games or automated-teller machines, you can sometimes see this faint, ghost-like image on the screen even though the screen may be turned off.

To prevent the screen from burning a static image into the glass, people used special programs called screensavers. The idea behind a screensaver was that by displaying a constantly changing image on the screen, there would be no chance that any image would appear on the screen long enough to burn into the glass.

Nowadays screensavers are far less important because flat-screen monitors pose far less risk of burning a static image onto the screen. Nevertheless, some people still prefer screensavers to make sure burn-in never occurs and to provide a pleasant display if you don't use your computer for a fixed period of time such as 5 minutes.

Since screensavers are still popular mostly for aesthetic reasons, Windows 10 provides a series of built-in screensavers from which you can choose. When choosing a screensaver, you need to choose a screensaver type and a time interval of inactivity to wait before the screensaver starts running.

To choose a screensaver for your computer, follow these steps:

1. Click the Windows icon in the lower left corner of the screen to open the Start menu.

2. Click the Settings icon. The Settings window appears.

3. Click the Personalization icon. A list of options appears.

4. Click Lock screen in the left pane. Scroll down on the right pane until you see the Screen saver settings, as shown in Figure 10-4.

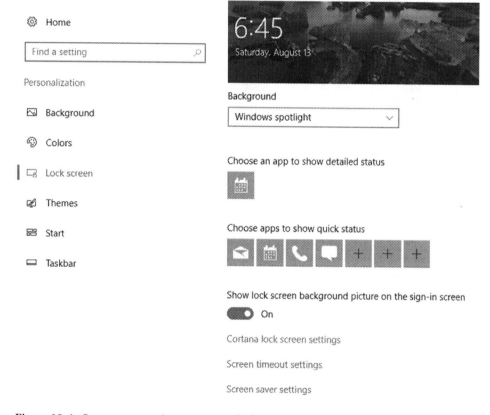

Figure 10-4. Screen saver settings appear at the bottom of the window

5. Click Screen saver settings. A Screen Saver Settings dialog box appears, as shown in Figure 10-5.

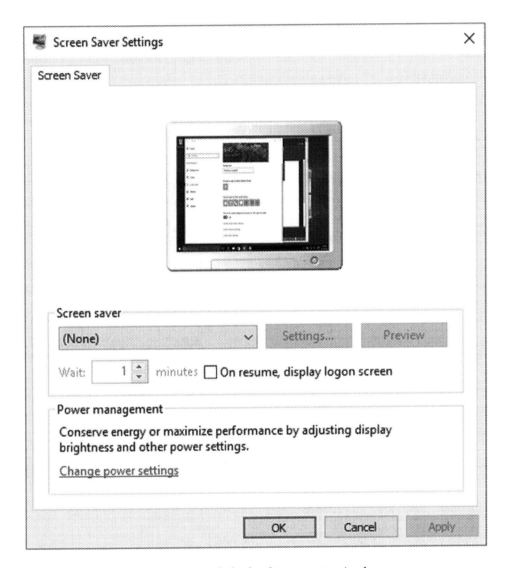

Figure 10-5. *The Screen Saver Settings dialog box lets you customize the screensaver*

6. Click the Screen saver list box and choose from options such as (None), 3D Text, Bubbles, or Ribbons.

7. Click the Settings button. Depending on the screensaver you chose (such as 3D Text), you may see another settings dialog box, as shown in Figure 10-6. (Remember, not all screensavers offer additional settings you can modify.)

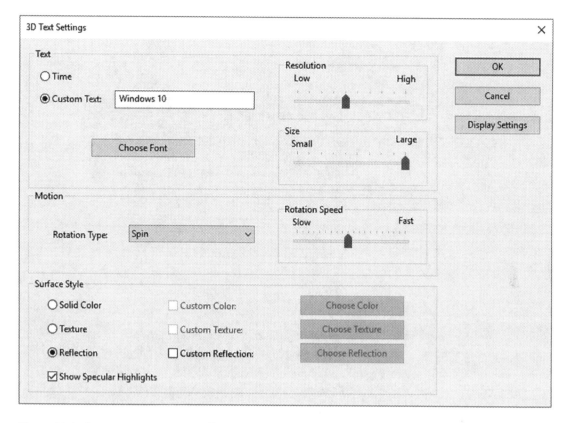

Figure 10-6. *Some screensaver types offer addition options you can modify*

8. Modify any options for your particular screensaver and click OK.

9. Click OK to make the Screen Saver Settings dialog box go away.

10. Click the close button (the X button) in the upper right corner of the Settings window to make it disappear.

Saving Power

If you have a laptop, you'll be especially concerned about saving power since it can prolong the life of your battery. Even if you have a desktop computer, you may still want to save power to reduce your electricity bill.

With a laptop, you can define two different power consumption settings. One setting is when your laptop is running on its battery power. The second setting is when your laptop is plugged into an electrical outlet.

To modify the energy settings of your computer, follow these steps:

1. Click the Windows icon in the lower left corner of the screen to open the Start menu.

2. Click the Settings icon. The Settings window appears.

3. Click the Personalization icon. A list of options appears.

4. Click Lock screen in the left pane.

5. Scroll down the right pane until you find the Screen timeout settings, as shown in Figure 10-7.

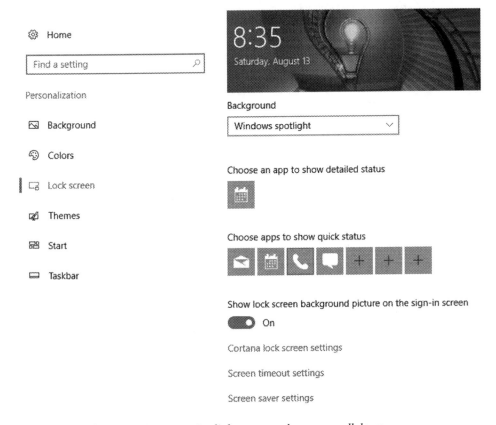

Figure 10-7. *The Screen timeout setting link appears when you scroll down*

6. Click Screen timeout settings. Another window appears showing various power setting options, as shown in Figure 10-8.

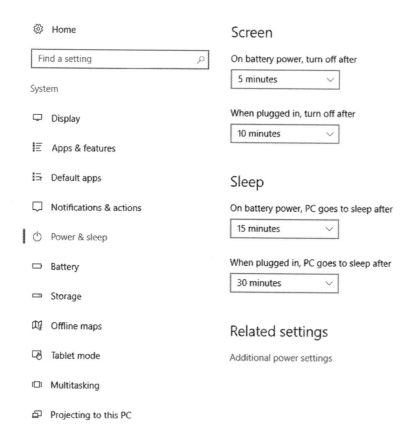

⚙ Home

Find a setting ⌕

System

▢ Display

☰ Apps & features

☷ Default apps

▢ Notifications & actions

⏻ Power & sleep

▭ Battery

▭ Storage

◫ Offline maps

▱ Tablet mode

▢ Multitasking

▱ Projecting to this PC

Screen

On battery power, turn off after

5 minutes ⌄

When plugged in, turn off after

10 minutes ⌄

Sleep

On battery power, PC goes to sleep after

15 minutes ⌄

When plugged in, PC goes to sleep after

30 minutes ⌄

Related settings

Additional power settings

Figure 10-8. You can modify the power settings for running on batteries and running on electrical power

7. Select the options you want such as turning the screen off after 5 minutes on battery power or after 20 minutes when plugged in.

8. Click the close button (the X button) in the upper left corner Settings window to make it disappear.

Using Themes

You can customize individual parts of Windows 10, but a faster way to modify the appearance of your screen is to use a theme. A theme changes the desktop background pictures, window colors, and sounds. Microsoft offers free themes you can download and use to modify the appearance of Windows 10 quickly and easily.

To choose a theme, follow these steps:

1. Click the Windows icon in the lower left corner of the screen to open the Start menu.

2. Click the Settings icon. The Settings window appears.

3. Click the Personalization icon. A list of options appears.

4. Click Themes in the left pane. A list of options appears.

5. Click Theme settings. A window appears, showing different themes you can choose, as shown in Figure 10-9.

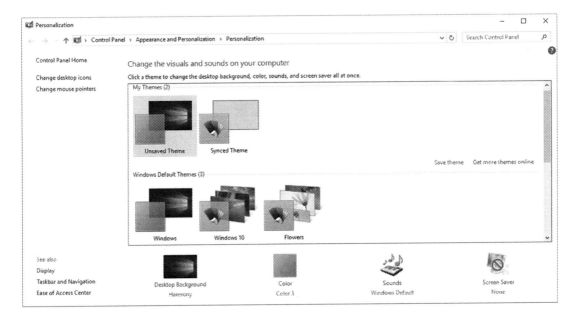

Figure 10-9. *Windows 10 provides different themes to choose from*

6. Click a theme. If you don't see a theme you like, continue to the next steps.

7. Click Get more themes online. Your browser loads the Microsoft web site listing more themes you can download and install on your computer, as shown in Figure 10-10.

BEACHES PANORAMIC

9 images in theme

Download

SUNNY SHORES

13 images in theme

Download

FORESTS

16 images in theme

Download

 Animal Affection

ANIMAL AFFFECTION

14 images in theme

Download

COMMUNITY SHOWCASE: AQUA 3

21 images in theme

Download

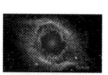

NASA HIDDEN UNIVERSE

14 images in theme

Download

FOREST PANORAMIC

8 images in theme

Download

NASA SPACESCAPES

14 images in theme

Download

EERIE AUTUMN

8 images in theme

Download

Figure 10-10. *Microsoft's web site offers more themes you can download and use on your computer*

8. Click a theme to download and save it to a folder on your computer that you can find again.

9. Open the File Explorer program and double-click the theme you just downloaded. Windows 10 displays your downloaded theme so you can click it.

10. Click the close button (the X button) in the upper right corner of the window to make it disappear.

Making the Pointer Easier to See

To use Windows 10, you need to use a mouse or trackpad, but some computers may include a touch screen so you can point with your finger. That means moving the pointer on the screen, but if you find the pointer too small or hard to see, you can make the pointer easier to find in two ways:

- Pointer trails

- Pointer location circles

Pointer trails mean that as you move the pointer, it leaves behind faint "ghost" images of the pointer, allowing you to easily spot the pointer on the screen.

Pointer location circles means that when you press and let go of the Control key, circles appear around the pointer so you can easily find it.

To turn on one or both features to make the pointer easier to see, follow these steps:

1. Click the Windows icon in the lower left corner of the screen to open the Start menu.

2. Click the Settings icon. The Settings window appears.

3. Click the Devices icon. A list of options appears.

4. Click Mouse & touchpad in the left pane. A list of mouse and trackpad options appears.

5. Scroll down the right pane until you see the Additional mouse options link, as shown in Figure 10-11.

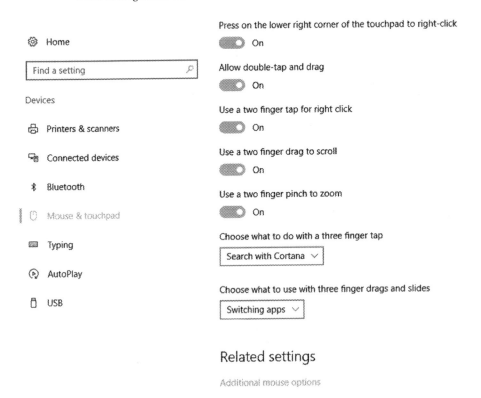

Figure 10-11. You must scroll down the right pane to find the Additional mouse options link

6. Click the Additional mouse options link. A Mouse Properties dialog box appears.

7. Click the Pointer Options tab to view a list of options, as shown in Figure 10-12.

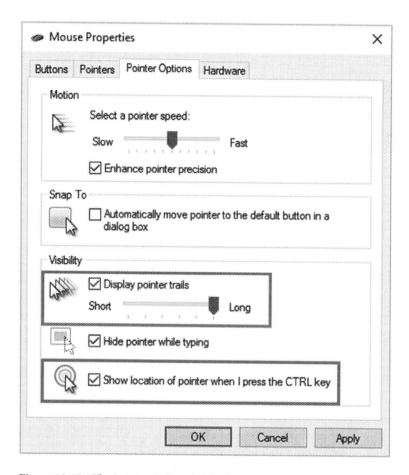

Figure 10-12. The Pointer Options tab in the Mouse Properties dialog box

8. Select the Display pointer trails check box and/or the Show location of pointer when I press the CTRL key check boxes.

▦ **Note**   You can also change how fast the pointer moves on the screen or turn on the Snap To feature, which automatically moves the pointer over the default button of a dialog box.

---

9. Click OK to close the Mouse Properties dialog box.

10. Click the close button (the X button) in the upper right corner of ther Settings window to make it disappear.

Summary

The appearance of your screen doesn't have to be boring. You can customize its look and behavior to make your computer uniquely your own. The simplest way to change the look of your computer is to select a Desktop wallpaper. This can be an image provided by Microsoft or any picture you may have copied off the Internet or captured with a digital camera.

Another way to customize your screen is to choose a screensaver. A screensaver can automatically run after a period of inactivity when you don't touch the keyboard, mouse, or trackpad. When Windows 10 detects inactivity for a fixed amount of time, it can run the screensaver.

Don't worry about every possible option available for customizing your computer. Just choose the features you need and ignore the rest. By customizing your computer, you can make your computer easier and more fun to use every day.

▓ ▓ ▓

CHAPTER 11

Customizing the File Explorer Window

No matter what you may need to do, the program you'll likely use most often is the File Explorer. The main purpose of the File Explorer is to help you organize and manipulate files stored on your computer. Those files may include word processor documents or databases, or they may include actual programs such as a game or a spreadsheet like Microsoft Excel.

With the File Explorer you can find, open, rename, copy, move, and delete files and folders. You can also modify or view information about each file as well as the file name or size. By customizing the File Explorer, you can make it easier to manipulate the files on your computer.

Some different ways to customize the File Explorer include:

- Hiding or showing File Explorer panes
- Changing the toolbar at the top of the File Explorer window
- Changing the type of information displayed about each file or folder

---

▓ **Note** When you customize the way your computer looks and behaves, it won't look or behave like another computer. If you use multiple computers, you may want to customize all of them identically.

Customizing the Panes

The File Explorer offers three different panes, as shown in Figure 11-1:

- Navigation pane
- Preview pane
- Details pane

© Wallace Wang 2016
W. Wang, *Absolute Beginners Guide to Computing*, DOI 10.1007/978-1-4842-2289-8_11

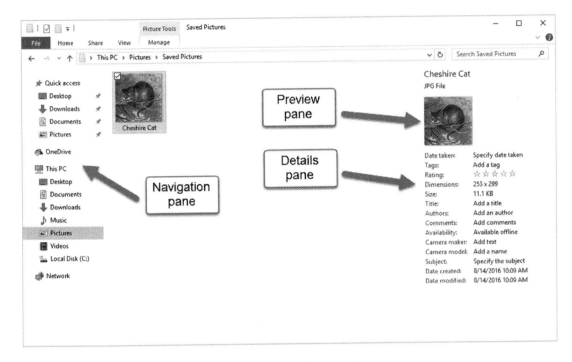

Figure 11-1. *The location of the three panes of the File Explorer window*

The Navigation pane appears on the left side of the File Explorer window and lists all the drives available on your computer, where each drive contains folders and each folder contains files and other folders.

The Preview pane lets you click a file and view its contents. This Preview pane works best for graphic files and Microsoft Word documents. If you click other types of files created by other programs, such as Microsoft Access, the Preview pane may not be able to show the contents of that file.

The Details pane displays information about the file such as its name, size, date created and modified, and even the type of camera that captured the image if it is a picture. Such detailed information can be helpful to identify which file may be the latest version if you have identical files.

To hide or display the three different File Explorer panes, follow these steps:

1. Click the Windows icon in the lower left corner of the screen to open the Start menu.

2. Click the File Explorer icon. The File Explorer window appears.

3. Click the View tab, as shown in Figure 11-2.

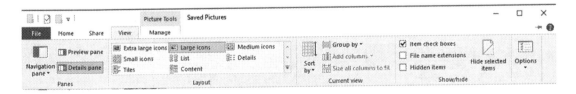

Figure 11-2. *The View tab lets you choose which panes to hide or display*

4. Click the pane you want to hide or display. Clicking each pane button toggles that pane so if it's currently hidden, clicking the pane button once again displays that pane.

Using the Navigation Pane

The Navigation pane is most useful to identify the different drives available on a computer. While most computers have a hard drive, they may also be connected to a CD/DVD drive, OneDrive, an external hard drive, a USB flash drive, or even a network.

▓ **Note**   OneDrive is Microsoft's online storage. You can get a free OneDrive account with limited storage but if you want more storage, you'll need to pay a monthly fee. Think of OneDrive as a hard disk connected to the Internet that you can access from any Internet-connected computer.

The Navigation pane typically displays the following categories, as shown in Figure 11-3:

- *Quick access*: Lists commonly accessed folders such as Documents or Pictures
- *OneDrive*: Lists the files and folders stored on your OneDrive account
- *This PC*: Lists all of the physical drives connected to your computer such as a USB flash drive or a CD/DVD drive
- *Network*: Lists the files and folders available if your computer is connected to a network

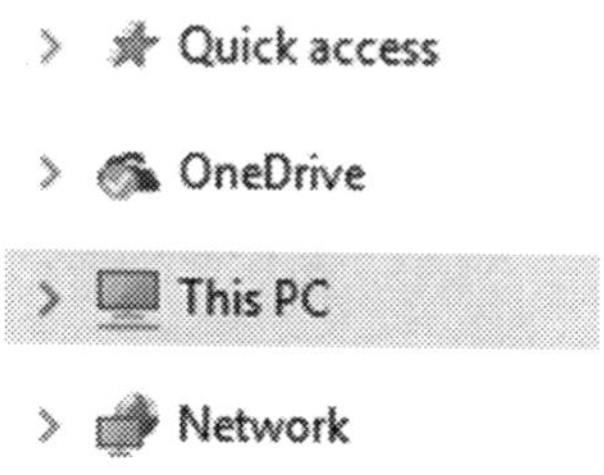

> ✱ Quick access

> ☁ OneDrive

> 🖥 This PC

> 🖧 Network

Figure 11-3. *The different categories in the Navigation pane*

For most people, the two categories they'll use most often are Quick access and This PC. The Quick access category gives you fast access to your commonly used folders, which you can customize. The This PC category gives you access to all of the drives and folders on your computer.

▓ **Note**   It's possible to view the exact same folder under both the Quick access and This PC categories. Although the same folder can be displayed under two different categories, they do not represent two different folders but the same folder.

An arrow appears to the left of each category. If you click that arrow, you can toggle between displaying all the devices stored in that category, as shown in Figure 11-4. The left arrow lets you keep hiding or displaying items under each category.

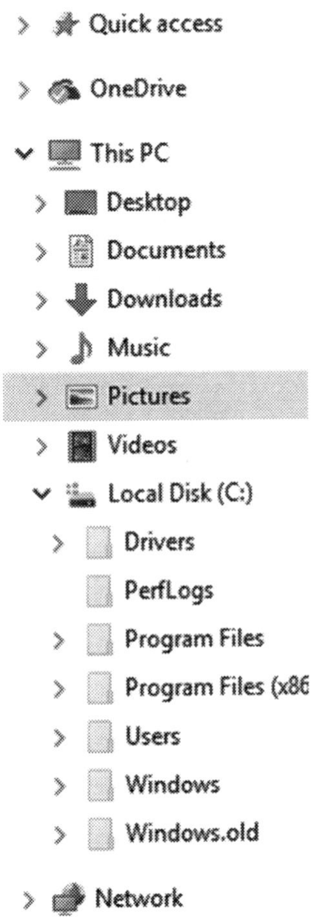

> ⭐ Quick access

> ☁ OneDrive

∨ 🖥 This PC
  > 🖳 Desktop
  > 📄 Documents
  > ⬇ Downloads
  > ♪ Music
  > 🖼 Pictures
  > 🎞 Videos
  ∨ 💾 Local Disk (C:)
    > 📁 Drivers
      📁 PerfLogs
    > 📁 Program Files
    > 📁 Program Files (x86
    > 📁 Users
    > 📁 Windows
    > 📁 Windows.old

> 🖧 Network

Figure 11-4. You can hide or display all devices connected to a category

Resizing the Navigation Pane

You can widen or shrink the Navigation pane to help you better see anything displayed. To resize the Navigation pane, follow these steps:

1. Open the File Explorer program.

2. Make sure the Navigation pane is visible on the left side of the File Explorer window.

3. Move the pointer over the right edge of the Navigation pane until the pointer turns into a two-way pointing arrow.

4. Drag (hold down the left button and move the mouse or slide your finger across the trackpad surface) to resize the Navigation pane.

Adding and Removing the Quick Access Category

The Quick access category is designed to list the folders you use most often. Initially this Quick access category contains several common folders such as Downloads and Music, but you can add or remove folders from this Quick access category.

To remove folders from the Quick access category, follow these steps:

1. Open the File Explorer program.

2. Make sure the Navigation pane is visible on the left side of the File Explorer window.

3. Click the arrow to the left of the Quick access category to display a list of folder names.

4. Right-click a folder, under the Quick access category, that you want to remove. A pop-up menu appears, as shown in Figure 11-5.

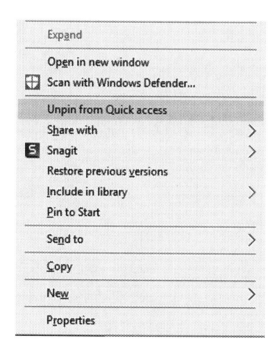

Figure 11-5. Right-clicking a folder displays a pop-up menu to allow you to unpin a folder

5. Choose Unpin from Quick access. Your chosen folder disappears from the Quick access category.

▨ **Note** When you remove a folder from the Quick access category, you don't physically delete or affect the folder or any of its contents. All you're doing is removing a shortcut link to that folder.

Once you've removed any folders you don't want displayed in the Quick access category, you can add new folders to this Quick access category. To add a folder to the Quick access category, follow these steps:

1. Open the File Explorer program.

2. Make sure the Navigation pane is visible on the left side of the File Explorer window.

3. Right-click a folder you want to place in the Quick access category. A pop-up menu appears, as shown in Figure 11-6.

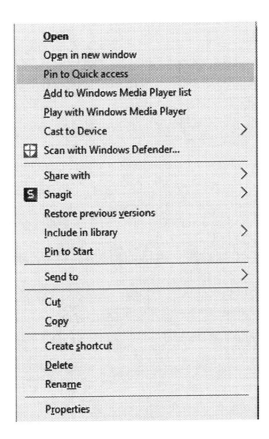

Figure 11-6. *Right-clicking a folder displays a pop-up menu to allow you to pin a folder*

4. Choose Pin to Quick access. Your chosen folder now appears in the Quick access category.

Customizing the Quick Access Toolbar

The Quick access category in the Navigation pane lets you open your most commonly used folders easily. To help you choose common types of commands for manipulating files and folders, such as Rename or Delete, the upper left corner of the File Explorer window displays a list of icons organized in the Quick Access toolbar, as shown in Figure 11-7.

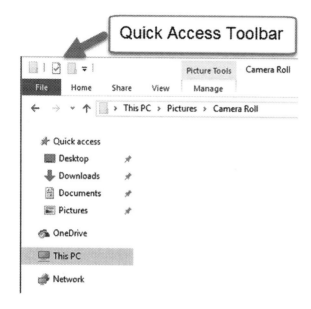

Figure 11-7. *The toolbar in the File Explorer window*

The Quick Access toolbar can show (or hide) icons that represent the following commands:

- *Undo*: Undoes the last command (equivalent to pressing Ctrl+Z)
- *Redo*: Redoes the last Undo command
- *Delete*: Deletes a selected file or folder
- *Properties*: Displays the Properties dialog box that contains information about a file or folder such as its date of creation or date last modified
- *New folder*: Creates a new folder
- *Rename*: Renames a selected file or folder

To customize the Quick Access toolbar, follow these steps:

1. Open the File Explorer program.
2. Click the Customize Quick Access toolbar icon, which looks like a downward-pointing arrow. A menu appears, as shown in Figure 11-8.

Figure 11-8. *The Customize Quick Access toolbar menu*

3. Click the commands you want to add (or remove) from the Quick Access toolbar. A check mark to the left means that command appears on the toolbar.

Customizing the File Explorer Ribbon Interface

The File Explorer window displays commands in a Ribbon interface that consists of tabs where each tab contains icons that represent different commands. The four different tabs of the Ribbon interface are labeled:

- *File*: Commands for opening additional windows or switching to another folder

- *Home*: Commands for copying, moving, renaming, or deleting files and folders

- *Share*: Commands for sharing files or folders with others

- *View*: Commands for changing how File Explorer displays the contents of a folder

If you click the name for a graphic file, a Picture Tools Manage tab appears, displaying commands for rotating the graphic or setting it as a background image, as shown in Figure 11-9.

Figure 11-9. *The Ribbon interface consists of tabs that group related commands together*

Normally the Ribbon interface displays tabs. If you want to see the icons on each tab, you need to click the tab. This keeps the icons out of the way until you need them.

However, some people prefer seeing the icons on each tab without having to click the tab. To toggle between making tab icons appear all the time or keeping them hidden, choose one of the following:

- Double-click any tab on the Ribbon interface.

- Press Ctrl+F1.

- Click the Expand/Minimize Ribbon icon in the upper right corner of the File Explorer window, as shown in Figure 11-10.

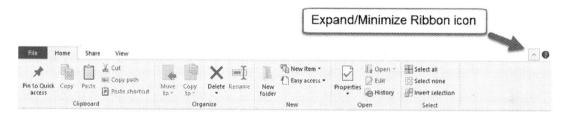

Figure 11-10. *The Expand/Minimize icon*

Customizing How to Open Folders

The File Explorer program has several settings that you might want to modify:

- The default category to highlight when the File Explorer program first starts up (Quick access or This PC)

- Whether to open a new folder within the same File Explorer window or in a new File Explorer window

- Whether to open a folder by single-clicking or double-clicking

In most cases, you want the File Explorer program to select the Quick access category so you can click the folder you use most often.

Each time you select another folder, the File Explorer displays that folder's contents in the same window. While this can be convenient, you may still want to view the contents of the previously displayed folder. By making File Explorer open a new window each time you select another folder, you can keep all previously opened files in view, but at the expense of having multiple File Explorer windows on the screen.

Most people are used to double-clicking to open a folder, but you can redefine File Explorer to open a folder by single-clicking. This can be handy for people who have trouble double-clicking or simply prefer to open a folder with a single click.

To customize the behavior of File Explorer, follow these steps:

1. Open the File Explorer program. Notice that it automatically selects either the Quick access or This PC category in the Navigation pane.

2. Click the View tab and click the top of the Options icon. A Folder Options dialog box appears, as shown in Figure 11-11.

Figure 11-11. The Folder Options dialog box lets you customize the behavior of File Explorer

3. Click the arrow for Open File Explorer to: list box and choose Quick access or This PC.

4. Click a radio button under the Browse folders group to define whether to open a folder in the same window or in a separate window.

5. Click the radio button under the Click items as follows group to define whether to open a folder with a single-click or double-click.

6. Click OK.

Summary

You'll likely use the File Explorer every time you use a computer to manipulate files and folders, so take some time to understand how you can customize its features so it will be easier for you. Place your favorite folders in the Quick access category of the Navigation pane for easy access. Modify the Quick Access toolbar so your most frequently used commands are available at all times.

Take some time to customize the behavior of the File Explorer program such as single- or double-clicking to open a folder and whether to open a new folder in the same window or in a separate window.

The File Explorer is one of the most crucial programs you'll use to manage files on your computer. A little time spent modifying the File Explorer today will make your computer much easier to use.

■ ■ ■

CHAPTER 12

Organizing Windows

No matter how big your screen may be (even if you have multiple screens), there never seems to be enough room to show everything. You can minimize windows or temporarily hide them, but a more elegant solution might be to use multiple Desktops.

When you first start your computer, you'll see the Desktop displaying its wallpaper background image. Any program windows you open will appear on this Desktop. Eventually if you open too many windows, your Desktop will get cluttered.

To solve this problem, you have several options:

- Minimize one or more windows to tuck them out of sight

- Use Task View to view all open windows

- Create multiple virtual Desktops

Minimizing, Maximizing, and Closing a Window

A window typically covers part of the screen. You can drag the edges or corners of the window to resize it. However, three other options for manipulating a window are:

- Minimize the window (hides the window from sight)

- Maximize the window (expands the window to fill the entire screen)

- Close the window (removes the window from the screen and may close the program that opened the window)

To minimize, maximize, or close a window, use the three icons located in the upper right corner of every window, as shown in Figure 12-1.

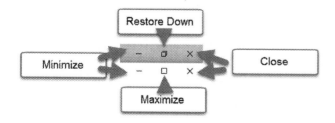

Figure 12-1. *The Minimize, Maximum/Restore Down, and Close buttons of a window*

© Wallace Wang 2016

W. Wang, *Absolute Beginners Guide to Computing*, DOI 10.1007/978-1-4842-2289-8_12

Minimizing a Window

The main advantage of opening multiple windows is so you can see information from one window while working in another window. However, too many windows on the screen can clutter the screen, so you can temporarily tuck a window out of sight by minimizing it.

When you minimize a window, it appears as a thumbnail image on the Dock next to the Trash icon. When you want to use a minimized window again, just click its thumbnail image on the Dock.

To minimize a window, you have several options:

- Click the minimize button that appears in the upper right corner of every window (see Figure 12-1)

- Press the Windows key plus the Down arrow key

- Click the program icon on the Taskbar that opened the window you want to minimize (this only works if a program has just one open window)

When you minimize a window, it disappears from view. To open a minimized window again, move the pointer over a program icon on the Taskbar. When you hover the pointer over a program icon, thumbnail images appear to show you all currently open windows, even if one or more of those windows is minimized. When you want to open a minimized window, just click its thumbnail image.

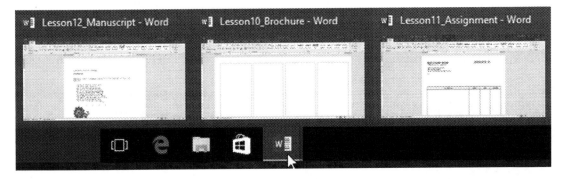

Figure 12-2. *View all currently open windows of a program*

Maximizing a Window

Maximizing a window fills the entire screen with that one window. This can help you focus on a single window without the distraction of other windows on the screen. To maximize a window, choose one of these commands:

- Click the Maximize icon in the upper right corner of the window

- Press the Windows key plus the Up arrow key

Once you've maximized a window to fill the entire screen, you can restore the window back to its previous size by choosing one of these commands:

- Click the Restore Down icon in the upper right corner of the window

- Press the Windows key plus the Down arrow key

▓ **Note** When a window is maximized, the Restore Down icon appears. When a window is not maximized, the Maximize icon appears (see Figure 12-1).

Closing a Window

Once you've opened a window, you can close that window at any time by doing one of the following:

- Click the Close icon in the upper right corner of the window

- Press Alt+F4 (On some keyboards, you may need to press the Fn key before pressing the F4 key)

Organizing Windows with Task View

While minimizing windows can help you keep your Desktop organized, it can be troublesome to minimize windows individually. The more minimized windows you tuck out of sight, the harder it can be to keep track of all your open windows. Rather than minimize one or more windows, Windows 10 lets you view all open windows as thumbnail images on the screen known as Task View, as shown in Figure 12-3.

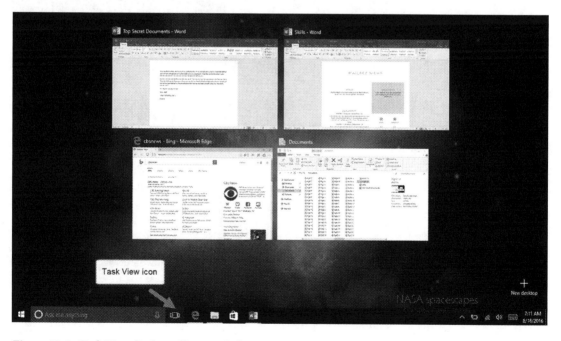

Figure 12-3. *Task View displays all open windows at once*

Task View lets you see all open windows on the screen. Now you can click the thumbnail image of the window you want to use. To toggle between opening (and closing) Task View, choose one of these options:

- Click the Task View icon on the Taskbar

- Press the Windows key plus the Tab key

Snapping Windows

The main advantage of opening multiple windows at the same time is so you can see information in two different windows or copy and paste information from one window to another. For example, you might want to copy text from your browser and paste it into your word processor.

Unfortunately, the more windows you open, the more cluttered your screen can get. Even if you get a larger monitor, there will always be a limit to the number of open windows you can comfortably display on the screen at the same time. That's why Windows 10 offers a feature called Snapping.

Snapping displays one window on the side of the screen while displaying any other open windows as thumbnail images, as shown in Figure 12-4.

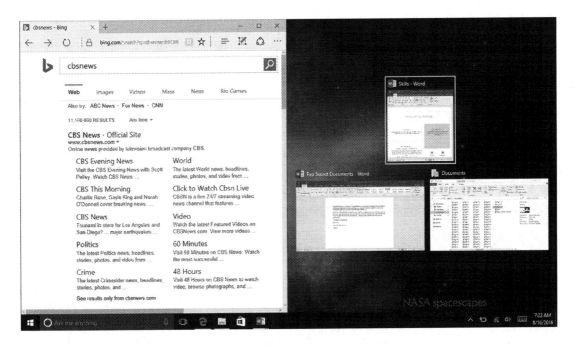

Figure 12-4. *Snapping highlights one window on the side of the screen*

To use Snapping windows, follow these steps:

1. Open Task View using one of these methods:

    a. Click the Task View icon on the Taskbar

    b. Press the Windows key plus the Tab key

2. Click the window you want to view. Windows 10 displays your chosen window on the screen.

3. Press one of the following keystrokes:

   a. Windows plus Left arrow key (to place the selected window on the left side of the screen)

   b. Windows plus Right arrow key (to place the selected window on the right side of the screen)

   Your chosen window appears on the left or right side of the screen.

4. Release the Windows and arrow keys. Thumbnail images of all other open windows appear on the other side.

5. Click another thumbnail image to open a second window side by side.

⬛ **Note**   You can also press Windows plus Up arrow to move an open window to the top of the screen or press Windows plus Down arrow to move an open window to the bottom of the screen. If a window isn't snapped to the left or the right, pressing Windows plus Up arrow maximizes a window and pressing Windows plus Down arrow minimizes a window.

Using Virtual Desktops

Most people only use one Desktop. Any windows you open appear on that one Desktop, so the more programs you use, the more windows clutter that one Desktop. As an alternative to organizing windows on one Desktop, you can create virtual Desktops.

The idea behind virtual Desktops is to help you organize related programs together. For example, you might open your word processor documents in one Desktop, your browser and e-mail program in a second Desktop, and a game in a third Desktop.

Now instead of having all open windows cluttering a single Desktop, you can organize programs in different Desktops and switch between Desktops.

Creating Additional Desktops

Each time you turn on your computer for the first time, it always displays a single Desktop. To create additional Desktops, follow these steps:

1. Open Task View using any method you like (such as pressing Windows plus Tab). Task View displays all open windows as thumbnail images along with a + New Desktop button in the lower right corner, as shown in Figure 12-5.

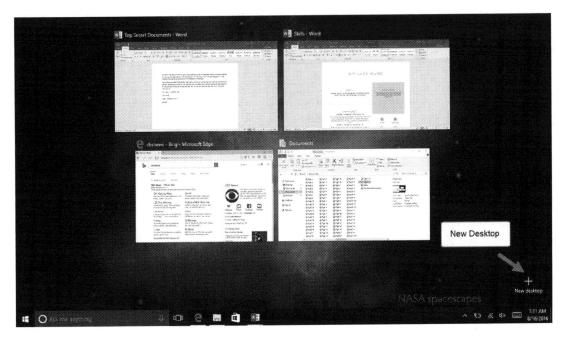

***Figure 12-5.** Clicking the + New Desktop button creates a new Desktop*

░ **Note** You can also press Windows+Ctrl+D to create a new virtual Desktop.

---

2. Click the + New Desktop button. Thumbnail images of two Desktops appear at the bottom of the screen, as shown in Figure 12-6.

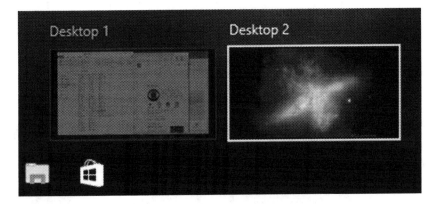

***Figure 12-6.** Virtual Desktops appear as thumbnail images in the center bottom of the screen*

3. Click the newly created Desktop thumbnail image, such as Desktop 2. Your Desktop appears.

4. Open Task View again and then click your first Desktop, such as Desktop 1. Notice that if you open any windows on Desktop 1, they appear again.

Rather than constantly managing multiple open windows on a single Desktop, virtual Desktops let you create multiple Desktops. Now you can isolate related windows in separate Desktops and each Desktop won't appear cluttered with so many open windows.

Switching Between Desktops

Once you've created two or more Desktops, you can switch between them. Each time you create another virtual Desktop, Windows 10 numbers each one and organizes them in a line where the first Desktop is numbered 1, the second Desktop is numbered 2, and so on. The ways to switch between Desktops are:

- Open Task View and click the Desktop thumbnail image that you want to use

- Press Windows+Ctrl+Right arrow to view the next Desktop (if you're currently viewing Desktop 3, this would display Desktop 4)

- Press Windows+Ctrl+Left arrow to view the previous Desktop (if you're currently viewing Desktop 3, this would display Desktop 2)

Moving Windows Between Desktops

On each Desktop you can open programs and arrange windows any way you like. If you open a program in one Desktop, you can later move it to a different Desktop. By moving open windows from one virtual Desktop to another, you can arrange each Desktop to display exactly the windows you want to see.

To move an open window from one Desktop to another, follow these steps:

1. Open Task View to display all open windows as thumbnails.

2. Right-click a window that you want to move to another Desktop. A pop-up menu appears.

3. Choose Move to, which will display a submenu. This submenu lists all other virtual Desktops available, as shown in Figure 12-7.

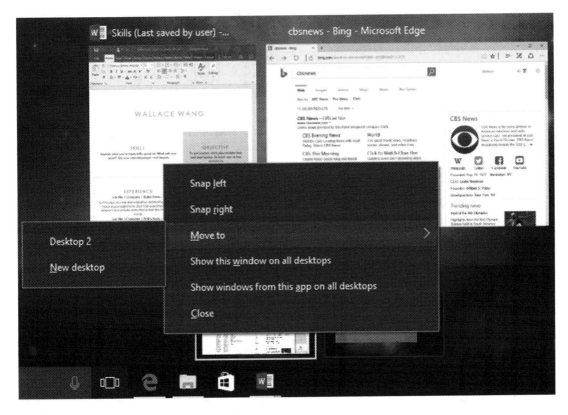

Figure 12-7. *Moving a window to another Desktop*

4. Choose a Desktop such as Desktop 2. (If you choose New Desktop, Windows 10 creates another virtual Desktop and places your chosen window in that Desktop.) Your chosen window now appears in the other Desktop.

5. Exit out of Task View (press Windows plus Tab).

By moving windows from one Desktop to another, you can have different windows from the same program in separate Desktops. For example, you might open two documents in Microsoft Word and place one document window in one Desktop and a second document window in another Desktop.

Deleting a Desktop

Once you've created two or more Desktops, you may eventually want to delete a Desktop. If you delete a Desktop that has open windows in it, they'll appear in another Desktop automatically, but you may want to move all windows to a specific Desktop yourself before deleting a Desktop.

To delete a Desktop, follow these steps:

1. Open Task View using any method you like (such as pressing Windows plus Tab). Task View displays all open windows as thumbnail images.

2. Move the pointer over the Desktop thumbnail you want to delete at the bottom of the screen. A close button (an X) appears in the upper right corner of each Desktop thumbnail, as shown in Figure 12-8.

Figure 12-8. *When hovering the pointer over a Desktop thumbnail image, a close button (X) appears*

3. Click the close button of the Desktop you want to delete. Your chosen Desktop disappears and any open windows on that Desktop move to another Desktop.

Summary

The ability to open multiple windows lets you multitask and refer to the contents of one window while working in another. However, too many windows can clutter the screen and prove more confusing than helpful.

That's why Windows 10 offers several ways to help organize and reduce the clutter. You can minimize individual windows to temporarily tuck them out of sight on the Dock. You can also hide windows completely and make them appear again when you want them.

If you have multiple open windows on the screen, you might want to use Task View, which can display all open windows as thumbnail images. By letting you see all open windows at once, you can click the one you want to use.

Another handy feature is virtual Desktops, which let you organize separate Desktops with different windows and switch between Desktops. This lets you keep each Desktop organized for a specific task.

With so many different ways to organize windows, you can use the methods you like best to keep yourself from getting distracted and getting overwhelmed by so much information displayed on the screen at once. By taking the time to learn different ways to organize your program windows, you can find the way that helps you to be more efficient and productive.

PART III

▪ ▪ ▪

Having Fun

The real reason people buy any computer isn't just to do more work, but to have fun. Even if you don't play video games, you can still find different ways to have fun with your computer by viewing and organizing pictures captured with a digital camera. In addition to letting you view and modify still images, your computer also lets you watch video.

Perhaps the most common trait everyone enjoys is listening to music. Whether you listen to classical, jazz, country, hip hop, rock, or rap, you can store, organize, and listen to your favorite songs and recording artists by turning your computer into a sophisticated jukebox or radio.

Computers are supposed to be fun to use, so find what you enjoy most and chances are good you'll find a way to have fun using your computer.

CHAPTER 13

Playing with Photos

Taking pictures can be fun. With digital cameras in every smartphone and tablet, it's easy to capture pictures wherever you go without worrying about taking a camera with you.

Since so many people take pictures, one of the biggest problems is finding a place to store those pictures. If you take too many pictures, you'll eventually run out of room to store them, so you need to know how to get photos off a smartphone, tablet, or camera and onto a computer for safe keeping.

There are two ways to transfer pictures from an external device (such as a smartphone or tablet) to a computer:

- Use the Photos program

- Use the File Explorer to copy individual pictures into a folder

Using the Photos Program

Included with Windows 10 is a program called Photos, which can store pictures, organize them, and edit them. Best of all, Photos can import pictures off a smartphone or tablet to make transferring photos fast, simple, and easy.

The Photos program can automatically display pictures stored in a folder such as the Pictures folder. Once you've stored pictures in the Pictures folder (or any other folder you define for Photos to automatically use), Photos lets you view pictures in chronological order, as shown in Figure 13-1, or grouped together in albums. You can also do light editing on pictures, such as adjusting the brightness or enhancing part of a picture.

© Wallace Wang 2016

W. Wang, *Absolute Beginners Guide to Computing*, DOI 10.1007/978-1-4842-2289-8_13

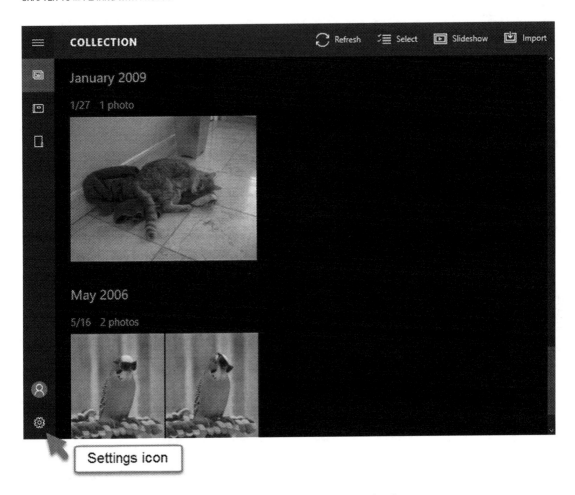

Figure 13-1. *The Photos program can organize pictures in chronological order*

For many people, Photos can be the only program you need to save, modify, and view your pictures, whether you get those pictures off the Internet, from your smartphone or tablet, or from files others may give you.

Adding Pictures to Photos

The Photos program knows how to access pictures stored in the Pictures folder on your computer or on your OneDrive account. To add pictures to the Photos library file, you just need to copy pictures into either of these Pictures folders. That means you can either connect a cable to an external camera (such as a smartphone or tablet) or retrieve pictures off a USB flash drive.

The Photos program uses the Pictures folder to retrieve images, but you can modify this setting. This lets you choose additional folders to retrieve pictures. To modify which folders the Photos program uses to look for images, follow these steps:

1. Open the Photos program.

2. Click the Settings icon in the bottom left corner (see Figure 13-1). The Settings window appears, as shown in Figure 13-2.

Figure 13-2. *The Settings window lets you customize the Photos program*

3. Scroll down until you see the Sources category.

4. Choose one of the following:

    a. Click the X icon (close) to the right of any folder you no longer want the Photos program to access automatically.

    b. Click + Add a folder. A dialog box appears, as shown in Figure 13-3.

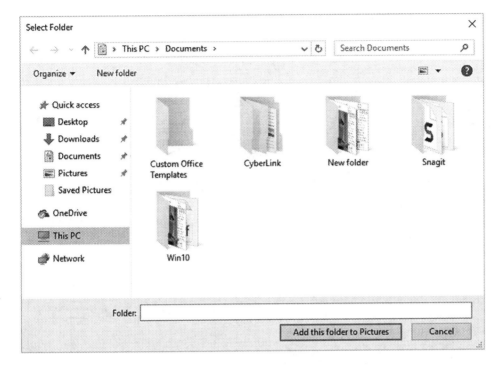

Figure 13-3. *A dialog box lets you select a folder for the Photos program to access*

5. Click a folder you want Photos to access and click the Add this folder to Pictures button.

Importing Pictures in Photos

If you have pictures stored on a memory card or flash drive, you can plug it into your computer and import them into Photos. Photos will copy those pictures into a folder (such as the Pictures folder) and give you the option of deleting the pictures off the external storage device.

To import pictures into Photos, follow these steps:

1. Open the Photos program.

2. Plug in the external storage device (flash drive, memory card, etc.) that contains the pictures you want to import into Photos.

3. Click the Import icon in the upper right corner of the Photos window, as shown in Figure 13-4. A Select dialog box appears, as shown in Figure 13-5. Photos automatically assumes you want to import all pictures unless you specify which pictures you do not want to import.

Figure 13-4. *Photos can detect and import pictures stored on an external device.*

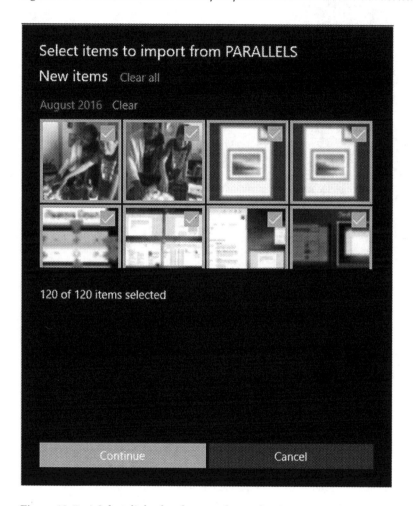

Figure 13-5. *A Select dialog box lets you choose the pictures you want to import*

4. Clear the pictures you don't want to import by clicking Clear All, Clear, or by clicking individual pictures.

5. Click the Continue button. A Start importing? dialog box appears, as shown in Figure 13-6.

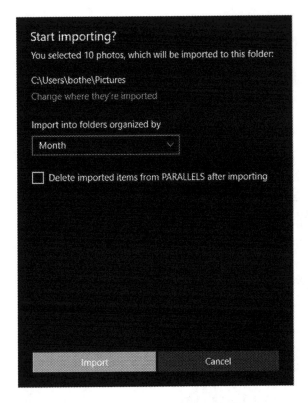

Figure 13-6. *The Start importing? dialog box lets you define which folder to store pictures and how to organize them*

6. (Optional) Click the Change where they're imported link and specify a different folder to store all your imported pictures.

7. (Optional) Click the Import into folders organized by list box and choose Month or Day.

8. (Optional) Select (or clear) the Delete imported items from PARALLELS after importing check box if you want to automatically delete pictures off the external device afterward.

■ **Note**　For maximum safety, it's better to leave this Delete imported items check box unchecked. Once you've verified that the Photos program has imported all your pictures correctly, then delete those files off the external device using the File Explorer program.

---

9. Click the Import button. Photos imports your pictures.

Viewing Pictures in Photos

Once you've saved pictures in the Photos program, you can view them in chronological order or by albums. Since most cameras place a date and time stamp on each photo, the Photos program can organize pictures by the date they were captured. Now you can easily find the most recent pictures at the top and older pictures by scrolling down, as shown in Figure 13-7.

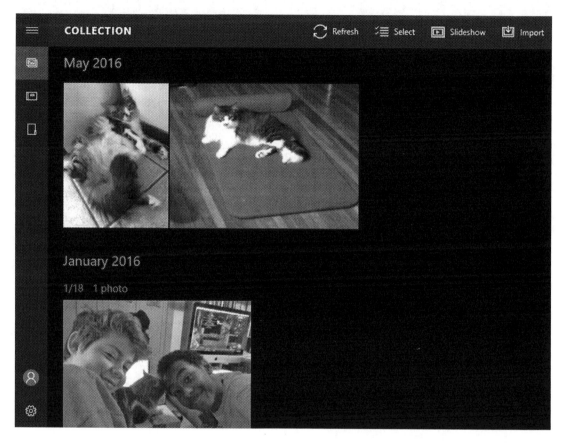

Figure 13-7. *The Photos program displays most recent pictures first*

When you scroll through pictures individually, it can become cumbersome if you have stored hundreds of pictures. As a faster alternative, you can view a list of all months by following these steps:

1. Open the Photos program.

2. Click the Collections icon in the upper left corner of the Photos window to make Photos display all your pictures organized by the month and year they were taken, such as May 2016 (see Figure 13-7).

3. Click the month category you want to view (such as May 2016). Photos displays a list of all months, as shown in Figure 13-8.

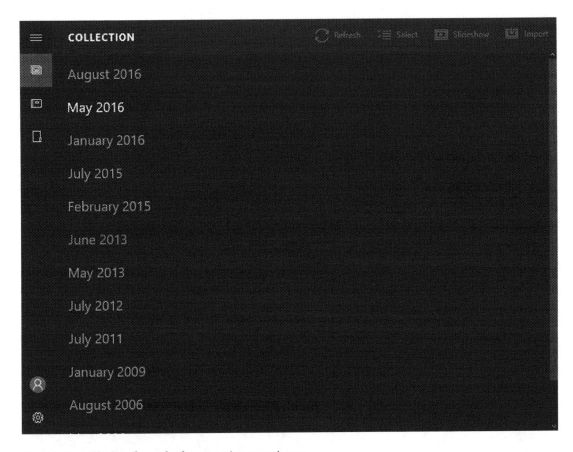

Figure 13-8. *The list of months that organize your pictures*

▓ **Note**   If you don't see certain months listed, that means you don't have any pictures that were captured in that particular month or year.

---

4.   Click a month and year to view the pictures captured during that time. Photos displays thumbnail images of all the pictures captured during your chosen month and year.

5.   Click a picture. Photos displays that one picture on the screen.

Editing Pictures in Photos

Editing a picture lets you fix slightly flawed pictures such as changing brightness, cropping pictures to cut out unwanted parts, or rotating images. Some different options for editing a picture include:

- *Enhance*: Brightens an image to correct pictures that are too dark

- *Rotate*: Flips a picture on its side

- *Crop*: Lets you select a rectangular part of the image to keep

- *Filters*: Lets you change the appearance of a picture as seen through different visual filters

- *Color*: Lets you change the color of an image

- *Retouch*: Lets you drag the pointer over parts of an image you want to remove such as eliminating blemishes on a person's face

- *Red-eye*: Lets you remove the red glow in a person's eyes that occurs when a picture is captured using flash

Each type of editing tool displays different options for modifying an image in different ways. To edit a picture stored in Photos, follow these steps:

1. Display the picture you want to edit. (Follow steps 1-5 in the previous section "Viewing Pictures in Photos.")

2. Click the picture to edit it. A list of buttons (Share, + Add to album, Enhance, Edit, Rotate, and Delete) appears at the top of the screen, as shown in Figure 13-9.

Figure 13-9. Clicking a picture displays buttons for editing that image

3. Click an editing tool on the right edge of the screen such as Enhance or Edit. If you click Edit, additional tool icons appear on the left and right sides of the screen to let you modify the image, as shown in Figure 13-10.

Figure 13-10. *Choosing Edit gives you access to multiple editing tools*

4. Click the Save button in the upper right corner when you're done, or click the Save a copy button if you want to retain your original image and save your modified image under another name.

Organizing Pictures in Albums

Just as you can organize physical pictures into albums, you can also organize digital pictures into different albums. The big difference is that physical photos can only appear in one album at a time. With digital albums, you can place the same photo in multiple albums.

For example, you might have one album containing only pictures of your pet dog and a second album containing only pictures of your son. Yet the same dog picture could appear in both albums if there's a picture of your dog with your son.

Albums simply give you a way to group related photos together so you can easily find them again. Photos automatically creates an album of your last imported pictures and all your saved pictures, but you can create your own albums to organize pictures based on your own criteria.

Creating an Album

To create an album, follow these steps:

1. Open the Photos program.

2. Click the Albums icon in the upper left corner of the Photos window. A list of all available albums appears, as shown in Figure 13-11.

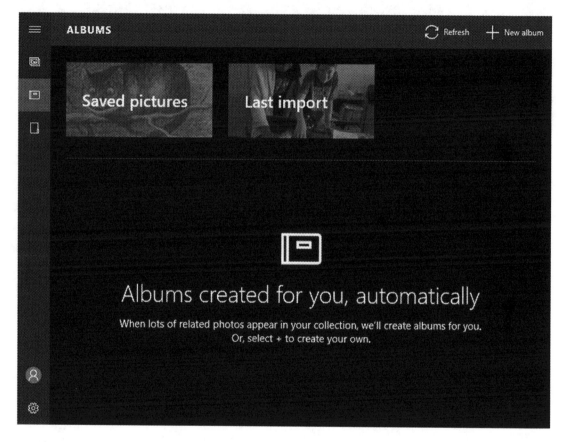

Figure 13-11. *Viewing all available albums*

3. Click the + New album button in the upper right corner of the Photos window. Photos displays all your pictures so you can select the ones you want to add to the album, as shown in Figure 13-12.

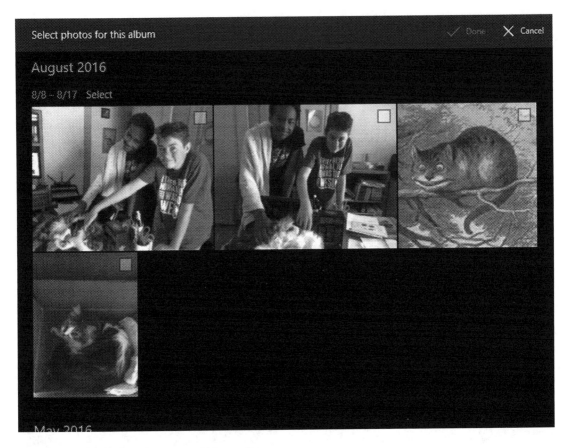

Figure 13-12. *Selecting pictures to add to an album*

4. Click the check box in the upper right corner of each picture that you want to add to the album.

5. Click the Done button in the upper right corner of the Photos window. Photos displays a text box for defining a name for your album, as shown in Figure 13-13.

Figure 13-13. *After you select pictures for an album, you need to name your album*

6. Type a name for your album.

7. (Optional) Click the Change cover button and select a picture to act as your album cover.

8. Click the Save button in the upper right corner of the Photos window to save your album.

Adding (or Removing) Pictures to an Album

Once you've created an album, you can add pictures to it. Adding pictures essentially means making a copy of that picture and storing it in an album, so if you ever delete that album (or that picture in that album), you'll still have a copy of that picture stored in the Photos Saved pictures main album.

To add pictures to an album, follow these steps:

1. Open the Photos program.

2. Click the Albums icon in the upper left corner of the Photos window. A list of all available albums appears (see Figure 13-11).

3. Click an album you created to which you want to add more pictures.

4. Scroll down all the pictures in your album until you see an Add or remove photos button in the bottom left corner, as shown in Figure 13-14. Photos displays all the pictures available for adding to the album.

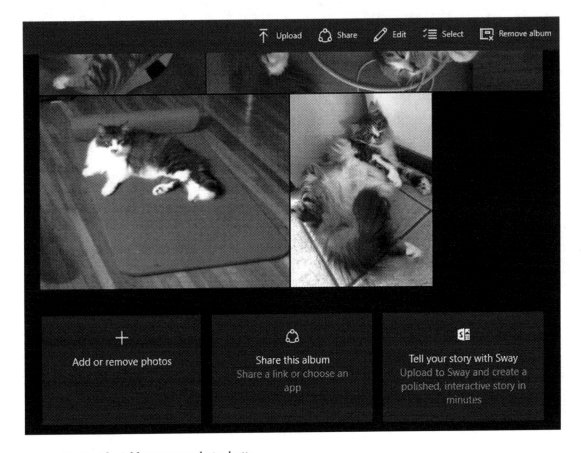

Figure 13-14. The Add or remove photos button

5. Select the pictures you want to add to the album (or select the pictures you want to remove from the album). The check box in the upper right corner of each picture shows whether or not a picture is selected.

6. Click the Done button in the upper right corner of the Photos window when you're done.

Removing an Album

After you've created an album, you can always remove that album later. When you remove an album, you do not delete any pictures displayed in that album. To remove an album, follow these steps:

1. Open the Photos program.

2. Click the Albums icon in the upper left corner of the Photos window. A list of all available albums appears (see Figure 13-11).

3. Click the album you want to remove. Photos displays all the pictures in your chosen album.

4. Click the Remove album button in the upper right corner of the Photos window. A dialog box appears, asking if you want to remove the album, as shown in Figure 13-15.

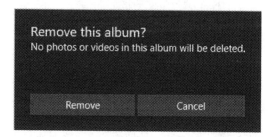

Figure 13-15. *A dialog box asks if you want to remove the album or cancel the removal process*

5. Click the Remove button. The Photos program removes your chosen album.

Viewing File Information

Each time you capture a photo with a digital camera, it may tag that file with a generic file name along with a date and the location where it was captured. To view this file information, follow these steps:

1. Open the Photos program.

2. Click the Albums icon in the upper left corner of the Photos window. A list of all available albums appears (see Figure 13-11).

3. Click an album you want to view. If you want to view all saved pictures, click the Saved pictures album.

4. Click a picture that you want to view file information on.

5. Click the three dots icon that appears in the upper right corner. A pull-down menu appears, as shown in Figure 13-16.

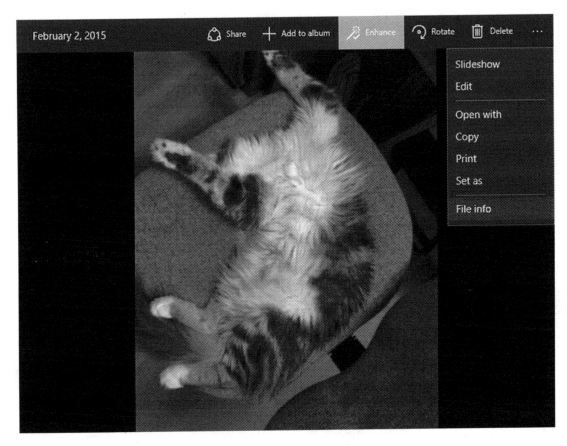

Figure 13-16. *A pull-down menu appears when you click the three dots icon*

6. Click File info. The bottom of the Photos window displays detailed information about that file, as shown in Figure 13-17.

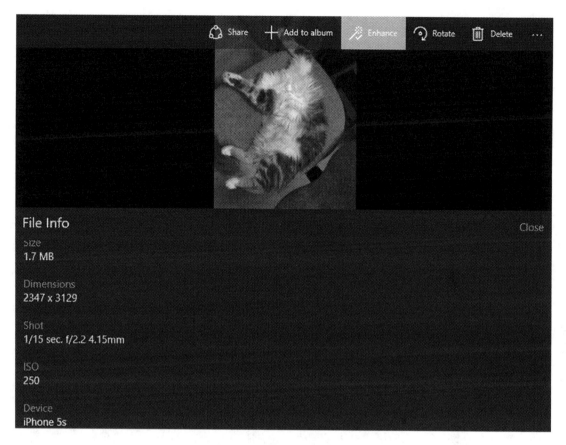

Figure 13-17. *File information appears at the bottom of the Photos window*

7. Click Close when you're done viewing the file information.

Sharing a Picture

Photos can be handy for storing pictures, but you'll likely want to share them with others. Photos can send a picture directly to e-mail or Twitter.

▓ **Note**   Before you can share a picture by e-mail or Twitter, you must set up an e-mail or a Twitter account.

To share a picture, follow these steps:

1. Open the Photos program.

2. Click the Albums icon in the upper left corner of the Photos window. A list of all available albums appears (see Figure 13-11).

3. Click an album you want to view. If you want to view all saved pictures, click the Saved pictures album.

4. Click a picture that you want to share.

5. Click the Share button. A Share pane appears on the right side of the screen, as shown in Figure 13-18.

Figure 13-18. *Clicking the Share icon displays a menu offering different ways to share a picture*

6. Click Mail or Twitter.

Making a Slideshow

In the olden days, people used to have their pictures turned into slides so they could show their pictures as a slideshow on a big screen. To mimic physical slides, the Photos program can create a slideshow on your computer screen out of any album such as the Saved pictures album (that contains all your pictures) or an album you created to organize related pictures together.

To show a slideshow of all pictures in an album, follow these steps:

1. Open the Photos program.

2. Click the Albums icon in the upper left corner of the Photos window. A list of all available albums appears (see Figure 13-11).

3. Click an album that contains the pictures you want to view in a slideshow.

4. Click the Slideshow button in the upper right corner of the Photos window. Photos starts showing your pictures, one at a time, on the screen.

5. Tap any key to stop the slideshow.

Summary

Almost every smartphone and tablet comes with a built-in camera, which means you can easily capture pictures at any time. The Photos program can help you organize any pictures stored in one or more folders. The default folder for organizing pictures is the Pictures folder, but you can define a different folder or several folders if you wish.

You can create albums to store related pictures together. It's possible for a single picture to appear in more than one album. If you delete an album, you do not delete any of the pictures grouped in that album.

The Photos programs can not only organize pictures but edit them as well. Such editing might not rival the complex features of a dedicated graphics editor, but Photos offers basic editing features that can correct pictures that may be under- or overexposed.

If you have pictures, use the Photos program to help you organize your pictures so you can find them again. You will find the Photos program is simple enough to use without being too complicated to understand.

CHAPTER 14

■ ■ ■

Watching Video and Playing Audio

One of the most popular uses for a computer is to play video or listen to music and other types of audio files. Most cameras can capture both still images and video, or you can download videos off the Internet. Likewise, you can download many different types of audio files or record your own audio to play back.

However you get video and audio files onto your computer, you'll need to be able play them. The two main video and audio playing apps on Windows 10 include the Movies & TV app for playing video and the Groove Music app for playing audio.

The Movies & TV app can play the following video formats:

- .mpg, .m4v (MPEG-4 format)

- .mpg, .mpeg (MPEG-1 format)

- .mov (QuickTime format)

- .avi (Audio Video Interleave format)

- .asf (Advanced Systems Format)

- .wmv (Windows Media Video format)

- .m2ts (MPEG-2 Transport Stream, used in Blu-ray discs)

- .3g2, .3gp2, .3gpp (Multimedia format used on 3G mobile phones)

These aren't all of the possible video file formats, so if you run across an obscure video file format that you can't play on Windows 10, you might be able to convert that file to a format the Movies & TV app can play such as .mpg or .wmv formats. Once you get a video in a format your computer can recognize, then you can play that video.

The Groove Music app can play the following audio formats:

- .mp3 (MPEG-2 Audio Layer III format)

- .flac (Free Lossless Audio Codec format)

- .m4a (MPEG-4 Part 14 format)

- .aac (Advanced Audio Coding format)

- .wav (Waveform Audio File format)

- .wma (Windows Media Audio format)

- .ac3 (Audio Codec 3 format)

- .amr (Adaptive Multi-Rate Codec format)

- .3gp, .3g2 (Multimedia format used on 3G mobile phones)

© Wallace Wang 2016
W. Wang, *Absolute Beginners Guide to Computing*, DOI 10.1007/978-1-4842-2289-8_14

Two popular audio formats are .mp3 and .flac because both compress files but .flac retains audio quality when compressing files while .mp3 does not.

Playing Video in the Movies & TV App

The Movies & TV app can be handy for playing video files stored on your computer. To play a video file, follow these steps:

1. Click the Windows icon in the lower left corner of the screen. The Start menu appears.

2. Click Movies & TV. The Movies & TV window appears.

3. Click the Videos icon on the left pane, as shown in Figure 14-1. If you have video files stored in the Videos folder, you'll see thumbnail images of your video files

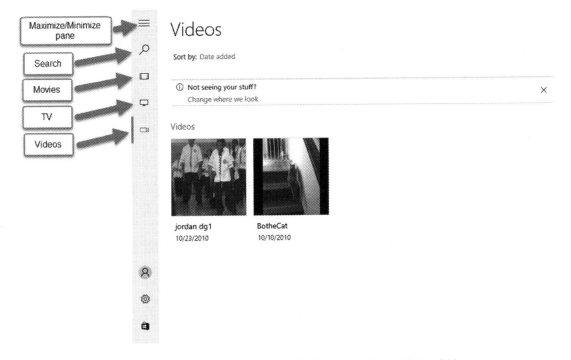

Figure 14-1. *The Movies & TV app can automatically find videos stored in the Videos folder*

4. Click the video you want to watch.

5. Once the Movies & TV app starts playing a video, moving the pointer over the video displays controls at the bottom of the screen, as shown in Figure 14-2.

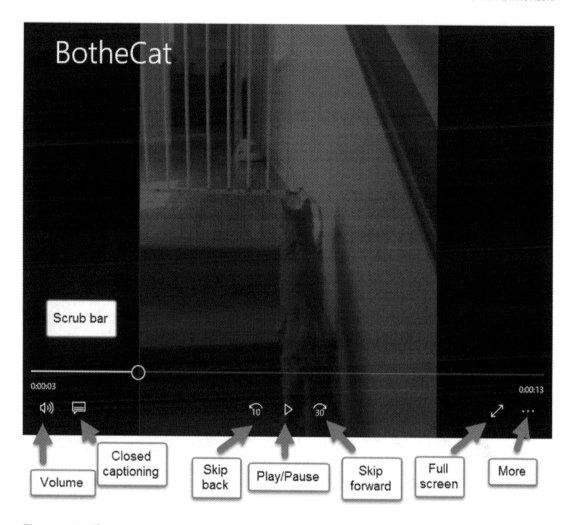

Figure 14-2. *The Movies & TV app displays controls when the pointer hovers over the video*

6.   To play a video, you can use the following onscreen controls:

   - *Play/Pause*: Toggles between playing and pausing a video

   - *Scrub bar*: Lets you drag back or forward to view different parts of a video

   - *Volume*: Lets you adjust the volume of a video

   - *Closed captioning*: Toggles between displaying or hiding closed captioning (if available)

   - *Skip back*: Reverses the video

   - *Skip forward*: Advances the video

- *Full screen*: Toggles between expanding the window to full screen or back down to a smaller window

- *More*: Displays a menu of additional options to repeat the video, stretch it to fill the size of the window, or play the video on a connected device such as a television screen

7. Click the Back arrow in the upper left corner of the Movies & TV window when you're done playing the video. This returns you back to the Movies & TV app window (see Figure 14-1).

While you could start the Movies & TV app and then open the video file you want to watch, you can also find the video file you want to watch in the File Explorer program. Then double-clicking a video file in File Explorer will open the Movies & TV app for playing that video.

To open a video in the Movies & TV app using the File Explorer, follow these steps:

1. Open the File Explorer window.

2. Find the folder that contains your video files such as the Videos folder. The File Explorer identifies video files by showing them as if they were clips in a film strip, as shown in Figure 14-3.

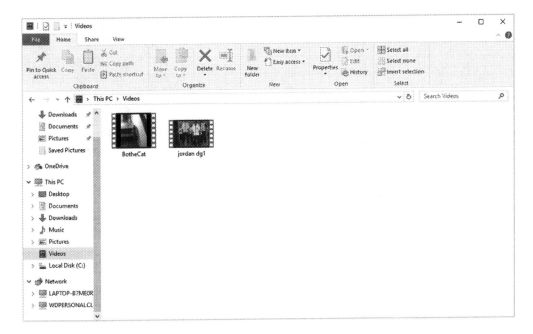

Figure 14-3. *The File Explorer uniquely identifies video files*

3. Double-click a video file. The File Explorer launches the Movies & TV app.

Watching Movies and TV Shows (For a Price)

The Movies & TV app can play video files stored on your computer, but you can also use the Movies & TV app to browse through the latest Hollywood movies and TV shows. Once you click a movie or TV show in the Movies & TV app, the Microsoft Store window appears where you can purchase that movie or TV show.

To browse the latest movies and TV shows in the Movies & TV app, follow these steps:

1. Open the Movies & TV app. The Movies & TV app window appears.

2. Click the Movie or TV icon on the left pane. The right side lists the latest movies or TV shows available to purchase or rent, as shown in Figure 14-4.

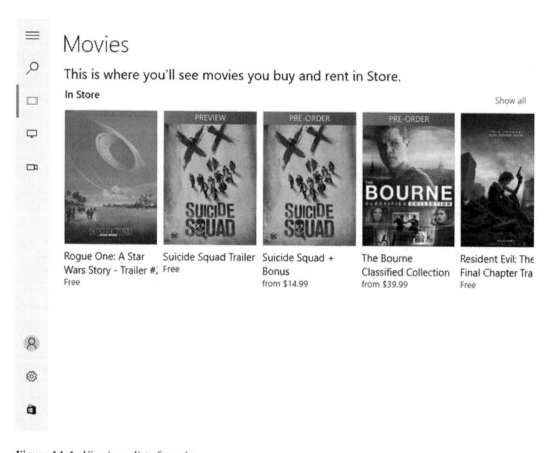

Figure 14-4. *Viewing a list of movies*

3. Click a movie or TV show you want to watch. The Microsoft Store window appears, allowing you to purchase your chosen movie or TV show, as shown in Figure 14-5.

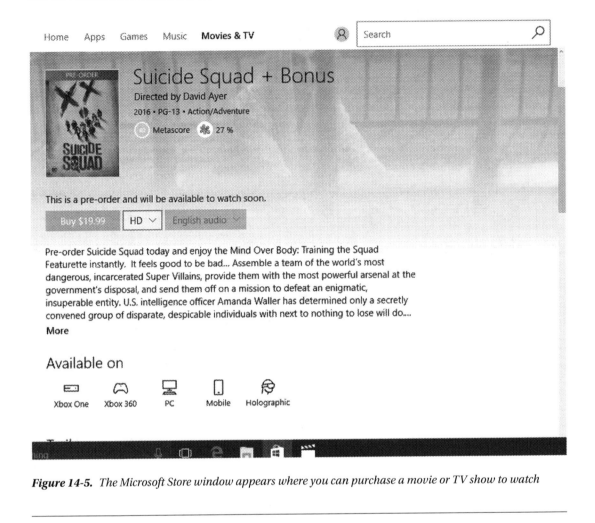

Figure 14-5. The Microsoft Store window appears where you can purchase a movie or TV show to watch

---

▓ **Note**   When the Microsoft Store window appears, the Movies & TV app window will still be open.

Playing DVDs

Curiously, Windows 10 won't let you play DVDs on your computer. If you want to play DVDs on your Windows 10 computer, you'll need a separate DVD player.

First, check if your PC's manufacturer (Dell, Toshiba, Hewlett-Packard, etc.) included a third-party DVD player on your computer. One popular third-party DVD player is Cyberlink Media Player, but you may need to search your Start menu in case you have a different third-party media player.

▓ **Note**   Insert a DVD into your computer drive and see if a program opens and recognizes that DVD. If so, then you'll know if you have a DVD player already installed on your computer.

Second, if you upgraded your computer to Windows 10 from an earlier version of Windows, you may also get the Windows DVD Player app for free (otherwise it costs $14.99 from the Microsoft Store).

Third, you can download and install several free DVD players. Some popular and free DVD players include:

- VideoLAN (`http://www.videolan.org`)

- 5K Player (`https://www.5kplayer.com`)

- KMPlayer (`http://www.kmplayer.com`)

In general, don't pay for a DVD player unless you absolutely want to because there are plenty of free alternatives you can use instead.

Playing Audio Files

The Groove Music app can play any audio files stored in the Music folder of your computer. You can play multiple audio tracks either in the order they appear or in random order, known as shuffling.

To play audio files, follow these steps:

1. Click the Windows icon in the lower left corner of the screen. The Start menu appears.

2. Click Groove Music. The Groove Music window appears.

3. Click the Songs icon on the left pane to display all the audio files stored in the Music folder of your computer, as shown in Figure 14-6.

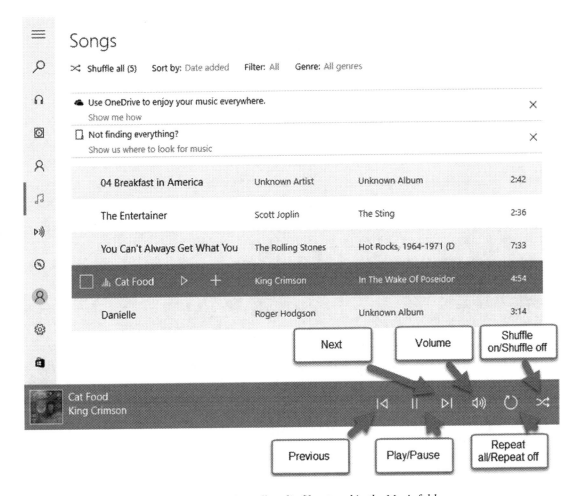

Figure 14-6. *The Groove Music app recognizes all audio files stored in the Music folder*

4. Move the pointer over the first audio file you want to hear and click the Play
    button that appears to the right of that audio track title. Groove Music starts
    playing your chosen audio file and all other audio files underneath.

When playing audio, you can use the following onscreen controls:

- *Play/Pause*: Toggles between playing and pausing an audio file

- *Previous*: Plays the previous song

- *Next*: Plays the next song

- *Volume*: Adjusts the volume separately from the computer's volume control

- *Repeat all/Repeat off*: Repeats playing the list of songs from the beginning

- *Shuffle on/Shuffle off*: Plays the list of songs in random order or plays them from top
  to bottom

Creating a Playlist

The more audio tracks you store in the Music folder, the more difficult it can be to find any particular audio track. Even more difficult, you may only want to hear a handful of audio tracks, such as those from a particular artist. To help you organize your audio files into groups, you can create playlists.

A playlist lets you group related audio files together where one audio file can belong to more than one playlist. By using playlists, you can play a handful of audio tracks rather than trying to pick and choose from every audio file stored in the Music folder.

To create a playlist and then add audio tracks to it, follow these steps:

1. Open the Groove Music window and look for the + New Playlist icon in the left pane, as shown in Figure 14-7. (You may need to scroll down to find the + New Playlist icon.)

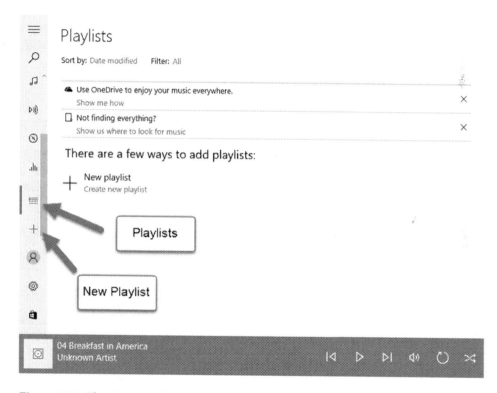

Figure 14-7. *The + New Playlist icon appears on the left pane*

2. Click the + New Playlist icon. A dialog box appears letting you name your playlist, as shown in Figure 14-8.

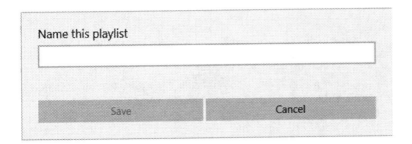

Figure 14-8. *You can give your playlist a descriptive name*

3. Type a name for your playlist and click the Save button. The Groove Music window displays your empty playlist as an icon, as shown in Figure 14-9.

Music for Cats

0 songs

Figure 14-9. *A playlist appears as an icon and lists the number of songs stored inside*

4. Click the Songs icon in the left pane to view all audio tracks stored in your Music folder.

5. Right-click any audio track to display a menu and choose Add to and then the name of the playlist you want to add the song to, as shown in Figure 14-10.

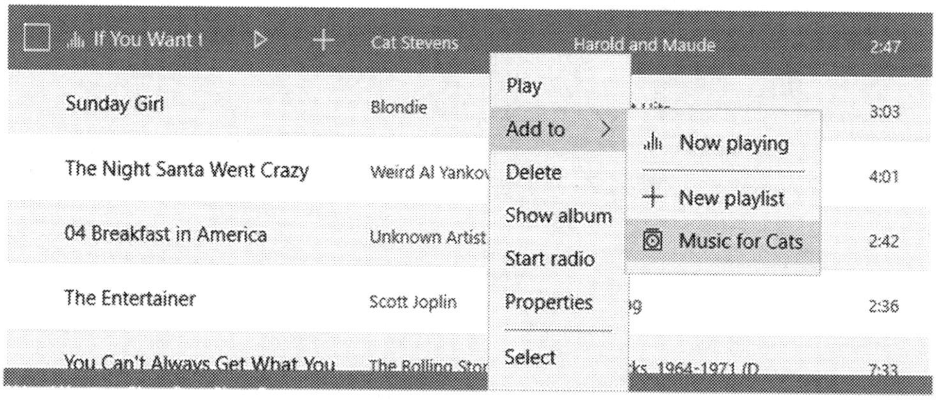

☐	�𝗂𝗅𝗂 If You Want I	▷	＋	Cat Stevens	Harold and Maude	2:47
Sunday Girl			Blondie			3:03
The Night Santa Went Crazy			Weird Al Yankov			4:01
04 Breakfast in America			Unknown Artist			2:42
The Entertainer			Scott Joplin			2:36
You Can't Always Get What You			The Rolling Stor			7:33

Play
Add to   >   �𝗂𝗅𝗂 Now playing
Delete   ＋ New playlist
Show album   ⊙ Music for Cats
Start radio
Properties
Select

Figure 14-10. *Right-clicking displays a menu to add an audio track to an existing playlist*

Creating an empty playlist and then adding audio tracks might seem slow and cumbersome, so you might prefer selecting the audio tracks you want and then creating a playlist.

To select audio tracks and then add them to a new playlist:

1. Open the Groove Music window.

2. Click the Songs icon in the left pane of the Groove Music window.

3. Click the check box to the left of every audio track you want to add to the playlist. The Groove Music window displays icons in the bottom right corner, as shown in Figure 14-11.

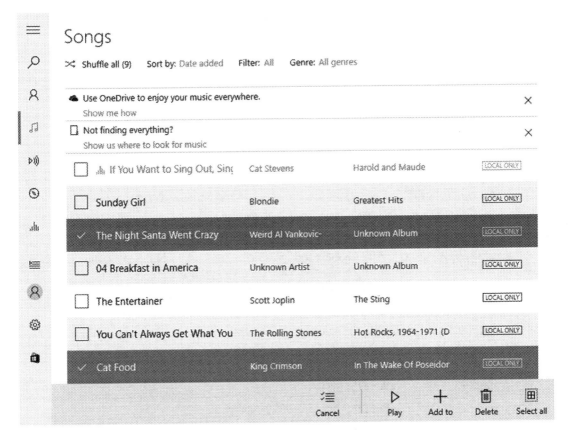

Figure 14-11. *Groove Music displays controls for manipulating audio tracks*

4. Click the + Add to icon in the bottom right corner. A pop-up menu appears, listing all your existing playlists.

5. Click the playlist where you want to add the audio track.

Playing a Playlist

Once you've created a playlist, you can play the audio tracks stored in that playlist. To play audio tracks in a playlist, follow these steps:

1. Open the Groove Music window.

2. Click the Playlist name in the left pane. (You may need to scroll down to find all your playlists.)

3. Double-click the playlist you want to play. The Groove Music window lists all the audio tracks in your chosen playlist. (If you hover the pointer over the playlist icon, a Play button appears so you can click this Play button to play all audio tracks in the playlist.)

4. (Optional) Click the Shuffle on icon in the bottom right corner if you want to play the audio tracks in your playlist in random order.

5. Click the Play icon.

Modifying a Playlist

When you have audio tracks stored in a playlist, you may later want to modify that playlist by adding more audio tracks, removing some audio tracks, or rearranging the order of the audio tracks.

▒ **Note** When you remove audio tracks from a playlist, you do not delete those audio tracks from your computer.

To add more audio tracks to a playlist, follow these steps:

1. Open the Groove Music window.

2. Click the Songs icon in the left pane of the Groove Music window.

3. Right-click the audio track you want to add to the playlist. A pop-up menu appears.

4. Choose Add to and then choose the name of the playlist where you want to add the audio track.

To remove audio tracks from a playlist, follow these steps:

1. Open the Groove Music window.

2. Click the Playlist icon in the left pane of the Groove Music window (see Figure 14-7). A list of playlists appears.

3. Double-click the playlist you want to modify. The audio tracks of your chosen playlist appears.

4. Move the pointer over the audio track you want to remove from the playlist. A Play button and minus sign (–) icon appear, as shown in Figure 14-12.

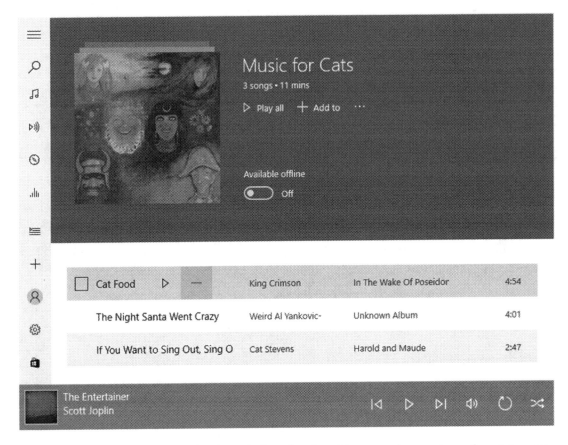

Figure 14-12. *A Play button and Delete from playlist minus icon (-) appear when you hover the pointer over an audio track*

5. Click the Delete from playlist icon (-). Your chosen audio track disappears from your playlist.

To rearrange the order of audio tracks in a playlist, follow these steps:

1. Open the Groove Music window.

2. Click the Playlist icon in the left pane of the Groove Music window (see Figure 14-7). A list of playlists appears.

3. Double-click the playlist you want to modify. The audio tracks of your chosen playlist appears.

4. Move the pointer over an audio track you want to move.

5. Drag the mouse/trackpad up or down to move the audio track within your playlist.

6. Release the mouse/trackpad to place the audio track in its new order in the playlist.

Deleting or Renaming a Playlist

After you create a playlist, you may eventually want to delete or rename it. Remember, deleting a playlist does not delete any audio tracks stored on your computer. To delete or rename a playlist, follow these steps:

1. Open the Groove Music window.

2. Click the Playlist icon in the left pane of the Groove Music window (see Figure 14-7). A list of playlists appears.

3. Right-click the playlist you want to delete. A pop-up menu appears.

4. Choose Delete or Rename. A dialog box asks if you really want to delete the playlist.

5. Click OK or Cancel.

Searching Your Audio Library

The more audio tracks you store on your computer, the harder it can be to find the audio tracks you want. Organizing audio tracks into playlists can help, but if you want to find a specific audio track, you have two ways to search for it.

First, you can search by artist. This lets you view all audio tracks by a particular recording artist. Second, you can search for a particular audio track by name (either the audio track name or the recording artist name).

To search for a particular audio track by artist, follow these steps:

1. Open the Groove Music window.

2. Click the Artists icon on the left pane. A list of all recording artists appears in alphabetical order, as shown in Figure 14-13.

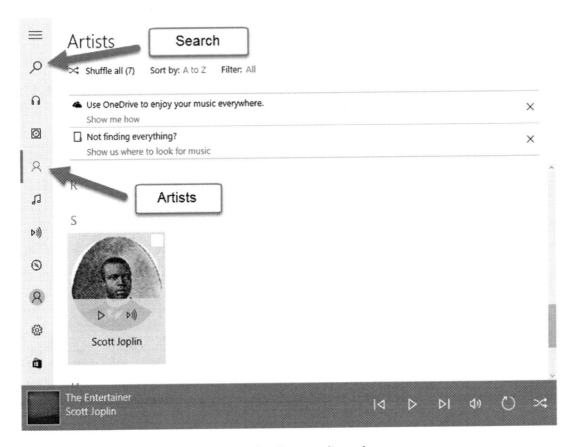

Figure 14-13. Viewing a list of recording artists for all your audio tracks

3. Move the pointer over the artist picture to display a Play and a Volume icon. Now you can click the Play icon to play all audio tracks by that particular recording artist.

To search for a particular audio track by title or recording artist, follow these steps:

1. Open the Groove Music window.

2. Click the Search icon on the left pane (see Figure 14-13). A Search text box appears, as shown in Figure 14-14.

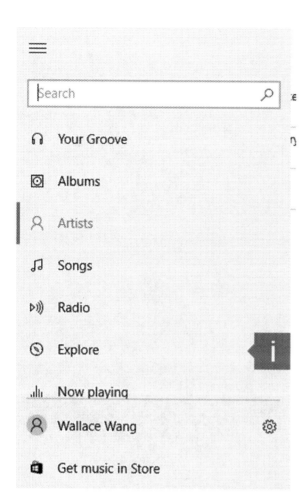

Figure 14-14. *A Search text box lets you type all or part of an audio track or recording artist name*

3. Type all or part of an audio track or recording artist name and press Enter.
Groove Music displays all matches for audio tracks and recording artist names, as
shown in Figure 14-15.

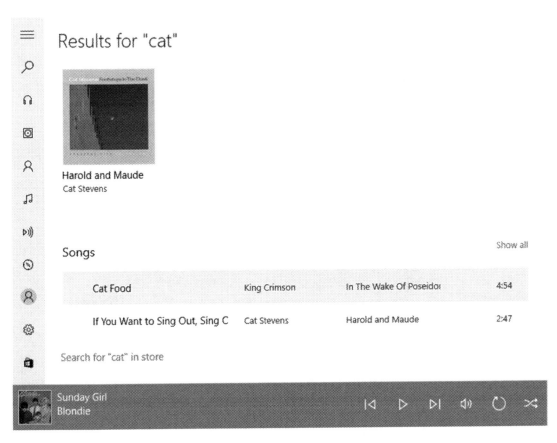

Figure 14-15. *Groove Music matches the search criteria to existing audio tracks and recording artist names*

4.   (Optional) Move the pointer over an audio track or recording artist picture and click the Play button that appears.

Summary

If you have video or audio files, you can play them on Windows 10. The Movies & TV app lets you play video files and the Groove Music app lets you play audio files. As long as your video or audio file is stored in one of many popular formats, chances are good you'll be able to watch or listen to any video or audio file you may find.

Windows 10 stores video files in its Videos folder and audio files in its Music folder. While it's possible to store files in other folders, it's best to keep your video and audio files organized so you can easily find them again.

Even though Windows 10 can't play DVDs, you can always download a free DVD player or check if your computer already comes with a DVD player installed. With Windows 10, you can enjoy your video and audio files and turn your computer into a TV screen or stereo.

CHAPTER 15

▓ ▓ ▓

Drawing and Editing Pictures

Besides letting you type and edit text, computers allow you to draw pictures as well. Even if you have no desire to become an artist or can't draw anything beyond a stick figure, you might still need to draw simple pictures to capture your ideas and show them to others.

If you have a digital camera or a smartphone, chances are good you've taken pictures that you've stored on your computer. Just as you might scribble text and arrows on a printed picture, so too you can scribble text and simple shapes such as arrows on a digital picture.

To create and edit pictures, Windows 10 provides a simple Paint program. This Paint program lets you draw and edit individual pixels, which are the tiny dots that make up everything you see on the screen. By coloring and deleting individual pixels, you can draw or edit any picture, whether it's one you've captured with a digital camera or one you've downloaded off the Internet.

The Windows 10 Paint program can't replace a dedicated graphics editor like Adobe Photoshop, but it can introduce you to the world of digital drawing and editing. Some of the popular file formats the Paint program supports include:

- .bmp

- .jpeg, .jpg

- .gif

- .tiff

▓ **Note**   There are two types of graphics programs: bitmap or raster graphics and vector graphics. Bitmap or raster graphics lets you draw and edit individual pixels. Vector graphics lets you draw and edit entire shapes such as lines, circles, and squares. Programs such as the Paint program and Adobe Photoshop are bitmap or raster graphics editors. Programs such as Adobe Illustrator are vector editors.

Finding the Paint Program

Unlike most programs that you can easily find on the Start menu, Windows 10 buries the Paint program under the Windows Accessories category, as shown in Figure 15-1.

© Wallace Wang 2016
W. Wang, *Absolute Beginners Guide to Computing*, DOI 10.1007/978-1-4842-2289-8_15

Figure 15-1. *The Paint program is under the Windows Accessories category on the Start menu*

To start the Paint program, follow these steps:

1. Click the Windows icon in the lower left corner of the screen. The Start menu appears.

2. Click Windows Accessories. A list of different programs under the Windows Accessories category appears (see Figure 15-1).

3. Click Paint. The Paint program appears, as shown in Figure 15-2.

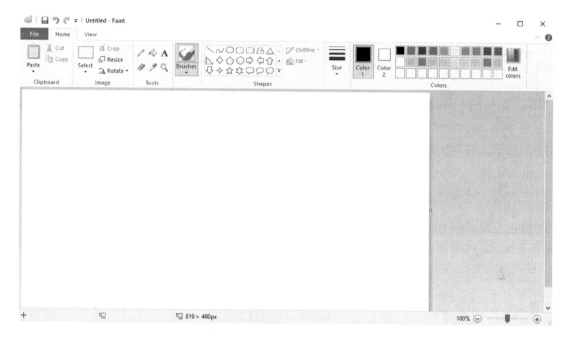

Figure 15-2. *The Paint program user interface*

The Paint program displays three tabs that contains related commands as follows:

- *File*: For saving, sharing, or printing the currently displayed drawing

- *Home*: For creating and editing a drawing

- *View*: For changing the magnification of a drawing or displaying (or hiding) rulers and gridlines

The basic idea behind the Paint program is to let you create or modify a picture. When using the Paint program, the most common commands you'll use appear on the Home tab (see Figure 15-2). The main groups of commands on the Home tab include:

- *Clipboard*: For copying, cutting, and pasting selected items

- *Image*: For selecting an image or manipulating it such as resizing, cropping, or rotating it

- *Tools*: For choosing different ways to modify the functions of the mouse or trackpad

- *Shapes*: For drawing an object such as a line, circle, or triangle

- *Colors*: For choosing a color for your drawn object

Learning to Paint

Imagine dipping a paintbrush in a bucket of paint and smearing the paint on a piece of paper. That's essentially how the Paint program works on your computer. First, you must choose a color. Second, you need to use the mouse or trackpad to draw a line or object on the screen. Once you've painted something, you can go back and delete all or part of that object.

The main difference painting something in real life and painting on the computer is that the computer gives you the option of changing your painting later. You can delete individual pixels or entire chunks of a painting. You can copy all or part of your painting and paste it in the same file or in a different file. Computer painting gives you more flexibility (and less mess) than a real paintbrush and bucket of paint.

Choosing a Painting Tool

Your mouse/trackpad acts like a paintbrush. By choosing a different painting tool, you can create different visual effects. The three main types of painting tools are:

- *Paintbrush*: Simulates different size brushes, pens, and airbrush tools

- *Pencil*: Simulates a thin pencil tip

- *Shapes*: Makes it easy to draw lines and shapes like triangles, octagons, and stars, as shown in Figure 15-3

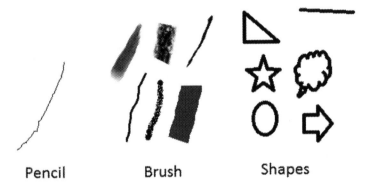

Pencil   Brush   Shapes

Figure 15-3. *The three types of output from different painting tools*

The paintbrush is the most common painting tool. To choose a painting tool, follow these steps:

1. Open the Paint program. The Paint window appears.

2. Click the Home tab.

3. Click one of the following:

   - Pencil

   - Brushes

   - Shapes

The Brushes icon displays two halves. If you click the top half, you'll select the last paintbrush tool you used. If you click the bottom half, a menu of different paintbrush types appears, as shown in Figure 15-4. The Shapes gallery displays three rows of common shapes such as circles, triangles, and arrows. If you click the More icon, you can view all possible shapes, as shown in Figure 15-5.

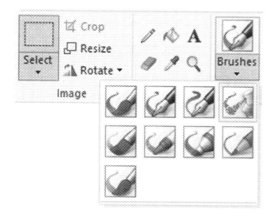

Figure 15-4. *Clicking the bottom half of the Brushes icon displays a menu of brush types*

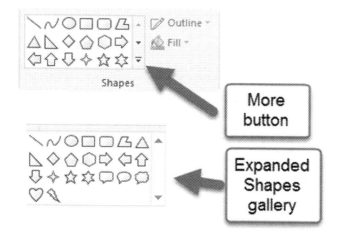

Figure 15-5. *The More button displays the entire gallery of shapes*

Defining the Size and Color of a Painting Tool

Once you've chosen a painting tool, the next step is to choose a size and color. The size of the painting tool determines the width of the lines the painting tool creates. The color defines the color of the lines you paint.

To choose a size and color for a painting tool, follow these steps:

1. Click the Home tab.

2. Click a painting tool (pencil, brush, or shape).

3. Click the Size icon. A menu of different options appears, as shown in Figure 15-6.

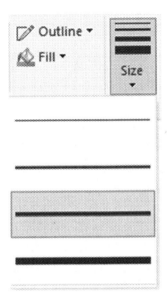

Figure 15-6. *The Size options for defining the width of the painting tool*

4. Click a width.

5. Click a color displayed in the palette that appears in the right corner of the Paint window.

6. Draw something with the painting tool (mouse/trackpad) by moving the pointer where you want to draw an item, holding down the left button, and moving the mouse or sliding your finger across the trackpad.

Drawing with the pencil or brush tool draws a line wherever you drag the mouse/trackpad. Drawing with the shape tool defines a box that represents the height and width of a shape such as a star or rectangle, as shown in Figure 15-7.

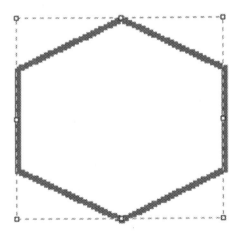

Figure 15-7. *Dragging the mouse/trackpad defines the height and width of a shape*

▓ **Note** Immediately after drawing a shape, you can click the Size icon or a different color to change the line width and color of that shape.

Typing Text

Although the Paint program is mostly designed for drawing and painting, you can also type text. Unlike a word processor, any text you type can only be edited while you're typing it. The moment you choose a different painting tool, your text remains frozen in the color, size, and font you chose for it initially.

To type text, follow these steps:

1. Click the Home tab.

2. Click the Text tool, as shown in Figure 15-8.

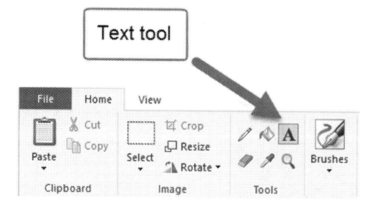

Figure 15-8. *The Text tool appears in the Tools group*

3. Click where you want to type text. A text box appears on the screen and a Text tab appears, as shown in Figure 15-9.

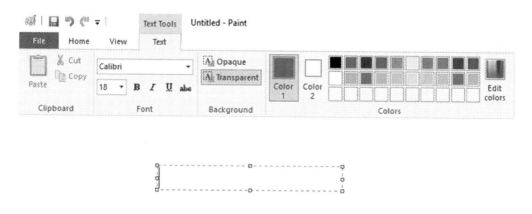

Figure 15-9. *Typing text displays a Text tab with additional text formatting commands*

4.   (Optional) Click the font and font size list boxes to choose a font and size for your text.

5.   (Optional) Click the bold, italics, underline, or strikethrough icons to define a style for your text.

6.   (Optional) Click either Opaque or Transparent. Opaque displays a background behind your text while Transparent only displays text, allowing any background image to appear behind the text.

7.   Click a color for your text.

8.   Type your text. As long as the cursor remains inside the text box, you can edit the text. The moment you click outside this text box, your text will become a graphic image that can't be edited anymore.

Selecting Items

After you've painted something on the screen, you may want to cut, copy, and paste parts of your painting. To do that, you need to select that item.

Selecting involves dragging the mouse/trackpad to define a portion of the screen. A rectangle shown as a dotted line indicates the part of a picture you have selected, as shown in Figure 15-10.

Figure 15-10. *Dragging with the Selection tool defines a rectangular portion*

Since selecting a rectangular portion of the screen may be clumsy, you can also choose a free-form selection tool. This lets you drag the mouse/trackpad to select an enclosed area, such as an oval or triangular area.

To select a rectangular or free-form portion of the screen, follow these steps:

1.   Click the Home tab.

2.   Click the bottom half of the Select tool icon to display a menu, as shown in Figure 15-11.

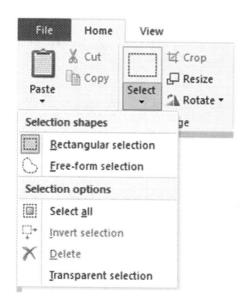

Figure 15-11. *The Select tool menu lets you choose between a Rectangular or Free-form selection tool*

3. Click Rectangular or Free-form selection.

4. Drag the mouse/trackpad to define the area you want to select. A dotted line appears around your selected area (see Figure 15-10).

Once you've selected an area, you can then choose a command to manipulate that selected area such as:

- Copy (Ctrl+C)

- Cut (Ctrl+X)

- Delete (Delete key)

- Crop (deletes all parts of the picture outside the selected area)

- Resize

- Rotate

▓ **Note**   If you choose a command on a selected area and don't like how it looks, press Ctrl+Z to choose the Undo command and reverse the last command you chose.

Deleting Parts of a Picture

There are two ways to delete part of a picture. First, you can select an area to delete and then press the Delete key. Second, you can use the Eraser tool, as shown in Figure 15-12.

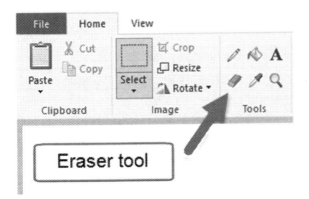

Figure 15-12. The Eraser tool

To use the Eraser tool, follow these steps:

1.   Click the Home tab.

2.   Click the Eraser tool.

3.   (Optional) Click the Size icon and choose a width to define the width of the Eraser tool.

4.   Drag the mouse/trackpad. Wherever you drag the mouse/trackpad, that's what you'll erase, as shown in Figure 15-13.

Figure 15-13. The Eraser tool lets you drag to delete parts of a picture

Using the Fill Tool

If you have a large area where you want to paint a specific color, you could choose a wide brush tool and drag the mouse/trackpad around to color that area. However, a faster solution is to use the Fill tool. The Fill tool lets you fill an enclosed area with a single color.

The Fill tool is often used with a shape or an enclosed area created by the pencil or brush tool. To use the Fill tool, follow these steps:

1. Click the Home tab.

2. Draw a shape or an enclosed area using the pencil or brush tool.

▧ **Note**   Make sure you have a completely enclosed area. If there's a gap, the Fill tool will "leak" out and fill the surrounding area as well. If this happens, press Ctrl+Z to undo the Fill tool.

---

3. Click the Fill tool (it looks like a tipping paint bucket), as shown in Figure 15-14.

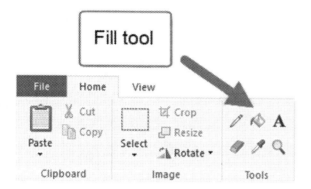

Figure 15-14.   *The Fill tool floods an enclosed area with a single color*

4. Click any color to select it.

5. Click inside any enclosed area. The Fill tool floods that enclosed area with your chosen color.

Picking a Custom Color

The color palette displays common variations of color, but if you want to create a custom color of your own, you can do that. To create custom colors, you can choose from different color variations or define the following values:

*   Red, Green, and Blue

*   Hue, Saturation, and Luminosity

To define a specific color, follow these steps:

1. Click the Home tab.

2. Click the Edit colors icon. An Edit Colors dialog box appears, as shown in Figure 15-15.

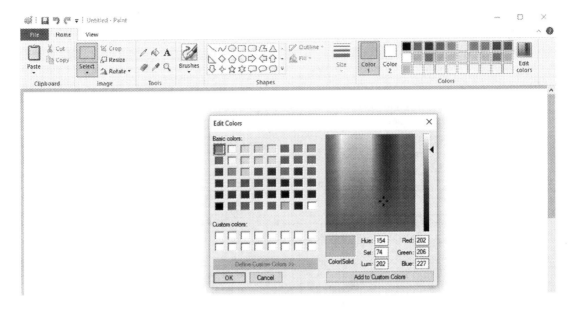

Figure 15-15. *The Edit colors icon displays the Edit Colors dialog box*

3. Choose one of the following:

    • Click a color displayed in the upper right corner of the Edit Colors dialog box

    • Type in values in the Red, Green, and Blue text boxes

    • Type in values in the Hue, Saturation, and Luminosity text boxes

4. Click OK.

If you have an existing picture and want to use a color in that picture, you can use the Color picker tool. The Color picker tool lets you click an existing color to select that color. Now you can use that color with any other tool such as the pencil, brush, or shape tool.

To use the Color picker tool, follow these steps:

1. Click the Home tab.

2. Open a picture that contains the color you want to use.

3. Click the Color picker tool (it looks like an eyedropper), as shown in Figure 15-16.

216

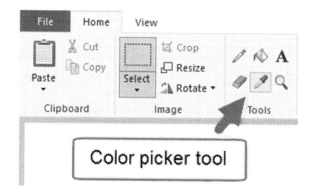

Figure 15-16. The Color picker tool appears in the Tools category

4. Click the color in the existing picture that you want to use. At this point, you can now choose another tool (such as the shape or brush tool) to use the color you just selected with the Color picker tool.

Magnifying a Picture

To help you view and edit a picture, you can magnify that picture. Three ways to magnify a picture include:

- Clicking the Magnifier tool, as shown in Figure 15-17
- Dragging the Zoom slider in the bottom right corner of the Paint window (see Figure 15-17)

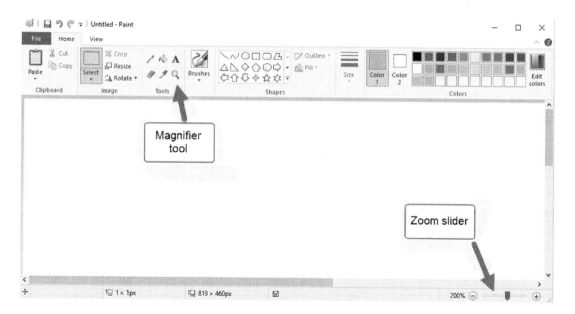

Figure 15-17. The Magnifier tool and Zoom slider

- Clicking the View tab and clicking the Zoom in/Zoom out icons, as shown in Figure 15-18

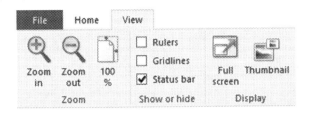

Figure 15-18. *The magnifier commands on the View tab*

Summary

You can use the Paint program to create pictures. Even if you're not an artist, you can create simple diagrams and images that you can copy and paste into a word processor document or presentation file.

If you have existing pictures downloaded from the Internet or pictures you've captured with a digital camera, you can add text, arrows, and other objects to those images. This lets you modify an image or edit it in simple ways such as deleting parts of that picture.

Think of the Paint program as a simple drawing and doodling electronic notepad. Whatever you could scribble on a piece of paper, you can doodle in the Paint program using your mouse/trackpad. Even if you have no artistic training or skill, don't worry. The Paint program is simple enough that anyone can create decent looking images with just a little patience and practice.

■ ■ ■

PART IV

Getting on the Internet

Back in the olden days, every computer was isolated from everyone else's computer. Fortunately, those primitive dark ages of computing are over because now almost everyone's computer can connect with anyone else's computer throughout the world through the magic of the Internet.

In this part of the book, you'll learn how to connect your computer to the Internet. Once you're connected to the Internet, you can send and receive e-mail from people all over the world, explore the world by visiting different web sites, chat with your friends and family members through text messages, and talk to each other through video and audio so you can see the person you're talking to.

The Internet can literally be your gateway to making your computer even more fun and productive than ever before.

CHAPTER 16

Browsing the Internet

Back in the olden days, you had to read a newspaper or magazine, listen to the radio, or watch television to get the latest news. Today, you can get the latest news, often within minutes of it happening, right on your computer.

The secret to accessing information all over the world lies with the Internet. By connecting to the Internet, you can access a wealth of information that rivals anything your library could offer.

To access the Internet, you need to use a special program called a browser. Windows 10 comes with a browser called Edge, which lets you browse web sites on the Internet.

Note   Edge is the default browser for Windows 10 but you can always install and use another browser such as Chrome or Firefox since all browsers work in similar ways. Windows 10 also comes with a second, older browser called Internet Explorer. You should only use Internet Explorer in the rare case that a web site does not work with the Edge browser.

Connecting to the Internet

Besides a browser such as Edge, you will also need an Internet connection. Two ways to connect to the Internet are through an Ethernet cable that physically plugs into your computer or through Wi-Fi, which doesn't require any wires at all.

An Ethernet connection is the most secure and reliable way to connect to the Internet but is mostly useful only for desktop computers that don't need to be moved.

Wi-Fi connections are less secure and reliable than Ethernet connections, but far simpler to use, especially for laptops that may not have an Ethernet port. Wi-Fi is often available at public places such as libraries, coffee shops, or airport terminals.

© Wallace Wang 2016
W. Wang, *Absolute Beginners Guide to Computing*, DOI 10.1007/978-1-4842-2289-8_16

To make sure you have an Internet connection, follow these steps:

1. Click the Windows icon in the left corner of the screen. The Start menu appears.

2. Click Settings. The Settings window appears, as shown in Figure 16-1.

Figure 16-1. *The Network window identifies if you have an Internet connection*

3. Click the Network & Internet icon. The Network window appears.

4. Click Status in the left pane to see your current Internet status, as shown in Figure 16-2.

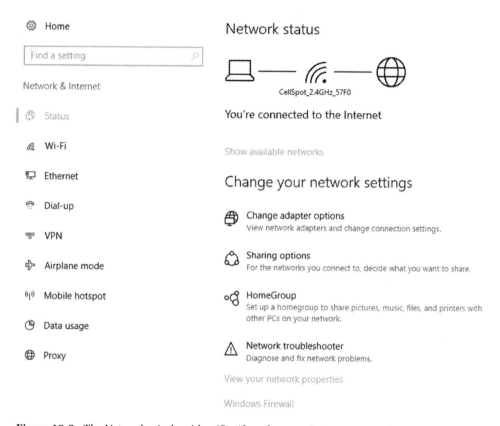

Figure 16-2. *The Network window identifies if you have an Internet connection*

5. Click the close button (the big X icon) in the upper right corner of the Settings window to close it.

By checking your Internet status, you can see if you're connected through an Ethernet cable or Wi-Fi. If you're connected by Ethernet, you can click Ethernet in the left pane to view various Ethernet options, as shown in Figure 16-3.

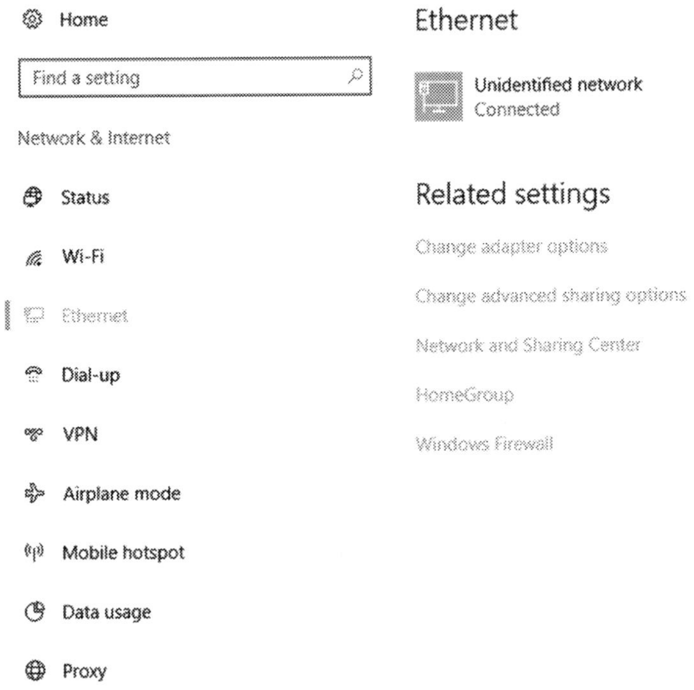

⚙ Home	**Ethernet**
Find a setting 🔎	
Network & Internet	Unidentified network
⊕ Status	Connected
ⓖ Wi-Fi	**Related settings**
⌑ Ethernet	Change adapter options
☎ Dial-up	Change advanced sharing options
⦸ VPN	Network and Sharing Center
✈ Airplane mode	HomeGroup
⦿ Mobile hotspot	Windows Firewall
◕ Data usage	
⊕ Proxy	

Figure 16-3. Settings for an Ethernet connection

If you're connected by Wi-Fi, you can click Wi-Fi in the left pane to view various Wi-Fi options, as shown in Figure 16-4. If you click Show available networks, you can view a list of Wi-Fi networks you can connect to. Just remember that some Wi-Fi networks require a password and that just because a Wi-Fi network is available doesn't mean it's necessarily secure.

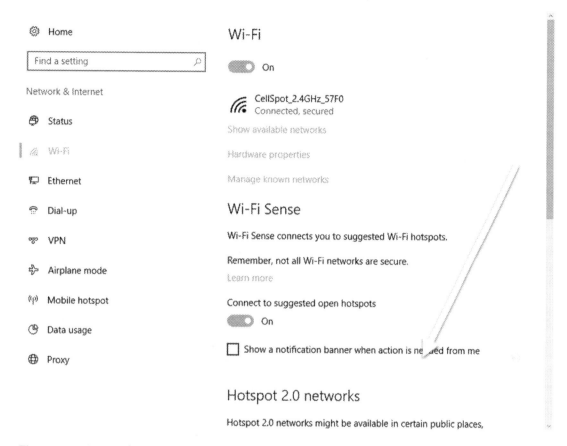

Figure 16-4. *Settings for a Wi-Fi connection*

■ **Note** For maximum security, don't type anything sensitive, like credit card numbers or passwords, over a public Wi-Fi network. That's because it's possible for someone to intercept your data as it's sent from your computer to the Wi-Fi network.

Defining a Default Browser

Edge is the default browser for Windows 10. However, if you have installed other browsers such as Chrome or Firefox, you may want to use those browsers instead. To define a default browser for your computer, follow these steps:

1. Click the Windows icon in the left corner of the screen. The Start menu appears.

2. Click Settings. The Settings window appears (see Figure 16-1).

3. Click the System icon. The System window appears.

4. Click Default apps in the left pane, as shown in Figure 16-5.

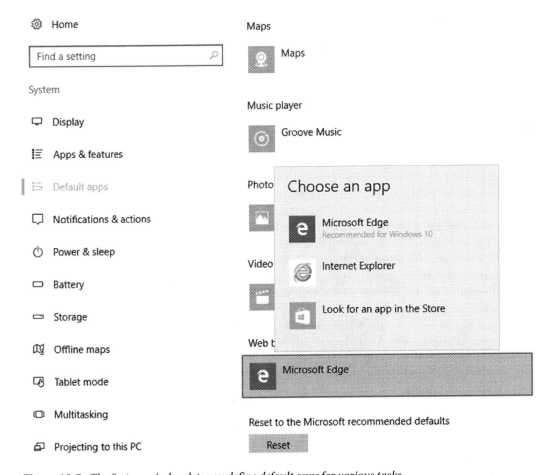

Figure 16-5. *The System window lets you define default apps for various tasks*

5. Click the currently displayed web browser name under the Web browser category. A pop-up menu appears, listing all browsers currently installed on your computer. If you have installed other browsers such as Chrome or Firefox, you can choose one of those browsers instead.

6. Click the close button (the big X) in the upper right corner of the System window to close the window.

Visiting Web Sites

The main purpose of a browser, such as Edge, is to let you view web sites anywhere on the Internet. Two common ways to find a web site is to either type in the web site address (such as www.microsoft.com) or type a search query such as looking for all web sites that contain information about "Best laptops."

In general, searching for a web site is easier because you just type one or more keywords that you want to find such as "unclogging a sink drain" or "cat breeding."

Typing a web site address means knowing the exact web site address you want to find and spelling it correctly. If you misspell a web site address, you won't find the web site you want. The advantage of typing a web site address is that it gets you directly to the web site you want to view.

▓ **Note**   Be especially careful when typing a web site address. Malicious hackers often create web sites with domain addresses that match commonly misspelled web site addresses. If you visit a malicious web site, it could lock up your browser and try to install malware on your computer.

To visit a web site by typing its address, follow these steps:

1. Open your browser such as the Edge program.

2. Click in the Search text field at the top, middle of the browser window, as shown in Figure 16-6.

Figure 16-6. *The Search text field appears at the top middle of the window*

3. Type a web site address (such as **www.apress.com**) or type a search query (such as "books on Windows") and press Enter. Your browser either displays the web site at the address you specified or a search page of web sites that matchs your search query ("books on Windows 10").

▓ **Note**   When typing a search query, use as many words as possible to avoid finding web sites containing irrelevant information. So rather than just search for "pig," search for "raising pigs" or "origin of piggy banks" to find more web sites that exactly match your search criteria.

Defining a Default Search Engine

When you type a search query, Edge sends your query to its default search engine, which is Bing. If you want, you can choose a different search engine.

Different search engines return different results for the exact same query, so many people have a favorite search engine they prefer to use. Google is the most popular search engine, but some people prefer DuckDuckGo as their search engine because it doesn't track your search queries like Google does.

Baidu is the most popular search engine in Asia, so if you search Asian web sites frequently, you may want to switch to Baidu instead. If for some reason you simply don't like the results Google consistently provides, you can try switching to Yahoo! or any search engine you choose.

▓ **Note**   If you define a default search engine for Edge, this won't change the default search engine for any other browsers you may have installed such as Chrome or Firefox.

To define a default search engine for Edge, follow these steps:

1.   Open the Edge program.

2.   Visit the search engine you want to make as the default search engine such as www.google.com.

3.   Click the More icon in the upper right corner of the Edge window (it looks like three dots). A pull-down menu appears, as shown in Figure 16-7.

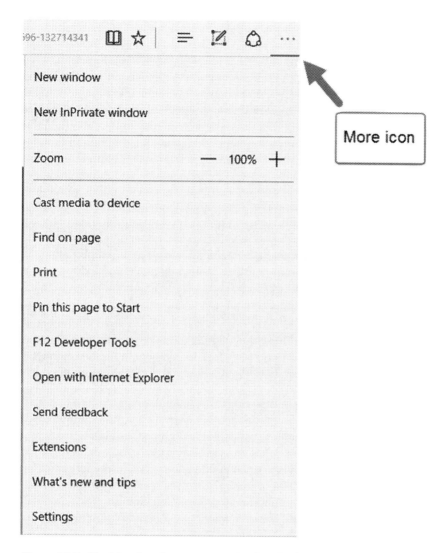

Figure 16-7. The More icon lets you customize the Edge browser

4. Choose Settings. A Settings pane appears, as shown in Figure 16-8.

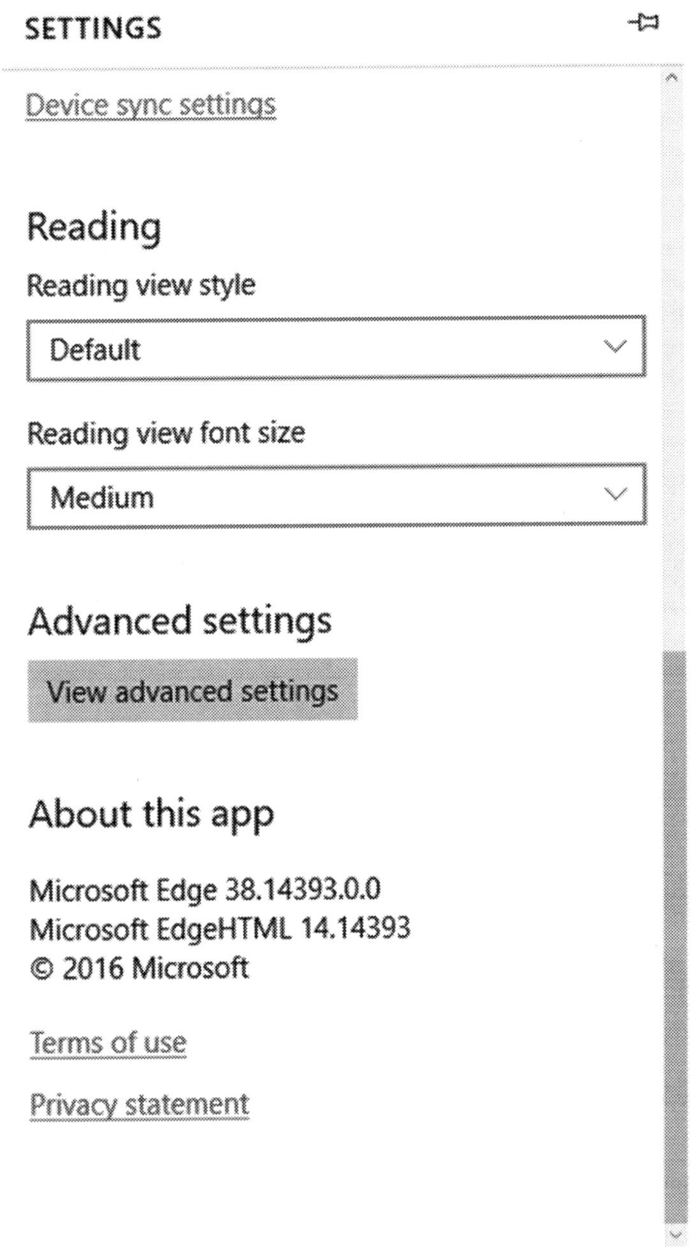

SETTINGS   ⇥

Device sync settings

Reading

Reading view style

| Default | ⌄ |

Reading view font size

| Medium | ⌄ |

Advanced settings

View advanced settings

About this app

Microsoft Edge 38.14393.0.0
Microsoft EdgeHTML 14.14393
© 2016 Microsoft

Terms of use

Privacy statement

Figure 16-8. *The Settings pane displays options for customizing Edge*

5. Scroll down the Settings pane and click the View advanced settings button. An Advanced settings pane appears, as shown in Figure 16-9.

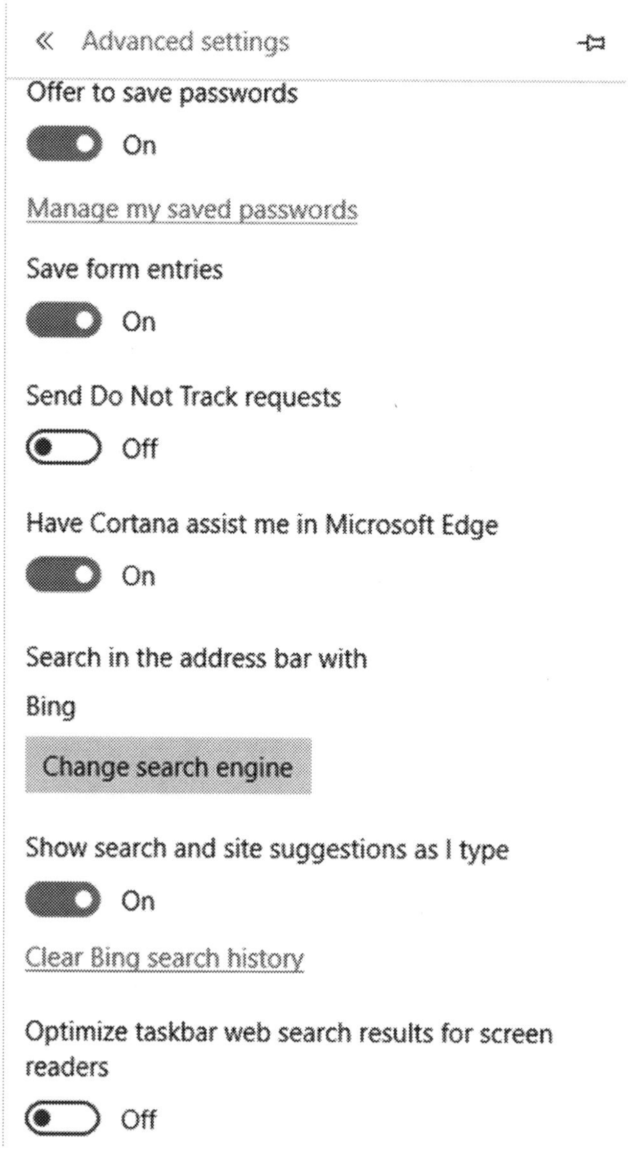

《 Advanced settings

Offer to save passwords

⬤━ On

Manage my saved passwords

Save form entries

⬤━ On

Send Do Not Track requests

━⬤ Off

Have Cortana assist me in Microsoft Edge

⬤━ On

Search in the address bar with

Bing

Change search engine

Show search and site suggestions as I type

⬤━ On

Clear Bing search history

Optimize taskbar web search results for screen readers

━⬤ Off

Figure 16-9. *Scrolling down the Advanced settings pane displays a Change search engine button*

6. Click the Change search engine button. A list of all past search engines you've visited appears, as shown in Figure 16-10.

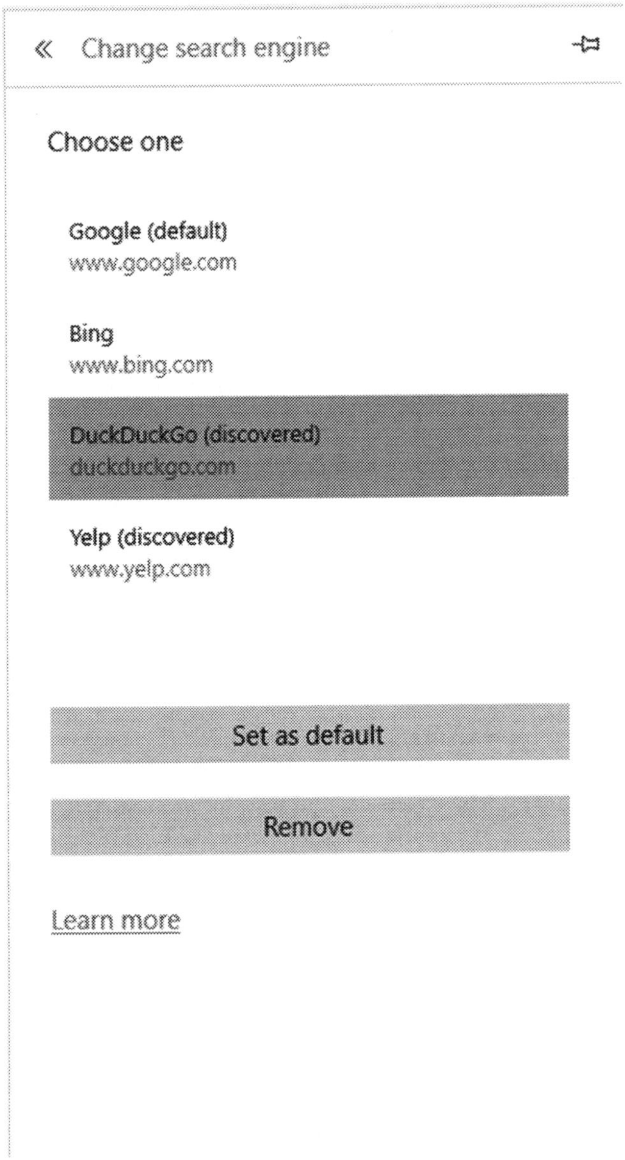

«   Change search engine   ⊏⊐

Choose one

Google (default)
www.google.com

Bing
www.bing.com

DuckDuckGo (discovered)
duckduckgo.com

Yelp (discovered)
www.yelp.com

Set as default

Remove

Learn more

Figure 16-10. *The Change search engine lists all search engines you've visited*

7. Click a search engine that you want to use as the default and then click the Set as default button.

8. Click the More icon again to close the right pane.

Opening Multiple Web Sites

When you first start Edge, you can open and view a single web site. If you want to view another web site, the new web site appears and your previously viewed web site disappears.

In some cases, this might be what you want, but if you want to keep a web site visible while looking at more web sites at the same time, you may need to open additional web sites inside of multiple windows or tabs.

When you open multiple windows, you can arrange the windows on the screen so you can view them side by side. However, multiple windows can clutter your screen so another alternative is to open multiple web sites as separate tabs inside a single window, as shown in Figure 16-11.

Figure 16-11. *Multiple tabs let you view several web sites within a single window*

Opening a Web Site in Another Window

Displaying multiple web sites in separate windows can come in handy when you want to view two or more web sites at the same time. The larger the screen, the more open windows you can comfortably display.

To open another web site in a separate window, follow these steps:

1. Open the Edge program.

2. Press Ctrl+N. Edge displays another window.

3. Click in the Search text field in the top middle of the new Edge window, type a web site address or search query into the Search text field, and press Enter.

4. Click the close button (the big X) in the upper right corner of the Edge window when you're done using it.

Opening a Web Site in a Tab

Multiple windows make it easy to view two or more web sites side by side. However, if you don't need to view two or more web sites at the same time, you can open multiple web sites in tabs.

Tabs appear in a single window so they take up less space and make it easy to quickly switch from one web site to another. If you want, you can even open multiple windows where each window has two or more tabs.

To open a web site in a tab, follow these steps:

1. Open the Edge program.

2. Create a new tab by choosing one of the following:

   a. Click the Add new tab button (it looks like a plus [+] sign) (see Figure 16-11)

   b. Press Ctrl+T

3. Click in the Search text field in the top middle of the new Edge tab, type a web site address or search query into the Search text field, and press Enter.

4. When you're done with a tab, move the pointer over the tab so a close button (an X) appears to the right of that tab, as shown in Figure 16-12.

Figure 16-12. *A close button appears to the right of a tab when you move the pointer over that tab*

5. Click the close button on a tab that you want to close. The tab disappears.

Defining Default Web Sites for New Windows and Tabs

Each time you open another web site in a separate window or tab, Edge can display a default web page. You can define the start page when you first open Edge, and you can define the default web page when you open a new window or tab.

To define default web pages in Edge, follow these steps:

1. Open the Edge program.

2. Click the More icon in the upper right corner of the Edge window (it looks like three dots). A pull-down menu appears (see Figure 16-7).

3. Choose Settings. A Settings pane appears (see Figure 16-8).

4. Click the Open Microsoft Edge with list box and choose an option, as shown in Figure 16-13:

    • *Start page*: Displays the default Edge start page

    • *New tab page*: Displays the web page defined by the Open new tabs with list box (step 5 below)

- *Previous pages*: Opens the last page displayed before exiting out of Edge the last time you used it

- *A specific page or pages*: Lets you type a specific domain address of a web page

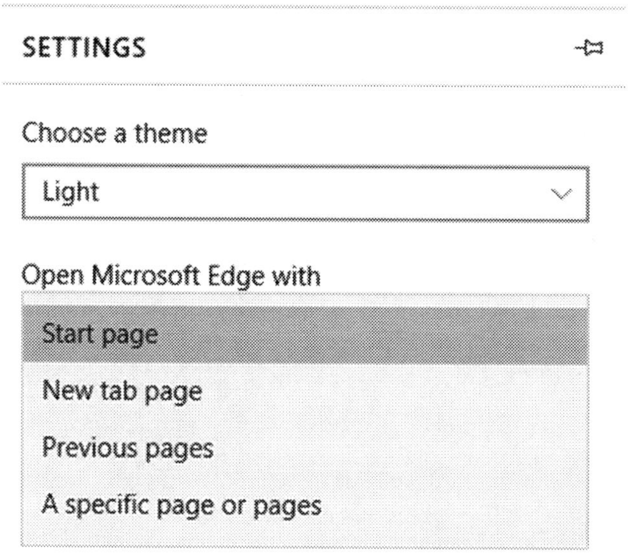

SETTINGS   ⇥

Choose a theme

Light   ∨

Open Microsoft Edge with

Start page
New tab page
Previous pages
A specific page or pages

Figure 16-13. *The Settings window lets you define a default start page*

5. Click the Open new tabs with list box and choose an option, as shown in Figure 16-14:

    • *Top sites and suggested content*: Displays icons for popular sites such as Facebook and Yahoo Mail along with various news articles from MSN

    • *Top sites*: Only displays icons for popular sites such as Facebook and Yahoo Mail

    • *A blank page*: Displays an empty page

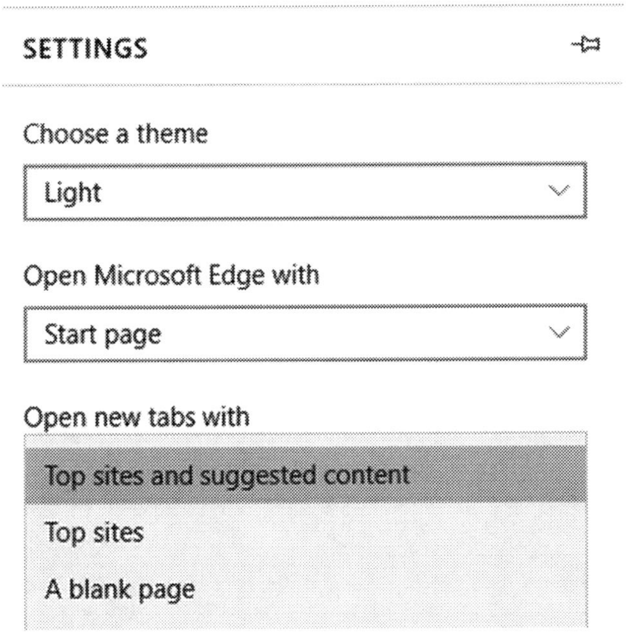

SETTINGS   ⇥

Choose a theme

| Light | ⌄ |

Open Microsoft Edge with

| Start page | ⌄ |

Open new tabs with

| Top sites and suggested content |
| Top sites |
| A blank page |

Figure 16-14. The Settings window lets you define default web pages for new windows and tabs

6. Click the More icon again to close the right pane.

Turning Tabs into Multiple Windows (and Vice Versa)

If you open another web site in a separate window, you can always merge all open Edge windows into one and display those web sites as tabs within a single Edge window.

Likewise, if you open multiple web sites in separate tabs, you can always display those tabs as different windows instead. By switching between multiple windows and tabs, you can view your web sites the way you like best.

To merge multiple Edge windows into tabs, follow these steps:

1. Open two or more separate windows in Edge.

2. Move the pointer over the top of one of the open Edge windows (the gray area to the right of the tabs).

3. Drag the mouse/trackpad over the tabs of another open Edge window and release the mouse/trackpad. Edge displays both windows as tabs in a single window.

To display a tab as a separate window, follow these steps:

1. Open a window in Edge that displays two or more tabs.

2. Move the pointer over the tab that you want to display as a separate window.

3. Drag the mouse/trackpad anywhere outside the open Edge window and release the mouse/trackpad. Edge displays your chosen tab as a separate window.

Going Back to Previously Viewed Web Sites

The Internet encourages you to browse by clicking various links to see something new. The problem is that as you explore the Internet, you may want to return back to a previous web site that you had just looked at.

Fortunately, Edge offers two ways to go back to previous viewed web sites:

*   Use the Back and Forward buttons

*   View the History of your viewed web sites

The Back and Forward buttons appear in the upper left corner of the Edge window, as shown in Figure 16-15.

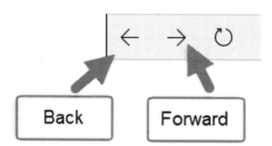

Figure 16-15. *The Back and Forward buttons*

Each time you click a web page link that displays a new web page, you can go back to the previous web page by clicking the Back button.

Suppose you visit a financial web page and then visit an animal web page. With the animal web page displayed, clicking the Back button would return you to the financial web page. Now clicking the Forward would display the animal web page again.

Essentially the Back/Forward buttons let you go back one web page at a time to web pages you previously viewed. Until you go back at least one web page, the Forward button remains dimmed and unavailable.

As an alternative to clicking the Back/Forward buttons, you can also press the following keystroke shortcuts:

- Alt+Left arrow (Back)

- Alt+Right arrow (Forward)

Going back and forth one web page at a time can be slow. If you want to go back to a web site you viewed earlier in the day but browsed through dozens of other web sites since then, going back one web page at a time is clumsy. A faster alternative is to view your browsing history.

Each time you visit a web site, Edge keeps track of the site in its history list. By viewing this history list, you can see a list of previously visited web sites and just click the one you want to return to.

To use Edge's history list, follow these steps:

1. Start Edge and browse different web sites.

2. Click the Hub icon. A menu appears.

3. Click the History icon, as shown in Figure 16-16.

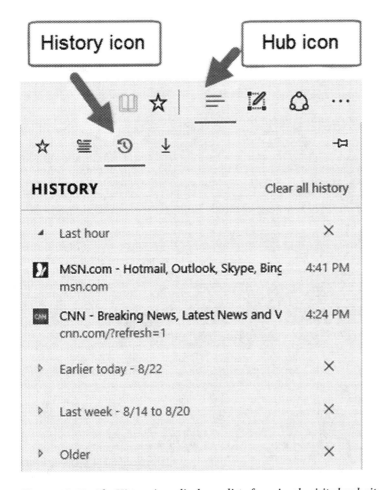

Figure 16-16. *The History icon displays a list of previously visited web sites*

4. Click a web site that appears in the History menu list. You can also click the different categories such as Earlier today or Last week to view web sites you visited farther in the past.

Protecting Your Privacy

One drawback of storing your browsing history is that you may not want anyone else to see which web sites you may have visited. Since you can't always keep people from away from your computer, you can protect your privacy in two ways.

First, you can erase your browsing history. Second, you can use a special private browsing feature of Edge.

The drawback of erasing your browsing history is that you might delete a web site that you may want to visit again later. If you use the private browsing feature of Edge, you can never go back to previously viewed web sites since Edge won't keep track of them.

Erasing Your Browsing History

Some of the data you can erase from Edge include:

-   *Browsing history*: The web sites you've visited recently

-   *Cookies and saved web site data*: Information web sites may have stored on your computer to make it easy to return to that site in the future

-   *Cached data and files*: Information web sites may have stored on your computer to speed up access to that site in the future

-   *Download history*: The files you have downloaded recently

-   *Form data*: Information you may have typed in a form such as your name or address

-   Passwords: Passwords you may have typed to access a web site

To erase your history, follow these steps:

1. Start Edge.

2. Click the Hub icon.

3. Click the History icon (see Figure 16-16).

4. Click Clear all history. A pane appears showing you all the data Edge can delete, as shown in Figure 16-17.

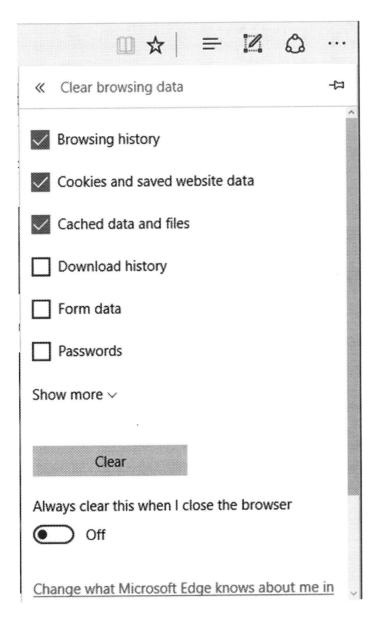

Figure 16-17. *Deleting your browsing history in Edge*

5. Select (or clear) check boxes for the data you want to keep or delete.

6. Click the Clear button.

▓ **Note** When you delete data from Edge, the deleted data still remains on your hard disk. That means someone could still retrieve this deleted data using special forensics tools.

Private Browsing

If you really want to protect your privacy, use Edge's private browsing feature. This doesn't save any of your browsing history at all so it's impossible to retrieve it later.

To use private browsing, follow these steps:

1. Start Edge.

2. Click the More icon. A pane appears, as shown in Figure 16-18.

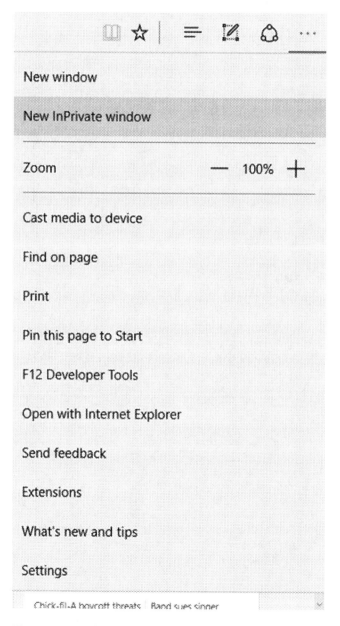

Figure 16-18. *Choosing the New InPrivate window option*

3. Choose New InPrivate window. A Browsing InPrivate window appears, as shown in Figure 16-19.

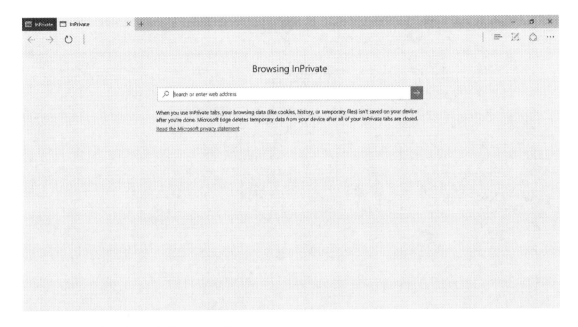

Figure 16-19. *Opening an InPrivate window*

4. Type a domain address or search query. To remind you that you're in private browsing mode, Edge displays InPrivate in the upper left corner of the Edge window.

A private browsing window lets you create additional tabs as well where each tab also lets you browse privately without saving your history. When you're done with a private browsing window, click the close button (the big X) in the upper right corner of the private browsing window.

Defining Browser Privacy Settings

When you browse the Internet, many web sites use small files known as cookies to track your behavior. In addition, some web sites can even identify your location. While this can be handy to help you find directions on a map, it can also be used to pinpoint your location, which you might not want.

To further protect your privacy, you can block cookies, passwords, and form entries. It may not block particularly devious web sites, but it can provide an additional level of privacy for you.

The most secure setting is to always block cookies, but if you always block cookies, you'll lose the convenience of web sites recognizing you when you return. You may want to experiment with different settings so you can determine what tradeoff between convenience and privacy you're willing to accept.

To define browser privacy settings for Edge, follow these steps:

1. Start Edge.

2. Click the More icon. A pane appears.

3. Click Settings. Another pane appears.

4. Scroll down and click the View advanced settings button. Another pane appears.

5. Scroll down to view the Privacy and services settings, as shown in Figure 16-20.

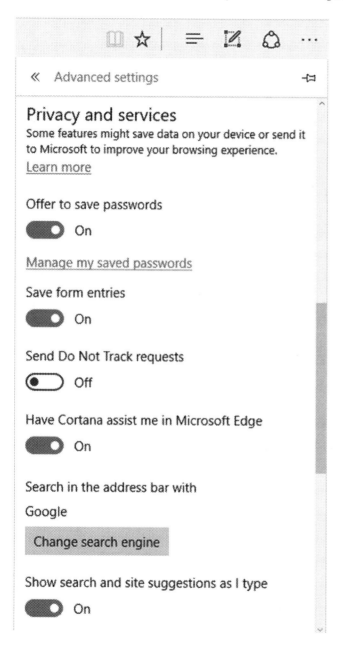

Figure 16-20. Edge's Privacy settings

6. (Optional) Click the switch to turn on (or off) the Offer to save passwords.

7. (Optional) Click the switch to turn on (or off) the Save form entries

8. (Optional) Scroll down and click the Cookies list box and choose one of the following options, as shown in Figure 16-21:

- *Block all cookies*: Stops all web sites from storing cookies on your computer (may keep some web sites from working)

- *Block only third-party cookies*: Allows web sites to store cookies but blocks other sites that you haven't visited from storing cookies on your computer (recommended option for most people)

- *Don't block cookies*: Allows any web site to store cookies on your computer (least secure option)

9. Click the More icon again to close the right pane.

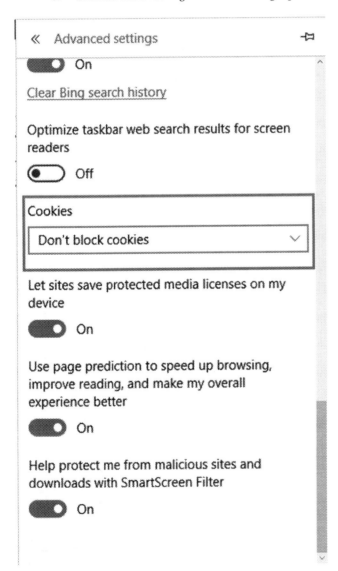

Figure 16-21. *Changing how Edge manages cookies*

Using Bookmarks

Jumping to a web site from your history list can be convenient, but if there are web sites you visit frequently, it's far easier to save those web sites as bookmarks instead. When you bookmark a web site, you can return to that web site later with just one click of the mouse (or trackpad) on your stored bookmark.

Bookmarking a Web Site

When you find a favorite web site, create a bookmark so you'll always be able to find that web site again. When bookmarking a web site, you can give it a descriptive name and choose where to store it. By default, Edge stores bookmarks in the Favorites folder but you can choose a different folder if you wish.

To bookmark a web site, follow these steps:

1. Start Edge.

2. Open any web site that you want to visit repeatedly.

3. Click the Favorites icon (it looks like a star). (You can also press Ctrl+D.) A menu appears, asking for a bookmark name and where you want to store that bookmark, as shown in Figure 16-22.

4. Click in the Name text field and edit or type a descriptive name for your bookmark.

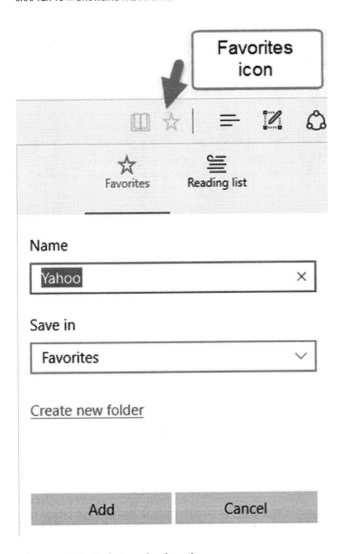

Figure 16-22. *Defining a bookmark*

5. (Optional) Click the Create new folder link if you want to store your bookmark in a different folder than the Favorites folder.

6. Click the Add button.

Viewing Bookmarks

Once you've saved your bookmark, you'll eventually want to view it. To revisit a bookmarked web site, follow these steps:

1. Start Edge.

2. Click the Hub icon. A menu appears.

3. Click the Favorites icon. A list of your bookmarked web sites appears, as shown in Figure 16-23.

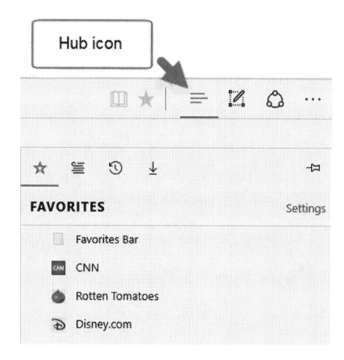

Figure 16-23. *Choosing a bookmark*

4. Click a bookmark. Edge loads your bookmarked web site.

Editing Bookmarks

After you've created a bookmark, you can always modify that bookmark later such as changing its descriptive name. Editing also lets you rearrange your bookmarks by dragging them with the mouse or trackpad.

To edit a bookmark, follow these steps:

1. Start Edge.

2. Click the Hub icon. A menu appears.

3. Click the Favorites icon. A list of your bookmarked web sites appears (see Figure 16-23).

4. Right-click the bookmark you want to edit. A pop-up menu appears, as shown in Figure 16-24.

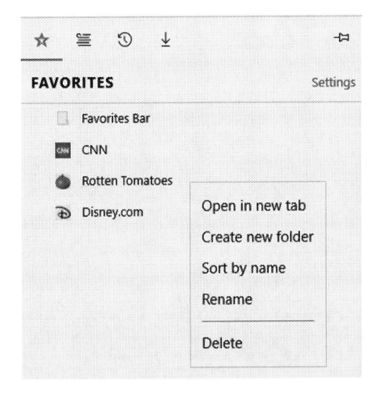

Figure 16-24. *Right-clicking a bookmark displays a pop-up menu*

5. Choose one of the following:

    a. *Rename*: Lets you rename the bookmark

    b. *Delete*: Lets you remove a bookmark from Edge

6. (Optional) Drag a bookmark up or down with the mouse/trackpad to rearrange the order in which your bookmarks appear.

Importing Bookmarks

If you've been using Internet Explorer before upgrading to Windows 10, you probably have bookmarks stored in Internet Explorer. Fortunately, you can export them out from Internet Explorer and import them into Edge. To import bookmarks, follow these steps:

1. Start Edge.

2. Click the Hub icon to display a menu.

3. Click the Favorites icon to display the Favorites pane.

4. Click Settings. The Favorites settings pane appears, as shown in Figure 16-25.

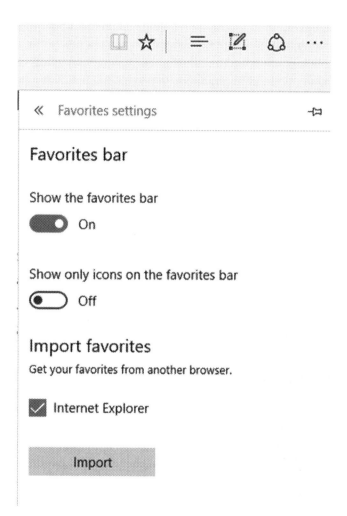

Figure 16-25. *The Favorites settings pane lets you choose to import bookmarks from Internet Explorer*

5. Select the Internet Explorer check box.

6. Click the Import button.

7. Click the Hub icon to close the pane.

Creating a Reading List

Bookmarks are meant to store web sites that you plan to visit regularly in the future. However, if you only want to save a web page to read but don't necessarily want to visit that site later, you can use Edge's reading list feature instead.

A reading list essentially acts like bookmarks. The main difference is that a bookmark takes you to a specific domain address, which may display different content than the last time you visited it, such as the latest headlines news. A reading list takes you to a specific web page that displays the content you saw when you stored it in the reading list.

To place a web page on a reading list, follow these steps:

1. Start Edge.

2. Open a web page you want to temporarily save to read later.

3. Click the Favorites icon (it looks like a star). A menu appears.

4. Click the Reading list icon. The reading list pane appears, as shown in Figure 16-26.

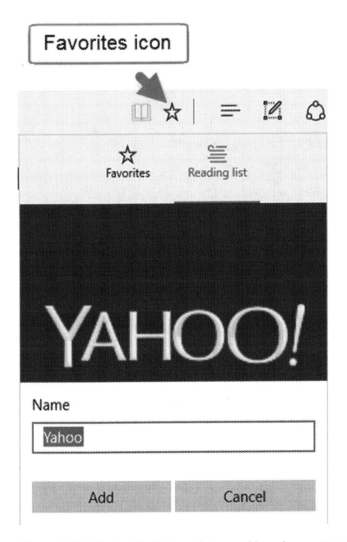

Figure 16-26. The Reading list pane lets you add a web page to save

5. Click in the Name text box and type a descriptive name for your saved web page.

6. Click the Add button.

Once you've saved one or more web pages on your reading list, you can return to that web page at any time. To read a saved web page in your reading list, follow these steps:

1. Start Edge.

2. Click the Hub icon. A menu appears.

3. Click the Reading list icon. A list of your saved web pages appears, as shown in Figure 16-27.

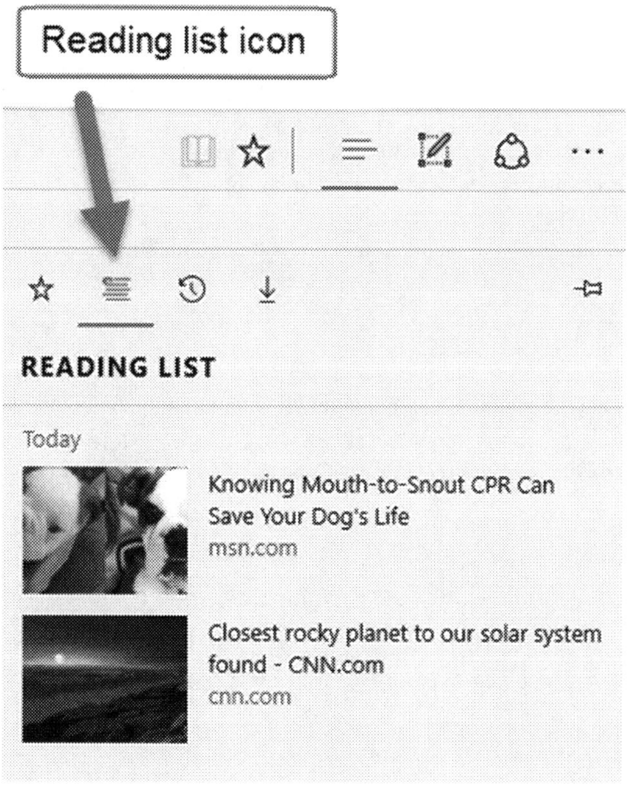

Figure 16-27. *The saved reading list*

4. Click the saved web page you want to read.

To remove a web page from the reading list, right-click the web page you want to remove in step 4. When a pop-up menu appears, choose Delete.

Using AutoComplete

If you often need to type the same information into different web sites, you may want to use AutoComplete. AutoComplete lets you store common information such as your name, street address, and credit card number. Now if you need to fill in this information on a web page, AutoComplete can type all of this information for you automatically.

AutoComplete can store four different types of information:

- Your contact information including your name, address, e-mail address, and phone number

- User names and passwords for different web sites

- Additional sign-in information

The advantage of AutoComplete is that it can simplify typing information needed to order products online or access different types of web sites such as those that require a user name and password.

The disadvantage of AutoComplete is if someone accesses your computer without your permission, they could impersonate you by letting AutoComplete automatically type in your personal data.

AutoComplete works automatically as soon as it detects you're filling out a form in Edge. That's when AutoComplete will ask if you want to save your recently typed data, as shown in Figure 16-28.

Figure 16-28. AutoFill appears automatically when you start filling out a form

When you save passwords using AutoComplete, you might need to edit that password later if you choose a new password. To edit passwords stored in AutoComplete, follow these steps:

1. Start Edge.

2. Click the More icon and choose Settings. A Settings pane appears.

3. Scroll down the right pane and click the View advanced settings button.

4. Scroll down and click the Manage my saved passwords link, as shown in Figure 16-29. A Manage passwords pane appears, listing all the web sites AutoComplete has saved a password to access.

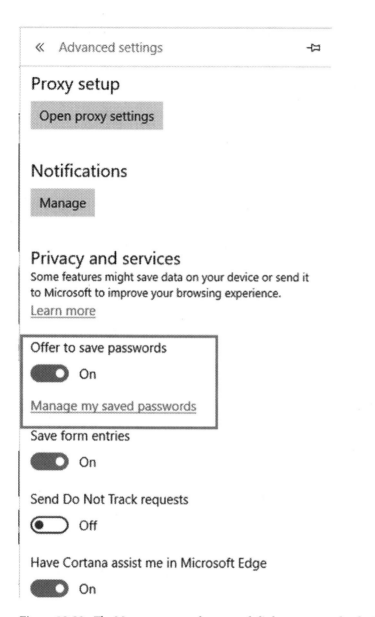

Figure 16-29. *The Manage my saved passwords link appears under the Offer to save passwords option*

5. Click a web site that you want to edit. (If you click the close icon [the big X] to the right of a web site, you can delete that saved web site's data from Edge.) The URL, Username, and Password text boxes appear, as shown in Figure 16-30.

Figure 16-30. Editing saved password data for a web site

6. Click in the URL, Username, or Password text box and edit the data.

Reducing Internet Annoyances

Two of the biggest problems with the Internet are pop-up ads and Flash animation, which are often used to display obnoxious ads. Besides being annoying, Flash animation can also run down the battery of your laptop if it's not connected to an electrical outlet. That's because displaying animation takes constant processing power. On a desktop computer that's plugged in all the time, Flash animation isn't a problem, but if you're running off batteries, running Flash animation can drain your laptop's batteries over time.

To fix these two problems, Edge lets you block pop-up ads and turn off Flash animation. Blocking pop-up ads can let you browse without distracting pop-up ads getting in the way, and turning off Flash can save your laptop's batteries, prevent annoying ads from appearing, and also protect your computer from malware that often infects your computer through Flash animation.

To block pop-up ads and turn off Flash animation in Edge, follow these steps:

1. Start Edge

2. Click the More icon. A pane appears.

3. Scroll down and click Settings. A Settings pane appears.

4. Scroll down and click the View advanced settings button. An Advanced settings pane appears, as shown in Figure 16-31.

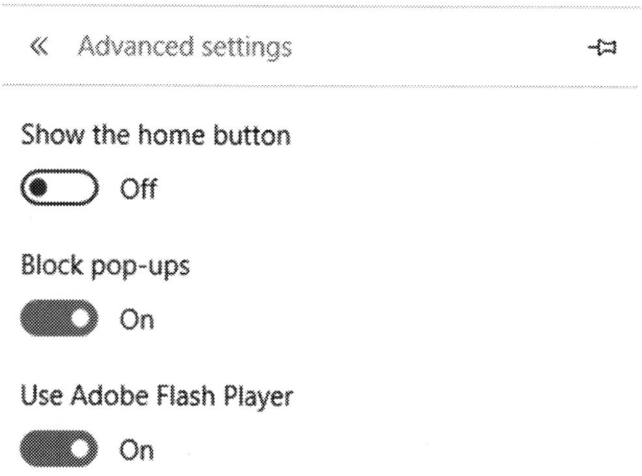

« Advanced settings   -⊏⊐

Show the home button

⬤⬭ Off

Block pop-ups

⬤⬤ On

Use Adobe Flash Player

⬤⬤ On

Figure 16-31. *The Advanced settings pane lets you block pop-up ads and turn off Flash animation*

5. (Optional) Click the Block pop-ups switch to turn the pop-up blocker on or off.

6. (Optional) Click the Use Adobe Flash Player switch to turn Flash on or off.

7. Click the More icon again to close the pane.

Summary

Although you can always install and use any browser such as Chrome or Firefox, Edge is optimized for Windows 10 and will become the standard browser for Windows in the future.

With Edge, you can browse web sites and save them later as bookmarks or part of a reading list. If you need to open and view multiple web sites at the same time, you can open them in separate windows or in multiple tabs within each window.

To protect your privacy, Edge offers a special privacy browsing window or you can define various privacy settings so you control what web sites can track from your activities.

If you frequently fill out information such as your name, address, and credit card number, you can use Edge's AutoComplete feature to automatically fill in that information.

Edge acts like a gateway to the Internet so be sure you know how to use this program so you can access the world of information scattered all over the world.

CHAPTER 17

Talking to Cortana

The main purpose of the Internet is to find information such as sports scores, driving directions, or national and international news. While it's easy to load the Edge browser and search the Internet for specific web sites on your own, it can be faster and easier to just use Cortana instead.

Cortana is a natural language recognition program that lets you type or speak a question. Cortana then understands your question and searches for an answer on the Internet. By using Cortana, you can avoid the hassle of wading through multiple web sites and web pages, and just find the information you want.

Besides making it easier to search the Internet for information, Cortana can also work as a personal assistant to set alarms, launch programs, and send e-mail. If you find the keyboard, mouse, or trackpad clumsy to use, then you might appreciate the ability to speak commands directly to Cortana and get the information you want.

Think of Cortana as your Windows 10 virtual assistant. Whenever you need to use your computer, chances are good you can do your computer tasks faster and easier with Cortana's help.

Searching the Internet with Cortana

Here's how searching works without Cortana. First, you have to load a browser such as Edge. Second, you have to type your query. Third, you have to wade through a list of different web sites until you find the answer you want.

Here's how searching with Cortana works. You either type or speak your query. Then Cortana shows you the result. It's that simple and it eliminates the nuisance of visiting different web sites or finding a search engine to use. When you search, you want results right away instead of going through several intermediary steps that get in your way and slow you down.

To search with Cortana, make sure your computer has an Internet connection and then follow these steps:

1. Click in the Cortana search text box that appears next to the Windows icon in the lower left corner of the screen, as shown in Figure 17-1.

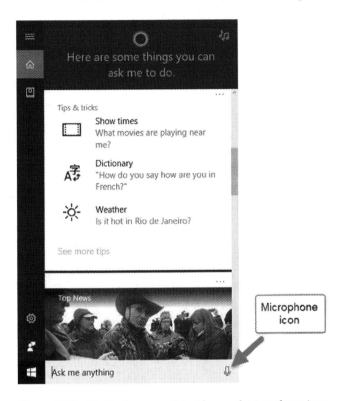

Figure 17-1. *The Cortana search text box and microphone icon*

2. Choose one of the following:

- Click the Microphone icon and speak your query

- Click in the Cortana search text box and type your query

Cortana displays the results of your query, as shown in Figure 17-2.

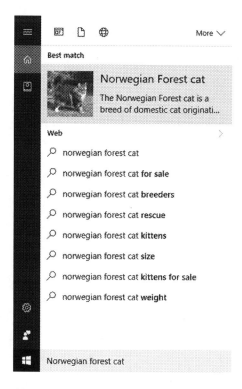

Figure 17-2. *Cortana displays the result of your query*

3. Click any information displayed to open the Edge browser and see more details, or press ESC or click away from the Cortana window to make the results disappear.

Tracking Flights and Packages

If you want to know the arrival time of a package or airline flight, you would normally have to visit the delivery company's web site or the airline's web site and type in the package tracking number or flight number. Rather than do that, you can just type or speak the package tracking number or flight number.

Flight numbers typically consist of the airline code followed by the flight number. The airline code is either a two- or three-letter code such as KE or KAL for Korean Airlines or WN or SWA for Southwest airlines. To find a list of airline codes, visit the Wikipedia web site of airline codes (https://en.wikipedia.org/wiki/List_of_airline_codes).

To track a package or flight with Cortana, type the tracking number or flight number in the Cortana search text box. Cortana displays the results of your query, as shown in Figure 17-3.

Figure 17-3. Cortana displays information about your flight or package

---

░ **Note** Since many package delivery services send you tracking numbers by e-mail, it's easier and more accurate to copy this tracking number from your e-mail message and paste it in the Cortana search text box.

When tracking packages, you may need to click the displayed information to open the Edge browser and see more details from the delivery service, as shown in Figure 17-4.

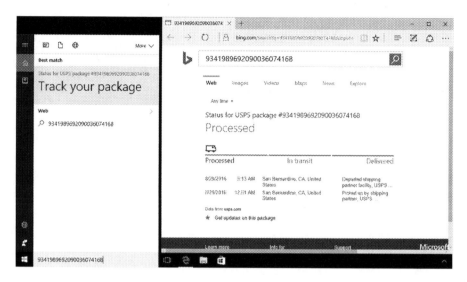

Figure 17-4. *Tracking a package often requires seeing more details in a browser*

Performing Calculations and Conversions

A surprising number of people not only don't like math but actually fear doing any math at all. Related to math are conversions from one measuring system to the other. While most of the world uses the metric system, the United States still clings to the English system of measurement involving pounds, inches, and pints.

Trying to convert inches to centimeters or pounds to kilograms involves finding the right conversion formula and then doing the actual math. To spare you the trouble of doing math at all, you can ask Cortana to do math and conversions for you.

Cortana can do simple arithmetic operations that you can find on the built-in calculator in Windows 10 such as addition, subtraction, division, and multiplication. In addition, Cortana can also do percentages, square roots, and square.

▓ **Note**   Although Cortana lets you recite numbers, it's probably easier and more accurate to type them out instead.

When giving Cortana math commands, type an equation as follows:

- 2 + 54

- 12 - 8

- 3.4 * 7

- 903.4 / 28

- square root of 8 or sqrt 8 ($\sqrt{8}$)

- 9.12 ^ 2 or 9.12 squared (9.12^2)

- 1.39 ^ 4 (1.39^4)

When typing exponentials, you can type the caret (^) symbol followed by any number such as 3 ^ 4 (3^4) or 8.37 ^ 3 (8.37^3), as shown in Figure 17-5.

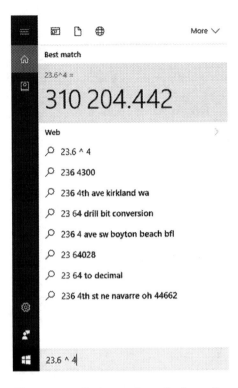

Figure 17-5. *Typing mathematical equations into Cortana*

When typing a conversion, you need to type four items in order, as shown in Figure 17-6:

- The numerical amount you want to convert into another measurement unit (such as 100)

- The measurement unit name or abbreviation (such as kilogram or the abbreviation such as kg)

- The word "to"

- The measurement unit name or abbreviation that you want to convert to (such as pounds or lbs)

Figure 17-6. *Typing a conversion into Cortana*

Check the Weather

If you frequently travel, you may want to know the weather in different cities around the world. You could visit a weather site and type in a different city name each time, but it's faster to ask Cortana the weather instead.

Just type in the following:

- weather in

- a city name (such as Paris, London, Hong Kong, or Toronto)

So if you wanted to know the weather in Dallas, you would type "weather in Dallas" in the Cortana search text box, as shown in Figure 17-7.

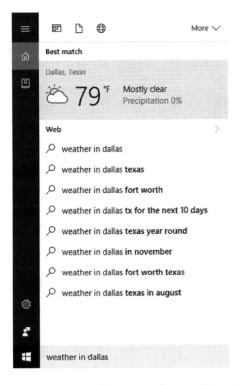

Figure 17-7. Looking up weather conditions in Cortana

Getting Directions

In the olden days if you wanted directions to a place you've never been to before, you either had to get a map or ask someone for directions. While you could visit a mapping web site for directions, it's faster to ask Cortana directly.

To get driving directions, you must first give Windows 10 permission to identify your current location. To do this, follow these steps:

1.   Click the Windows icon in the lower left corner of the screen. The Start menu appears.

2.   Click the Settings icon. The Settings window appears.

3.   Click the Privacy icon. The Privacy settings appear.

4.   Click Location in the left pane.

5.   Click the Maps switch to turn it on, as shown in Figure 17-8.

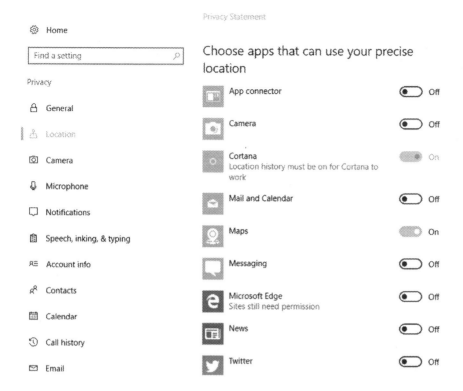

Figure 17-8. *Turning on locations for the Maps app*

6. Click the close button (the big X) in the upper right corner of the Settings window to close it.

Once you've given the Maps app permission to use your location, you can get driving directions from Cortana by following these steps:

1. Click in the Cortana search text box that appears next to the Windows icon in the lower left corner of the screen (see Figure 17-1).

2. Type or say the following:

   • Directions to

   • Your destination such as an address or a place

Cortana displays the results of your query, as shown in Figure 17-9.

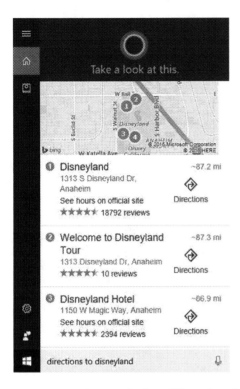

Figure 17-9. *Cortana displays different locations to choose*

3. Click the location you want directions to. The Maps app displays driving directions, as shown in Figure 17-10.

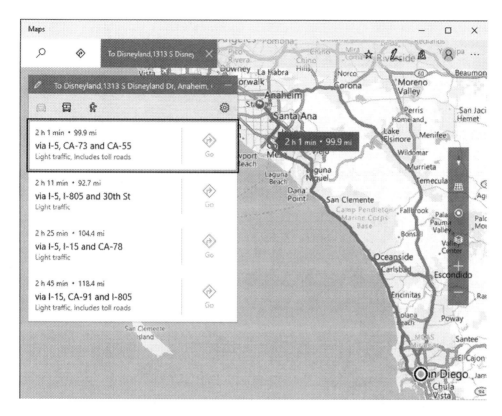

Figure 17-10. *The Maps app displays directions that you can print and view*

Setting Reminders

Most people get bombarded by ideas and tasks every day. If you don't write your thoughts down, you'll risk forgetting or losing them. Rather than hunt around for a pencil and paper, or jot your ideas down in a word processor, just tell them to Cortana instead.

Cortana can remind you about three types of items:

- *People*: Displays a reminder for meeting a specific person

- *Places*: Displays a reminder when you arrive or leave a specific location

- *Times*: Displays a reminder at a certain time such as one hour later

To set a reminder, follow these steps:

1. Click in the Cortana search text box that appears next to the Windows icon in the lower left corner of the screen (see Figure 17-1).

2. Type or say "Remind me." Cortana asks what you want to be reminded about, as shown in Figure 17-11.

Figure 17-11. *Cortana asks what you want to be reminded about*

3. Click the Person, Place, or Time button.

If you click the Person button, follow these steps:

1. After clicking the Person button, a Contacts window appears.

2. Click the name of the person you want to set a reminder for. The Cortana menu appears again with the name of the person you selected, as shown in Figure 17-12.

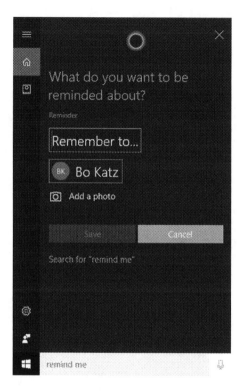

Figure 17-12. *Cortana lists the name of the contact you choose*

3. Click in the Remember to... text box and type your reminder.

4. Click the Remind button, as shown in Figure 17-13. Cortana lists your reminder.

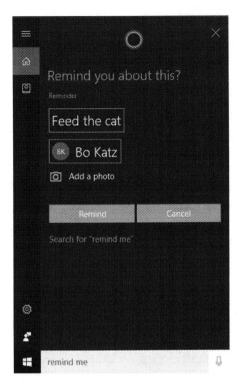

Figure 17-13. Completing a reminder for meeting a person

If you click the Place button, follow these steps:

1. After clicking the Place button, a window appears displaying various locations you've recently searched for driving directions, as shown in Figure 17-14.

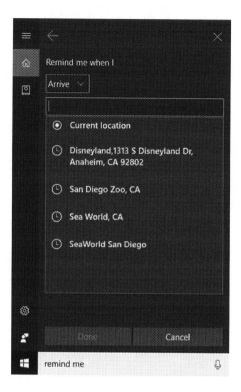

Figure 17-14. *Viewing a list of recently searched locations*

2. Click a displayed location or type a new location.

3. Click in the Arrive list box and choose either Arrive or Leave.

4. Click the Done button. The Cortana menu appears again displaying your chosen location, as shown in Figure 17-15.

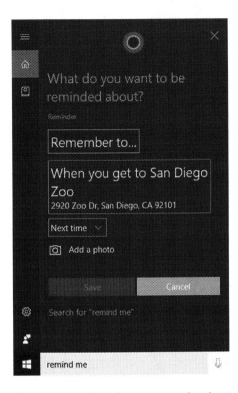

Figure 17-15. *Completing a reminder about a location*

5. Click in the Remember to... text box and type your reminder.

6. Click in the Next time list box and choose an option such as Next time or On Mondays.

7. Click the Remind button. Cortana lists your reminder.

If you click the Time button, follow these steps:

1. After clicking the Time button, a pop-up menu appears, as shown in Figure 17-16.

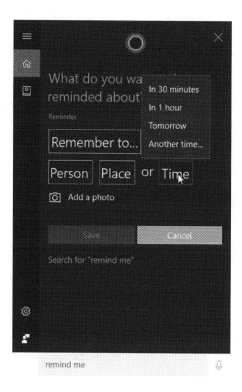

Figure 17-16. *Choosing a time for your reminder*

2. Click a time such as In 30 minutes. If you click Another time, you can specify a specific time and date, as shown in Figure 17-17.

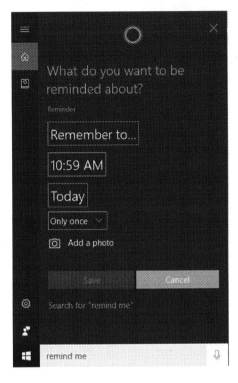

Figure 17-17. *Setting a specific time*

3. Click in the Remember to... text box and type your reminder.

4. Click the Remind button. Cortana lists your reminder.

If you set a reminder with an alarm, Cortana will display a reminder window in the bottom right corner of the screen, as shown in Figure 17-18.

Figure 17-18. *A time reminder appears on the screen*

You can then click the Snooze icon to set the alarm for a later time or click the Complete icon. Once you've set a reminder, you can view it at any time. To view your reminder, follow these steps:

1. Click the Cortana icon in the left of the Cortana search text box, as shown in Figure 17-19. The Cortana menu appears.

Figure 17-19. *The Cortana icon*

2. Click the Notebook icon in the left pane of the Cortana menu, as shown in Figure 17-20.

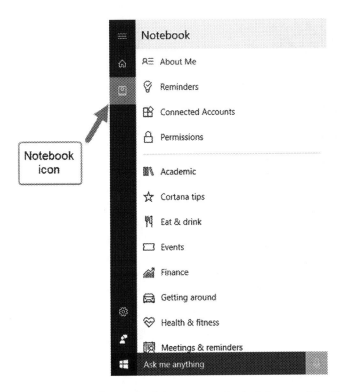

Figure 17-20. *The Notebook icon appears in the left pane of the Cortana menu*

3. Click Reminders. Cortana displays a list of your saved reminders, as shown in Figure 17-21.

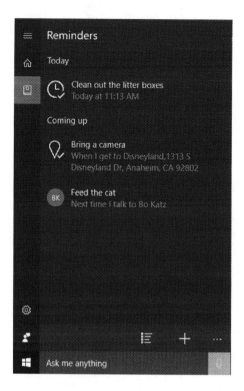

Figure 17-21. *Viewing a list of saved reminders*

To delete a reminder you no longer need, follow these steps:

1. Click the Cortana icon in the left of the Cortana search text box (see Figure 17-19). The Cortana menu appears.

2. Click the Notebook icon in the left pane of the Cortana menu (see Figure 17-20).

3. Click Reminders. Cortana displays a list of your saved reminders (see Figure 17-21).

4. Click the reminder you want to delete. Cortana shows your reminder, as shown in Figure 17-22.

Figure 17-22. *The Trash icon lets you delete a reminder*

5. Click the Trash icon. Cortana deletes your reminder.

Identifying Songs

Because Cortana recognizes spoken language, it can also recognize songs. If you hear a song but you don't know the song's title or recording artist, you can ask Cortana to find this information for you.

To identify a song, follow these steps:

1. Play a song near your computer's microphone.

2. Click the Cortana icon in the left of the Cortana search text box (see Figure 17-19). The Cortana menu appears.

3. Click the Home icon in the left pane of the Cortana menu (see Figure 17-20).

4. Click the Song icon in the upper right corner of the Cortana menu, as shown in Figure 17-23. Cortana displays a message that it's listening to the currently playing song, as shown in Figure 17-24.

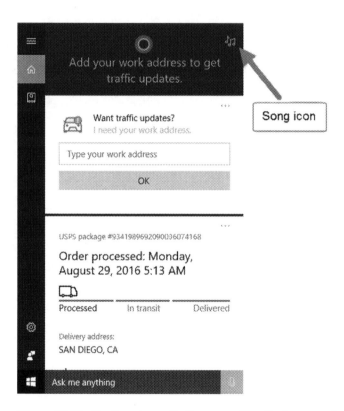

Figure 17-23. *The Song icon tells Cortana to identify the currently playing song*

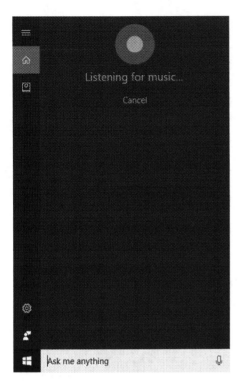

Figure 17-24. *Cortana listens to the currently playing song*

5. If Cortana can identify the song, it displays the song title, album name, and recording artist, as shown in Figure 17-25.

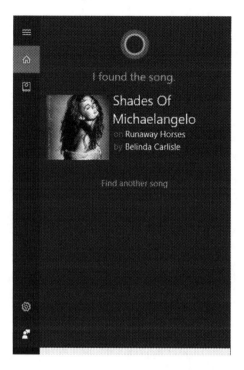

Figure 17-25. *Cortana displays information about the currently playing song*

▓ **Note**   Cortana may not be able to identify all types of songs such as songs by obscure artists or live music.

Finding Movie Showtimes

If you want to know which movies may be showing in your area, you don't have to search for movie listings on the Internet. To view movie showtimes, follow these steps:

1. Type "showtimes" in the Cortana search text box. A list of popular movies showing near you appears, as shown in Figure 17-26.

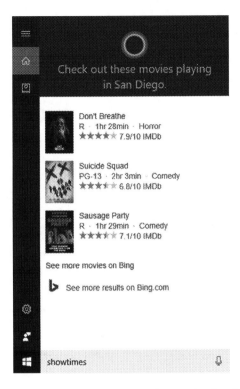

Figure 17-26. *Viewing popular movies showing near you*

2. Click a movie you're interested in. Cortana loads Edge to show you showtimes for your chosen movie at theaters near you.

Summary

If using a computer seems too complicated or cumbersome, then use Cortana as a shortcut to common tasks. You can either type or speak commands into Cortana, but make sure you're in a quiet area or else Cortana might pick up surrounding noise and interpret them as commands instead.

Think of Cortana as a virtual assistant. Any time you want to jot down reminders, look up movie showtimes, get driving directions, check the weather, or do simple unit conversions, ask Cortana to do them for you. By using Cortana's natural language capabilities, you can make your computer seem less like a machine and more like an eager assistant ready to give you answers whenever you need them.

CHAPTER 18

Using E-mail

Beyond browsing various web sites, the second most common use for the Internet is sending and receiving e-mail. To help you create and receive e-mail, Windows 10 comes with a program called Mail.

Besides letting you send and receive text messages, Mail also lets you send and receive files. This gives you a simple way to share files between two different computers as long as both computers can open that file.

There are two common ways to access an e-mail account:

- Through a browser

- Through an e-mail program

The advantage of accessing your e-mail account through a browser is that you can read messages using any computer connected to the Internet. The disadvantage of using a browser is that you can't read any messages if you don't have an Internet connection.

The advantage of using an e-mail program is that your messages will be stored on your computer so you can read them any time you want, whether or not you have an Internet connection. The disadvantage is that your messages are stored on one computer so you can't access those messages from another computer unless you copy or download them to another computer.

In this chapter, you'll learn how to use Windows 10's e-mail program called Mail. If you don't like Mail, you can always use a different e-mail program.

Setting Up an E-mail Account

To send and receive e-mail, you must first have an e-mail account. You can create an e-mail account with major web sites (such as Google or Yahoo!), your Internet service provider, or your company. To set up your browser to access an e-mail account, you need to know the following information:

- *Your e-mail address such as JohnSmith@mycompany.com*: You can often choose the first part of your e-mail address (such as JohnSmith or JSmith) but the second part of your e-mail address will be defined by the e-mail provider such as Google (@gmail.com) or your Internet service provider such as your cable company (@cox.net).

- *Password*: This is the password that gives you access to your account.

▒ **Note** Make sure you save all the information you needed to set up your e-mail account or else you won't be able to send or receive e-mail.

© Wallace Wang 2016
W. Wang, *Absolute Beginners Guide to Computing*, DOI 10.1007/978-1-4842-2289-8_18

Once you have all the information about your e-mail account, you can set up Mail to use that e-mail account. The Mail program can automatically set up e-mail accounts for popular e-mail services such as Google or AOL, but you might need to manually set up an account.

To run the Mail program for the first time, follow these steps:

1. Open the Mail program. A window appears, asking you to assign an existing e-mail account to work with the Mail program, as shown in Figure 18-1.

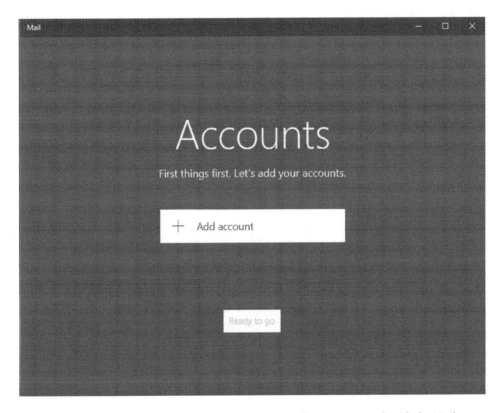

Figure 18-1. *You need to define at least one existing e-mail account to work with the Mail program*

2. Click the + Add account button. An Add an account dialog box appears, as shown in Figure 18-2.

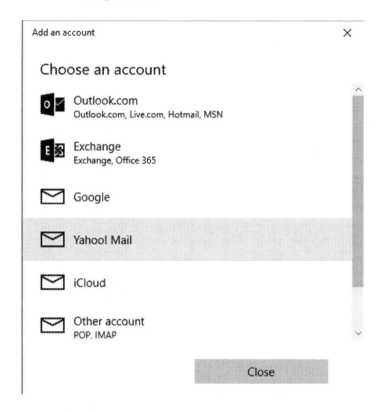

Figure 18-2. The Add an account dialog box can recognize common e-mail accounts

3. Click an e-mail provider such as Yahoo! Mail, Google, or iCloud. (If your e-mail provider isn't listed, click Other account.) Another window appears, asking for your e-mail address, name, and password, as shown in Figure 18-3.

Add an account   ✕

Yahoo! Mail

Email address

someone@example.com

Send your messages using this name

Password

We'll save this information, so you don't have to sign in every time.

Cancel   Sign in

Figure 18-3. *Defining an e-mail address, name, and password to use for an account*

4. Type your e-mail address, name, and password and then click the Sign in button. A dialog box appears to let you know you've successfully assigned an existing e-mail account to work with the Mail program.

5. Click the Done button.

If you aren't using a common e-mail provider, you'll need to type additional information into Mail yourself such as:

- *Your e-mail account type*: Common account types are IMAP and POP, but many corporations may use other e-mail account types such as Microsoft Exchange.

- *Incoming mail server name*: This is the name of the computer that sends e-mail to you, which usually has a name like mail.server.com or pop.server.com, where server.com is the name of the mail server.

- *Outgoing mail server name*: This is the name of the computer that lets you send e-mail to others, which usually has a name like smtp.server.com, where server.com is the name of the mail server.

To get this information, you'll need to contact your e-mail provider.

▨ **Note**　When you connect the Mail program to an e-mail account, you can still access your e-mail through a browser or through the Mail program so you can use whichever method might be most convenient for you at the time.

Sending E-mail

Once you've set up an e-mail account, you'll likely want to send e-mail to other people. To create a new message, you need to define three items:

- *An e-mail address*: This is the e-mail address of the person who will receive the message.

- *A subject*: This identifies the topic of your message.

- *The message itself*: This contains the text of your message that can be as long or short as you wish.

To create a new message and send it, follow these steps:

1. Open the Mail program.

2. Choose one of the following methods to create a new message, as shown in Figure 18-4:

   a. Press Ctrl+N

   b. Click the New mail button

A new message window appears, as shown in Figure 18-4.

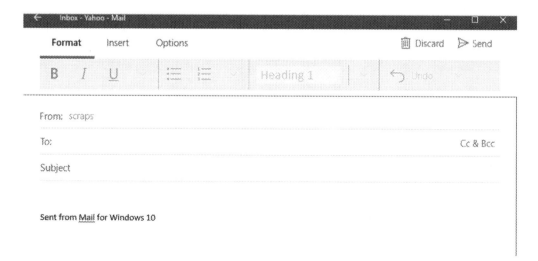

Figure 18-4. *The New message window*

3. Click the To: text field and type an e-mail address. (Make sure you type the e-mail address correctly or else your message will not be sent to the person you want to receive it.)

4. Click in the Subject: text field and type the topic of your message.

5. Click in the message text box and type your message. (Remember, you can paste text in here from other programs such as a word processor or spreadsheet.)

6. Click the Send icon in the upper right corner. To view all your sent messages, click the Sent folder in the left pane of the Mail window.

To send a message, you must have an e-mail address in the To: text field. If you want to send the same message to multiple people, you can use the carbon copy (cc:) or blind carbon copy (bcc:) feature. Carbon copy means everyone who receives your message can see all the e-mail addresses of everyone you sent that message to. Blind carbon copy means everyone who receives your message can only see your e-mail address but no one else's e-mail address. For privacy, use blind carbon copy instead of carbon copy.

To add additional e-mail addresses to send a message to, click the Cc & Bcc button in the far right of the To: text field.

Once you've displayed the Cc or Bcc Address Field, you can type additional e-mail addresses into either of these fields to send the same message to multiple recipients.

Saving Drafts

Rather than write a message and send it off right away, you can save your message by clicking the Back arrow that appears in the upper left corner of the New message window. This stores the message in your Drafts folder that appears on the left pane of the Mail window, as shown in Figure 18-5.

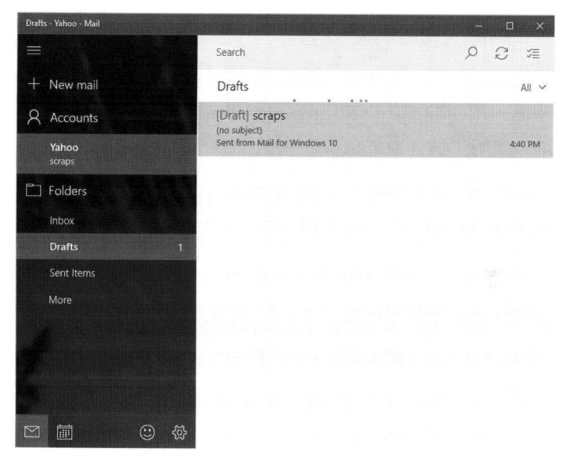

Figure 18-5. *The Drafts folder*

By saving messages as drafts, you can edit them later. To open a message stored in your Drafts folder, just click the Drafts folder and then double-click the message you want to edit. Now you can edit your message and click the Send icon when you're ready to send it.

Formatting Text

Most people just type ordinary text in their e-mail messages. However, you may want to format text in fancy ways such as choosing different fonts and font sizes, using bold or italics, or making bullet or number lists.

To format text, follow these steps:

1. Create a new message in the Mail program.

2. Click in the message text box. (You can only format text that's part of your message, not the text that defines the recipient's e-mail address or the subject line.)

3. Click the Format tab. The Mail program displays your formatting options, as shown in Figure 18-6.

Figure 18-6. *The Format tab displays formatting options*

4. Click the Font Formatting icon to display a list of formatting options, as shown in Figure 18-7.

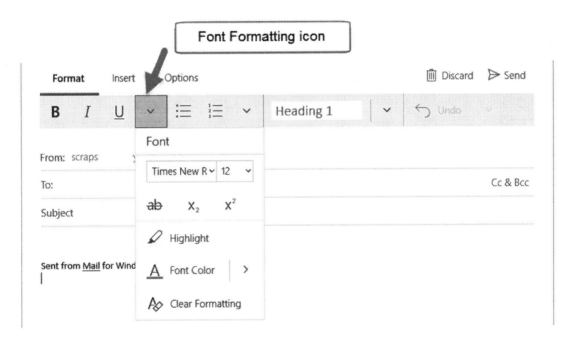

Figure 18-7. *The Font Formatting menu*

You can either choose different formatting options and then start typing, or you can type your message text and then highlight the text you want to change before choosing a formatting option.

Attaching a File

Oftentimes you might want to include an actual file such as a word processor document, a database file, or a spreadsheet to an e-mail. When you want to send someone a file created by another program such as Microsoft Excel, you can attach a file to a message and send that file by e-mail.

▓ **Note**   Depending on your e-mail provider, there may be a maximum file size limit you can send such as 10MB.

You can attach multiple files of any type to a single message. However, if you plan on sending multiple files, it's best to compress them by opening the File Explorer, selecting all the files you want to send, clicking the Share tab, and clicking the Zip icon.

Compressing creates a single ZIP file that you can attach to a message. When someone receives a ZIP file, they can unzip it to access the multiple files stored inside.

To attach a file to a message, follow these steps:

1.   Create a new message in the Mail program to open a message window.

2.   Click the Insert tab to display a list of options, as shown in Figure 18-8.

Figure 18-8. *The Insert tab displays options for adding a file attachment*

3. Click the Files icon. An Open dialog box appears.

4. Click the file you want to attach to the e-mail message and click the Open button. Your chosen file attachment appears as an icon, as shown in Figure 18-9. If you click the X icon that appears to the right of a file attachment, you can delete the file from the e-mail message.

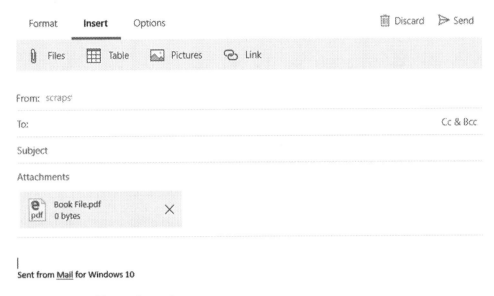

Figure 18-9. *A file attachment in a message*

You can attach as many files as you want to a single e-mail message. The only limitation may be the combined file size of all your attachments (as specified by your e-mail provider), such as a maximum file size of 10MB.

Viewing Sent Messages

Whenever you send a message, the Mail program saves a copy of that message in its Sent Items folder, which appears in the left pane of the Mail program. If you click the Sent Items folder icon in the left pane, you can see a list of messages you've sent in chronological order.

If you click a specific message, you can read the contents of that message. Now you can review any of your past messages to see exactly what you sent and the time and date that you sent it as well.

Saving E-mail Addresses

Typing an e-mail address can get cumbersome because if you misspell one character, your e-mail won't go through (or go to someone you do not intend to e-mail). Rather than type an e-mail address in, it's far easier to type it once, save it, and then just click the saved e-mail address you want to use.

To save e-mail addresses, you use the People program. You can open the People program through the Start menu and then manually type in someone's name and e-mail address.

To save e-mail addresses in the People program, follow these steps:

1. Open the People program from the Start menu. The People window appears, as shown in Figure 18-10.

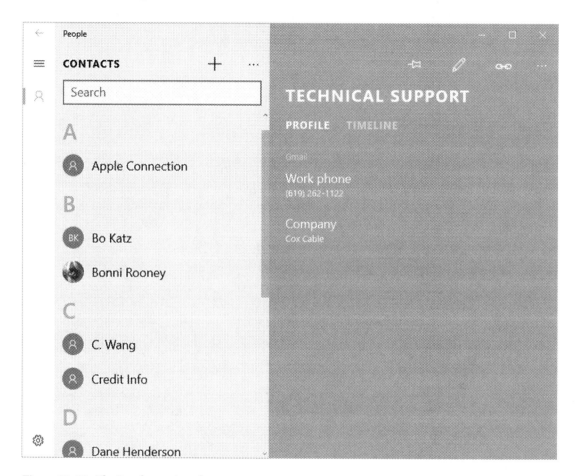

Figure 18-10. *The People user interface*

2. Click the + icon to add a new contact. A new contact pane appears in the right side of the People window, as shown in Figure 18-11.

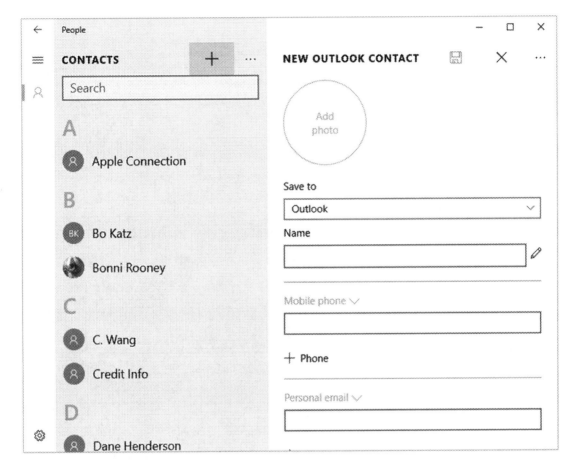

Figure 18-11. *The new contact pane lets you add a new name and contact information*

3. Type a person's name and e-mail address. You choose between adding a Personal, Work, or Other label for the saved e-mail address.

4. Click the Save icon when you've typed all the contact information about that person. You've now saved an e-mail address into the People program.

Once you've saved an e-mail address in the People program, you can now use that saved e-mail address to create a new message.

To send a message to a saved e-mail address, follow these steps:

1. Open the People program.

2. Click the name of the person you want to send an e-mail to.

3. Click that person's saved e-mail address. A menu pops up, asking which app you want to use to send the e-mail, as shown in Figure 18-12.

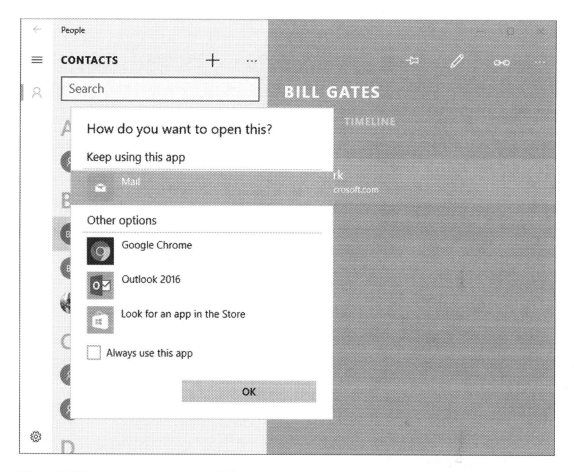

Figure 18-12. *A menu lets you choose which program to use to send an e-mail message*

4. Click the Mail app icon (or whatever program you want to use to send e-mail such as Outlook) and click the OK button. Your chosen e-mail program opens with the saved e-mail address already typed into the To: text field.

Getting New Mail

Even if your computer is connected to the Internet, you may still need to tell the Mail program to retrieve your messages from your e-mail account. To get any new e-mail messages, follow these steps:

1. Start the Mail program.

2. Click Inbox in the left pane.

3. Click the Sync this View icon, as shown in Figure 18-13. This will load any new e-mail messages into your Inbox.

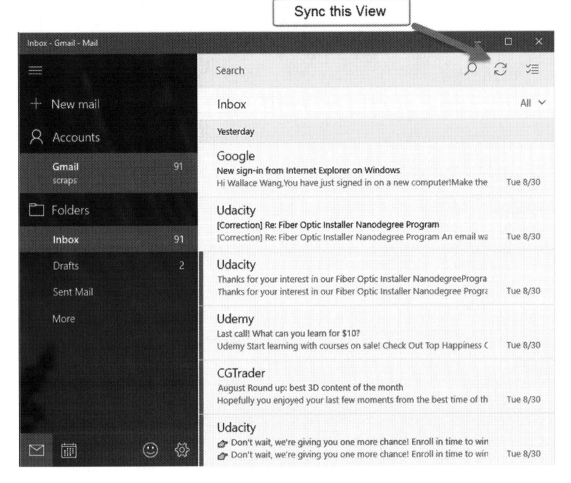

Figure 18-13. *The Sync this View icon lets you retrieve messages from your e-mail account*

Replying to Messages

When you receive messages, you can reply back or create a new message altogether. When you reply to a message, you don't save the sender's e-mail address but you do quote the previous contents of the message back for the recipient's reference.

For example, suppose you receive a message asking, "Are you coming to my birthday party this Saturday?"

If you reply to this message, Mail will display the message contents within your reply, as shown in Figure 18-14.

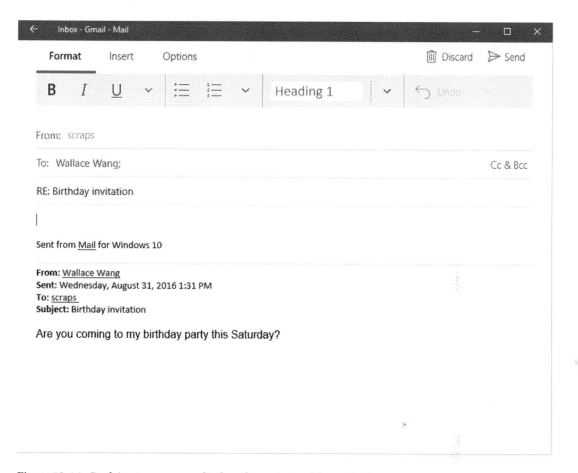

Figure 18-14. *Replying to a message displays the contents of the received message*

To make the previous message contents easy to find, the Mail program displays the previous message at the bottom.

Mail gives you three ways to reply to a message:

- *Reply*: Lets you send a message back to the e-mail address of the person who sent the message.

- *Reply All*: Lets you send a message back to all e-mail addresses stored in the To: and Cc: text fields.

- *Forward*: Lets you share a message with someone else, typically not the person who sent you the original message.

The main difference between Reply and Reply All is that Reply sends a message to one person while Reply All sends a reply to everyone who received the original message (except for any e-mail addresses stored in the Bcc: text field).

To reply to a message, follow these steps:

1. Start the Mail program.

2. Click the message you want to reply to.

3. Choose one of the following:

    a. Click the Reply button

    b. Click the Reply to All button

    c. Click the Forward button

4. Type a message and click the Send button to send your reply.

Searching Messages

Normally the Mail program lists your messages in the chronological order that it received them. While this can be fine when you know the date of a particular message, what if you don't remember the exact date you received a particular message?

Since you may want to find a particular message later, you can search for a particular message by using the sender's name, e-mail address, subject, or any keyword in the message itself.

To search for a message, follow these steps:

1. Start the Mail program.

2. Click in the Search text box that appears in the top of the Mail window.

3. Type part or all of the text you want to find such as a person's name, e-mail address, or subject.

4. Click the Search icon (it looks like a magnifying glass) to view a list of messages that match your criteria, as shown in Figure 18-15.

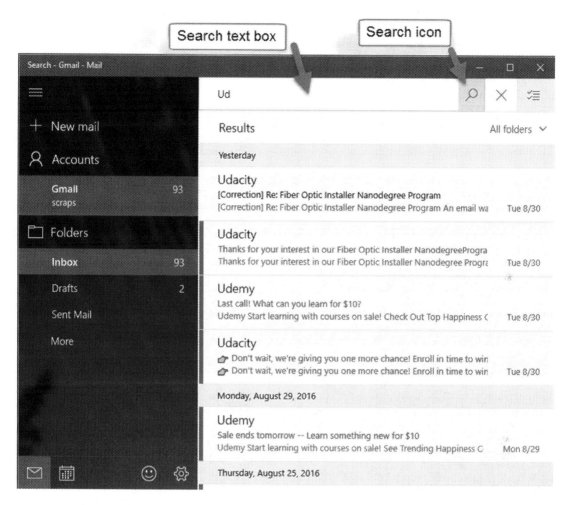

Figure 18-15. Searching for messages in the Mail program

5. The Mail program displays all messages that match your search criteria. Click the message that you want to view.

6. Click the Close search icon (it looks like an X) that appears on the far right of the Search text box to clear out the Search text field. When you clear the Search text box, the Mail program displays all your messages again, not just the messages that match your search criteria.

Deleting Messages

When you're done reading a message and don't need to keep it for future reference, delete it. Each time you delete a message, the Mail program stores it in the Trash folder. This gives you one last chance to retrieve a message if you need to.

To delete a message, follow these steps:

1. Start the Mail program.

2. Click a message that you want to delete. (If you want to delete multiple messages at once, click the Selection mode icon and then click in the check boxes of the messages you want to delete, as shown in Figure 18-16.)

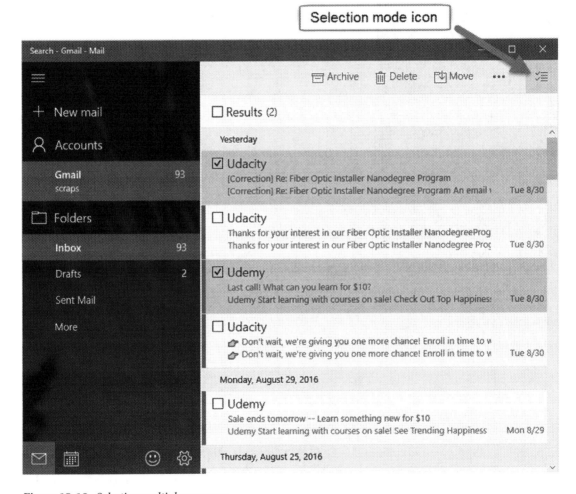

Figure 18-16. *Selecting multiple messages*

3. Click the Trash icon. Your chosen message now appears in the Trash folder.

⬚ **Note**   You can also right-click a message and when a pop-up menu appears, choose Delete.

Retrieving Deleted Messages

If you delete a message by mistake, you can undo the delete command by pressing Command+Z. Unfortunately, the Undo command only works if you choose it immediately after deleting a message by mistake. If you deleted a message a long time ago and then suddenly decide you need it after all, you can undelete a message by retrieving it from the Trash folder.

To retrieve a message from the Trash folder, follow these steps:

1. Click More in the left pane of the Mail window. A menu appears, as shown in Figure 18-17.

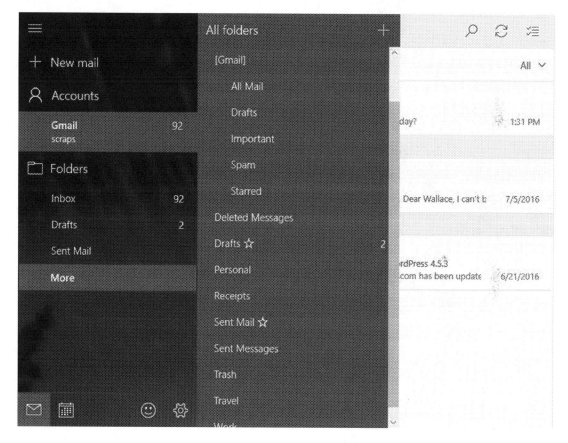

Figure 18-17. *The More menu*

2. Click Trash.

3. Right-click a message in the Trash folder that you want to retrieve. A menu appears, as shown in Figure 18-18.

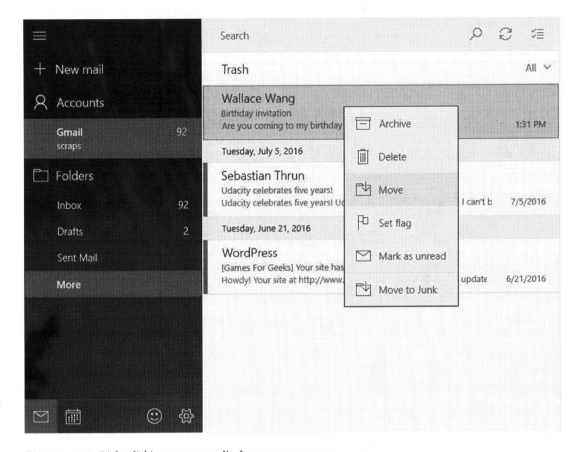

Figure 18-18. *Right-clicking a message displays a pop-up menu*

4. Click Move and choose Inbox. The message is then moved back to your Inbox.

Erasing Deleted Messages for Good

You can always retrieve deleted messages no matter how long ago you deleted them. However, you may eventually want to delete messages for good to save space on your computer and to avoid the risk of other people reading them if they ever gain access to your computer.

To erase deleted messages for good, follow these steps:

1. Start the Mail program.

2. Click More in the left pane of the Mail window. A menu appears (see Figure 18-17).

3. Click Trash.

4. Click a message in the Trash folder that you want to delete and click the Trash icon. This then permanently removes the e-mail.

Summary

The Mail program lets you retrieve messages from an e-mail account so you can view and read them without connecting to the Internet. You can connect more than one e-mail account to the Mail program.

You can send messages by typing e-mail addresses each time, or store commonly used e-mail addresses in the People program that you can use so you don't have to type them in again.

You can send a message to one e-mail address at a time, or send the same message to multiple e-mail addresses at once. When sending the same message to multiple people, you can use either Cc: (carbon copy) or Bcc: (blind carbon copy). Carbon copy lets everyone see all the e-mail addresses who received the same message while blind carbon copy does not.

To help you find a particular message, you can search for it. If you no longer need a message, delete it, but you can still retrieve it again from the Trash folder if necessary. To permanently delete a message, you must delete all previously deleted items in the Trash folder. Once you remove all the deleted items in the Trash folder, you can never retrieve those deleted messages again.

The Mail program can connect to any e-mail account such as Google or AOL. Use the Mail program as an alternative to reading your e-mail messages through a browser.

CHAPTER 19

Getting News

Many people use the Internet so they can get the latest news. While you could visit different news web sites such as ESPN, BBC News, or The New York Times, you may only want to retrieve specific types of news. Since many people want to keep up with the latest sports, financial, or international news, Windows 10 comes with several specialized apps dedicated to helping you retrieve news without the hassle of loading a browser, visiting a search engine, and looking for the information you want.

The four main apps for retrieving and displaying news include:

- *Money*: Financial news

- *News*: All types of news

- *Sports*: Sports news

- *Weather*: Weather-related news

To use each of these specialized news apps, you need to take time to customize them so they'll retrieve only the type of information you want. For example, if you only want news about baseball, you could customize the Sports app so it would only show you news about baseball while ignoring sports you may not care about such as hockey or ice skating. By taking the time to customize these specialized news apps, you can retrieve the information you want faster and easier than ever before.

Note   For faster access, you might want to store the various news apps on the Start menu as live tiles or as an icon on the Taskbar.

© Wallace Wang 2016
W. Wang, *Absolute Beginners Guide to Computing*, DOI 10.1007/978-1-4842-2289-8_19

Getting Financial News

If you want to track stocks, stay up to date on the latest financial news from Wall Street, London, or Hong Kong, or track foreign currencies, you can do all that with the Money app. The Money app consists of several categories, as shown in Figure 19-1:

- *Markets*: Lets you view charts of the major financial indexes around the world

- *Watchlist*: Lets you follow your favorite stocks

- *Currencies*: Lets you follow the value of foreign currencies

- *Mortgage Calculator*: Lets you chart various mortgage loans and interest rates

- *World Markets*: Lets you view financial news from around the world

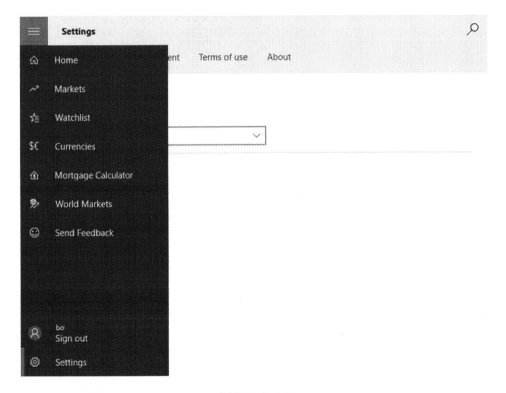

Figure 19-1. *The various categories available in the Money app*

The Markets category consists of four views, as shown in Figure 19-2:

- *Summary*: Displays a chart of the major financial indexes around the world

- *Movers*: Lists the biggest winners and losers in the stock market for that day

- *Commodities*: Lists information about various commodities such as natural gas or cattle

- *Bonds*: Lists changes in various government bonds

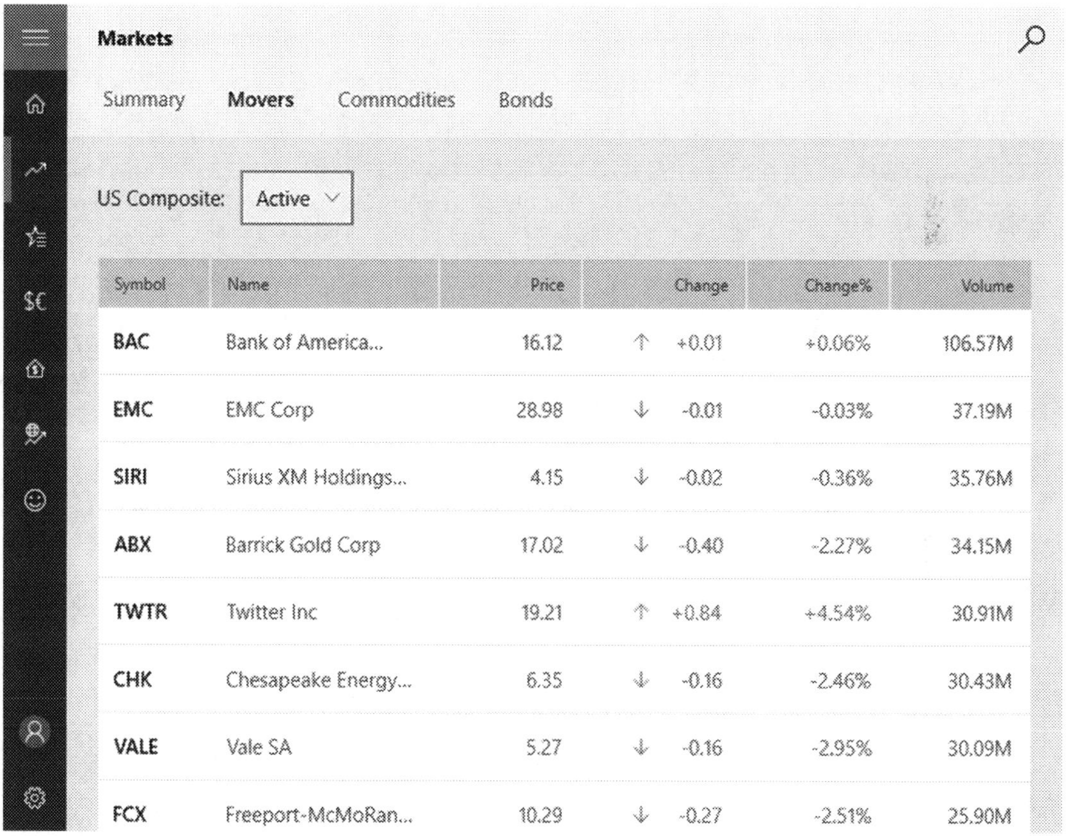

Markets

Summary   **Movers**   Commodities   Bonds

US Composite: Active ∨

Symbol	Name	Price		Change	Change%	Volume
BAC	Bank of America...	16.12	↑	+0.01	+0.06%	106.57M
EMC	EMC Corp	28.98	↓	-0.01	-0.03%	37.19M
SIRI	Sirius XM Holdings...	4.15	↓	-0.02	-0.36%	35.76M
ABX	Barrick Gold Corp	17.02	↓	-0.40	-2.27%	34.15M
TWTR	Twitter Inc	19.21	↑	+0.84	+4.54%	30.91M
CHK	Chesapeake Energy...	6.35	↓	-0.16	-2.46%	30.43M
VALE	Vale SA	5.27	↓	-0.16	-2.95%	30.09M
FCX	Freeport-McMoRan...	10.29	↓	-0.27	-2.51%	25.90M

Figure 19-2. The various categories available in the Money app

The Watchlist category consists of eight views, as shown in Figure 19-3:

- *Watchlist*: Lets you customize a list of stocks to follow

- *News*: Lists financial news stories

- *Investing*: Lists information about investing in different areas

- *Personal Finance*: Lists information about spending and saving money

- *Real Estate*: Lists news about real estate

- *Careers*: Lists news about jobs and careers

- *Videos*: Displays videos covering financial news

- *Rates*: Lists current mortgage rates

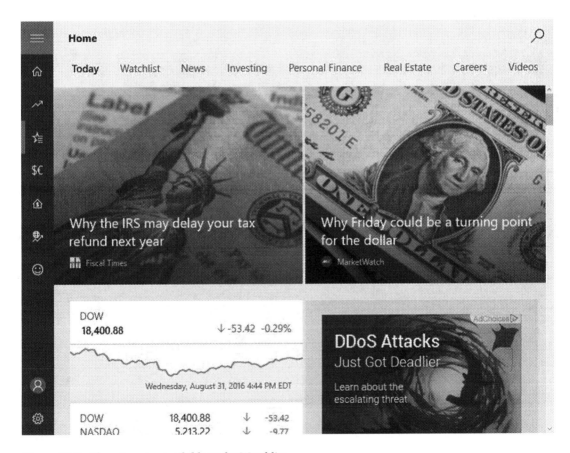

Figure 19-3. *The categories available under Watchlist*

The Currencies category consists of two views, as shown in Figure 19-4:

- *Currency Converter*: Lets you convert the value of one currency into another
- *Currency Rates*: Lists the latest values of various currencies around the world

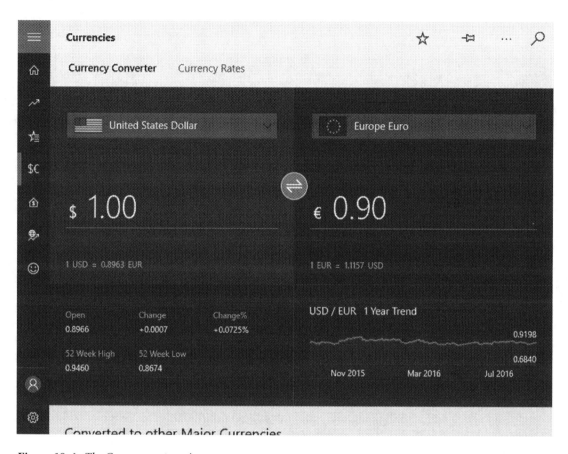

Figure 19-4. *The Currency categories*

The Mortgage Calculator lets you experiment with different loan amounts, interest rates, and loan lengths, as shown in Figure 19-5.

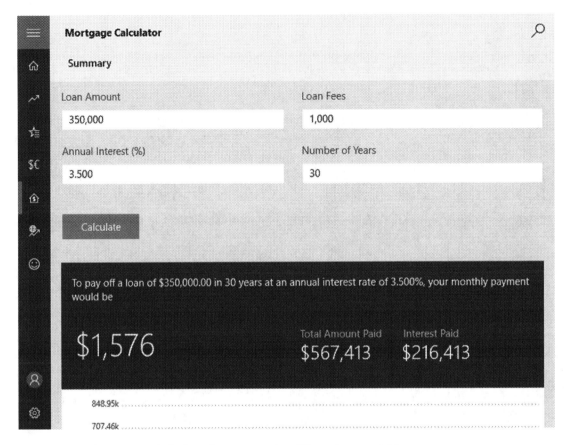

Figure 19-5. *The Mortgage Calculator lets you examine different loan variables*

The World Markets consists of four views, as shown in Figure 19-6:

- *Major*: Lists major financial indexes from around the world
- *Americas*: Lists major financial indexes in North America
- *EMEA*: Lists major financial indexes in Europe
- *Asia Pacific*: Lists major financial indexes in Asia

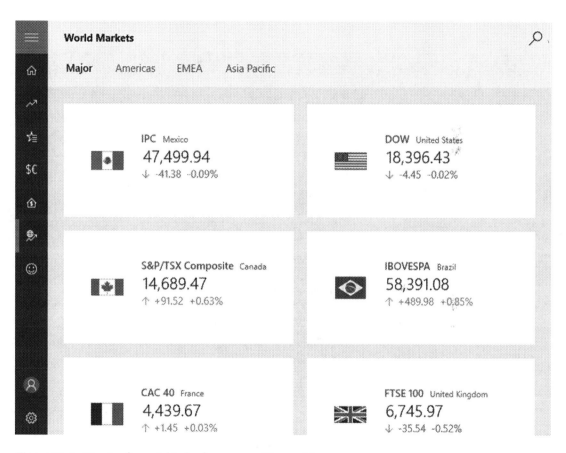

Figure 19-6. *Viewing financial index from around the world*

Getting Custom News

Everyday there's more news than you could read in a lifetime. While you could visit several popular news sites, it's much easier to let the News app find the type of news you like reading the most. Everyday the News app can retrieve your favorite types of news stories and display them for your browsing convenience.

The first time you start the News app, it will ask you to define the type of news you're most interested in such as Entertainment, Food, Medical, or Music. By choosing the topics that interest you the most, you can spend more time reading and less time searching for what you want.

The first time you start the News app, it will ask you to choose the topics you enjoy the most, as shown in Figure 19-7.

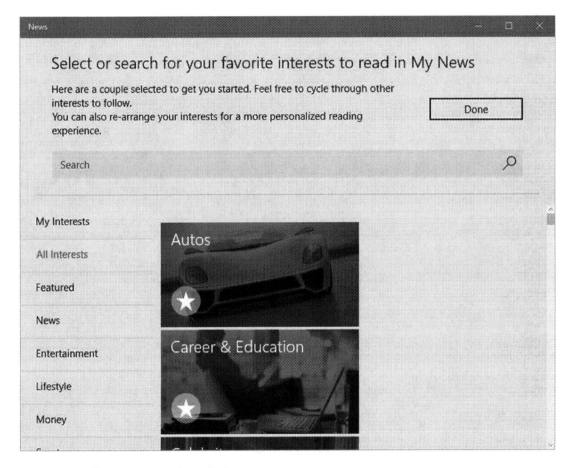

Figure 19-7. *Choosing news topics to display*

The News app consists of several categories, as shown in Figure 19-8:

- *Today*: Displays the latest news

- *Interests*: Displays news about specific news categories such as entertainment, lifestyle, and sports

- *Sources*: Lets you define the web sites where you want to retrieve news

- *Local*: Lets you follow news around a specific location such as your home

- *Video*: Lets you view videos of the latest news stories

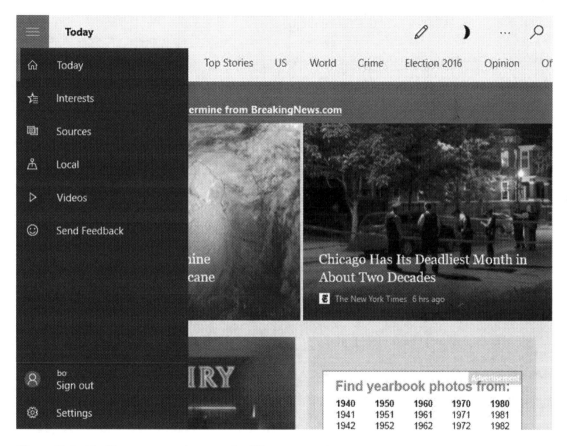

Figure 19-8. *The News app organizes news by different categories*

The first step to customizing the News app is to define the web sites where you want to retrieve your news. To define your news sources, follow these steps:

1. Open the News app.

2. Click the Sources icon in the left pane. A list of categories such as Gaming, National & World News, and Science appears, as shown in Figure 19-9.

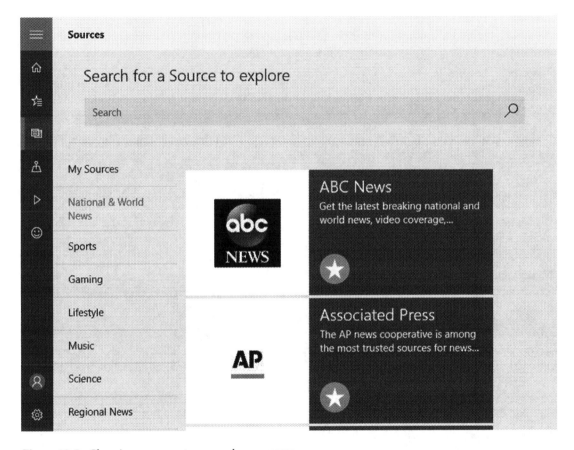

Figure 19-9. *Choosing a news category and news source*

3. Click a news category such as Regional News or Music. A list of news web sites appears on the right.

4. Click a news web site that you want to use for your chosen category.

5. (Optional) Click the Back arrow in the upper left corner of the News app window and repeat steps 3 and 4 for each additional news web site you want to add.

The bigger news web sites can be fine for national or international news, but what if you just want news about your particular city? To view local news, follow these steps:

1. Open the News app.

2. Click the Local icon in the left pane.

3. Click again to display a Search dialog box.

4. Type a city name in the Search text box. A list of matching city names appears, as shown in Figure 19-10.

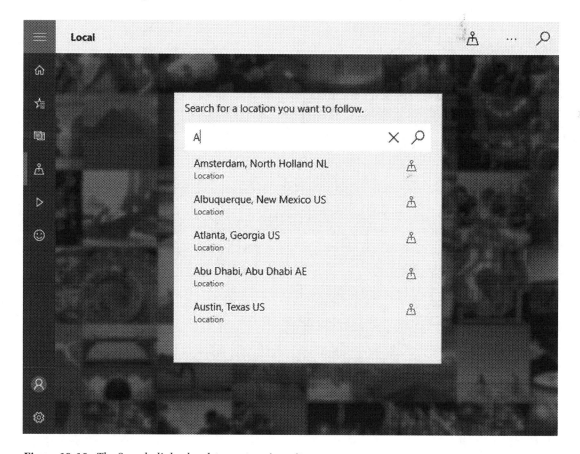

Figure 19-10. *The Search dialog box lets you type in a city name*

     5.   Click a city name. The News app displays news related to your chosen city.

Each time you click the Local icon in the left pane, you can select a different city to focus on. That way you can check news around your hometown as well as read news about other places you may be planning to visit soon.

Getting Sports News

Tracking the latest sports scores is one of the most popular news items people want no matter what particular sport they may enjoy. If you want to follow the latest sports scores or just enjoy following news about your favorite sport, use the Sports app.

The Sports app lists popular sports categories in the left pane that you can scroll down, as shown in Figure 19-11.

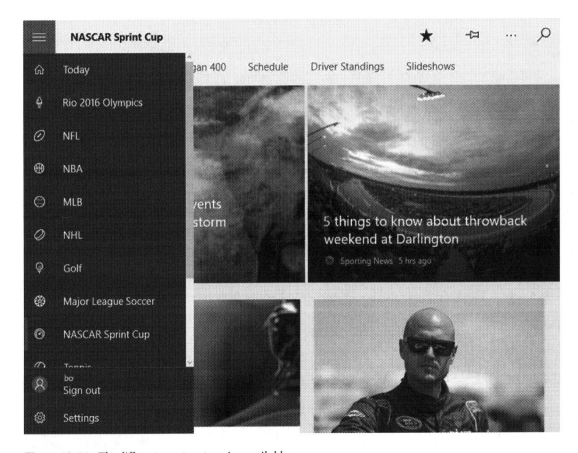

Figure 19-11. *The different sports categories available*

If you don't see the sport you like listed in the left pane, scroll down and click More Sports to view more sports categories, as shown in Figure 19-12.

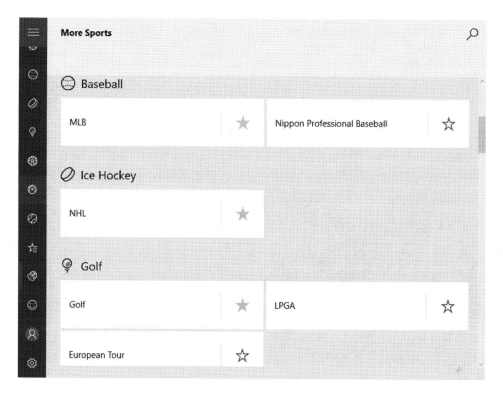

Figure 19-12. *The More Sports category lets you view sports from other countries*

Since the Sports app doesn't know what your favorite team or sport might be, it tries to retrieve news about all types of sports. To customize the sport or team the Sports app will cover, follow these steps:

1. Open the Sports app.

2. Click the My Favorites icon in the left pane. A list of different sports appears, as shown in Figure 19-13. You may need to scroll down to view all the sports the Sports app will cover.

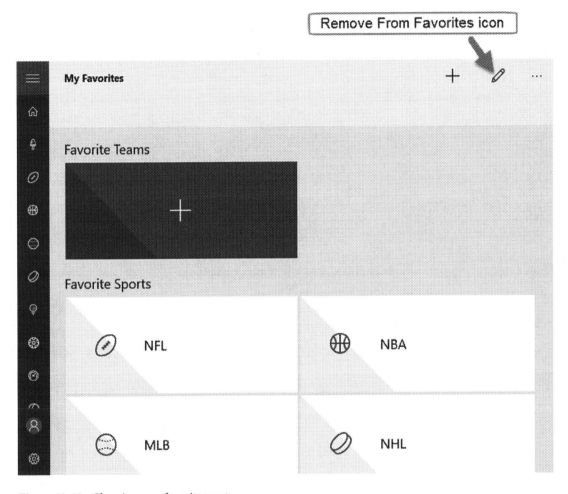

Figure 19-13. Choosing your favorite sports

3. Click the Remove from Favorites icon. Close icons (a big X) appear in the upper right corner of each listed sport. Notice also that the Remove from Favorites icon changes appearance to a check mark that represents the Done icon, as shown in Figure 19-14.

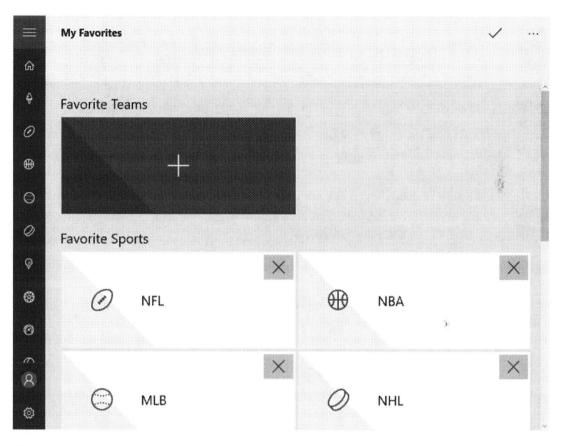

Figure 19-14. *The close icon lets you remove sports you don't care about*

4. Click the close icon of any sport you don't want news on.

5. Click the Done icon when you're finished.

6. (Optional) Click the + button under the Favorite Teams category and then type the name of your favorite team to get news on, as shown in Figure 19-15.

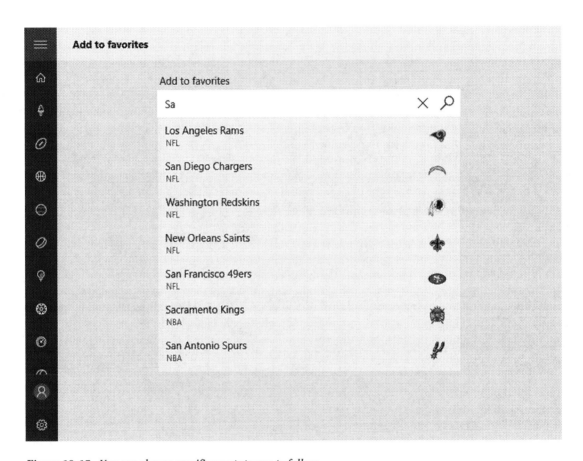

Figure 19-15. *You can choose specific sports teams to follow*

To view the latest sports scores, click the sports icon in the left pane such as Baseball or Basketball. Then click Scoreboard, as shown in Figure 19-16.

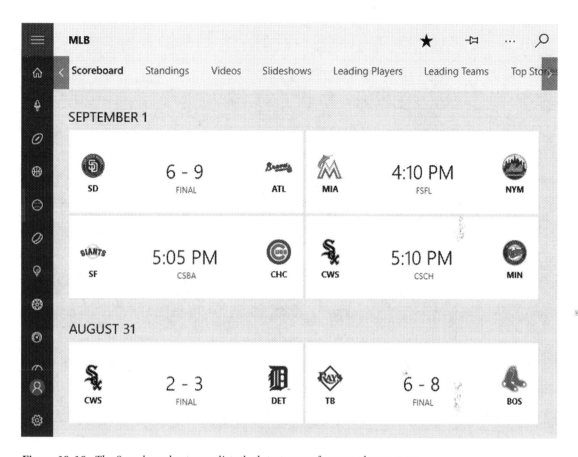

Figure 19-16. *The Scoreboard category lists the latest scores for your chosen sport*

Getting Weather News

No matter where you live, you need to know the current weather and the latest weather forecasts for your area. If you frequently travel, you'll need weather forecasts for different regions around the world. To help you find weather information easily, you can use the Weather app.

The first time you launch the Weather app, it will ask for your preferences such as whether to use Celsius or Fahrenheit and which location you want weather information about, as shown in Figure 19-17.

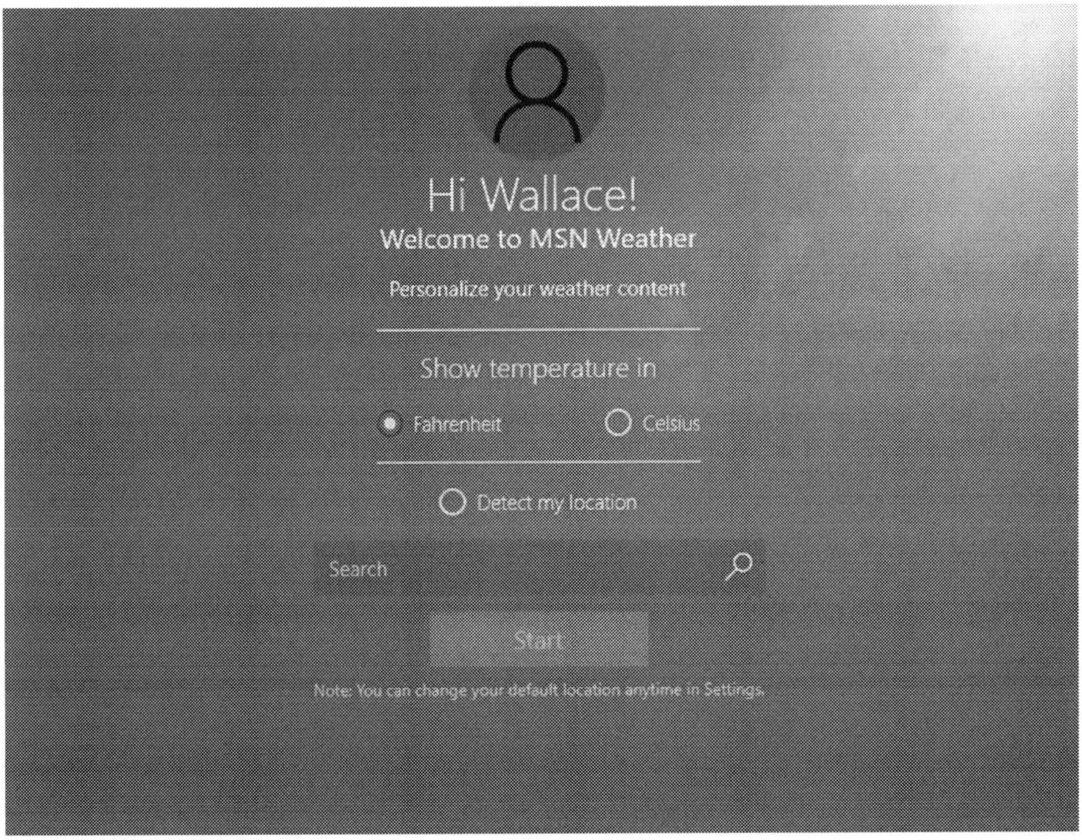

Figure 19-17. *Defining settings for the Weather app*

If you want to change these settings later, click the Settings icon in the left pane and click General, as shown in Figure 19-18.

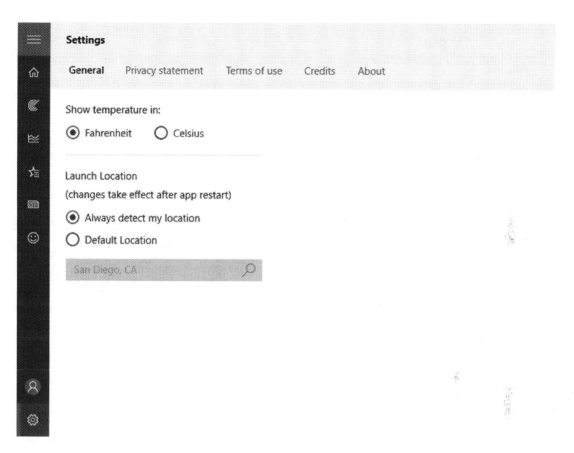

Figure 19-18. *Defining settings for the Weather app*

Once you've defined how to display temperatures (Celsius or Fahrenheit) and your location, you can view the different Weather categories, as shown in Figure 19-19:

- *Forecast*: Displays weather information for your specified location such as your home

- *Maps*: Displays different types of maps for your specified location

- *Historical Weather*: Displays past weather information for your specified location

- *Favorites*: Lets you define additional locations to get weather forecasts about such as cities you visit often

- *News*: Displays weather stories from around the world

Figure 19-19. *Viewing the different categories in the Weather app*

Summary

Reading news is one of the most popular uses for the Internet. Rather than visit different web sites individually or use search engines to find the news you want from different web sites, you can use the Money, News, Sports, and Weather dedicated apps instead.

These dedicated apps make it simple to retrieve the information you want as quickly and easily as possible. By taking the time to customize each app, you can filter out news you don't want to read and focus only on the news that's most interesting to you. Think of these dedicated news apps as your own private clipping service that gives you the news you want every day.

CHAPTER 20

Chatting with Skype

With the introduction of high-speed Internet in most places around the world, people now have a new way to communicate with each other. Instead of sending e-mail and waiting for a response, you can now communicate in real time using Skype.

Skype essentially gives you three ways to talk to other people:

- Video and audio

- Audio only

- Texting

By turning your computer into a video telephone, you can see the caller (and they can see you). If you prefer not looking at someone else while you chat, you can just use Skype to make audio calls or type text messages back and forth. Skype gives you the option to choose how you prefer to communicate instantly.

To use Skype, you need an Internet connection, the faster the better. As long as you have an Internet connection and the need to communicate with someone right away, you can choose which method will be best for you.

Note If you can't find the Skype Preview on the Start menu, you can visit the Microsoft Store and download the Skype Preview app for free, as shown in Figure 20-1.

© Wallace Wang 2016

W. Wang, *Absolute Beginners Guide to Computing*, DOI 10.1007/978-1-4842-2289-8_20

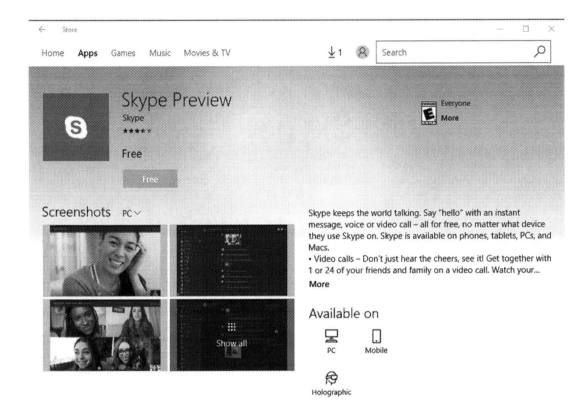

Figure 20-1. *The Skype Preview app is free on the Microsoft Store*

Setting Up a Skype Account

Before you can chat with Skype, you need to set up an account. Your account determines how people can reach you through Skype.

To set up a Skype account, follow these steps:

1. Click the Windows icon in the lower left corner of the screen. The Start menu appears.

2. Click Skype Preview. The Skype window appears, as shown in Figure 20-2.

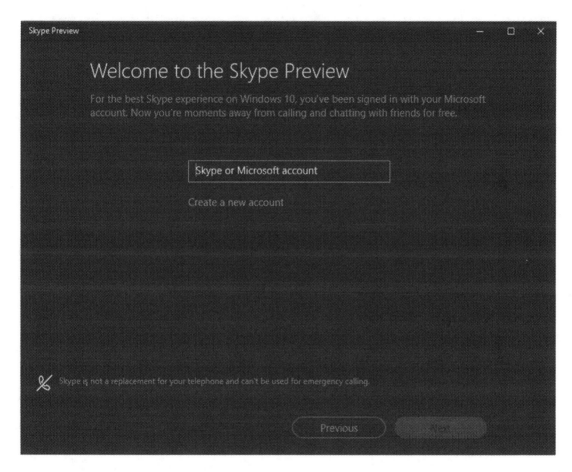

Figure 20-2. *Setting up a Skype account*

3. Click Create a new account (or type in your existing Skype account name if you have one).

4. Type in a password and phone number, or click Use your email instead, as shown in Figure 20-3.

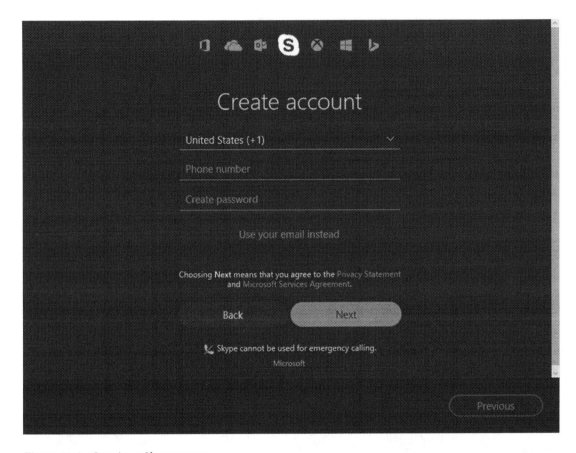

Figure 20-3. *Creating a Skype account*

5. Depending on which option you choose, follow the prompts to type in the requested information. When you're done, the Skype window appears, as shown in Figure 20-4.

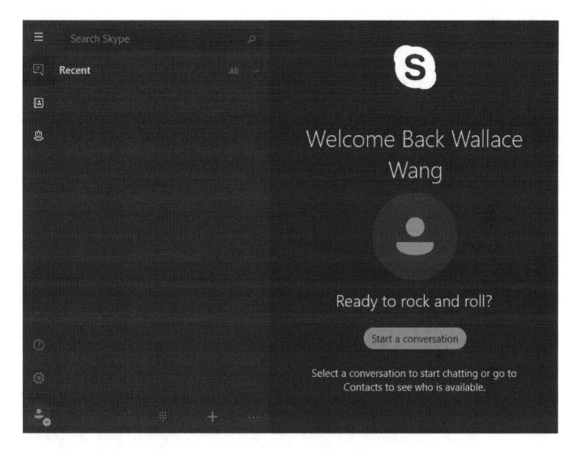

Figure 20-4. *The Skype window*

▓ **Note**   If you want other people to find you on Skype, you need to store an e-mail address and/or a phone number.

Testing Skype

Before you can use Skype, you should test to make sure Skype can connect to the Internet and that Skype can hear you speak through your computer's microphone. To test Skype, follow these steps:

1. Open Skype.

2. Click the Contacts icon in the left pane.

3. Click Echo/Sound Test Service, as shown in Figure 20-5.

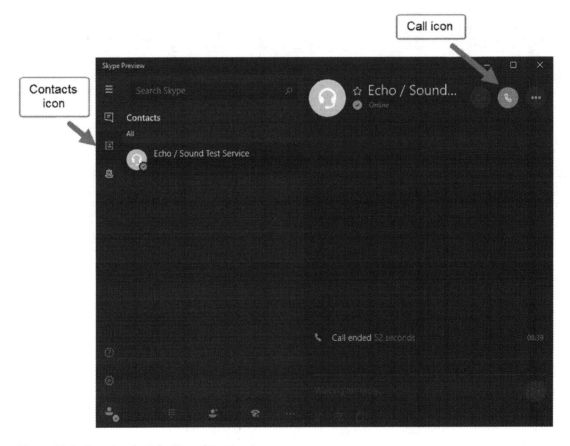

Figure 20-5. *Running the Echo/Sound Test Service*

4. Click the Call icon in the upper right corner of the Skype window. Skype calls an automated testing number, as shown in Figure 20-6.

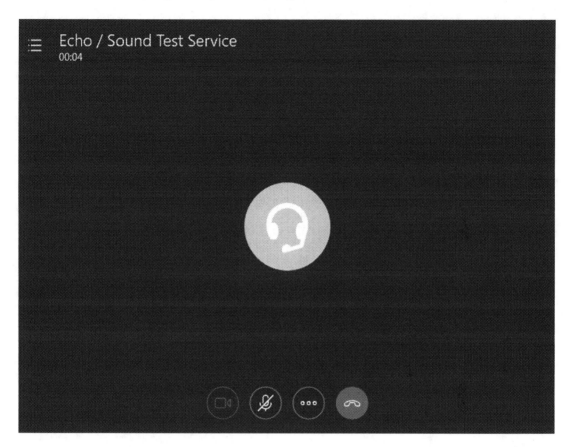

Figure 20-6. *Testing your Skype connection*

5. Speak a short message. If Skype is working properly with your Internet connection and microphone, you should hear your message repeated back.

Looking in the Skype Directory

Like a telephone or fax machine, Skype is only useful to connect with other people. Since calls made over the Internet are free, the least expensive way to make a call is to another person who also uses Skype. To help you find other Skype users to contact, Skype offers a directory.

To use the Skype directory, you need to know one or more of the following:

- A Skype user name

- An e-mail address

- A phone number

Remember, not all Skype users provide all three types of information to Skype so if you know someone's e-mail address but that person didn't store their e-mail address as part of their Skype account, the Skype directory won't find that person by their e-mail address.

If you search for someone in the Skype Directory but can't find them, you may need to search for them using a different method such as trying another e-mail address, phone number, or Skype user name.

To find someone in the Skype Directory, follow these steps:

1.   Open the Skype program.

2.   Click in the Search Skype text box in the upper left corner and type all or part of a Skype name, e-mail address, or phone number and then click the Search Skype button. A list of potential matches appears, as shown in Figure 20-7.

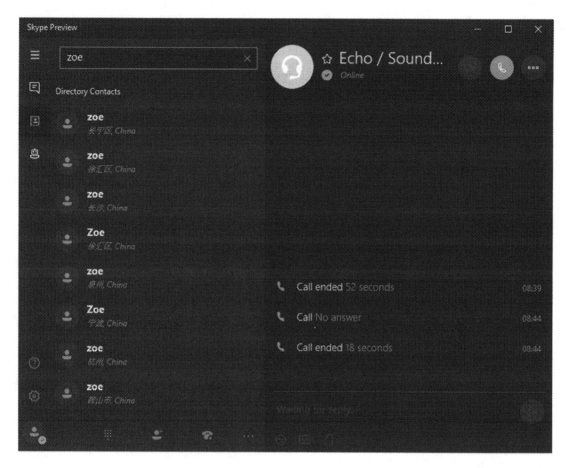

Figure 20-7. *Looking for other Skype users*

3. Click a name. The right pane of the Skype window displays a Video call icon (to use video and audio) and a Call icon (audio only) in the upper right corner of the Skype window, as shown in Figure 20-8.

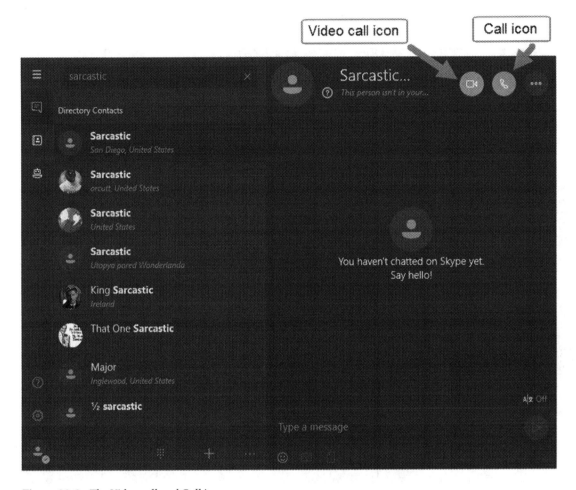

Figure 20-8. *The Video call and Call icons*

4. Click the Video call or Call icon to start a Skype call.

Making a Video Call

You can only make a video call if your computer includes a webcam. Many of the latest laptop computers include a webcam in the middle top of the screen, but many desktop computers may need a separate webcam. The person you're calling must also have a webcam to display video back to you.

▓ **Note**   Since both people need to be on Skype, you may need to plan ahead of time when to connect through Skype. If you just call someone at a random time, chances are good they won't be at their computer and running Skype at the moment you call.

To make a video call, follow these steps:

1. Follow steps 1-4 in the "Looking in the Skype Directory" section to find a Skype user.

2. Click the Skype user you want to call.

3. Click the Video call icon (see Figure 20-8). If the other person currently has Skype running, they'll hear a beeping noise and see a message dialog box, as shown in Figure 20-9. If the person receiving the Skype call clicks the Video button, you'll see their face on the screen. If the person receiving the Skype call clicks the Audio button, you'll just see a blank screen.

Figure 20-9. *When someone receives a Skype call, a message dialog box appears*

4.   (Optional) Move the mouse anywhere over the Skype window during a call to display icons at the bottom of the Skype window, as shown in Figure 20-10.

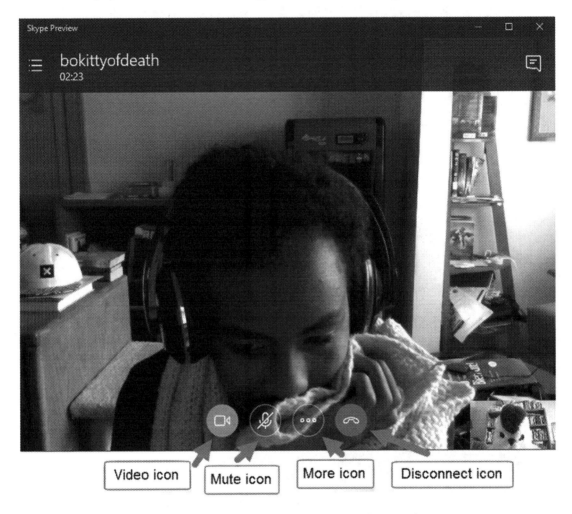

Figure 20-10. Icons appear when the mouse pointer appears over the Skype window

- The Video icon lets you toggle between turning your own webcam on or off

- The Mute icon lets you toggle between turning your microphone on or off

- The More icon displays a pop-up menu, as shown in Figure 20-11

- The Disconnect icon lets you disconnect from the Skype call

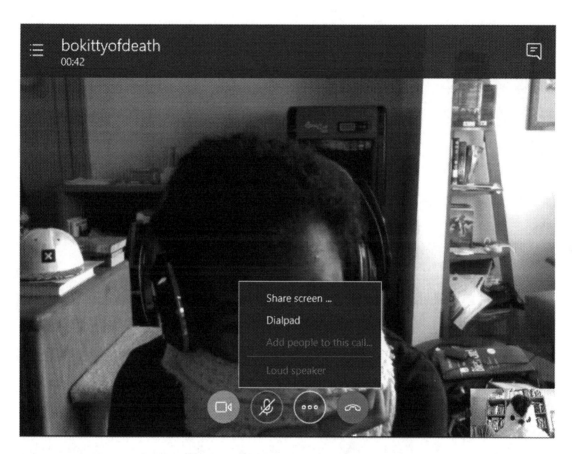

Figure 20-11. *The More icon displays a pop-up menu showing additional options*

5. Click the red Disconnect icon when you're done talking.

Making an Audio Call

Watching video can be interesting, but unless you absolutely need to show someone something, it's usually more comfortable (for both parties) to make an audio call instead. Besides being more like a regular telephone call, an audio only Skype call also requires less bandwidth so it's far more reliable than a video call especially if one or both parties has a slower Internet connection.

To make an audio call, follow these steps:

1. Follow steps 1-4 in the "Looking in the Skype Directory" section to find a Skype user.

2. Click the Skype user you want to call.

3. Click the Call icon (see Figure 20-8). If the other person currently has Skype running, they'll hear a beeping noise and see a message dialog box (see Figure 20-9). A blank Skype window appears, as shown in Figure 20-12.

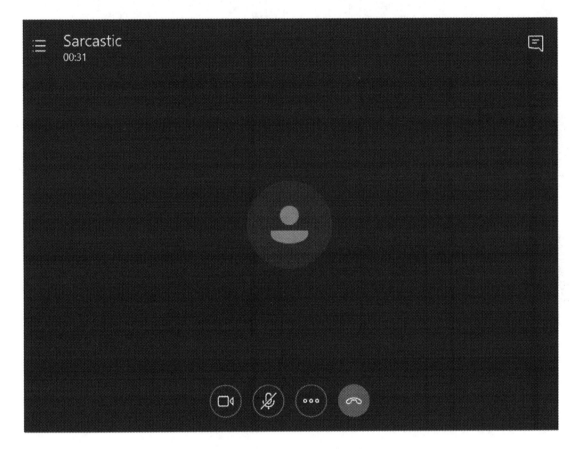

Figure 20-12. *During an audio call, the Skype window remains blank*

4. (Optional) Move the mouse anywhere over the Skype window during a call to display icons at the bottom of the Skype window (see Figure 20-10). If you click the Video icon, you can display video from your webcam to the other person.

5. Click the red Disconnect icon when you're done talking.

Sending Text Messages

If someone is currently on Skype, you can send them text messages rather than talk to them directly. Text messages can be handy as an alternative to video or audio calling, or as a supplement. With text messaging, you can use emojis, send images, or send files, so text messaging can be a way to share pictures and files while also making a video or audio call.

To send a text message, follow these steps:

1. Follow steps 1-4 in the "Looking in the Skype Directory" section to find a Skype user.

2. Click the Skype user you want to call.

3. Click in the Type a message text box at the bottom right corner of the Skype window and type a message.

4. Click the Send icon at the far right of the Type a message text box. Your text messages, along with any replies, appear, as shown in Figure 20-13.

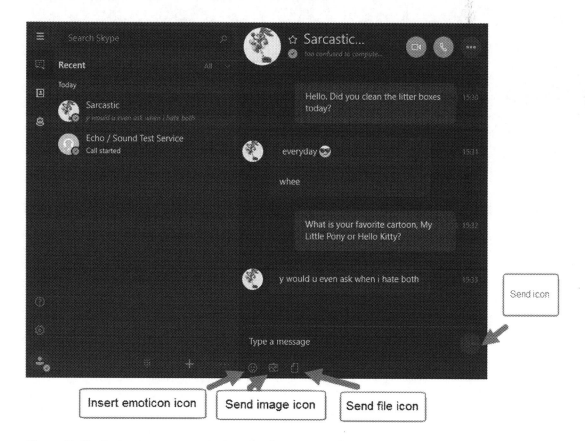

Figure 20-13. *Text messages appear in the order they were typed*

5.   (Optional) Click the Insert emoticon icon. A window appears, listing different emoticons you can choose, as shown in Figure 20-14.

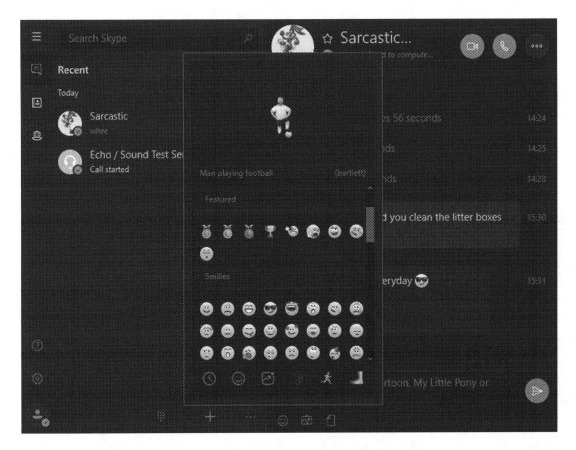

Figure 20-14. *Choosing an emoticon to send*

6. (Optional) Click the Send image icon. A dialog box appears where you can click a picture file and click the Open button to send that picture, as shown in Figure 20-15.

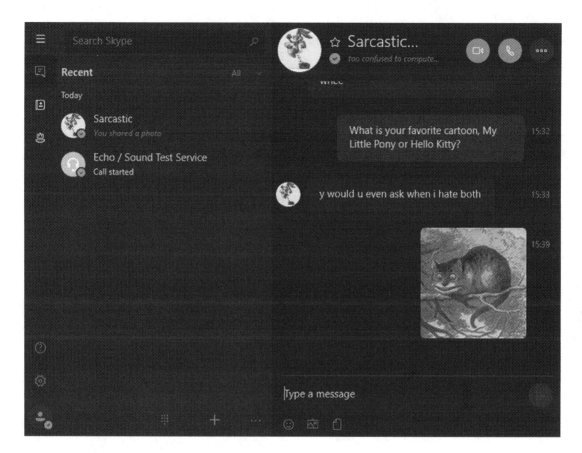

Figure 20-15. *Sending a picture*

7. (Optional) Click the Send file icon. A dialog box appears where you can click a file and click the Open button to send that file.

▩ **Note** If you're sending multiple files or a large file, you might want to compress the file before sending it.

When someone sends you a picture or a file, you can download that picture or file by clicking that picture or file. A download arrow appears on that picture or file, as shown in Figure 20-16.

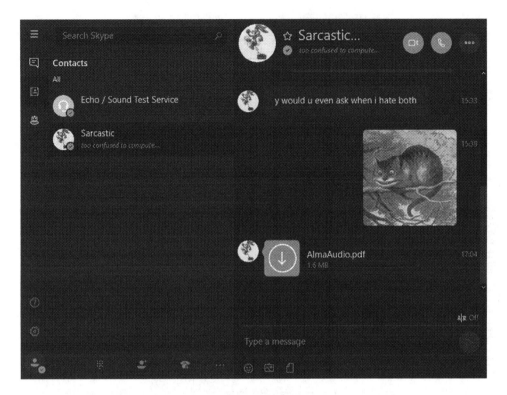

Figure 20-16. *You can download a picture or file to your own computer*

When you click a picture or file to download, a dialog box appears, asking if you trust the downloaded file, as shown in Figure 20-17. Click the Accept button if you trust the file or the Cancel button if you do not want to save the file on your computer.

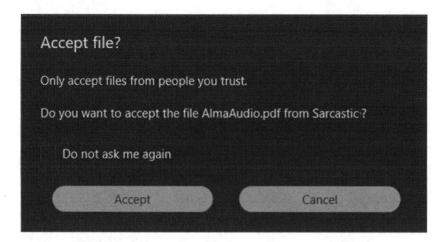

Figure 20-17. *A dialog box verifies whether you want to save the file*

▓ **Note**   Even if you trust a person, you may still not be able to trust any file sent to you. That's because a file could be infected but the person you trust may not know it, so be careful when downloading files even from people you trust.

Storing Names

Having to search for someone's Skype name, e-mail, or phone number to call them can be a nuisance. One faster alternative is to click the Recent Conversations icon in the left pane to show a list of all the people you've contacted with Skype in the past. Then you can just click the listed name again to call them once more.

Another solution is to store each person's name in a list. Each time you connect with someone through Skype, Skype keeps track of that person's name. Now you can view a list of all people you've chatted with in the past.

Another way to add a name to Skype's list is to manually add that person's name and phone number. To store a name in a list with a phone number, follow these steps:

1. Open the Skype program.

2. Click the Contacts icon in the left pane. A list of all previous callers you've connected to in the past appears.

3.   Click the Create a new phone number contact icon. An Add Phone Number Contact dialog box appears, as shown in Figure 20-18.

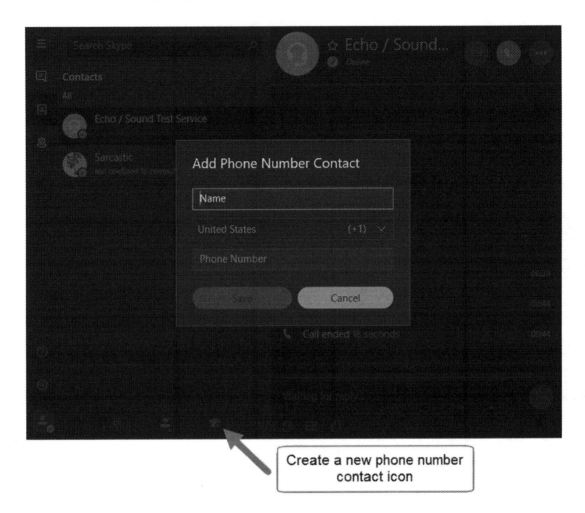

Figure 20-18. *Adding a name and phone number to Skype's list*

4.   Type a name and phone number.

5.   Click the Save button. Your contact now appears in the Skype contact list.

Blocking and Removing Callers

In a perfect world, everyone would get along. However, in this world, sometimes you may not want to receive calls from certain people. Rather than constantly declining their Skype calls, it's far easier to block them automatically. That way Skype won't bother to notify you when that person tries to call you.

Sometimes you may not want to block a caller but simply remove them from your Skype list. That way you don't have their name cluttering up your list of people you need to contact on a regular basis.

To block or remove a caller from the Skype list, follow these steps:

1. Start the Skype program.

2. Click the Contacts icon in the left pane to view your list of stored contacts.

3. Right-click a name you want to block or remove. A pop-up menu appears, as shown in Figure 20-19.

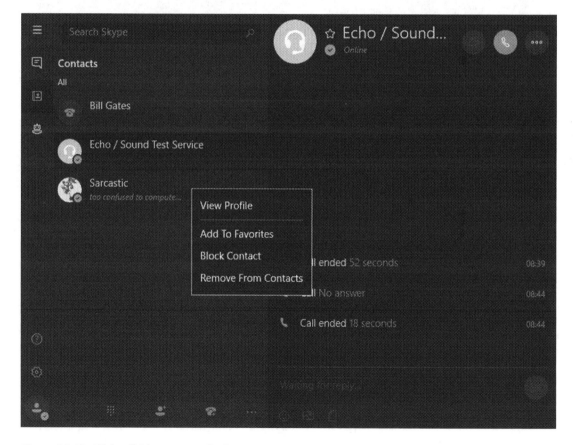

Figure 20-19. *Right-clicking a name displays a pop-up menu*

4. (Optional) Click Remove From Contacts. Skype removes your chosen name.

5. (Optional) Click Block Contact. A dialog box appears asking if you're sure you want to block the chosen caller, as shown in Figure 20-20. Click the Block button.

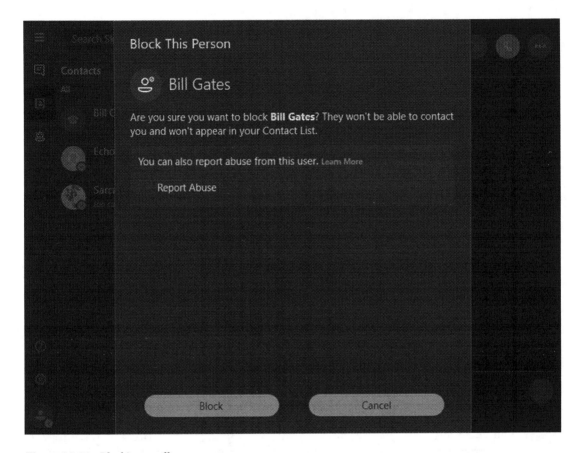

Figure 20-20. *Blocking a caller*

Summary

When sending and receiving e-mail is too slow, you can communicate using Skype. Skype essentially turns your computer into a phone where you can choose to chat with someone using audio or video. To use Skype, both people need Skype on their computers, whether it's a Windows PC or a Macintosh.

With Skype, you can communicate with anyone around the world absolutely free just as long as both of you have an Internet connection and a copy of Skype installed.

CHAPTER 21

Keeping Track of People

Everyone needs to keep track of someone, whether for business or for personal reasons. After all, you probably don't want to memorize someone's street address or e-mail address.

In the past, people stored contact information in Rolodex files or black books. To make it easier to store names, addresses, and other information about people, Windows 10 introduced a simple database called the People app.

The advantage of using the People app is that you can save names and contact information in one place so you can retrieve it whenever you need it again. Now you'll always have a simple way to save important names as long as you have your computer.

You can use the People app on its own or connected to an existing account. For example, many people store names and contact information in their Hotmail or Outlook e-mail account. Rather than retype this information into the People app, you can just import this information into the People app instead. To connect the People app to an existing list of names and contact information, you need to add an account to the People app.

Adding an Account

The People app can connect to an existing account that already contains names and contact information. The first time you start the People app, a screen appears, asking you to add an account, as shown in Figure 21-1.

© Wallace Wang 2016

W. Wang, *Absolute Beginners Guide to Computing*, DOI 10.1007/978-1-4842-2289-8_21

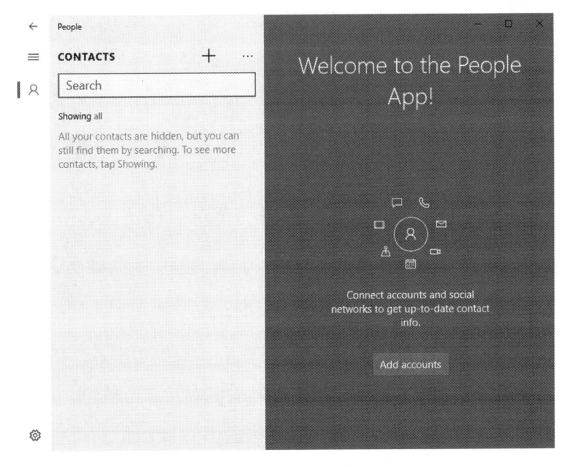

Figure 21-1. *The People app needs to connect to an existing account*

Once you click the Add accounts button, the People app gives you a choice of which account to connect to, as shown in Figure 21-2:

- Outlook.com (includes Outlook.com, Live.com, Hotmail, and MSN)

- Exchange, Office 365

- Google

- iCloud

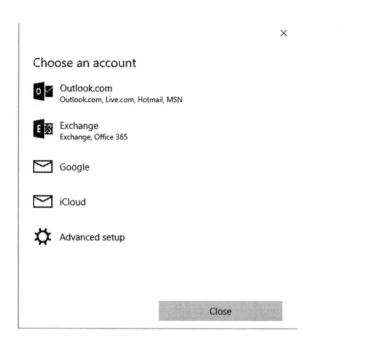

Figure 21-2. *A new card contains blank fields for storing contact information about a person*

If you use Google's Gmail often and have names and contact information stored there, you can connect to your Google account. If you use iCloud to store contact information on your computer or iPhone, you can connect to your iCloud account.

If you don't use any of the listed services, you can click Advanced Setup and define a Microsoft Exchange ActiveSync account or Internet POP or IMAP account to use instead, as shown in Figure 21-3.

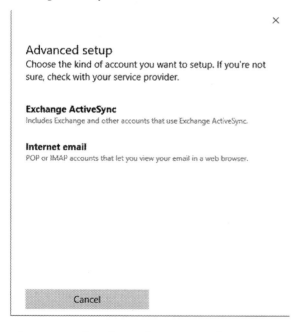

Figure 21-3. *The Advanced Setup option for defining an account to use*

Adding Names Manually

Besides or instead of importing names from an existing account, you can also add names manually into the People app. This lets you store a name along with additional information such as an e-mail address, phone number, or street address. For some people, you might only store a name and street address. For others, you might store a name, street address, e-mail address, Twitter name, web site address, and anything else that provides a way to contact that person.

The People app acts like an electronic version of a Rolodex file where it displays the name of one person at a time. Unlike physical Rolodex cards, the People app can store as much or as little information as you like.

To store a name manually into the People app, follow these steps:

1. Open the People app.

2. Click the + icon. The People app displays a name, phone number, and e-mail text boxes, as shown in Figure 21-4.

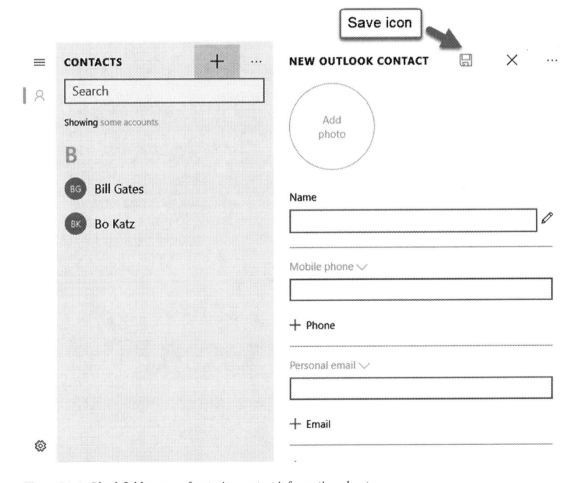

Figure 21-4. *Blank fields appear for storing contact information about a person*

3. Click in one or more of the following text boxes and type the information you
    want to save such as:

    • Name

    • Phone number

    • E-mail address

    • Other (notes, web site, job title, birthday, etc.)

4. Click in the Last text field and type the person's last name.

5. (Optional) Click the Add photo circle to choose a picture through the Photos
    program.

6. Click the Save icon to save your newly added data.

Editing Names

Once you've added information to the People app, you can always edit that information later. To edit a
person's contact information, follow these steps:

1. Open the People app.

2. Click the name of the person in the left pane whose information you want to edit.
    That person's information appears, as shown in Figure 21-5.

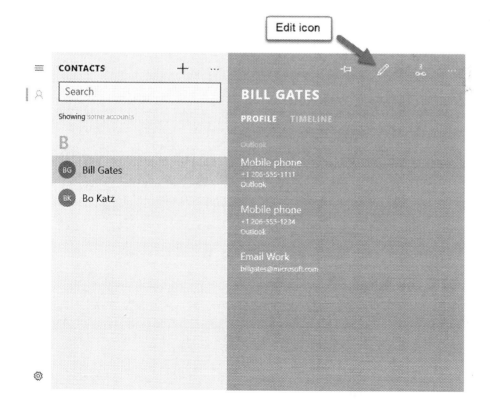

Figure 21-5. The Edit icon appears in the upper right corner as a pencil icon

3. Click the Edit icon (it looks like a pencil) in the upper right corner. The People app displays text boxes so you can edit existing information or click the + icon to add new information, as shown in Figure 21-6.

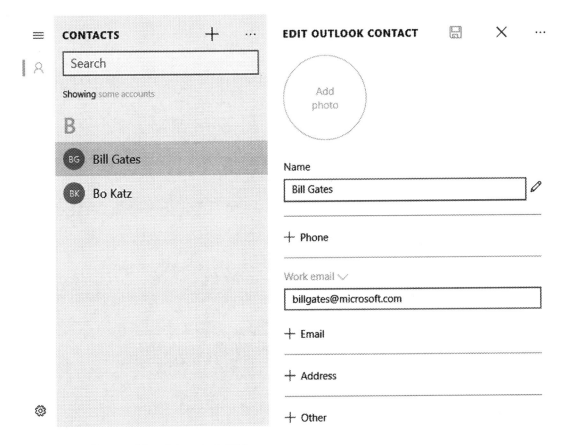

Figure 21-6. *You can delete data or just edit it*

4. Click in any existing data and use the arrow keys and Backspace key to edit the existing data.

5. Click the Save icon to save your changes.

Searching for a Name

The People app lets you search through names alphabetically. When you have a small number of stored names, you can easily find a name just by scrolling through the name list. However, once you start storing large numbers of names, then scrolling through the alphabetic list can become cumbersome.

That's why the People app provides a search text box. Just like searching on the Internet with a search engine, the search text box lets you type part or all of the information you want to find such as part of a person's name, telephone number, e-mail address, or street address. Just as long as you know some bit of information about someone and that information is stored in the People app, you'll be able to search and find it.

To search for a name in the People app, follow these steps:

1. Open the People app.

2. Click in the search text box that appears in the upper left corner of the People app window.

3. Type part or all of the information you know about the person you want to find such as the city where they live, their web site address, or their mobile phone number. As you type, the People app lists all matching data, as shown in Figure 21-7.

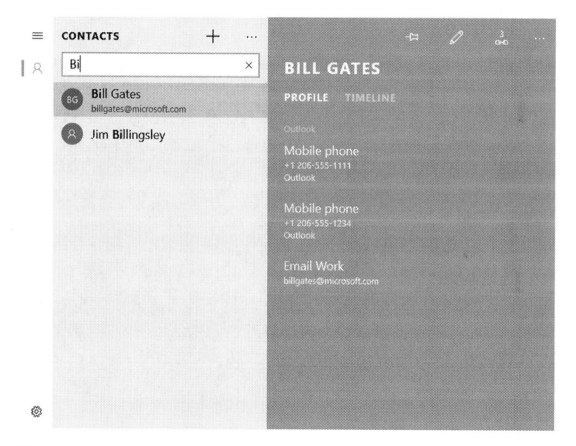

Figure 21-7. *As you type in the Search text box, the People app matches your existing data*

4. Click the close icon (it looks like an X) that appears to the right of the search text box to clear it and display all names in the People app once more.

Deleting Names

Although it's easy to add names, eventually you may want to delete names as well. To delete a name, follow these steps:

1. Open the People app.

2. Right-click a name you want to delete. A pop-up menu appears, as shown in Figure 21-8.

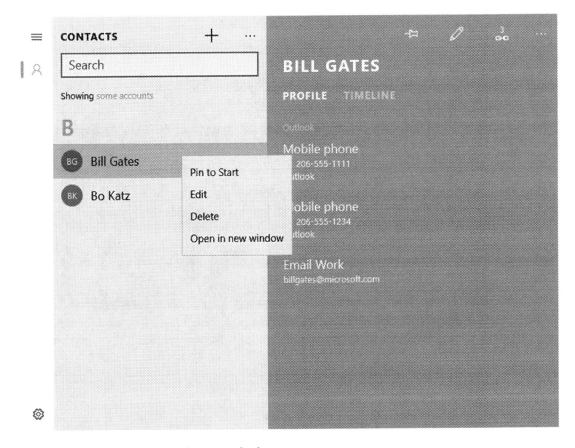

Figure 21-8. Right-click a person's name to display a pop-up menu

3. Click Delete. A message dialog box appears, asking if you're sure you want to delete the name, as shown in Figure 21-9.

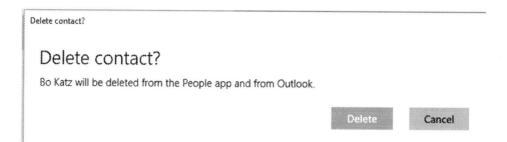

Figure 21-9. *A dialog box confirms whether you want to delete a name*

4. Click the Delete button (or Cancel if you don't want to delete the group after all).

■ **Note** If you delete a name, you can't undo this action, so make sure you really want to delete a name.

Pinning Information to the Start Menu

If a person is particularly important, you may want to pin their information as a tile in the Start menu, as shown in Figure 21-10. Then you can simply click this tile to view that person's contact information.

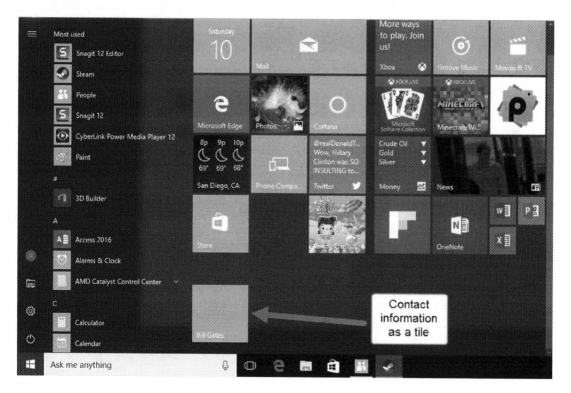

Figure 21-10. *A person's contact information can appear as a tile on the Start menu*

To pin contact information to the Start menu, follow these steps:

1. Open the People app.

2. Click the name you want to pin.

3. Click the Pin icon. A dialog box appears, asking if you want to pin your chosen name to the Start menu, as shown in Figure 21-11.

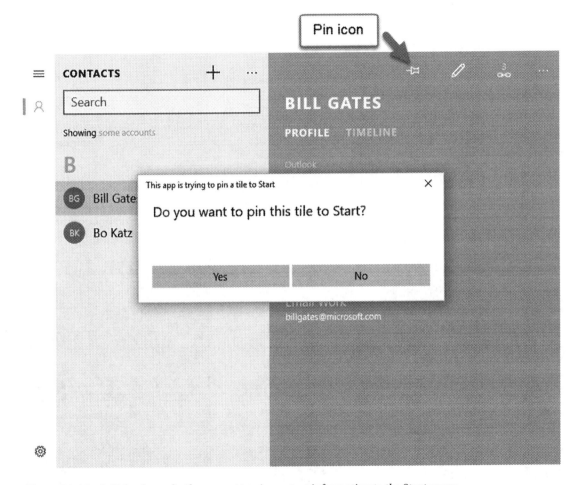

Figure 21-11. *A dialog box asks if you want to pin contact information to the Start menu*

4. Click the Yes button (or No if you change your mind). Your chosen contact information now appears as a tile on the Start menu.

To unpin contact information off the Start menu, repeat steps 1-3.

Customizing the People App

You can customize how the People app searches and displays names. The two options for displaying names are:

- Sort by first or last name
- Display as First Last or Last, First

To customize how the People app sorts and displays names, follow these steps:

1. Open the People app.

2. Click the Settings icon in the bottom left corner of the People app window. A Settings pane appears, as shown in Figure 21-12.

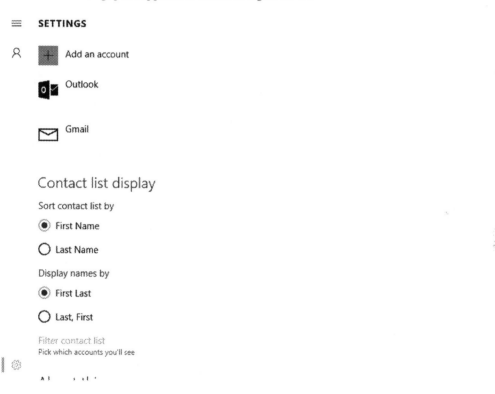

Figure 21-12. *The Settings pane lets you change how the People app sorts and displays names*

3. Click the options you want.

4. Click the Back arrow in the upper left corner of the People app window to return to the main People app screen.

Deleting an Account

If you have connected the People app to an account, such as your iCloud or Outlook account, you can always remove that account later if you wish. To remove an account, follow these steps:

1. Open the People app.

2. Click the Settings icon in the bottom left corner of the People app window. A Settings pane appears (see Figure 21-12).

3. Click the account name you want to delete. An Account settings window appears, as shown in Figure 21-13.

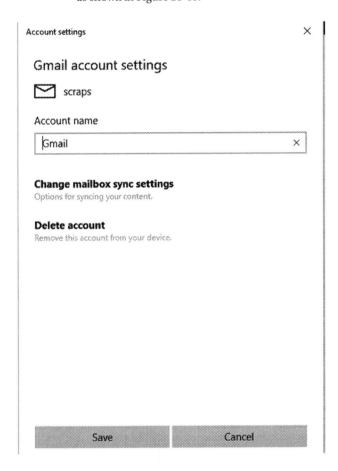

Figure 21-13. *The Account settings window*

4. Click Delete account. The People app asks you to verify you want to remove the chosen account.

5. Click the Delete (or Cancel) button.

Summary

The People app can be especially handy for storing the names and contact information of family members, friends, and business associates. You can store information such as e-mail addresses or telephone numbers, but you can also store unusual information such as important dates for a person (such as an anniversary or birthday) or text describing a project or idea related to a specific person.

The People app is nothing more than a simple database for helping you keep track of the people in your life who are most important to you, whether they're related to work or your personal life.

PART V

Getting Work Done

No matter how much you might like playing with your computer, eventually you may need to get some work done on it. Fortunately, using a computer doesn't have to be a drudgery. In fact, you may find that working on a computer can make any work-related task easier and even more enjoyable.

To help you keep track of important people in your life, you can use the People program so you'll never lose track of someone's phone number or e-mail address again.

To help you keep track of random thoughts and ideas, you can use the OneNote program that lets you organize related ideas in folders for quick access. By storing text or graphics in OneNote, you'll never risk losing a good idea ever again.

Work doesn't have to be dull. With the right programs, you may find yourself becoming more productive than ever before.

CHAPTER 22

Using OneNote

One way to keep track of random information is to write it down on scraps of paper and stuff them into your pocket or desk drawer. Of course if you do that, there's a good chance you'll lose your ideas or information. Even if you save these scraps of paper, you'll still likely want to store them on your computer so you can share, print, and e-mail them to others.

Paper solutions may work, but they can be clumsy and messy. A far better solution is to store everything electronically on your computer using OneNote, a note-taking program that lets you type or draw ideas. Unlike other programs that may store data in separate files, OneNote stores everything in a single location. As long as you stored it in OneNote, you'll never have the hassle of trying to find it again. With OneNote, you'll never risk losing important information.

Note   Windows 10 comes with OneNote for free, but if you purchase Microsoft Office, you may have a more advanced version of OneNote as well. This chapter focuses on the free version of OneNote.

Understanding OneNote

The basic idea behind OneNote is to mimic a paper notebook you might carry with you to jot down or sketch ideas as they come to you. Just as a paper notebook consists of separate pages, you can divide your ideas between multiple pages in OneNote.

Just like a paper notebook, OneNote lets you store text and drawings. Unlike a paper notebook, OneNote also lets you store links that you can click to visit web sites or files created by other programs such as Microsoft Excel or PowerPoint.

To share ideas when using a paper notebook, you might photocopy a page and hand it to someone. To share ideas when using OneNote, you can print individual pages and hand them to others, e-mail pages to someone, or even share a link to your OneNote page.

By connecting your Microsoft account to OneNote on a Windows PC, Macintosh, iPhone, iPad, or Android device, you can keep all your notes synchronized between multiple devices as long as each device is connected to the Internet.

© Wallace Wang 2016
W. Wang, *Absolute Beginners Guide to Computing*, DOI 10.1007/978-1-4842-2289-8_22

The first time you start OneNote, you can assign an account to OneNote. To add (or remove) accounts, follow these steps:

1. Open OneNote.

2. Click the Show Navigation icon (it looks like three horizontal lines). A left pane appears, as shown in Figure 22-1.

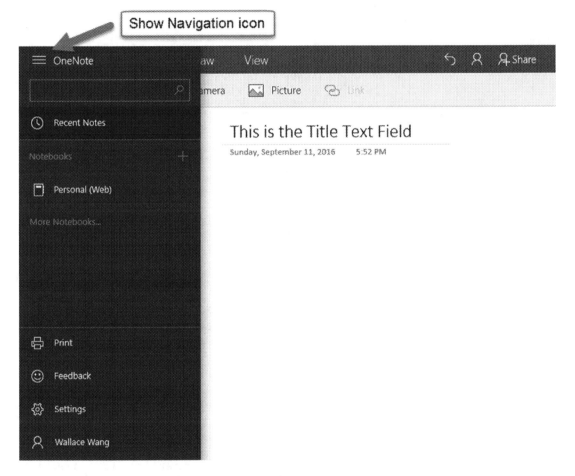

Figure 22-1. *The Show Navigation icon displays a left pane*

3. Click the Settings icon. A Settings pane appears in the right, as shown in Figure 22-2.

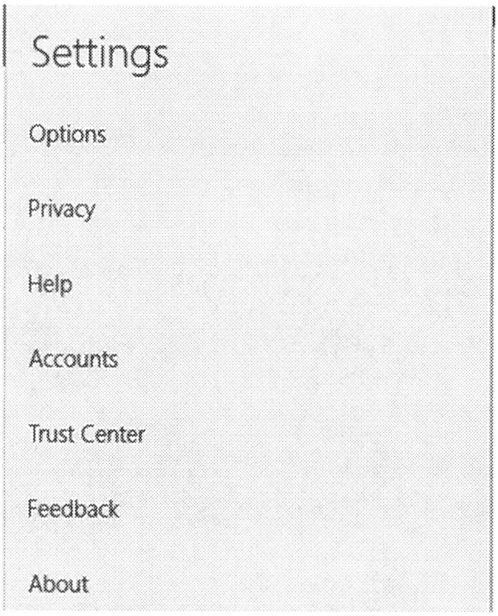

Figure 22-2. *The Settings pane*

4. Click Accounts. An Account window appears, listing all the accounts currently connected to OneNote.

5. Choose one of the following:

- To remove an account, click that account, click Sign out, and then click the Remove button.

- To add an account, click the Add account button and then type an e-mail address or phone number of the account you want to use with OneNote.

You can have zero or more accounts connected to OneNote. In general, it's best to have at least one account connected to OneNote if you plan on using OneNote on different devices such as a computer, an iPhone, an iPad, or an Android smartphone or tablet.

The OneNote user interface displays four tabs, as shown in Figure 22-3:

- *Home*: Displays basic text formatting commands

- *Insert*: Lets you insert files, tables, pictures, or web links

- *Draw*: Lets you choose colors and brush sizes for drawing pictures or typing text

- *View*: Lets you change the appearance of each page

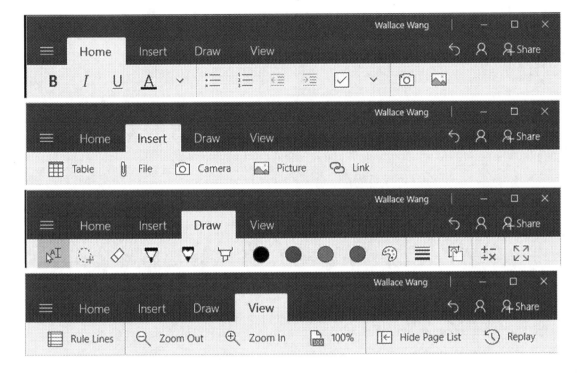

Figure 22-3. *The four tabs of OneNote*

The left pane displays the different pages available, as shown in Figure 22-4. You can delete, copy, rearrange, and create pages as necessary. As a general rule, give each page a descriptive name to make it easy to find your data again.

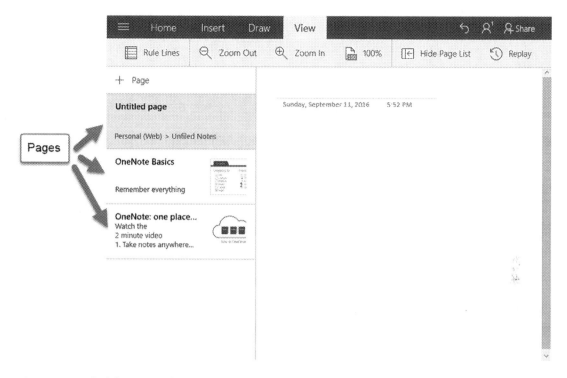

Figure 22-4. *The left pane displays the pages available in OneNote*

Unlike other programs such as a word processor or spreadsheet, OneNote always stores all notes together in a single file. This makes it easy to find your data again without wondering which file you stored them in and where you saved that file.

Using Pages in OneNote

Every time you type or draw something in OneNote, you need to store it on a page. You can create as many pages as you want and cram as much data as you want onto a single page. Generally, it's a good idea to separate ideas onto different pages.

To create a page in One Note, follow these steps:

1. Open OneNote.

2. Click the + Page button. OneNote creates a new page.

3. Click in the title text field and type a descriptive title for your page, as shown in Figure 22-5.

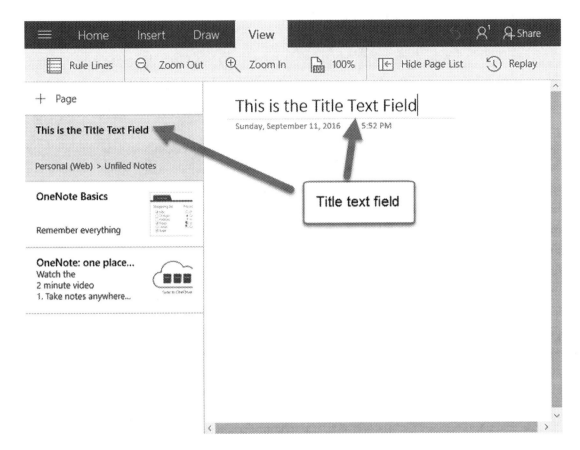

Figure 22-5. *Creating a title for a page*

Remember, you can always rename a page in two ways:

- Edit the title field text on the page
- Right-click a page in the left pane and when a pop-up menu appears, choose Rename Page, as shown in Figure 22-6.

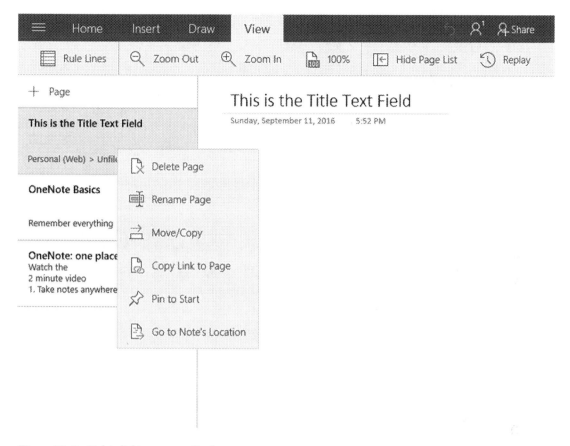

Figure 22-6. *Right-clicking a page displays a pop-up menu*

Typing Notes

Each time you type text on a OneNote page, OneNote stores the text in a text box that you can move anywhere on the page later. A single page can contain zero or more text boxes. To create a text box to type in, follow these steps:

1. Click the page in the left pane of OneNote to choose where you want to create text. OneNote displays the contents of your chosen page.

2. Click the Draw tab and click the Type Text icon, as shown in Figure 22-7.

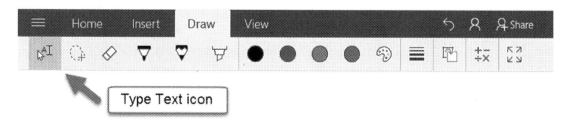

Figure 22-7. *The Type Text icon lets you choose to create a text box*

3. Click anywhere on the page, in the left pane, that you want to add text to.

4. Type your text. As you type, OneNote displays the text box border.

Moving Text Boxes on a Page

Once you've created and typed text into one or more text boxes on a page, you can always rearrange their position on the page. To move text boxes on a page, follow these steps:

1. Click the page in the left pane of OneNote that contains the text box you want to move.

2. Move the pointer over the text you want to move. OneNote displays a gray border at the top of the text box, as shown in Figure 22-8.

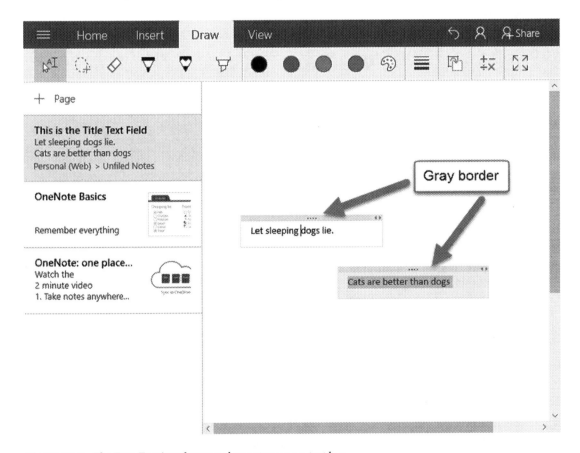

Figure 22-8. *The Type Text icon lets you choose to move a text box*

3. Move the pointer over the gray border of the text box and drag the mouse/trackpad to move the text box.

Formatting Text

After creating text, you can format text to choose different fonts, font sizes, and styles such as bold or italics. To format, follow these steps:

1. Click the page in the left pane of OneNote that contains the text box you want to move.

2. Click over the text you want to format.

3. Select the text you want to format by dragging the mouse/trackpad or holding down the Shift key and pressing the arrow keys.

4. Click the Home tab to view the different formatting options.

5. (Optional) Click the Font Formatting icon to display a pull-down menu of other formatting options such as choosing a different font or font size, as shown in Figure 22-9.

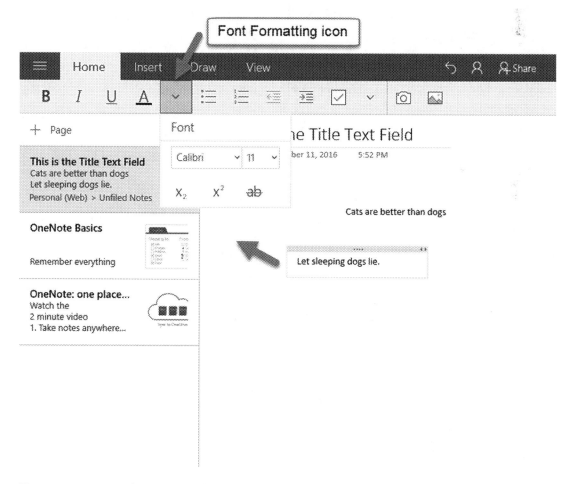

Figure 22-9. *You can format text in different ways*

Creating Lists

To help organize your ideas, OneNote lets you create three types of lists, as shown in Figure 22-10:

- Bullet lists

- Numbered lists

- To-do checklists

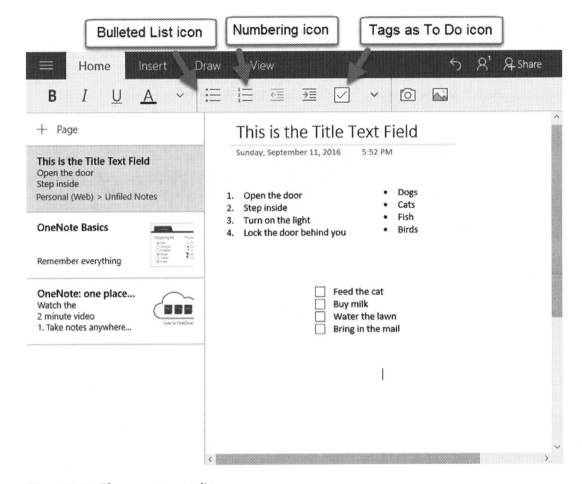

Figure 22-10. *Three ways to create lists*

You can either create a new text box and format it as a list or turn existing text into a list by selecting the text and then choosing a list option.

To create a list, follow these steps:

1. Click the page in the left pane of OneNote.

2. Choose one of the following:

   - Click anywhere to create a new text box

   - Select text in an existing text box

3. Click the Bulleted List, Numbering, or Tags as To Do icon to create a list.

Tagging Text with Icons

To emphasize the meaning of certain text, OneNote lets you tag text with icons that can identify phone numbers, addresses, or important text. To tag text with an icon, follow these steps:

1. Click the page in the left pane of OneNote.

2. Choose one of the following:

   - Click anywhere to create a new text box

   - Move the cursor in front of text in an existing text box

3. Click the Paragraph Formatting icon to display a pull-down menu of different icons to choose, as shown in Figure 22-11.

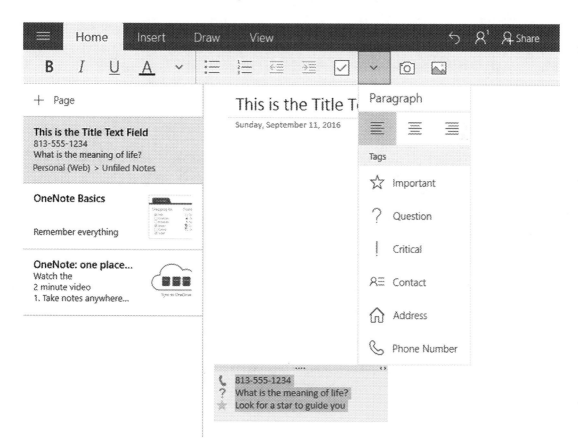

Figure 22-11. *Tagging text with icons*

4. Click an icon to insert that icon into your text box.

Deleting Text

After you've created text, you can delete select portions of your text or delete the entire text box altogether. To delete part of existing text, follow these steps:

1. Click the text that you want to edit.

2. Use the Backspace or Delete keys along with the cursor keys to delete text. You can also select text with the mouse/trackpad or the Shift key and the cursor keys before pressing the Backspace or Delete keys.

To delete an entire text box, follow these steps:

1. Move the pointer over the text box you want to delete until the gray border appears at the top.

2. Click the gray border of the text box. OneNote selects all the text inside the text box.

3. Press the Backspace or Delete key.

▓ **Note**   If you delete a text box by mistake, you can press Ctrl+Z or click the Undo icon in the upper right corner to undelete that text box right away.

Drawing Pictures

In addition to typing text, you can also draw pictures. When you draw a picture, you can choose a color and a width. Wherever you drag the mouse/trackpad, you can draw a line. Once you've drawn a line, you can select all or part of it and copy or move it to a new location. You can also erase all or part of that line.

Drawing pictures gives you a chance to capture your ideas solely as pictures or to mix text and pictures together to capture your different thoughts. At all times, OneNote treats your pictures and text as separate objects that you can move around on a page.

Drawing a Line

To draw a line, follow these steps:

1. Click the Draw tab.

2. Click the Pen icon.

3. (Optional) Click a color such as black or red. If you click the Color icon, you can choose from a variety of colors or unique color mixtures, as shown in Figure 22-12.

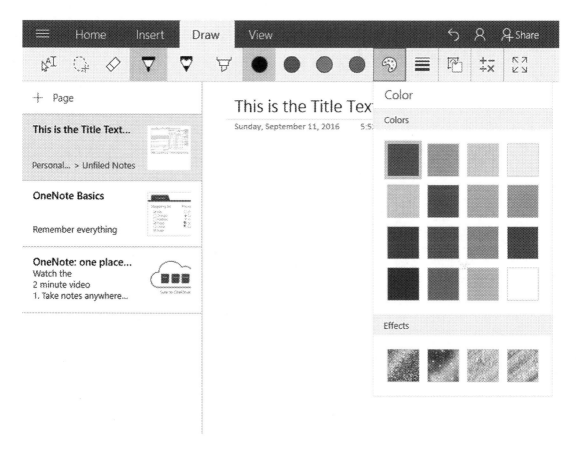

Figure 22-12. *The Color icon displays a palette of colors to choose from*

4. (Optional) Click the Thickness icon and choose a line thickness, as shown in Figure 22-13.

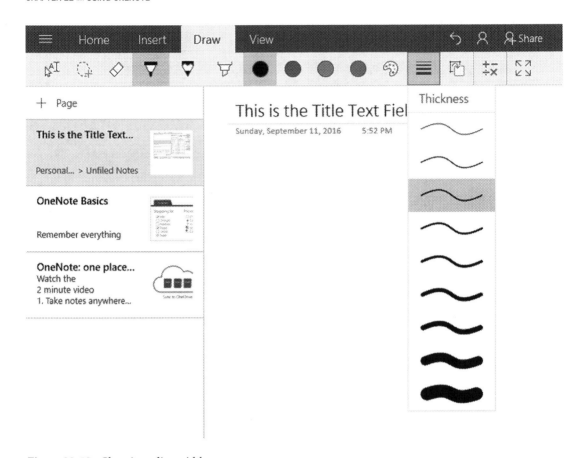

Figure 22-13. *Choosing a line width*

    5.   Drag the mouse/trackpad to draw a line.

Selecting a Line (to Delete, Copy, or Move)

Once you've drawn a line, you can select that line to delete it, copy it, or move it to another location. To select a line, you have two options. First, you can click the line using the Select Objects icon. Second, you can drag the mouse/trackpad to enclose the line using the Lasso Object icon, as shown in Figure 22-14.

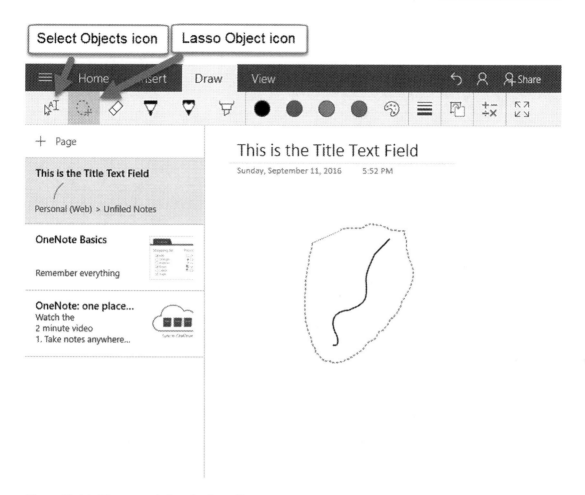

Figure 22-14. *The two tools for selecting a line*

The Select Objects icon lets you click a line to select the entire line. To use the Select Objects icon, follow these steps:

1. Click the Select Objects icon (see Figure 22-14).

2. Click the line you want to select. OneNote displays a dotted line box around your line, as shown in Figure 22-15.

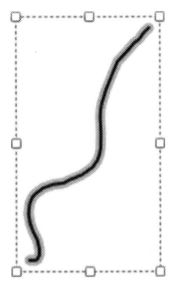

Figure 22-15. *Selecting a line displays a dotted line around it*

The Lasso Object icon lets you drag the mouse/trackpad completely around a line to select it. To use the Lasso Object icon, follow these steps:

1. Click the Lasso Object icon (see Figure 22-14).

2. Drag the mouse/trackpad entirely around the line you want to select. OneNote displays a dotted line box around your line (see Figure 22-15).

Once you've selected a line, you can do one of the following:

- Delete a line by pressing the Backspace or Delete key

- Move a line by dragging the mouse/trackpad

- Copy and paste a line by pressing Ctrl+C followed by Ctrl+V

Working with Tables

A table consists of rows and columns of equal width and height. By using a table, you can organize and sort data alphabetically or numerically by rows. You can create a table inside an existing text box or as a separate item altogether.

To create a table, you need to use the Insert tab. After you've created a table, you can modify that table by clicking in that table to make a Table tab appear that lists various commands, as shown in Figure 22-16.

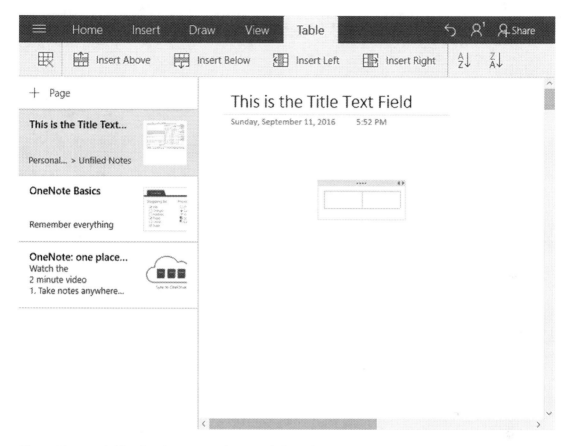

Figure 22-16. *A Table tab only appears when you click inside an existing table*

Creating a Table

When you create a table, it only contains one row and two columns but you can add more rows and columns later. To create a table, follow these steps:

1. Click the Insert tab.

2. (Optional) Click inside an existing text box and move the cursor where you want to insert the table.

3. Click the Table icon. OneNote creates a table, as shown in Figure 22-17.

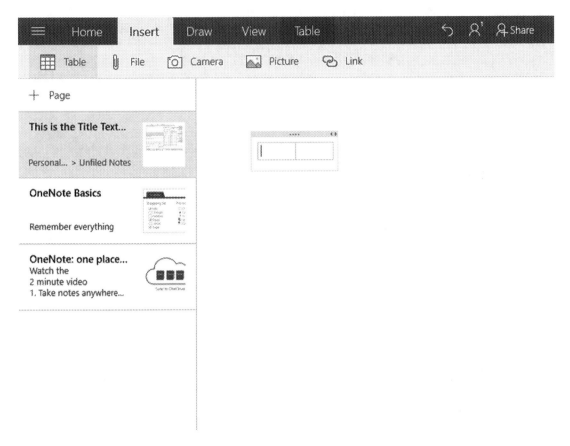

Figure 22-17. *Creating a table*

Adding Rows and Columns to a Table

Once you've created a table, you can add more rows and columns at any time. To add more rows using the Enter key, follow these steps:

1. Click in the table cell in the bottom right corner of the table.

2. Press Enter. OneNote creates a new row.

To add more rows or columns to a table using the Table tab, follow these steps:

1. Click in a row or column. Your newly created row or column will appear above/below or to the left/right of the current cursor location.

2. Click the Table tab (see Figure 22-16) and click one of the following:

    - *Insert Above*: Adds a new row above the current location of the cursor

    - *Insert Below*: Adds a new row below the current location of the cursor

    - *Insert Left*: Adds a new column to the left of the current location of the cursor

    - *Insert Right*: Adds a new column to the right of the current location of the cursor

Sorting by Rows

Once you've filled a table with data such as text or numbers, you can sort that table by rows in either ascending or descending order. Ascending order means text starting with the letter A appears at the top and text starting with the letter Z appears at the bottom, or lower numbers appear at the top and higher numbers appear at the bottom.

Descending order means text starting with the letter Z appears at the top and text starting with the letter A appears at the bottom, or higher numbers appear at the top and lower numbers appear at the bottom.

░ **Note**   OneNote ignores the top row of a table when sorting because the top row usually displays a heading.

To sort a table, follow these steps:

1. Click in the table you want to sort.

2. Click the Table tab and then click the Sort A-Z (ascending order) or Sort Z-A (descending order) icons, as shown in Figure 22-18.

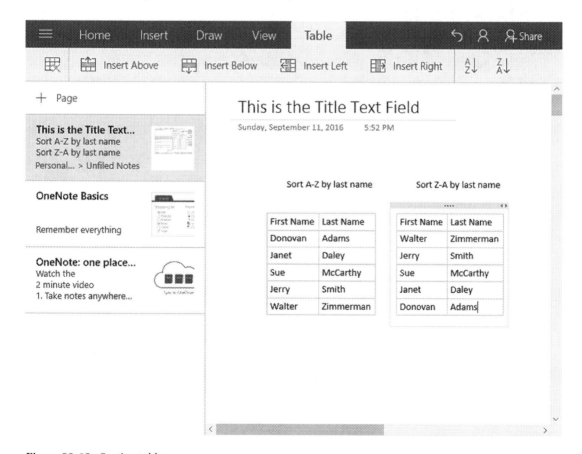

Figure 22-18. *Sorting tables*

Deleting Rows and Columns

Once you've created a table, you can always delete rows or columns from that table later. To delete an entire row or column using the keyboard, follow these steps:

1. Select the entire row or column you want to delete. (Make sure you select all cells in a row or column.)

2. Press the Backspace or Delete key.

To delete an entire row or column using the mouse/trackpad, follow these steps:

1. Click in any cell in the row or column you want to delete. (If you want to delete multiple rows or columns, select all cells in the rows or columns you want to delete.)

2. Click the Table tab and click the Delete icon. A pull-down menu appears, as shown in Figure 22-19.

Figure 22-19. *The Delete pull-down menu*

3. Click Delete Columns or Delete Rows. (If you click Delete Table, you can delete the entire table.)

▨ **Note**   If you accidentally delete a row or column, you can retrieve it by immediately clicking the Undo icon or by pressing Ctrl+Z.

Attaching Files

Many times you may have files created by other programs that are related to your ideas stored in OneNote. For example, you might jot down an idea and want to link your idea to word processor documents or presentations stored on your computer.

Rather than copying the data out of a file and pasting it into OneNote, it's easier to attach one or more files to a OneNote page. Then you can link your ideas in OneNote to any existing files created by other programs.

If you attach a .pdf (Portable Document Format) file, OneNote can display the contents of that .pdf file. However, if you attach any other file (such as a Microsoft Word or Excel file), OneNote simply displays that file's icon on the page, as shown in Figure 22-20.

Figure 22-20. *File attachments appear as icons*

To attach a file to a OneNote page, follow these steps:

1. Click the Insert tab.

2. Click the File icon. A pull-down menu appears, as shown in Figure 22-21.

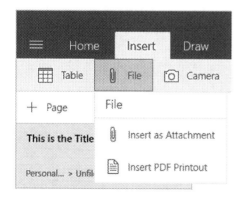

Figure 22-21. *The File icon pull-down menu*

3. Click Insert as Attachment or Insert PDF Printout (if you want to choose a PDF file). An Open dialog box appears.

4. Click the file you want to attach and click the Open button. OneNote displays your attached file as an icon or the entire contents of a PDF file (see Figure 22-20).

▨ **Note**   When you insert a PDF file, OneNote displays both its file icon and its contents. You can choose to delete either the PDF file icon or the PDF contents.

Viewing a File Attachment

After you've attached one or more files to a OneNote page, you may want to view the contents of those files by opening that file with another program. To view a file attachment, follow these steps:

1. Right-click the file icon. A toolbar appears, as shown in Figure 22-22.

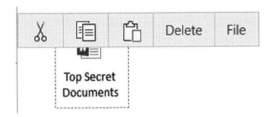

Figure 22-22. *Right-clicking a file icon displays a toolbar*

2. Click File. A pop-up menu appears, as shown in Figure 22-23.

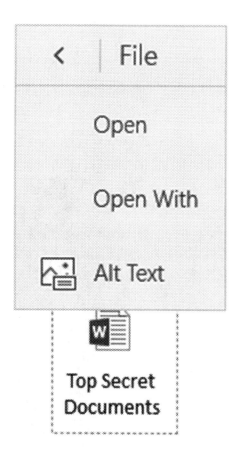

Figure 22-23. *You can open the file to view it in another program*

3. Click Open (to open the file with the program that created that file) or click Open With (to open the file with a different program). Your file attachment opens so you can edit it if you wish.

Removing a File Attachment

Once you've attached one or more files to a OneNote page, you may later want to remove those files from OneNote. When you remove a file from OneNote, you're only removing a link to that file, but you are not deleting or modifying the actual file itself.

To remove an attached file from a OneNote page, follow these steps:

1. Click the file icon or PDF file contents. A dotted line appears around the file icon or PDF file contents.

2. Press the Backspace or Delete key.

For another way to remove an attached file from a OneNote page, follow these steps:

1. Right-click the file icon or PDF file contents. A toolbar appears (see Figure 22-22).

2. Click Delete.

Inserting Pictures

OneNote lets you insert pictures stored on your computer, or pictures you can capture from your computer's webcam. To insert a picture from an existing file on your computer, follow these steps:

1. Click the Insert tab.

2. Click the Picture icon. An Open dialog box appears.

3. Click the picture file you want to insert into OneNote and click the Open button. A window appears showing the entire picture, as shown in Figure 22-24.

Figure 22-24. *Your chosen picture appears to let you verify whether you want to use it*

4. (Optional) Click the Crop icon and drag the circular handles around to define the rectangular portion of the picture you want to use, then click the OK button.

5. Click the Insert all icon. OneNote inserts your chosen picture file.

To capture a picture from your webcam, follow these steps:

1. Click the Insert tab.

2. Click the Camera icon. A window appears, showing the image currently visible by your computer's webcam.

3. Click the Camera icon to capture a picture. (You can repeat this step as often as you wish.)

4. Click the Insert all icon. OneNote inserts your captured images.

Add Web Links to Text

There may be times when you want to link your OneNote ideas to existing web pages. That's why OneNote lets you turn any text into a hyperlink. That way you can click that hyperlink and view a web page containing information related to your idea.

To create a hyperlink, follow these steps:

1. Create a new text box or click in an existing text box.

2. Select the text that you want to turn into a hyperlink.

3. Click the Insert tab.

4. Click the Link icon. A window appears, showing an Address text box, as shown in Figure 22-25.

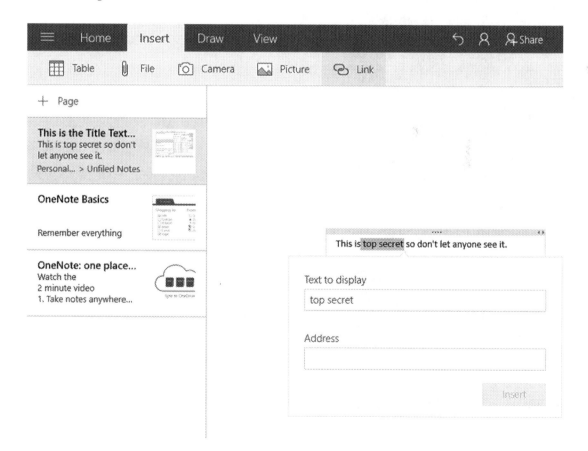

Figure 22-25. *Creating a hyperlink*

5. Type (or copy) a web page address in the Address text box and click the Insert button.

After you create a hyperlink, clicking that hyperlink will automatically load your browser and display the web page defined by the hyperlink.

Making Multiple Notebooks

To organize your ideas, OneNote lets you create multiple pages. However, you may want to keep those ideas stored in separate notebooks. To create a notebook, follow these steps:

1. Click the Show Navigation icon in the upper left corner of the OneNote window. The Navigation pane appears, as shown in Figure 22-26.

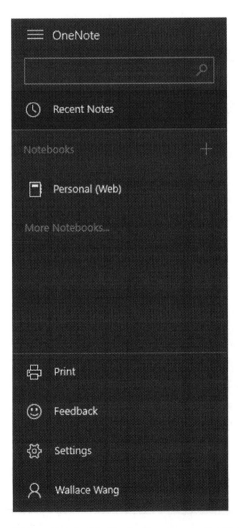

Figure 22-26. *The Navigation pane in OneNote. The + icon creates another notebook*

2. Click the + icon to add a new notebook. A dialog box appears, asking for a name for your new notebook, as shown in Figure 22-27.

New Notebook

Notebook name

Create Notebook   Cancel

Figure 22-27. *Defining a name for a new notebook*

3. Type a descriptive name for your notebook and click the Create Notebook button. OneNote creates a new notebook.

To switch between notebooks, click the Show Navigation icon and then click the notebook you want to use.

Viewing Pages

To help you view your pages, OneNote gives you several options:

- *Rule Lines*: Displays horizontal lines across the page to mimic lined notebook paper

- *Zoom In/Out*: Lets you magnify or shrink the appearance of a page

- *Hide Page List*: Toggles between showing or hiding the pages in your notebook in the left pane

- *Replay*: Lets you view the order that you created ideas on your page

Displaying Rule Lines

Lines can help you organize your text and pictures on a page. You can display different types of rule lines or display grid lines, which can be handy for drawing simple charts. To display rule lines on a page, follow these steps:

1. Click a page in the left pane of the OneNote window.

2. Click the View tab.

3. Click the Rule Lines icon. A pull-down menu of different rule/grid lines appears, as shown in Figure 22-28.

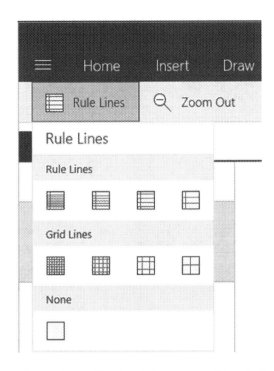

Figure 22-28. *Choosing different types of lines to display on a page*

4. Click a rule or grid line you want to appear on the currently visible page. OneNote displays your chosen rule/grid lines on the page.

Magnifying a Page

The View tab displays three ways to magnify a page:

- *Zoom Out*: Lets you see more of a page but shrinks all text and graphics on that page

- *Zoom In*: Lets you see a magnified view of a page

- *100%*: Quickly returns the page to its original magnification

Each time you click the Zoom Out icon, OneNote displays everything on your page smaller but lets you view the overall contents of a page.

Each time you click the Zoom In icon, OneNote displays your page in greater magnification, as shown in Figure 22-29.

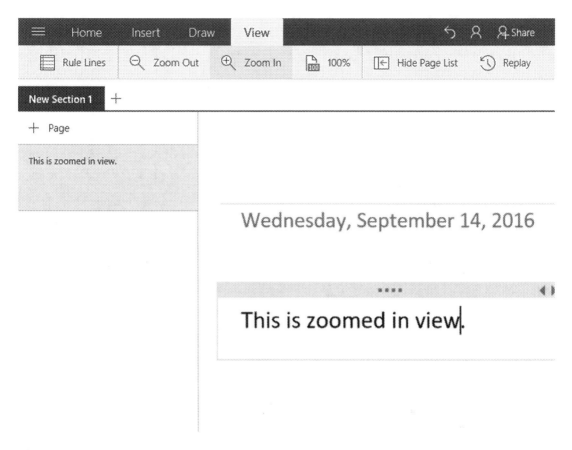

Figure 22-29. *Zooming in*

You can only Zoom In/Out a page a fixed number of times. To return the page to its original magnification, click the 100% icon.

Hiding/Showing the Page List

The left pane of the OneNote window displays a list of all the pages available. This lets you quickly switch to another page by clicking that page. However, displaying the page list also takes up room so you might want to hide the page list until you need it.

To toggle between hiding or displaying the page list, click the Hide Page List icon. Each time you click this Hide Page List icon, it toggles between showing or hiding the page list.

Replaying a Page

One unique and interesting feature of OneNote is its ability to replay all or part of a page so you can see the order that you created text and graphics on a page. To replay a page, follow these steps:

1.   Click a page that you want to replay in the left pane of the OneNote window.

2.   Click the View tab.

3. Click the Replay icon. OneNote asks you to either drag the mouse/trackpad over part of your page or click the Replay everything on the page link to see how you created the entire page.

Summary

When you have fleeting thoughts that you want to capture, store them in OneNote. You can store text, graphics, or a combination of the two along with pictures captured by you or someone else with a digital camera.

OneNote can organize your ideas on separate pages and you can create as many pages as necessary. To further organize your thoughts, create multiple notebooks so you can separate different ideas completely.

By using OneNote, you can turn your computer into an electronic notebook for sketching, doodling, or typing small amounts of text. Now you'll always have all the information you need at your fingertips just as long as you have your computer.

CHAPTER 23

Keeping Track of Dates and Times

Everyone needs to be somewhere on different days and at different times. While some people can keep track of appointments in their heads, most people need to write this information down. In the past, people used paper calendars and notebooks, which worked fine unless you lost your calendar or notebook.

That's why Windows 10 includes a Calendar program. Not only can you keep track of appointments for a particular date, but you can also view the calendar from a yearly, monthly, weekly, or daily view. That way you can spot appointments far in advance or check your daily schedule to see which appointments you might have and how long they might take.

To keep track of shorter amounts of time down to the second, you can use the Alarms & Clock app. Now you can time yourself to see how long you take to accomplish a task, such as running a lap, or set a timer to force yourself to do something until a specific amount of time passes.

By managing your time, you may find you actually have more time to do your favorite activities than you might have thought possible.

Connecting to an Account

To make sure you always have your calendar with you at all times, you should connect the Calendar app to an account. That way you can access your calendar data from multiple devices such as a desktop PC or a laptop.

The first time you run the Calendar app, it will ask you to connect to an account, but if you want to add (or remove) accounts from the Calendar app later, follow these steps:

1. Open the Calendar program.

2. Click the Settings icon in the bottom left corner of the Calendar window.
   A Settings pane appears, as shown in Figure 23-1.

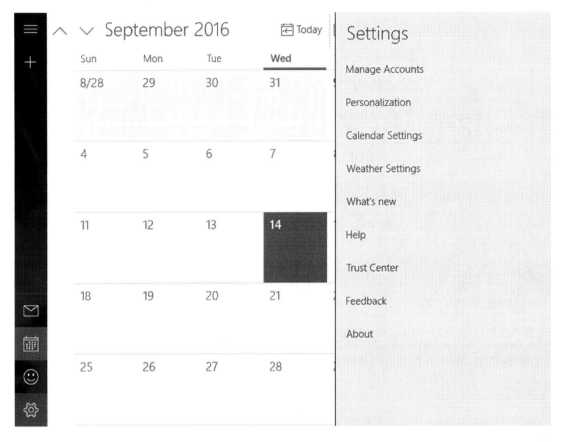

Figure 23-1. *The Settings pane*

3. Click Manage Accounts.

4. Choose one of the following:

- To remove an account, click that account and when an Account settings window appears, click Delete account.

- To add an account, click the Add account button and then choose an account to use, such as iCloud or Outlook.com.

Viewing a Calendar

With a paper calendar, you're stuck with viewing a monthly, weekly, or daily view. With the Calendar program, you can switch views any time by clicking one of the following in the upper right corner of the Calendar window, as shown in Figure 23-2:

- *Year*: Shows all the months of a single year

- *Month*: Shows all the days of a single month

▓ **Note**　The Month and Year buttons may sometimes be hidden behind a Show icon that appears as three dots in the upper right corner of the Calendar window.

- *Week*: Shows all seven days of the week
- Work week: Shows Monday through Friday of the week
- *Day*: Shows hourly time increments of a single day

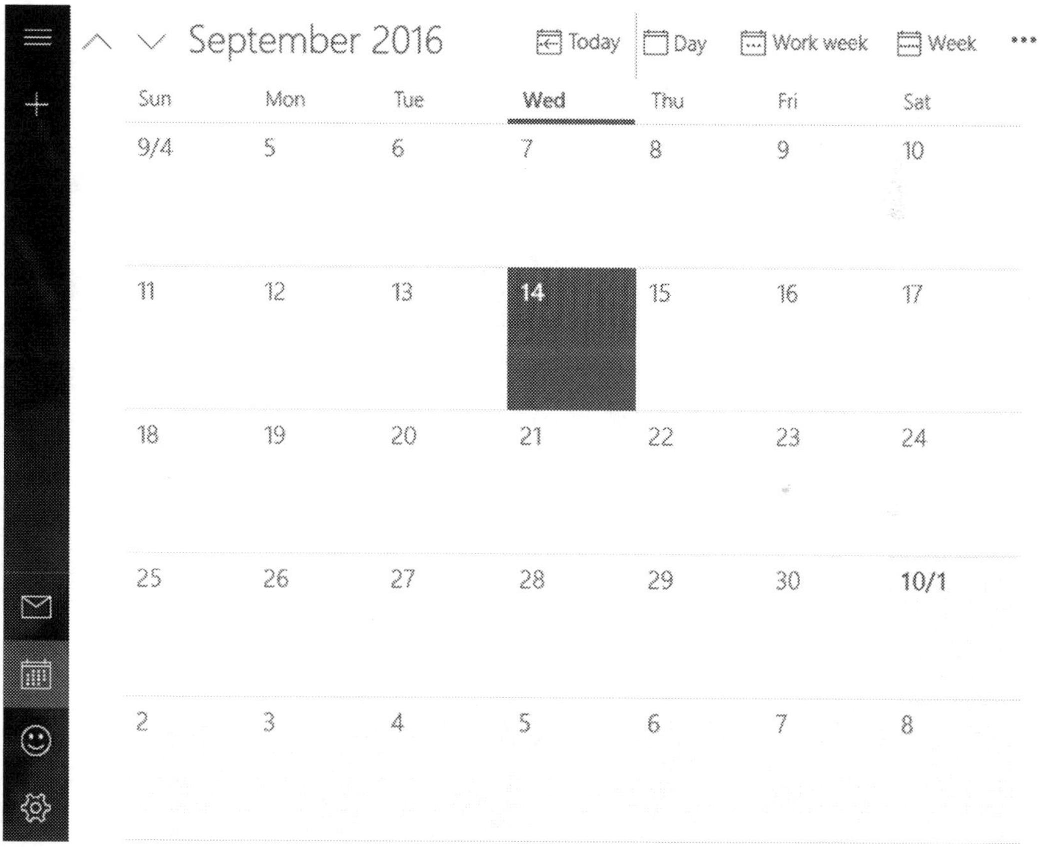

Figure 23-2.　*The Month view*

Viewing a calendar just gives you different ways of seeing your appointments. For example, the Month view lets you see what you might have scheduled in the upcoming weeks, while the Day view lets you see what's important for one particular day.

Setting an Appointment

No matter which calendar view you choose, you can create an appointment, also known as an event, for a particular date. To create an appointment, follow these steps:

1. Open the Calendar program.

2. Click the New event (plus sign [+]) icon in the upper left corner of the Calendar window. A new event window appears, as shown in Figure 23-3.

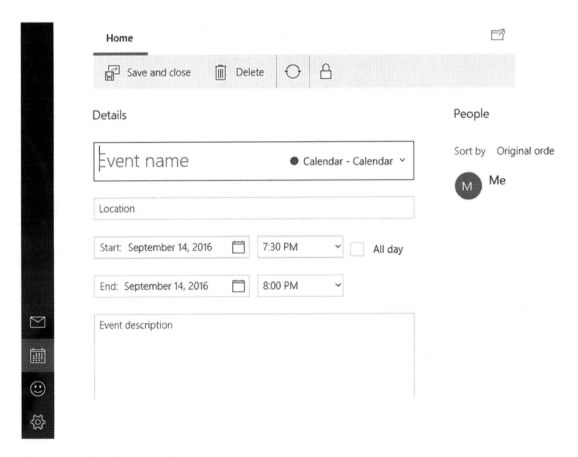

Figure 23-3. *Creating an appointment*

3. Click in the Event name text box and type a description of the event.

4. (Optional) Click in the Location text box and type where the event takes place.

5. Click in the Date Picker icon in the Start text box to display a monthly calendar, as shown in Figure 23-4.

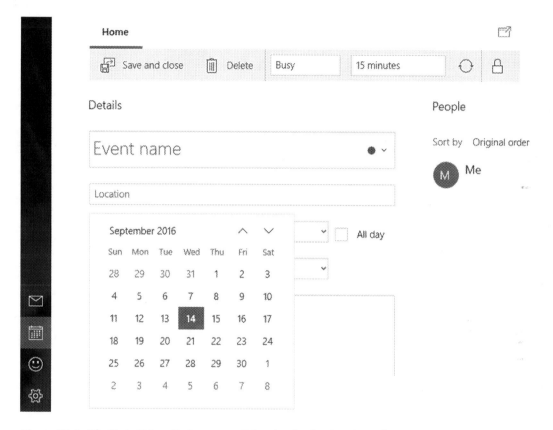

Figure 23-4. *The Date Picker displays a monthly calendar for choosing a date*

6. Click in the Time list box and choose a time such as 7:30 or 10:00. (You can also click the All day check box if the event will take the entire day.)

7. Repeat steps 5-6 for the End text box to define an ending time for the event.

8. Click in the Event description text box at the bottom and type any additional information about the event such as what you might need to bring or what your goals might be for that particular event.

9. Click the Busy list box and define a description of your time such as Busy, Tentative, or Out of office, as shown in Figure 23-5.

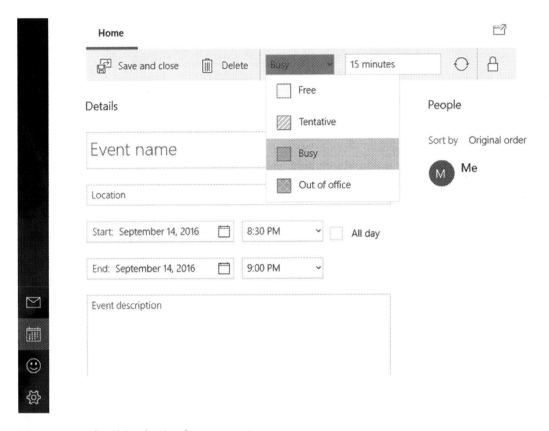

Figure 23-5. *Classifying the time for your event*

10.   Click in the time list box and choose a time to alert you to the event such as 5 or 15 minutes before the scheduled time, as shown in Figure 23-6.

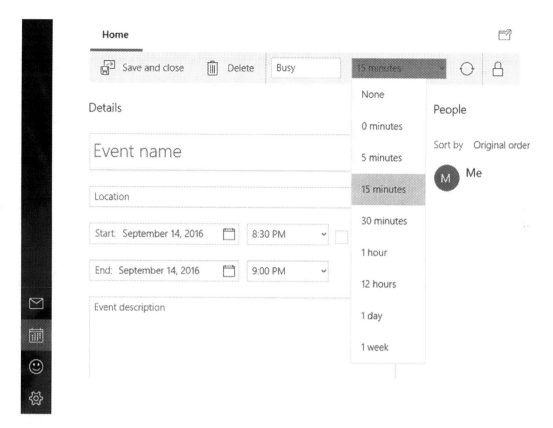

Figure 23-6. *Choosing a time to alert you before an event*

11.   Click the Save and close button. The Calendar app displays your defined event, as shown in Figure 23-7.

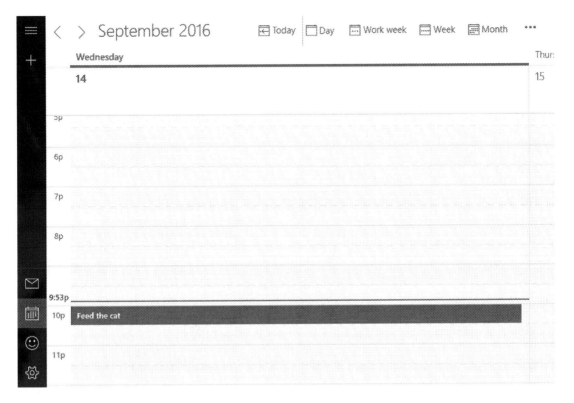

Figure 23-7. *Your defined event appears in the calendar*

Modifying an Appointment

Once you've created an appointment, you may want to modify it later. To modify an existing appointment, follow these steps:

1. Open the Calendar program.

2. Click the appointment you want to modify and make any changes such as choosing a different time or location.

3. (Optional) Right-click an appointment to display a pop-up menu and choose Show As and then choose a different way to identify your appointment such as Tentative or Busy, as shown in Figure 23-8.

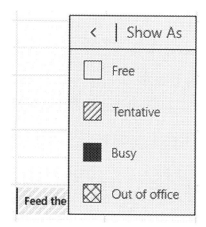

Figure 23-8. *You can display appointments as different categories such as Busy or Out of office*

    4.   Click the Save and close button.

Deleting an Appointment

When you're done with an appointment, you can delete it from your calendar. To delete an appointment, follow these steps:

    1.   Open the Calendar program.

    2.   Right-click the appointment you want to delete. A pop-up menu appears, as shown in Figure 23-9.

    3.   Choose Delete.

Figure 23-9. *Right-clicking an appointment displays a pop-up menu*

Tracking Time

When you create an appointment in the Calendar app, you can set an alarm to remind you of that appointment ahead of time. However, sometimes you may just need to track time without a specific appointment.

For example, suppose you like exercising a certain amount of time every day. With the Alarms & Clock app, you can measure time like a stopwatch or define when a certain amount of time has passed. The Alarms & Clock app lets you measure time in four ways:

- *Alarm*: Lets you set an alarm to go off at a certain time

- *World Clock*: Lets you view the current time around the world

- *Timer*: Lets you count down from a fixed amount of time such as 15 minutes

- *Stopwatch*: Lets you time how long an event lasts

Setting an Alarm

An alarm can be handy when you want to be notified at a certain time. For example, you might want to work on a project until 9:00 p.m. The Alarm feature in the Alarms & Clock app is handy for keeping track of when a certain time arrives.

▨ **Note**   The Alarms & Clock app can only notify you of an alarm if your computer is awake and turned on. If you turn your computer off or let it go to sleep, the alarm may not notify you, so alarms are best when you know you'll be using your computer at the time the alarm is set to go off.

To set an alarm, follow these steps:

1. Open the Alarms & Clock app.

2. Click the Alarm icon. All existing alarms appear, as shown in Figure 23-10.

3. Click the New (+) icon in the bottom right corner of the Alarms & Clock window. A New Alarm window appears, as shown in Figure 23-11.

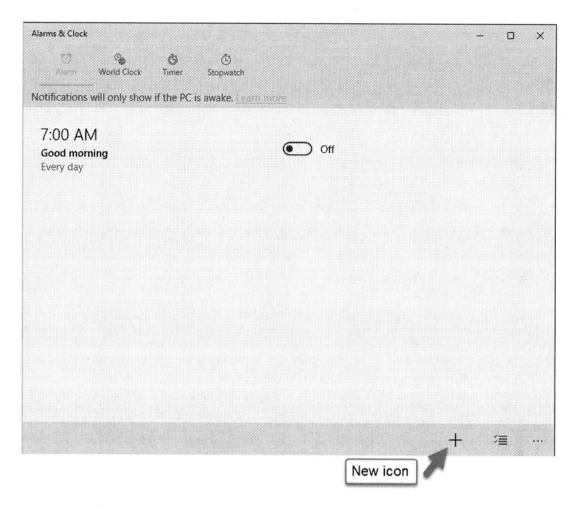

Figure 23-10. *The Alarm icon displays a list of currently defined alarms*

4. Select a time for your alarm such as 7:35 a.m. or 12:15 p.m.

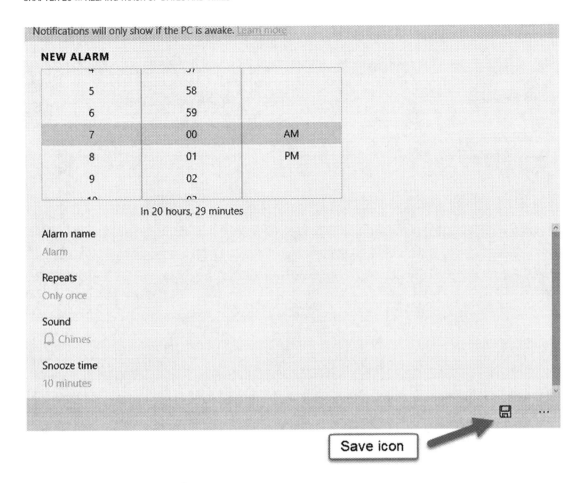

Figure 23-11. Creating a new alarm

5.   Click in the Alarm name text box and type a description of your alarm.

6.   (Optional) Click the Only once button under the Repeats category if you want to specify a day for your alarm, as shown in Figure 23-12.

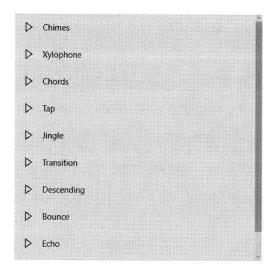

| ☐ Sunday |
| ☐ Monday |
| ☐ Tuesday |
| ☐ Wednesday |
| ☐ Thursday |
| ☐ Friday |
| ☐ Saturday |

Figure 23-12. *Defining an alarm for a specific day*

7. (Optional) Click the Chimes button under the Sound category if you want to specify a different sound for your alarm, as shown in Figure 23-13.

| ▷ Chimes |
| ▷ Xylophone |
| ▷ Chords |
| ▷ Tap |
| ▷ Jingle |
| ▷ Transition |
| ▷ Descending |
| ▷ Bounce |
| ▷ Echo |

Figure 23-13. *Defining a new chime for your alarm*

8. (Optional) Click the Snooze time button to define how many minutes can elapse before the alarm sounds again, as shown in Figure 23-14.

| 5 minutes |
| 10 minutes |
| 20 minutes |
| 30 minutes |
| 1 hour |

Figure 23-14. *Defining a snooze time*

9. Click the Save icon in the bottom right corner of the Alarms & Clock window.

Once you've set an alarm, you can modify it by clicking it. To remove an alarm, right-click it and choose Delete. To temporarily turn off an alarm, click its on/off switch to turn the switch to off.

Viewing the World Clock

If you need to call someone in another part of the world, you might want to check the local time in that area. That way you don't call them when they're sleeping. To check the local time around the world, follow these steps:

1. Open the Alarms & Clock app.

2. Click the World Clock icon.

3. Click the New (+) icon in the bottom right corner of the Alarms & Clock window.
   An Enter a location text box appears, as shown in Figure 23-15.

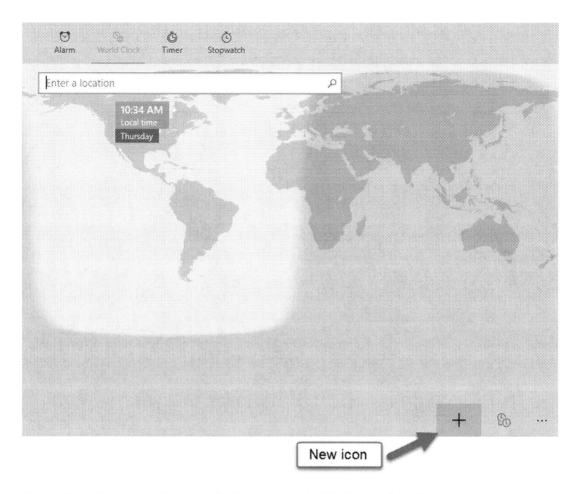

Figure 23-15. *You can type the name of a city to keep track of that location's local time*

4. Type all or part of the name of a city. A list of suggested matches appears, as shown in Figure 23-16.

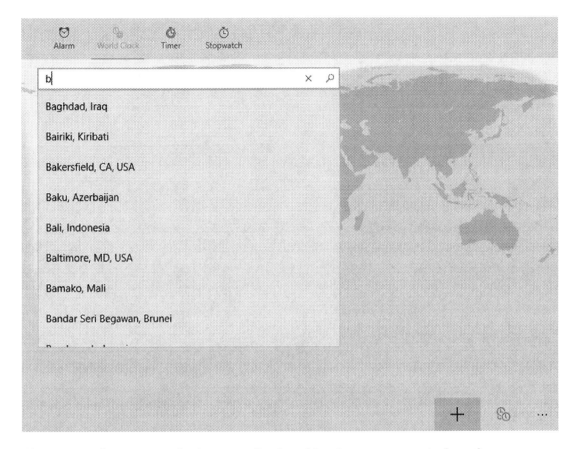

Figure 23-16. *If you type part of a city name, a list of matching city names appears to choose from*

5. Click the name of the city you want to track. The Alarms & Clock app displays your chosen city on the world map along with its local time, as shown in Figure 23-17.

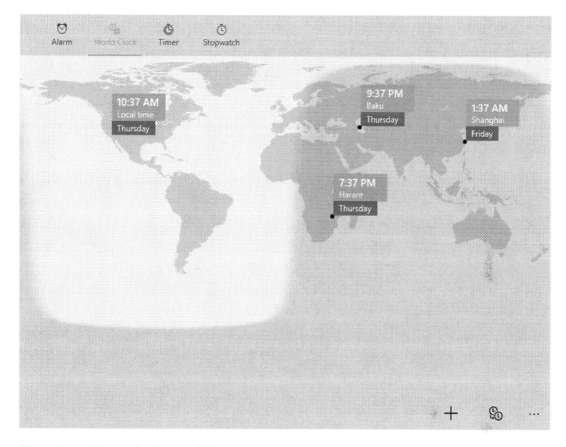

Figure 23-17. *Viewing local times of different cities around the world*

To remove a city from the world map, right-click that city and choose Delete. You can also right-click a city on the world map and choose Pin to Start to display the Alarms & Clock icon on the Start menu.

Setting a Timer

If you want to do a certain event within a fixed amount of time, such as working on a project for an hour or giving yourself 30 minutes to browse the Internet before getting back to work, you can set a timer. The timer lets you specify a time limit such as 15 minutes and then the timer counts down to zero. As soon as the timer hits zero, it alerts you that your time is up.

To set the timer, follow these steps:

1.   Open the Alarms & Clock app.

2.   Click the Timer icon. The timer window appears, as shown in Figure 23-18.

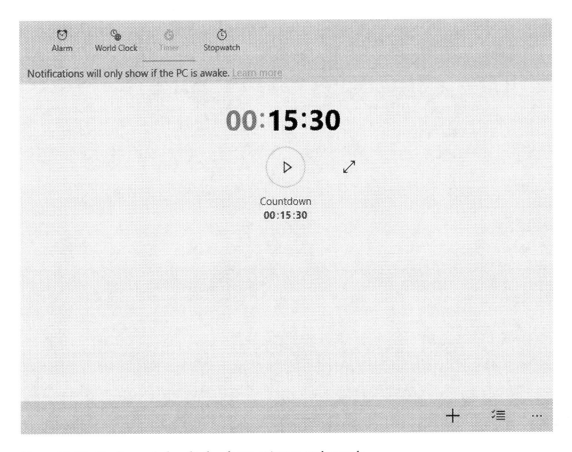

Figure 23-18. *The timer window displays hours, minutes, and seconds*

3. Click the displayed time to view the Edit Timer window, as shown in Figure 23-19.

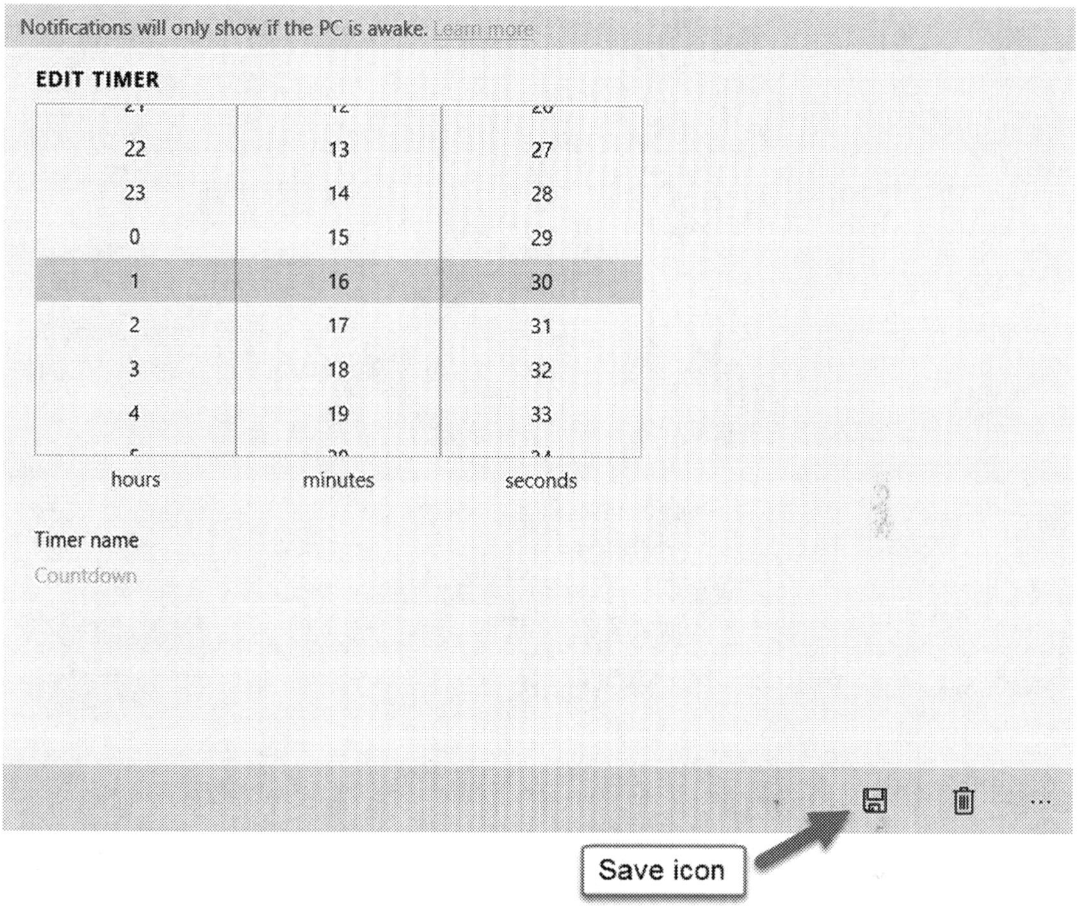

Notifications will only show if the PC is awake. Learn more

EDIT TIMER

hours	minutes	seconds
21	12	26
22	13	27
23	14	28
0	15	29
1	16	30
2	17	31
3	18	32
4	19	33
5	20	34

Timer name

Countdown

Save icon

Figure 23-19. You can set the timer for hours, minutes, and seconds

4. (Optional) Click in the Timer name text box and give your timer a descriptive name such as Exercise period or Study time.

5. Click the Save icon in the bottom right corner of the Alarms & Clock window.

You can create multiple timers so you can keep track of different timed events and even have multiple timers running at the same time. To start a timer, click the Play icon. To pause a timer, click the Pause icon, as shown in Figure 23-20. The Play/Pause icons toggle so if you click the Play icon, it toggles to the Pause icon and vice versa.

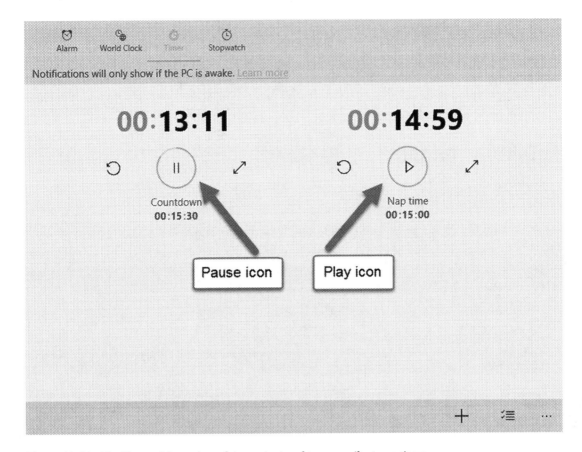

Figure 23-20. *The Play and Pause icons let you start and temporarily stop a timer*

To remove a timer, right-click the timer and choose Delete.

Timing an Event with the Stopwatch

If you want to time an event to track how long it goes on, you can use the Stopwatch feature of the Alarms & Clock app. The Stopwatch feature starts at zero and keeps counting time until you specifically click the Pause icon to stop it.

Initially, the Stopwatch displays a Play icon. Clicking the Play icon starts the stopwatch, displays the Pause icon, and also displays the Laps/Splits icon. Clicking the Pause icon then displays a Reset icon, as shown in Figure 23-21.

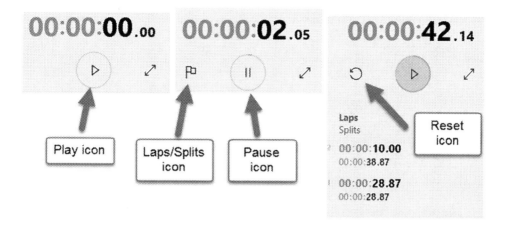

Figure 23-21. *The Play, Pause, Laps/Splits, and Reset icons*

Each icon lets you control the stopwatch in different ways:

- *Play*: Starts the stopwatch

- *Pause*: Temporarily stop the stopwatch until you click the Play icon again

- *Laps/Splits*: Lets you record different events (such as laps) while continuing to keep the stopwatch running

- *Reset*: Resets the stopwatch back to zero again

Summary

Everyone has the same amount of time every day. The huge difference is how you decide to spend your time. With the Calendar app, you can keep track of appointments during the day, week, month, or year. With the Alarms & Clock app, you can track time down to the second.

By scheduling your time, you can become more efficient and productive. More importantly, you'll find you can do more of what you like without wasting time. Time is precious, so use the Calendar and Alarms & Clock apps to keep yourself focused on whatever goals you want to achieve.

CHAPTER 24

Capturing Screenshots and Audio

In the business world, many people give presentations using programs like Microsoft PowerPoint. Usually such presentations consist of text and graphics, but sometimes you might need to capture images off your screen. Windows 10 provides two simple keyboard strokes to capture a screenshot:

- Print screen (PrtScr): Captures the entire screen
- Alt+PrtScr: Captures the currently active window

With either method, Windows 10 stores the captured screenshot in memory on the Clipboard. To access the screenshot, you need to use the Paste command, such as Ctrl+V, to paste the screenshot into another program.

If you want to save a screenshot as a .png file, you can also press the Windows key plus PrtScr. This saves the entire screen as a .png file stored in the Pictures folder.

The PrtScr key can be handy for capturing images off the screen but if you need more flexibility, Windows 10 includes two programs to capture screenshots: the Snipping Tool and the Steps Recorder. By capturing images directly off the screen, you can show people what your computer displays rather than just trying to describe it to someone.

Both the Snipping Tool and the Steps Recorder appear under the Windows Accessories category on the Start menu, as shown in Figure 24-1.

© Wallace Wang 2016

W. Wang, *Absolute Beginners Guide to Computing*, DOI 10.1007/978-1-4842-2289-8_24

Figure 24-1. *The Windows Accessories folder holds the Snipping Tool and Steps Recorder*

In addition to capturing screenshots, you can also capture audio. This lets you dictate and capture your thoughts so you can preserve them for later.

Capturing Screenshots with the Snipping Tool

When capturing a screenshot with the Snipping Tool, you can choose between four types of screen captures, as shown in Figure 24-2:

- *Free-form Snip*: Lets you drag the mouse/trackpad to define an irregular shape to capture

- *Rectangular Snip*: Captures any rectangular portion of the screen

- *Window Snip*: Captures a single open window on the screen

- *Full-screen Snip*: Captures the entire screen

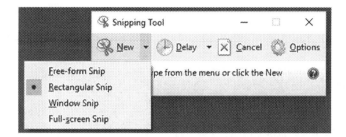

Figure 24-2. *The four ways to capture screenshots*

In addition, you can also delay a screen capture. This lets you set up the screen for a few seconds before actually capturing the image.

To capture a screenshot with the Snipping Tool, follow these steps:

1. Open the Snipping Tool program.

2. (Optional) Click the Delay button and choose a delay time such as 3 or 5 seconds, as shown in Figure 24-3.

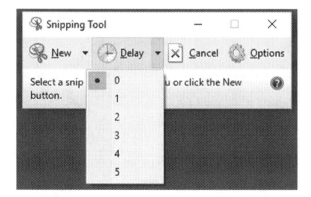

Figure 24-3. *Choosing a delay time*

3. Click the downward-pointing arrow to the right of the New button to display a pull-down menu (see Figure 24-2).

4. Click the type of screen capture you want (such as Window Snip or Full-screen Snip).

5. (Optional) If you chose Free-form Snip or Rectangular Snip, you'll need to drag the mouse to define the area you want to capture. If you chose Windows Snip, you'll need to click inside the window that you want to capture.

6. The Snipping Tool window displays the screen you've captured, as shown in Figure 24-4.

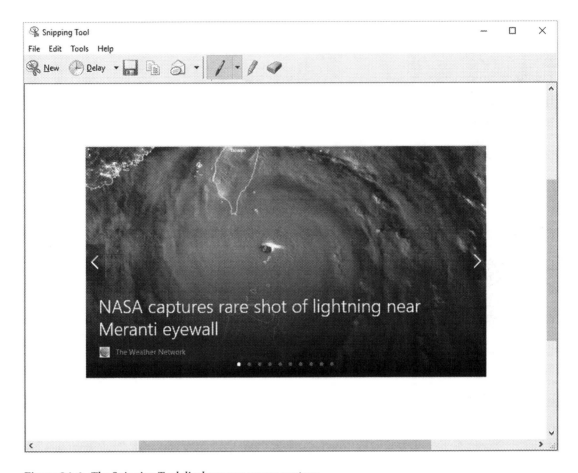

Figure 24-4. *The Snipping Tool displays your screen capture*

7.   Click the Save icon to save your screen capture. A Save As dialog box appears.

8.   Type a name for your file in the File name text box.

9.   Click in the Save as type list box and choose a file format (.png, .gif, .jpeg), as shown in Figure 24-5.

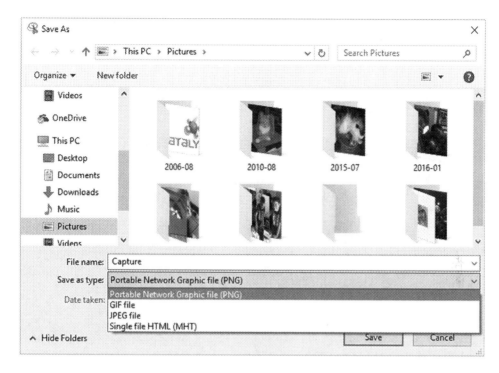

Figure 24-5. *The Save As dialog box lets you define a name and file type for your screen capture*

10. Click the Save button.

Editing Screen Captures

Once you've captured all or part of a screen, you can draw lines to point out important parts of the screen capture or highlight important areas with a yellow background using the Pen or Highlighter icons, as shown in Figure 24-6. If you make a mistake, you can erase a line or highlighted area using the Eraser icon.

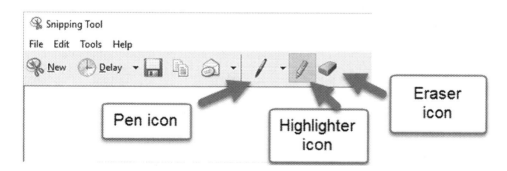

Figure 24-6. *The Pen, Highlighter, and Eraser icons*

If you click the downward-pointing arrow to the right of the Pen icon, a pull-down menu appears, letting you choose different colored pens, as shown in Figure 24-7.

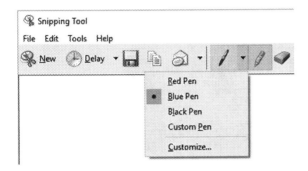

Figure 24-7. *Choosing different pen colors*

If you choose the Customize option, you can define your own pen features, as shown in Figure 24-8.

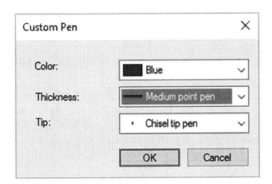

Figure 24-8. *Customizing a pen*

Once you've chosen the Pen or Highlighter icon, drag the mouse/trackpad to draw or highlight any part of your screen capture, as shown in Figure 24-9.

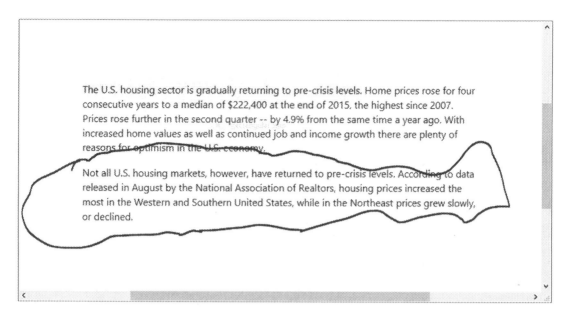

The U.S. housing sector is gradually returning to pre-crisis levels. Home prices rose for four consecutive years to a median of $222,400 at the end of 2015, the highest since 2007. Prices rose further in the second quarter -- by 4.9% from the same time a year ago. With increased home values as well as continued job and income growth there are plenty of reasons for optimism in the U.S. economy.

Not all U.S. housing markets, however, have returned to pre-crisis levels. According to data released in August by the National Association of Realtors, housing prices increased the most in the Western and Southern United States, while in the Northeast prices grew slowly, or declined.

Figure 24-9. *Drawing and highlighting with the Pen and Highlighter*

To erase a line, click the Eraser icon and click the line you want to delete. Clicking any part of a line or highlighted area erases that entire line or highlighted area.

Capturing Multiple Screenshots with the Steps Recorder

If you've ever tried to explain how something works on a computer, it can be frustrating. Rather than tell someone what to do, it's far easier to capture multiple screenshots that show people what to do. That's the purpose of the Steps Recorder.

You turn on the Steps Recorder and it captures every step you take with the keyboard and mouse/ trackpad. Now you can show someone step by step how to perform different tasks on their PC. Once you've captured these steps, the Steps Recorder saves your screenshots in a ZIP folder that you can share with others.

The actual screenshots get stored in an MHTML file that you can view in a browser. (Strangely, the Microsoft Edge browser cannot view MHTML files but the Internet Explorer browser, which also comes with Windows 10, can view and display MTHML files.)

To capture a video with the Steps Recorder program, follow these steps:

1. Open the Steps Recorder program. The Steps Recorder program appears, as shown in Figure 24-10.

Figure 24-10. *The Steps Recorder window*

2. Click the Start Record button. From this point on, the Steps Recorder saves everything you type or view.

3. (Optional) Click the Add Comment button to open a Highlight Area and Comment window where you can type a comment and click the OK button.

4. (Optional) Click the Pause Record button if you want to temporarily stop recording. The Pause Record button changes into the Resume Record button, so click the Resume Record button when you're ready to continue recording again.

5. Click the Stop Record button when you're done. Your captured screenshots appear in the Steps Recorder window, as shown in Figure 24-11.

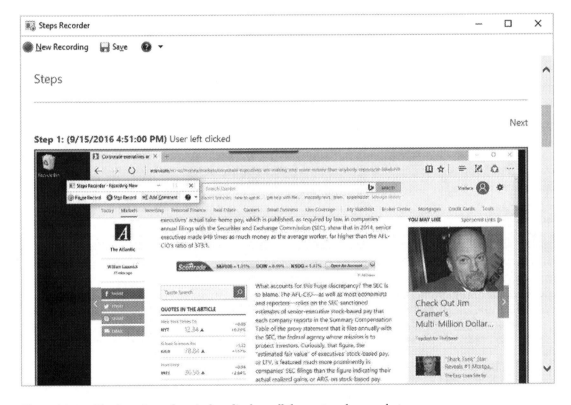

Figure 24-11. *The Steps Recorder window displays all the captured screenshots*

6. Click the Save button. A Save As dialog box appears.

7. Type a name for your file in the File name text box and then click the Save button.

The Steps Recorder saves your recorded screenshots as an MHTML file inside a ZIP folder. You can share this ZIP folder with others but they'll need to extract or unzip the MHTML file inside before they can view it.

Capturing Audio

Capturing audio can be useful when you're dictating a message. Once you've captured an audio file, you can then send it to someone else such as through an e-mail file attachment.

To capture audio, follow these steps:

1. Open the Voice Recorder program. The Voice Recorder window appears, displaying a microphone button, as shown in Figure 24-12.

Figure 24-12. *The Voice Recorder window*

2. Click the Record button and start talking. The Record button turns into a Stop button and also displays a Pause and an Add a marker icon, as shown in Figure 24-13.

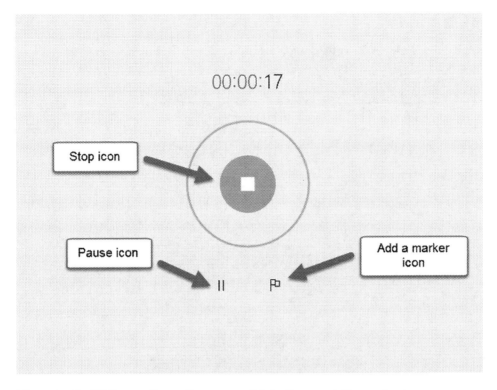

Figure 24-13. *While recording audio, you can click the Pause or Add a marker icon*

3. (Optional) Click the Add a marker icon to mark a specific point of time in your recording.

4. Click the Stop icon when you're done recording. The Voice Recorder window displays your recorded audio file with a Play button so you can hear what you recorded, as shown in Figure 24-14.

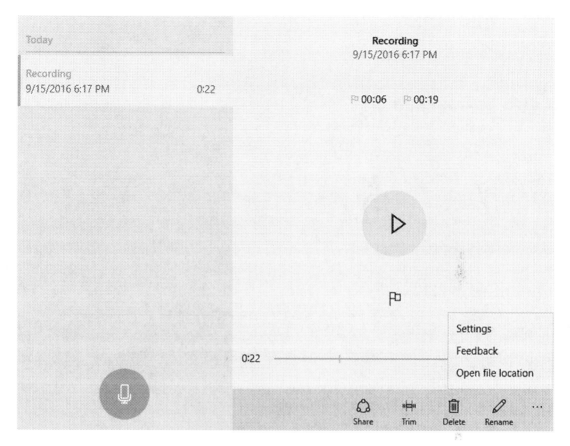

Figure 24-14. *The Voice Recorder window lets you play back or edit your recording*

5.   (Optional) Click the Trim icon. Black circular handles appear at the beginning and end of your audio file, which you can drag to trim the audio recording, as shown in Figure 24-15. Click the check mark (meaning OK) or X (meaning Cancel) icon when you're done.

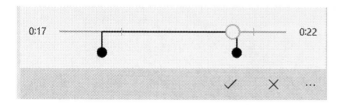

Figure 24-15. *You can trim the beginning or end of an audio recording*

6. (Optional) Click the Rename icon to display a text box where you can type a descriptive name for your audio recording, as shown in Figure 24-16. Type a descriptive name and click the Rename button.

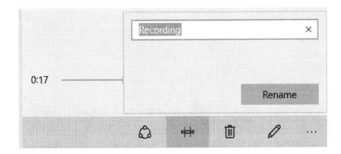

Figure 24-16. *Renaming an audio recording*

Viewing Audio Files

The Voice Recorder program saves your audio files in a Sound Recordings folder. To view your audio recordings, follow these steps:

1. Open the Voice Recorder program. The Voice Recorder window appears (see Figure 24-12).

2. Click the See more icon (it looks like three dots) in the bottom right corner of the Voice Recorder window. A menu appears (see Figure 24-14).

3. Click Open file location. The File Explorer window appears, listing all the audio files of your recordings. You can copy and share these audio files with others by e-mail or by copying them onto a flash drive.

■ **Note**   The Voice Recorder program saves audio files in the .m4a file format.

Deleting Audio Recordings

When you're done with an audio recording, you should delete it. To delete a recording, follow these steps:

1. Open the Voice Recorder program. The Voice Recorder window appears (see Figure 24-12).

2. Click the recording in the left pane that you want to delete.

3. Click the Delete icon. A dialog box appears, asking if you're sure you want to delete the recording.

4. Click the OK button.

Summary

Capturing images of your screen can help you show others how to use a computer or how to use a particular feature in a program. By capturing screenshots, you can create tutorials to show people exactly what they should see on their own computer.

If you can't type as fast as your thoughts flow, you can record your thoughts using the Voice Recorder program. This lets you turn your computer into a dictating machine so you can record your thoughts as an audio file to share them with others or to simply capture and listen to as often as you wish in the future. By capturing screenshots and audio, you have another way to communicate with others besides using ordinary text.

▓ ▓ ▓

CHAPTER 25

Using the Calculator

Oftentimes you may need to perform simple arithmetic calculations. While you could write them down on paper and calculate them yourself, you may not feel confident about your mathematical capabilities in addition to worrying about accuracy. Another quick solution might be to load a spreadsheet like Microsoft Excel, but that would likely take far more time than you'd like to take. A far simpler solution is to use the Calculator app that comes with Windows 10.

Besides letting you perform the four basic math functions like addition, subtraction, multiplication, and division, the Calculator app can also perform scientific functions such as logarithms, sine, cosine, and tangents. If you're a programmer, you can also use the Calculator app to manipulate data stored in hexadecimal or binary numbers.

Since most of the world uses the metric system but the United States does not, you may need to convert kilometers into miles or meters into feet. The Calculator app can make conversions between different measurement units easy, fast, and accurate.

Whenever you need to perform quick calculations that are too difficult to calculate by hand, use the Calculator app instead.

Changing the Calculator

Like most apps, you can start the Calculator app from the Start menu. Once you've launched the Calculator app, you'll see an icon that displays three horizontal lines (often referred to as a "hamburger" icon because it looks like two buns sandwiching a meat patty in the middle), as shown in Figure 25-1.

© Wallace Wang 2016

W. Wang, *Absolute Beginners Guide to Computing*, DOI 10.1007/978-1-4842-2289-8_25

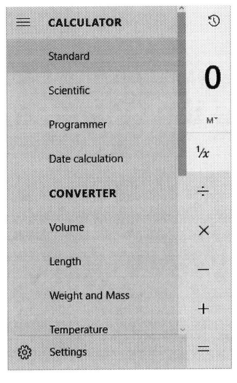

Figure 25-1. *The Calculator window*

Clicking this icon displays a menu that lets you choose the calculator you want to use such as:

- *Standard*: Offers the four common math functions (subtraction, addition, multiplication, and division)

- *Scientific*: Offers additional math functions such as square root, cosine, tangent, and logarithms

- *Programmer*: Offers calculations and conversions between decimal, hexadecimal, octal, and binary numbers

- *Date calculation*: Calculates the number of days between two dates

In addition, the Calculator app can also perform conversions among volume, length, area, and weight measurement units.

To change the type of calculator, follow these steps:

1. Open the Calculator app.

2. Click the icon displaying three horizontal lines. A menu appears (see Figure 24-1).

3. Click the type of calculator you want to use such as Standard or Scientific.

■ **Note**   You can open two or more Calculator windows by repetitively launching the Calculator app from the Start menu. That way you can have two or more different calculators on the screen at the same time, such as a Scientific and Standard calculators, side by side.

To change the size of the calculator, follow these steps:

1. Move the pointer over the edge or corner of the Calculator window until the pointer turns into a two-way pointing arrow.

2. Drag the mouse/trackpad to resize the Calculator window.

Using the Calculator

Most people understand the basics to using a calculator. Type in a number, choose a mathematical function such as addition or division, type in a second number, and click the equals (=) sign key to get the answer. For simple calculations involving two numbers, this process is straightforward, but if you need to calculate multiple numbers that involve multiple mathematical functions, you may need extra help.

Two often overlooked features that can help you use the Calculator app with less frustration are the way it can clear numbers and the way it can store numbers in memory.

Clearing Numbers

If you start typing a long equation and suddenly type the wrong number, you might have to start all over again. Since this can be annoying, the Calculator app offers three ways to clear a mistyped number, as shown in Figure 25-2:

- *Backspace*: Deletes the last typed number

- *C (Clear)*: Clears all numbers

- *CE (Clear Entry)*: Clears the last number typed in

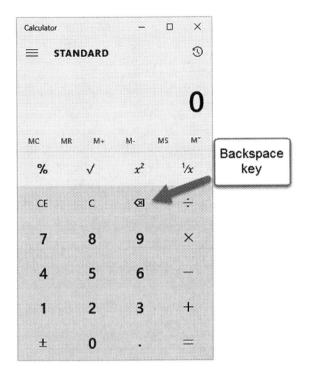

Figure 25-2. *The C, CE, and Backspace keys*

When you want to wipe out everything and start a new calculation, click the C (Clear) key.

When you're typing a number with multiple digits and mistakenly type a wrong digit (such as typing 935 instead of 937), click the Backspace key to delete the last typed number.

When you typed in a completely wrong number, you could click the Backspace key multiple times, but it's far faster to click the CE (Clear Entry) key instead.

To see how these different keys work, try the following exercise:

1. Open the Calculator app.

2. Type 123.

3. Click the Backspace key. Notice that the number changes from 123 to 12.

4. Click the + key.

5. Type 8. This would normally add 12 + 8 and calculate 20 if you pressed the = key next.

6. Click the CE key. This clears the 8 you just typed.

7. Type 3 and click the = key to see the results of 12 + 3, which is 15.

8. Click the C key to clear everything.

Storing Numbers in Memory

When you need to do multiple calculations, you probably don't want to retype one calculation's answer to use in a second calculation. Not only is this slow and inconvenient, but it could also be inaccurate if you mistype the number.

Instead, it's far easier to store a number in memory temporarily and then recall that number later. To use memory to store numbers, the Calculator app offers six keys:

- *MC (Memory Clear)*: Clears all numbers stored in memory

- *MR (Memory Recall)*: Retrieves a number stored in memory

- *M+ (Add)*: Adds a number to any other numbers stored in memory

- *M- (Remove)*: Removes a number stored in memory

- *MS (Save)*: Saves numbers stored in memory

- *M*: Lists all numbers stored in memory

To see how the different memory keys work, try the following exercise:

1. Open the Calculator app.

2. Type 12.

3. Click the M+ key to add the number to memory.

4. Type 3.

5. Click the M+ key to add 3 to the current number stored in memory, which is 12 so the total result should be 15.

6. Click the M key to view the contents of memory to verify that it holds 15, as shown in Figure 25-3.

7. Click the M key again and then type 2.4.

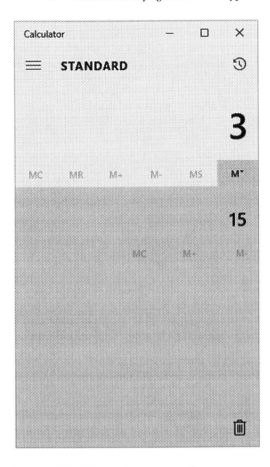

Figure 25-3. *Viewing the contents of memory*

8. Click the MS key. This saves the number 2.4 without modifying any other values in memory.

9. Click the M key to view the contents of memory. Notice that the memory now contains two values: 15 and 2.4.

10. Click the M key again.

11. Click the M- key.

12. Click the M key to view the contents of memory. Notice that the memory has now cleared the first value (2.4) and only displays the second value (15).

13. Click the M key again.

14. Click the MC key.

15. Click the M key to view the contents of memory. Notice that all the values have been cleared from memory.

By storing numbers in memory, you can temporarily save values created by calculations and then retrieve them to use in other calculations.

Viewing the Calculator History

When you type a mathematical function such as addition or division and click the equals sign (=) key, the Calculator app displays your calculation in its history list. By reviewing this history list, you can make sure you typed your calculations correctly (typing the right number and mathematical function).

To view the history list, click the History icon, as shown in Figure 25-4.

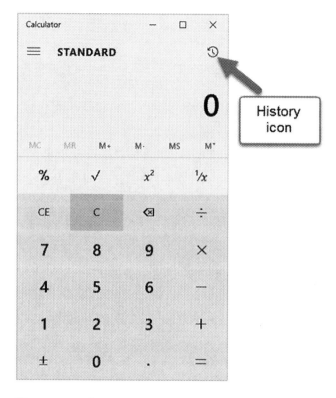

Figure 25-4. The History icon

Each time you perform a calculation, that calculation gets added to the history list, as shown in Figure 25-5. If the history list gets too long, a vertical scroll bar appears so you can scroll up and down and view all the calculations stored in the history list.

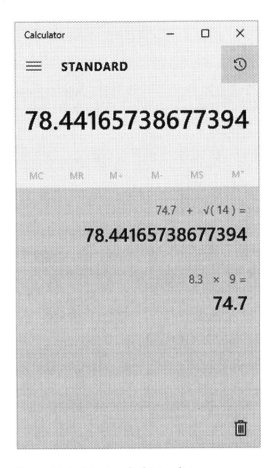

Figure 25-5. *Viewing the history list*

To clear the history list, follow these steps:

1. Click the History icon to display the history list.

2. Click the Delete icon (it looks like a trash can). The history list disappears.

Converting Units

If you need to convert measurement units, you probably don't want to calculate it by hand. Not only would you have to look up the right formula, but you'll also have to do the actual mathematical calculation. Since converting between different measurement units can be so cumbersome, the Calculator app provides several conversions for length, area volume, and other common types of measurements.

When converting measurement units, you need to define two items:

- The value and measurement unit you currently know

- The measurement unit you want to convert to

To convert the value of one measurement unit into another, follow these steps:

1. Open the Calculator app.

2. Click the three horizontal line icon in the upper left corner of the Calculator window. A menu appears (see Figure 25-1).

3. Click the type of measurement unit you want to convert such as temperature, speed, or volume. The Calculator app displays two different measurement units.

4. Click the downward-pointing arrow of the top measurement unit. A pull-down menu appears listing different measurement units, as shown in Figure 25-6.

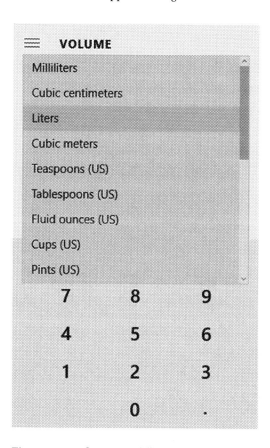

Figure 25-6. *Choosing a different measurement unit*

5. Repeat step 4 for the bottom measurement unit.

6. Click the 0 and type the value you currently know such as 7 liters. The Calculator app displays the equivalent value in the other measurement unit, as shown in Figure 25-7. You can type in either the top or bottom measurement unit.

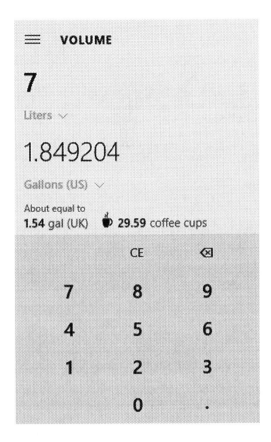

Figure 25-7. *Converting between measurement units*

7.   Click the CE key to clear your typed value and start with 0 again.

Summary

The Calculator app can be handy for performing a variety of short mathematical calculations. Most people will likely use the Standard calculator that displays the four common math functions (addition, subtraction, multiplication, and division), but if you need more specialized mathematical functions, you can switch to the Scientific or Programmer calculator.

Besides allowing you perform various mathematical calculations, the Calculator app can also convert between two different measurement units such as inches to centimeters or liters to quarts. By using these conversion features, you'll never have to look up conversion formulas again.

The Calculator app is designed for fast and short calculations. Use it whenever you'd rather let your computer worry about calculating numeric results accurately so you don't have to do it yourself.

PART VI

■ ■ ■

Useful Computer Information

A surprisingly large amount of information about using a computer often gets passed around by word of mouth but rarely printed in a book. That's why this part of the book includes useful information that more experienced Windows 10 users often know. By reading this part of the book, you'll learn what experienced Windows 10 users have known for years.

First, you'll learn about simple ways to back up your data so you'll never risk losing it again.

Second, you'll learn how to protect your computer from malware. By knowing how to identify various types of threats, you can learn to protect your computer as much as possible.

Third, you'll need to regularly maintain your computer to keep it running in optimum condition. By freeing up disk space or defragmenting your hard drive, you can squeeze a little extra performance out of your computer and make it work just a little bit faster than before.

By reading this part of the book, you'll learn hidden secrets that have taken most people years to learn on their own.

CHAPTER 26

Backing Up Your Data

Computers are like cars because they only work if you properly maintain them. While it's nice to think that your computer will just work all the time whenever you need it, the reality is that your computer may eventually fail if you don't take care of it. Perhaps the most important way to maintain your computer and all your critical data is to maintain your hard disk.

Older computers have physical hard disks, while newer models use solid-state drives that act like USB flash drives in that they have no moving parts. While solid-state drives are much faster than mechanical hard drives, they can be prone to failure too. One of the most common ways disks can fail is by corrupting or losing data.

Losing or corrupting data may never happen to you, but it's not a surprise when it does occur. That's because Windows 10 isn't perfect and it's possible that, through no fault of your own, Windows 10 will simply fail to correctly save a file in the right location, overriding or destroying other files you've saved.

Ultimately maintaining your disk is really about protecting your files. Two common ways you might lose a file is through deleting it by mistake or having Windows 10 corrupt your file somehow.

Retrieving Deleted Files

When you delete a file, Windows 10 doesn't physically erase that file. Instead, it stores that file in the Recycle Bin folder. As long as a file appears in the Recycle Bin folder, you'll be able to retrieve it later.

That means if you delete a file today and peek in your Recycle Bin folder five years later, you'll be able to find your file safe and sound. The only way you ever risk losing a file is if you dump it in the Recycle Bin folder and then empty the Recycle Bin folder.

The moment you empty the Recycle Bin folder, Windows 10 pretends that file never existed. However, that file still physically exists on your hard disk. That means if you buy special file recovery software, you may still be able to retrieve previously deleted files. However, the longer you wait to retrieve a deleted file, the lower your chances of actually recovering it.

© Wallace Wang 2016
W. Wang, *Absolute Beginners Guide to Computing*, DOI 10.1007/978-1-4842-2289-8_26

If you haven't emptied the Recycle Bin folder, you can recover deleted files by following these steps:

1. Right-click the Recycle Bin icon (looks like a trash can) on the Desktop. A pop-up menu appears, as shown in Figure 26-1.

Figure 26-1. *Right-clicking the Recycle Bin icon displays a pop-up menu*

2. Choose Open. A File Explorer window appears, listing all the deleted files still in the Recycle Bin folder.

3. Click the file you want to retrieve. (If you hold down the Control key, you can click and select multiple files.)

4. Click the Restore the selected items (or the Restore all items) button, as shown in Figure 26-2.

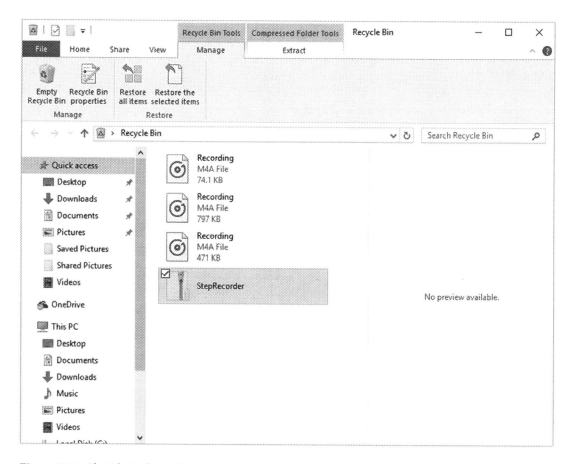

Figure 26-2. The File Explorer displays a special Recycle Bin Tools tab when viewing the Recycle Bin folder

Using File History

Retrieving files from the Recycle Bin folder works only as long as you don't empty the Recycle Bin folder. The moment you empty the Recycle Bin folder, you won't be able to retrieve any previously deleted files without buying special file recovery software.

Of course, you have to empty your Recycle Bin folder periodically or else all your deleted files will take up space until you might have so many deleted files on your computer that you can't store anything else. That's why you need to empty the Recycle Bin folder periodically, but only after you're sure you will never need any of those deleted files again.

If you want the option of retrieving deleted files in the future, then another solution is to use the File History program, which is a free backup program included with Windows 10.

To use File History, you need an external hard disk that's connected to your computer, typically through a USB cable. The idea is to save copies of your crucial files on the external hard disk so if anything happens to your computer, you'll still have your important files saved on the external hard disk.

▨ **Note**   For even greater security, store your critical files through your OneDrive account. That way if your house or office burns down and destroys both your computer and external hard disk, your important files will still be safe.

Once you have an external hard disk, you need to configure File History to work with that external hard disk. Ideally, you should only use that external hard disk solely for backing up your computer with File History.

Configuring an External Hard Disk with File History

Once you have an external hard disk connected to your computer, you need to configure File History to work with that external hard disk.

To configure a hard disk to work with File History, connect an external hard disk to your computer and then follow these steps:

1. Click the Windows icon. The Start menu appears.

2. Click Settings. The Settings window appears.

3. Click Update & security. The Update & security window.

4. Click Backup. The File History settings appear in the right pane, as shown in Figure 26-3.

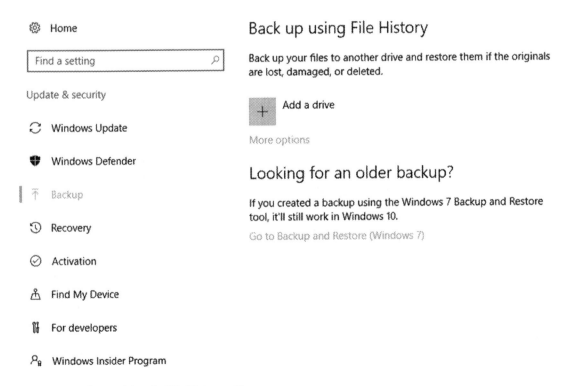

Figure 26-3. Customizing the File History settings

5. Click + Add a drive.

6. Click the Select Backup Disk button. A window appears, listing all available hard disks you can use.

7. Click a drive to use. The File History window now displays an Automatically back up my files switch, as shown in Figure 26-4.

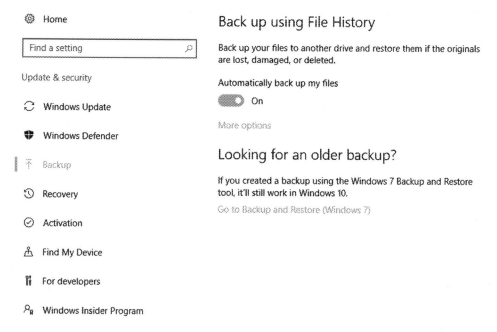

Figure 26-4. *The File History window lets you choose whether to automatically back up your files*

8. Click More options. The File History window displays various options you can choose such as how often to back up your files and which folders to back up, as shown in Figure 26-5.

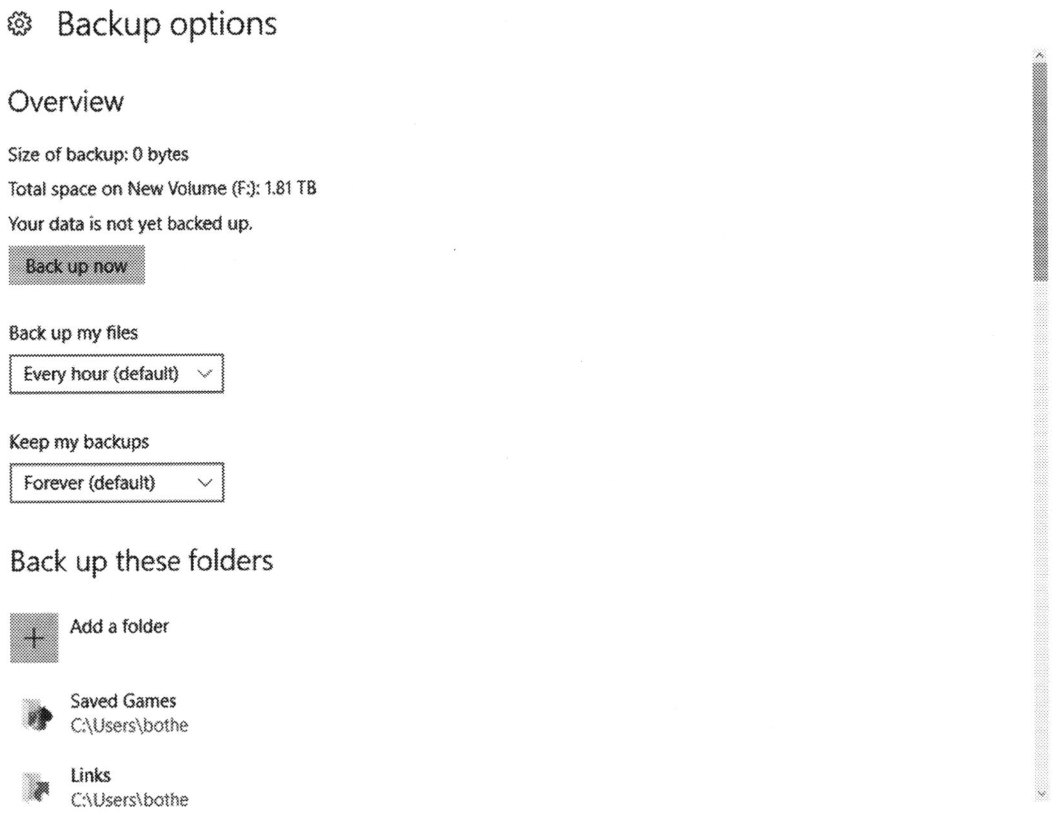

⚙ Backup options

Overview

Size of backup: 0 bytes

Total space on New Volume (F:): 1.81 TB

Your data is not yet backed up.

Back up now

Back up my files

| Every hour (default) ∨ |

Keep my backups

| Forever (default) ∨ |

Back up these folders

+ Add a folder

Saved Games
C:\Users\bothe

Links
C:\Users\bothe

Figure 26-5. *You can define a backup frequency along with the folders to back up*

9. (Optional) Click the Back up my files list box and choose how often you want to back up your files such as every hour or every 30 minutes.

10. (Optional) Click the Keep my backups list box and choose how long you want File History to save your backups, such as Forever or 2 years.

11. (Optional) Click a folder that you do not want to back up and click the Remove button.

12. (Optional) Click the + Add folder button and choose a folder to back up.

13. Click the Backup now button to back up your chosen folders.

Retrieving Deleted Files with File History

The larger the external hard disk, the more backups File History can save. Because of this, you want the largest external hard disk you can afford. If you get a small external hard disk, File History won't be able to store backups from too far in the past. If you get a large external hard disk, you'll be able to retrieve files from longer in the past such as several months or even several years ago.

The moment you realize you need a file that you once had, you don't have to panic or frantically search through your computer to see if another copy still exists. Instead, you can just load File History, go back to a specific time in the past when you know the file existed, and then retrieve the file.

To retrieve a file saved by File History, follow these steps:

1. Open the File Explorer program.

2. Click the folder that is used to contain the deleted file you want to retrieve.

3. Click the Home tab and click the History icon, as shown in Figure 26-6. A History window appears, showing the contents of that folder.

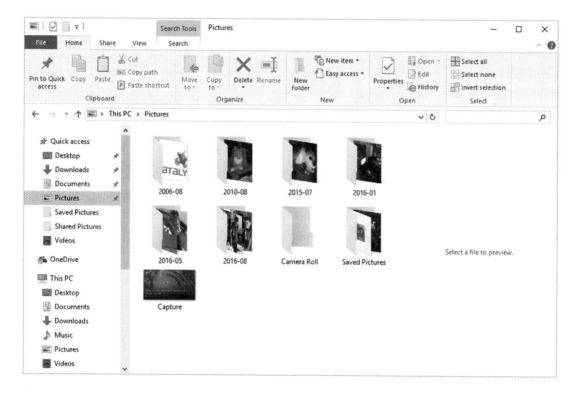

Figure 26-6. *The History icon appears on the Home tab*

4. Click the Previous version (Ctrl+Left arrow) or the Next version (Ctrl+Right arrow) icon to view the different backups saved by File History until you find the file you want to retrieve, as shown in Figure 26-7.

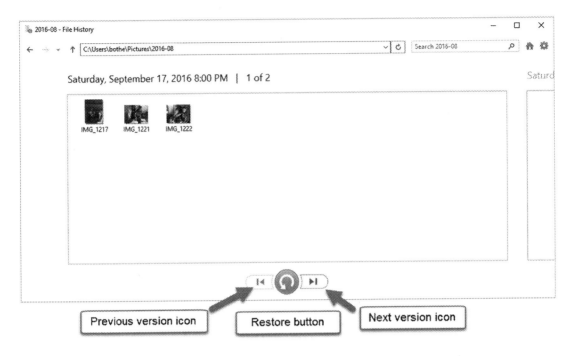

Figure 26-7. Reviewing the File History of a folder

5.   Click the file you want to retrieve and click the Restore button. File History retrieves your file and displays it in the File Explorer window.

Using Restore Points

Computers aren't perfect. It's entirely possible to use your computer one day and everything works just fine. Then the next day, the computer refuses to work at all. One solution is to exhaustively troubleshoot your computer to see what might have caused the problem, but if you're not familiar with computers, this approach is like telling the average person to just rebuild their car engine the next time their car won't start.

A far simpler solution is to create a restore point. Essentially a restore point freezes the past when your computer was working just fine. Now if something goes wrong with your computer, you can just revert to an earlier restore point when your computer was working. Restore points capture working configurations of your computer so you can return back to the past at any time.

Creating a Restore Point

You should always capture restore points right before you change anything such as installing a new program. That way if the latest changes to your computer somehow foul it up completely, you can go back to a restore point right before you made any changes.

To create a restore point, follow these steps:

1. Click in the Search text box in the Taskbar and type restore point. A menu appears, listing Create a restore point as an option, as shown in Figure 26-8.

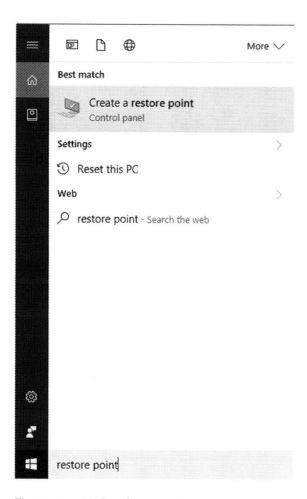

Figure 26-8. Finding the Restore Point program

2. Click Create a restore point in the menu. A System Properties dialog box appears, as shown in Figure 26-9.

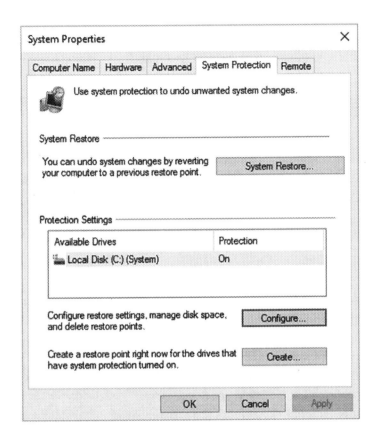

Figure 26-9. *The System Properties dialog box*

3. Click the Configure button. A Restore Settings window appears, as shown in Figure 26-10.

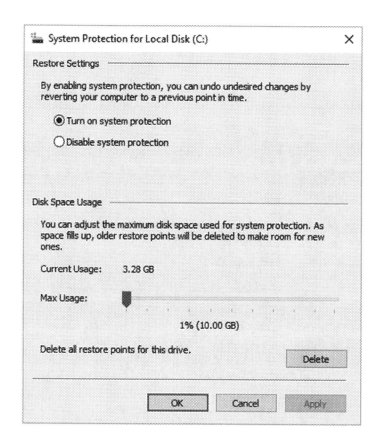

Figure 26-10. *Configuring restore settings*

4. Make sure the Turn on system protection radio button is selected and then click the OK button.

5. Click the Create button. A System Protection dialog box appears, asking for a descriptive name for your restore point, as shown in Figure 26-11.

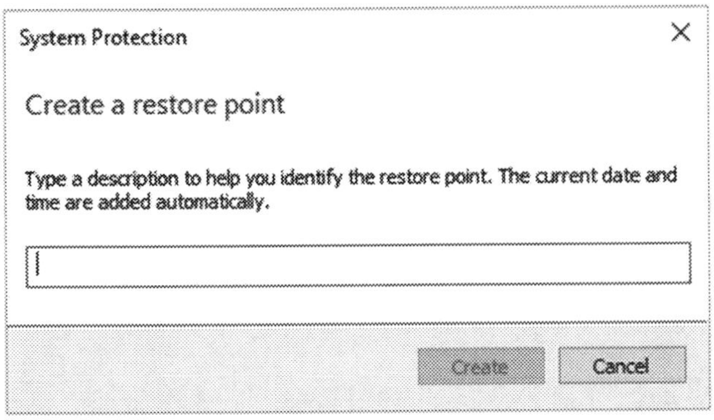

Figure 26-11. *Naming a restore point*

6. Type a descriptive name for your restore point such as a date, and click the Create button. A dialog box appears to let you know when the creation of the restore point is done.

7. Click the Close button to make this dialog box disappear.

Restoring a Restore Point

Once you've created at least one restore point, you can always return back to that restore point at any time. Just remember that any changes you might have made since creating that restore point, such as installing new programs, will be wiped out. So if you created a restore point and then installed Microsoft Office, returning to that restore point will create a working version of Windows 10 but without Microsoft Office installed.

To return to a restore point, follow these steps:

1. Click in the Search text box in the Taskbar and type restore point. A menu appears, listing Create a restore point as an option (see Figure 26-8).

2. Click Create a restore point in the menu. A System Properties dialog box appears (see Figure 26-9).

3. Click the System Restore button. A System Restore windows appears, as shown in Figure 26-12.

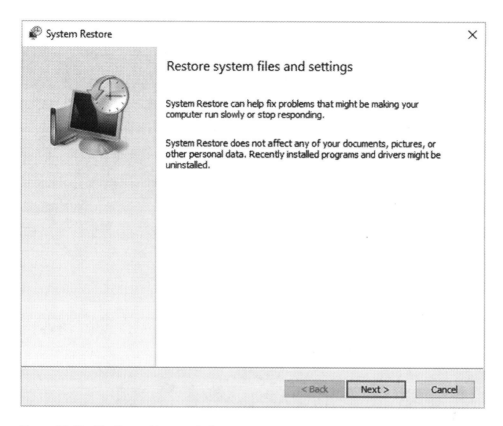

Figure 26-12. *The System Restore window*

4. Click the Next button. Another window appears, listing all your saved restore points, as shown in Figure 26-13.

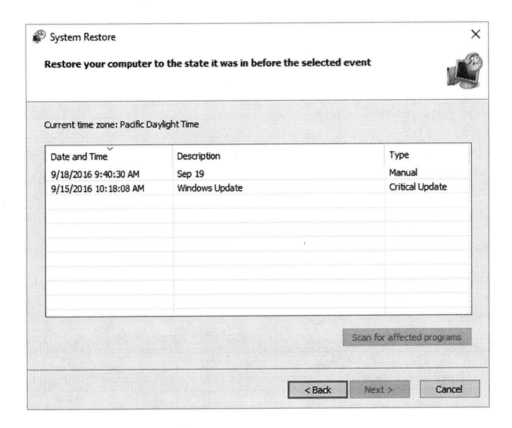

Figure 26-13. *Listing restore points*

5. Click a restore point and click the Next button. A confirmation window appears, as shown in Figure 26-14.

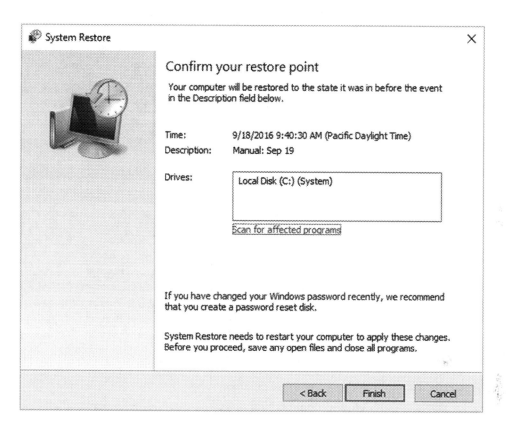

Figure 26-14. *Returning back to a restore point*

6. Click the Finish button.

Deleting a Restore Point

Each time you create a restore point, it takes up space. Eventually you'll want to wipe out all your restore points and start creating new ones. By deleting old restore points, you can free up space on your hard drive. By saving new restore points, you can capture the latest configuration of your computer.

To delete a restore point, follow these steps:

1. Click in the Search text box in the Taskbar and type restore point. A menu appears, listing Create a restore point as an option (see Figure 26-8).

2. Click on Create a restore point in the menu. A System Properties dialog box appears (see Figure 26-9).

3. Click the Configure button. A Restore Settings dialog box appears (see Figure 26-10).

4. Click the Delete button. A confirmation dialog box appears, asking if you're sure you want to delete all restore points.

5. Click the Continue button.

Create a Recovery Drive

Restore points work fine as long as you can start Windows 10 on your computer. However, sometimes your computer may foul itself up so badly that it won't even start. If that happens, then all the data on your hard drive may still exist, but remain out of your reach.

Before this happens to you, take time to create a recovery drive. The purpose of a recovery drive is to provide a way to start your computer if it fails to run correctly from your hard disk. From the recovery drive you can reinstall Windows and (hopefully) get your computer running so you can retrieve critical files and/ or return to an earlier restore point when Windows 10 was actually working right.

To create a recovery drive, you'll need a USB flash drive that has 4GB or more free space. Then to create a recovery drive, follow these steps:

1. Insert a 4GB or higher USB flash drive into the USB port of your computer. Make sure there are no important files on this USB flash drive because creating a recovery drive will delete any files stored on it.

2. Click the Windows icon and click Create USB Recovery under the Windows System category in the Start menu, as shown in Figure 26-15. A User Account Control dialog box appears, asking if you want to allow the Recovery Media Creator program to make changes to your computer.

Figure 26-15. *Finding the Create USB Recovery program on the Start menu*

3.   Click the Yes button. A Recovery Drive window appears, as shown in Figure 26-16.

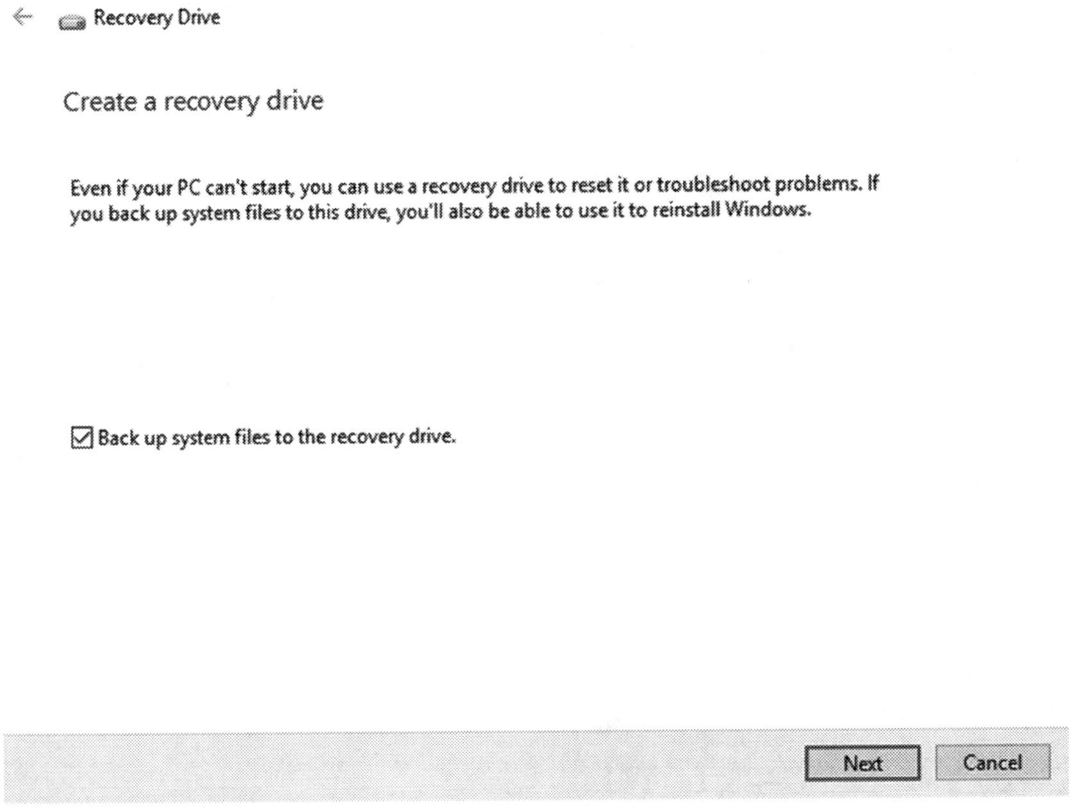

← 🖴 Recovery Drive

Create a recovery drive

Even if your PC can't start, you can use a recovery drive to reset it or troubleshoot problems. If
you back up system files to this drive, you'll also be able to use it to reinstall Windows.

☑ Back up system files to the recovery drive.

Next   Cancel

Figure 26-16. *The Disk Utility program displays additional details on what it has done*

4. Click the Next button. Another window appears, asking you to choose the USB drive to use, as shown in Figure 26-17.

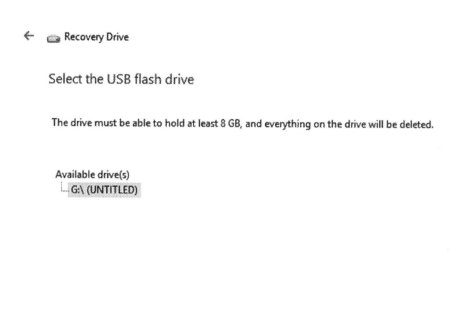

← 🖴 Recovery Drive

Select the USB flash drive

The drive must be able to hold at least 8 GB, and everything on the drive will be deleted.

Available drive(s)
  └ G:\ (UNTITLED)

Next   Cancel

Figure 26-17. *Choosing a USB drive to use*

5. Click the USB drive you want to use and click the Next button. A warning appears, letting you know that everything on the USB drive will be deleted, as shown in Figure 26-18.

 ←   Recovery Drive

Create the recovery drive

⚠ Everything on the drive will be deleted. If you have any personal files on this drive, make sure you've backed up the files.

Figure 26-18. You must verify that you want to use the USB drive solely as a recovery drive

6. Click the Create button.

Once you have created a recovery drive, you can boot up from that recovery drive later. When you first turn on a computer, you can press a key such as F1 or F10 to display a menu that lets you choose which drives to boot up from. Normally you always want to boot from the hard disk, but you can temporarily change the settings to boot from the USB recovery drive instead.

Once you've booted from the USB recovery drive, you can reinstall Windows and (hopefully) access your critical files again.

Summary

The two most common ways to lose files is through user error or computer failure. If you accidentally delete a file, you might be able to retrieve it from the Recycle Bin folder, provided you didn't empty the Recycle Bin folder.

If you did empty the Recycle Bin folder and you still need to retrieve a lost file, you might still be able to recover that file if you had connected an external hard disk to your computer and used the File History backup program.

With File History, you can retrieve files from days, weeks, months, or even years ago. Of course, File History can only protect your files if you set it up long before you actually need it.

To make sure you can use your computer if it develops an issue, create restore points. A restore point can literally turn back time to a point where your computer was working perfectly.

To guard against the possibility that you may not be able to boot up your computer at all, take the time now to make a USB recovery drive.

All of these different ways to protect your data will only work if you make a conscious effort to use them. So don't delay. Protect your data now before it's too late.

CHAPTER 27

▓ ▓ ▓

Protecting Against Malware

Malware is a category of software known as malicious software or viruses. Most malware can only attack specific operating systems. Since Windows PCs are still the most common computers in the world, most malware targets Microsoft Windows.

There are two ways to guard against malware. The most common way is to rely on technological solutions such as anti-virus software. Unfortunately, technological solutions can never provide 100 percent protection. That's because the weakest link in any computer's security is always the user.

If users fail to turn on or use technological solutions, then those technological solutions are useless. Even worse, users can often be tricked into installing malware. Ultimately, no amount of technological solutions can ever protect your computer, so that's why you also need a basic understanding of computer security so you don't accidentally infect your computer.

Malware can only infect your computer if it can access it. Some of the ways malware can get into a computer include:

- Sticking an infected USB flash drive into the USB port of your computer

- Downloading an infected file attachment sent to you by e-mail

- Visiting a malicious web site

Ultimately the best defense against malware is knowing the types of threats that could attack your computer and avoiding falling prey to their traps.

Password Protecting a Computer

The easiest way for malware to get on your computer is if a malicious person deliberately installs it on your computer. Beyond physically protecting your computer behind a locked door, the next best way to block access to your computer is to password protect it. When you first set up your computer, you have to choose a password, but you can always change it later.

▓ **Note**   The best passwords contain random letters, numbers, and symbols.

Windows 10 offers three ways to password protect your computer:

- Passwords

- PIN

- Picture

© Wallace Wang 2016
W. Wang, *Absolute Beginners Guide to Computing*, DOI 10.1007/978-1-4842-2289-8_27

A password consists of a string of characters that should be hard for someone to guess such as gd12@ptst92.

A PIN (Personal Identification Number) consists of a string of digits such as 3928. PINs must be at least four digits long but there is no maximum length, although the longer the PIN, the harder it will be to type correctly.

A Picture lets you display a picture on the screen and then create unique gestures on a touch screen (provided your computer has one) to unlock your computer.

To change the password settings on your computer, follow these steps:

1. Click the Windows icon. The Start menu appears.

2. Click Settings. The Settings window appears.

3. Click Accounts.

4. Click Sign-in options, as shown in Figure 27-1.

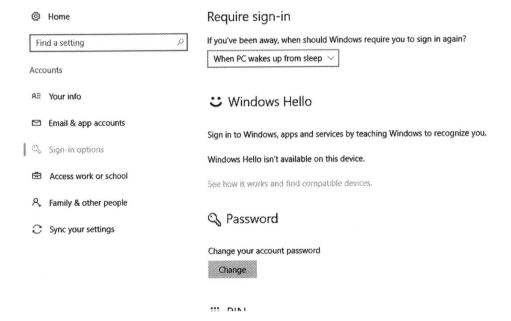

Figure 27-1. *The Sign-in options*

5. (Optional) Click the Require sign-in list box and choose one of the following:

- Never (not recommended)

- When PC wakes up from sleep (default)

6. Choose whether to use a password, PIN, or picture and follow the steps in the corresponding sections below.

Passwords are familiar to most people, but far too many people choose simple, easy to remember passwords that are also easy for someone to guess.

PINs are harder for someone to guess but may not be as easy to remember, especially if you create a long PIN consisting of several digits.

Pictures are much more secure than passwords or PINs because it's harder to guess both the picture to use and the gestures to make on them, but they can also be more cumbersome to use regularly.

▓ **Note** Before allowing you to change any password settings, Windows 10 may ask you to verify an e-mail address to send you a code. You will need to type this code in before you'll be able to modify password settings. This is to verify that someone else isn't trying to change your password settings without your knowledge.

Defining a Password

If you plan to use a password, choose one that consists of upper and lower case letters, plus numbers and symbols to make it harder to guess. To define a password, follow these steps:

1. Follow steps 1-6 in the "Password Protecting a Computer" section to change password settings.

2. Click the Change button under the Password category. A window appears, asking you to verify your current password. (This prevents someone else from changing your password without your knowledge.)

3. Type your current password and click the Sign in button. A new window appears, asking you to type in the new password twice, as shown in Figure 27-2.

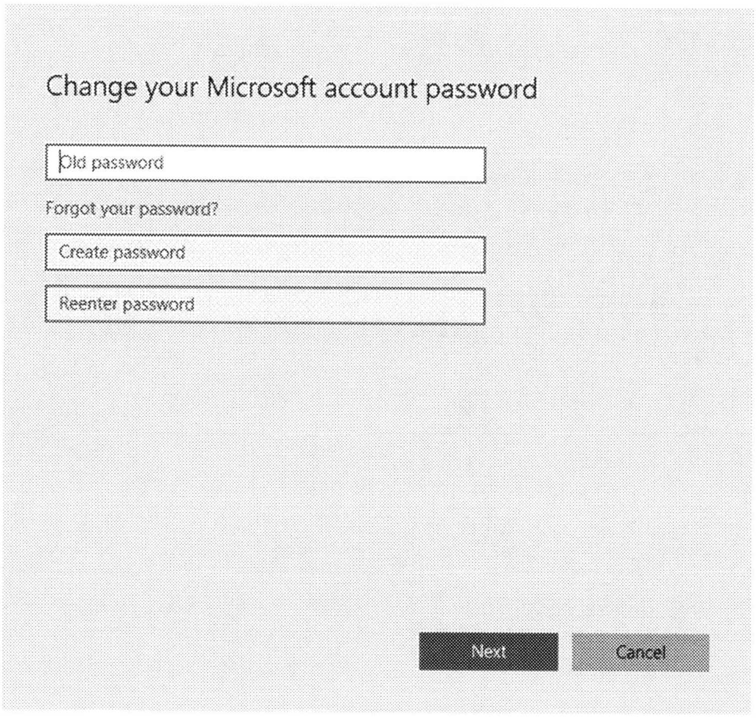

Change your Microsoft account password

Old password

Forgot your password?

Create password

Reenter password

Next   Cancel

Figure 27-2. Defining a new password

467

Defining a PIN

Most people choose passwords that consist of words, which mean they're easy to remember but also easy to guess. By using a PIN, you can choose a numeric code to unlock your computer. Just make sure you choose random numbers rather than a series of easily guessed PINs such as 1234 or 99999. To define a PIN, follow these steps:

1. Follow steps 1-6 in the "Password Protecting a Computer" section to change password settings.

2. Click the Add button under the PIN category. A Set up a PIN window appears, asking you to type a PIN that's at least four digits long, as shown in Figure 27-3.

Figure 27-3. *Defining a new password*

3. Type a PIN twice and click the OK button.

Defining a Picture Password

If your computer has a touch screen, you can choose to display a picture that requires a unique gesture swiped across the image to unlock the computer. Picture passwords are more secure than passwords or PINS because they're harder to guess. (Just be careful that someone doesn't watch your gestures over your shoulder and see the gestures needed to unlock the computer.)

The three types of accepted gestures for a picture password are:

- Circles

- Straight lines

- Taps

If you had a picture of a dog, you might define a circle gesture around the dog's right eye, a straight line gesture between its two eyes, and a tap on its nose.

▓ **Note**   Taps are the easiest gestures for Windows 10 to recognize while circles can be the trickiest to perform consistently.

To define a picture password, follow these steps:

1. Follow steps 1-6 in the "Password Protecting a Computer" section to change password settings.

2. Click the Add button under the PIN category. A dialog box appears, asking to verify your password.

3. Type your password and click OK. A Picture password window appears, as shown in Figure 27-4.

Figure 27-4. Defining a picture password

4. Click the Choose picture button. An Open dialog box appears, letting you choose any image stored on your computer. The Picture password window displays your chosen picture, as shown in Figure 27-5.

Figure 27-5. *Previewing a picture to use*

5. (Optional) Drag the picture on the screen until it's positioned the way you like in the window.

6. Click the Use this picture button. The Picture password window asks you to define three gestures (circle, straight line, or tap), as shown in Figure 27-6. The position and order of the gestures are important since you must do them in the right order and location on the picture.

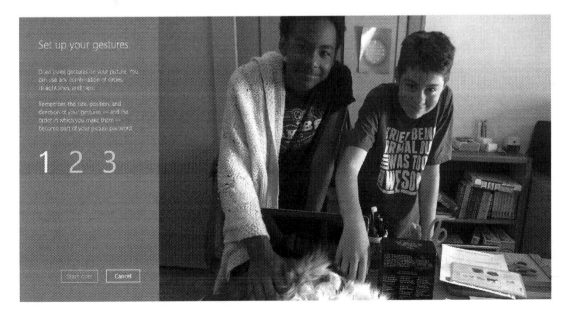

Figure 27-6. *Defining three gestures for a picture password*

7. Define three gestures. You'll need to do this a second time to confirm you can do the right gestures in the right order.

8. Click the Finish button.

Deleting a PIN or Picture Password

Once you've defined a PIN or picture password, you can always change or delete them later. To change or delete either a PIN or Picture password, follow these steps:

1. Follow steps 1-6 in the "Password Protecting a Computer" section to change password settings.

2. Click the Change or Remove button under the PIN or Picture password category, as shown in Figure 27-7. When removing a PIN, you may need to type in your password to verify this action.

⠿ PIN

You can use this PIN to sign in to Windows, apps, and services.

| Change | Remove |

I forgot my PIN

▨ Picture password

Sign in to Windows using a favorite photo

| Change | Remove |

Figure 27-7. Changing or removing a PIN or Picture password

Turning on the Firewall

Most malicious people won't have physical access to your computer, so it's far more common to sneak into your computer through the Internet instead. Every time you connect to the Internet, you're an open target for anyone around the world to hack into your computer.

To protect yourself when you're on the Internet, you need to turn on the firewall. A firewall essentially acts like a locked door that keeps hackers on the Internet from getting into your computer. Without a firewall, anyone on the Internet can get into your computer so it's crucial that you turn on your firewall.

Generally, if you turn on your firewall, you'll rarely have a reason to turn it off, so once you turn on the firewall, leave it on. Windows 10 turns the firewall on by default, but you may want to turn it off to use a different firewall, or you may need to turn it on in case someone else may have turned it off.

To turn on the firewall, follow these steps:

1. Right-click the Windows icon. A pull-down menu appears, as shown in Figure 27-8.

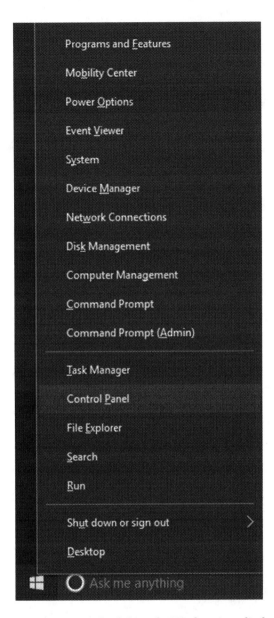

Figure 27-8. *Right-clicking the Windows icon displays a menu*

2. Click Control Panel. The Control Panel window appears, as shown in Figure 27-9.

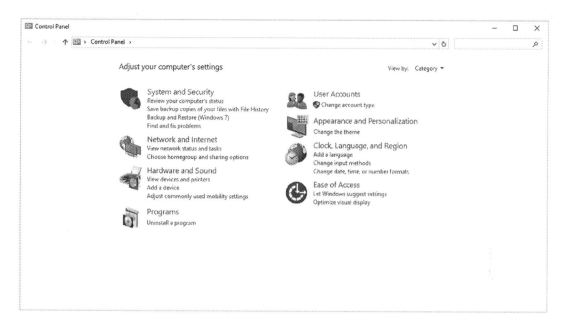

Figure 27-9. *The Control Panel window*

3. Click System and Security. The System and Security window appears, as shown in Figure 27-10.

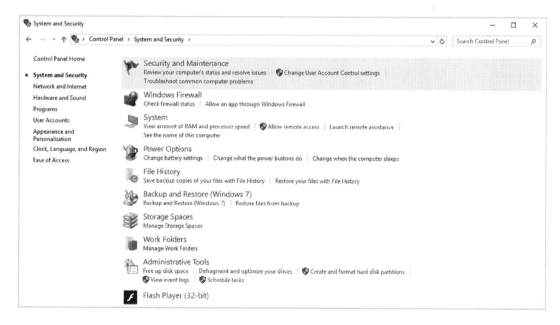

Figure 27-10. *The System and Security window*

4. Click Windows Firewall. The Windows Firewall window appears, showing you the current firewall settings, as shown in Figure 27-11.

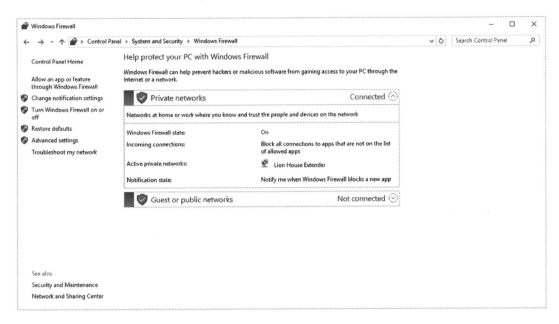

Figure 27-11. *The Windows Firewall window*

5. Click Turn Windows Firewall on or off in the left pane. The Customize Settings window appears, as shown in Figure 27-12.

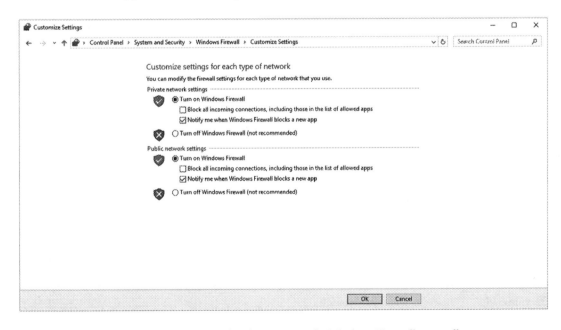

Figure 27-12. *The Customize Settings window lets you turn the Windows Firewall on or off*

6. Type your password and click the Unlock button.

7. Select the Turn on/Turn off Windows Firewall radio button for either or both private networks and public networks.

8. Click OK.

9. Click the close button (the X icon) in the upper right corner of the window to close it.

Using Windows Defender

Password protecting your computer can stop someone from installing malware on your computer and firewalls can block malicious hackers from sneaking malware on to your computer over the Internet. However, it's still possible to get tricked into installing malware.

Many malicious hackers set up booby trapped web sites that are similar to popular web sites. For example, instead of typing the correct microsoft.com, you might misspell it such as mircosoft.com. Because it's so easy to misspell a domain name, hackers can set up a malicious web site to look like the popular web site. The moment you visit a malicious web site, you could click a link that actually installs malware on your computer without your knowledge.

Other times malicious hackers may send you e-mail claiming you need to click a link or file attachment. If you follow the directions of this unsolicited e-mail, you might accidentally install malware on your computer.

The best way to protect yourself from malicious web sites is to type a domain address carefully and check its spelling before visiting the site. Then if it's a site you plan on visiting often, bookmark the site so you can safely visit that site in the future.

Of course, it's not always possible to avoid malicious web sites because sometimes hackers booby trap legitimate web sites as well. Because you can never be too safe on the Internet, expect that malware may slip on to your computer eventually and take the steps to prevent that.

To guard against this likelihood, Windows 10 comes with Windows Defender, an anti-malware program that can scan your computer for malware and wipe it out. Although Windows Defender works in the background to scan your computer, you may want to scan your computer periodically just to make sure your computer is free from malware.

To work, Windows Defender relies on a database of known malware. Since malicious hackers create malware every day that Windows Defender may not know about, you should update the Windows Defender database (called its definitions) periodically to make sure you're protected against the latest malware.

Updating Windows Defender's Database

You need to keep Windows Defender's database (definitions) up to date to ensure it can catch and delete the latest malware infecting Windows computers. If you fail to update Windows Defender's database, you'll risk thinking your computer is free of malware while it may actually be infected by newer malware.

To use Windows Defender, follow these steps:

1. Click the Windows icon and click Windows Defender in the Windows System category, as shown in Figure 27-13. The Windows Defender window appears.

Figure 27-13. *Finding Windows Defender on the Start menu*

2. Click the Update tab. The Update tab lists the latest definitions used to defend your computer, as shown in Figure 27-14.

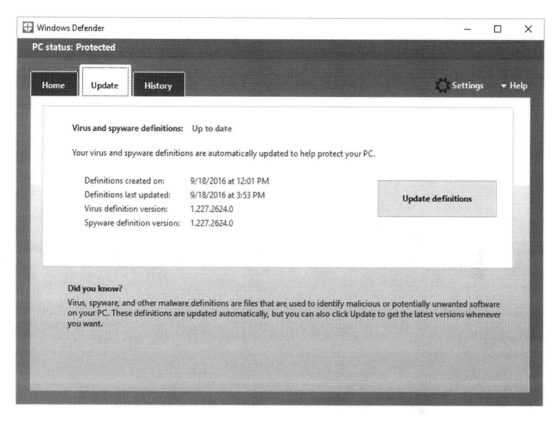

Figure 27-14. *Viewing a list of Windows Defender's latest malware definitions*

3. Make sure your computer is connected to the Internet and then click the Update definitions button.

Checking for Malware with Windows Defender

Once you've updated the malware database for Windows Defender, you might want to scan your computer to make sure it isn't infected by any malware. You can choose between three types of scanning options:

- *Quick*: Scans only the most common places where malware can hide

- *Full*: Scans the entire hard disk

- *Custom*: Lets you define the folders to scan

The Quick scan option is much faster than the Full scan option, but not as comprehensive. You should perform a Full scan periodically and then use Quick scan most of the time. If you suspect malware might be located in a specific folder, then use Custom scan.

▓ **Note**   Windows Defender can never detect all possible malware, so it's possible that Windows Defender will say your computer is clean but it could really be infected by malware. For maximum protection, you may want to install a second anti-malware program and run both anti-malware programs periodically.

To scan your computer using Windows Defender, follow these steps:

1. Click the Windows icon and click Windows Defender in the Windows System category (see Figure 27-13). The Windows Defender window appears.

2. Click the Home tab, as shown in Figure 27-15.

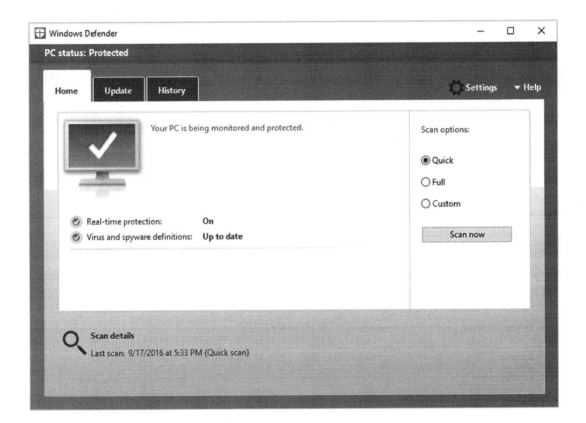

Figure 27-15. *Choosing a scanning option*

3. Click the Quick, Full, or Custom radio button under the Scan options category.

4. Click the Scan now button.

Summary

The best computer security starts with you. Don't visit suspicious web sites, don't open file attachments from strangers, and don't believe phony e-mail messages from seemingly legitimate organizations. In other words, trust no one on the Internet.

At the very least, password protect your computer so nobody but you can use it. Then make sure the Windows 10 firewall is turned on to block malicious hackers from breaking into your computer over the Internet.

Finally, run Windows Defender periodically to scan for malware and make sure you keep the Windows Defender database up to date so it can catch the latest malware.

Ultimately, the best form of security is knowing how malware might attack your computer and then taking steps to minimize the risk. You'll never be completely free from attacks, but you can always do whatever is possible to make your computer a little harder for hackers and malware to attack.

CHAPTER 28

▓ ▓ ▓

Maintaining Your Computer

If you bought a car and never changed its oil, checked its tire pressure, or refilled its radiator, eventually the car will fail. The same holds true with computers. Just because a computer may work perfectly when you first get it doesn't mean that it will continue to work unless you take some time periodically to maintain it.

One way to keep your computer running smoothly is to install the latest Windows updates. Updates typically fix problems with Windows and offer additional features. However, updates can occasionally keep certain programs from working or even wreck a computer altogether.

Despite these problems, it's generally a good idea to update Windows periodically for greater security and reliability. To protect against catastrophic update problems, you should diligently make backups of your most critical files.

Besides updates, another common maintenance task involves keeping your hard disk optimized. The more programs and data you store, the more cluttered your hard disk can get. Eventually a hard disk can get cluttered with so much data that the computer will take a lot of time to find anything. To fix this problem, you may need to clean up and defragment your hard drive periodically to maximize the efficiency of your hard disk.

Maintaining your computer isn't difficult, but it is something you'll need to do on a regular basis. As long as you regularly maintain your computer, your computer should continue working whenever you need it.

Updating Windows

Microsoft recommends that you install updates whenever they're available. While flawed updates can cause problems, the latest updates also increase the security and reliability of your computer. For that reason, you should make backups of your critical files before updating Windows.

Usually after an update, Windows will need to reboot your computer. Since this can take time, you probably don't want to install an update and reboot your computer during the day when you need to use it. To avoid this problem, you can schedule times when Windows 10 will not update itself.

To modify the update schedule of Windows 10, follow these steps:

1. Click the Windows icon. The Start menu appears.

2. Click Settings. The Settings window appears.

3. Click Update & security. The update settings window appears.

4. Click Windows Update in the left pane. Various update settings appear, as shown in Figure 28-1.

© Wallace Wang 2016
W. Wang, *Absolute Beginners Guide to Computing*, DOI 10.1007/978-1-4842-2289-8_28

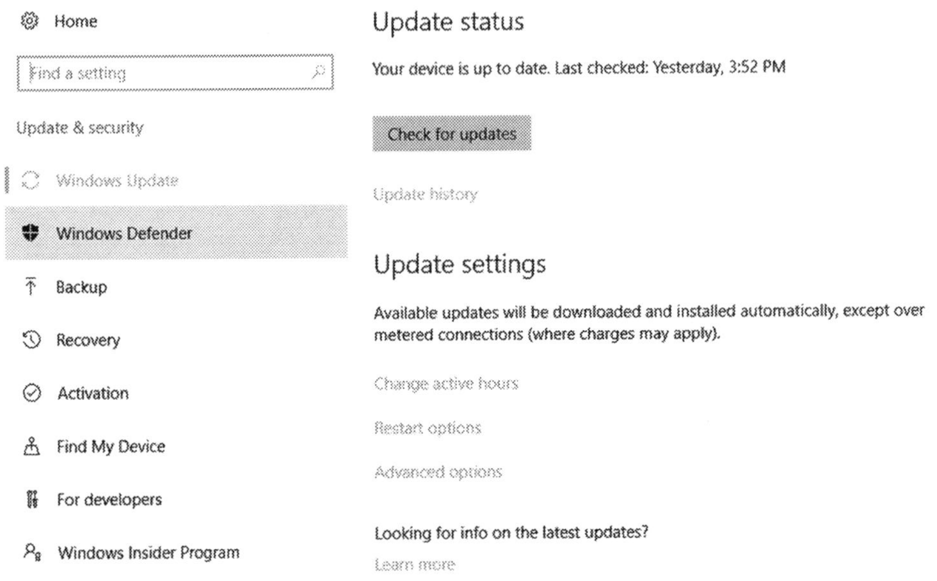

Figure 28-1. *The Update settings*

5. Click Change active hours under the Update settings category. An Active hours window appears, letting you define the start and end times when you do not want Windows to restart and update, as shown in Figure 28-2.

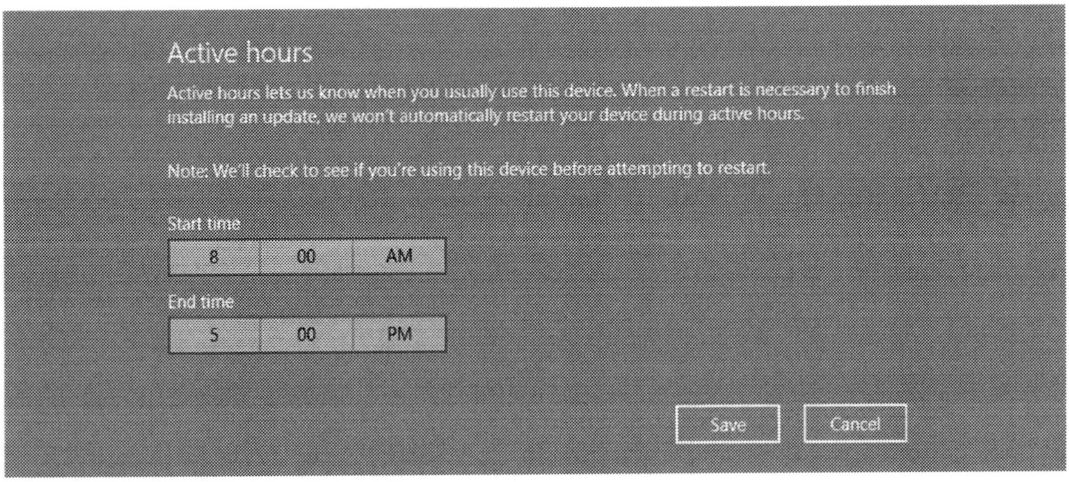

Figure 28-2. *Defining active hours for not updating Windows*

6. Click in the Start and End time boxes and define a new starting and ending time for when you'll likely be using your computer.

7. Click the Save button

8. Click the Check for updates button if you want to update your computer.

Optimizing the Hard Disk

If you dumped your clothes in a big pile on the floor, you would likely have a hard time finding a particular outfit to wear later. That's why most people hang their clothes in a closet or fold their clothes and organize them in drawers.

Unfortunately, your computer isn't always so neat. Each time you store data on your hard disk, Windows 10 stores that data in the first available spot it can find. Eventually as you save and delete data, your data may not be stored neatly anymore. Instead, you may have gaping holes where you deleted old files. Such gaps mean that Windows 10 must skip over them when searching for particular data.

When a hard disk no longer stores files neatly, that's called fragmentation. The longer you use a computer, the more your files will get deleted and modified, creating larger and larger gaps between files. To speed up your computer, you need to defragment your computer.

Another problem is that as you use a computer, many programs create and save temporary files on the hard disk. When you stop using many programs, they leave these temporary files behind. Eventually, these numerous temporary files can start cluttering up your hard disk and prevent you from saving important data instead.

To fix this problem, you need to clean up your hard disk periodically. Such a disk clean up deletes temporary files that are no longer needed, which frees up more space and makes your computer run a little faster.

By defragmenting your hard disk and cleaning up unnecessary files from your hard disk, you can make your hard disk run as efficiently as possible.

Defragmenting a Hard Disk

You can manually defragment a hard drive or schedule Windows 10 to defragment a hard drive automatically at fixed intervals. To defragment a hard drive, follow these steps:

1. Click the Windows icon. The Start menu appears.

2. Click Defragment and Optimize Drives under the Windows Administration Tools category. The Optimize Drives window appears, as shown in Figure 28-3.

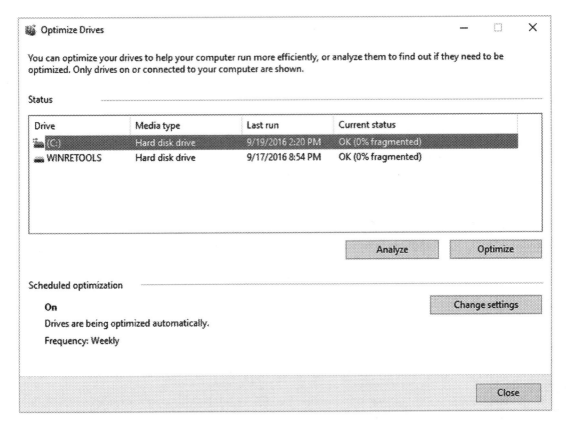

Figure 28-3. *The Optimize Drives window*

3. Click a drive you want to defragment and click Analyze to determine whether you need to defragment the hard drive, or click Optimize to start defragmenting immediately.

4. (Optional) Click the Change settings button. An Optimization schedule dialog box appears, as shown in Figure 28-4.

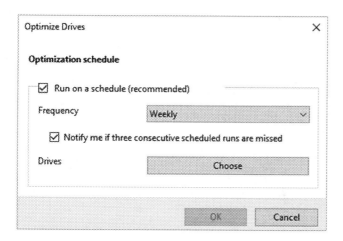

Figure 28-4. *The Optimization schedule dialog box*

5. Make any changes to the optimization schedule such as defining which drives to defragment and when.

6. Click OK.

Cleaning Up a Hard Disk

Ideally, it is best to get the largest hard disk possible for your computer. If you ever run out of space, you can always buy external hard drives to connect to your computer, but no matter how large your hard drive may be, it's always best to clean up unnecessary files periodically.

To clean up files on a hard drive, follow these steps:

1. Click the Windows icon. The Start menu appears.

2. Click Disk Cleanup under the Windows Administration Tools category. The Disk Cleanup window appears, as shown in Figure 28-5.

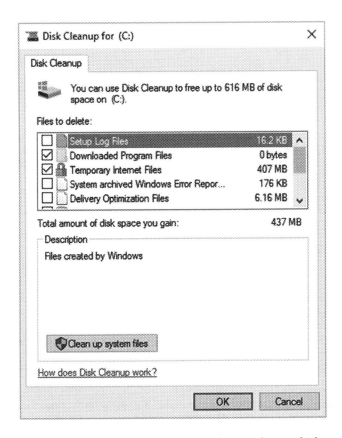

Figure 28-5. *The Disk Cleanup window lets you choose which types of files to delete*

3. Click the check boxes to select the different files to delete. In most cases, you can safely select all these types of files to delete.

4. Click OK. A dialog box asks if you're sure you want to delete the selected files.

5. Click the Delete Files button. The Disk Cleanup program deletes those chosen files.

Uninstalling Programs

The more you use your computer, the more likely you'll install new programs. Eventually you may find that you don't use some programs at all. In that case, you can uninstall that program to free up space on your hard disk for storing more data or newer programs that you will use more often.

▒ **Note**   Unlike ordinary files that you can delete, never delete a program file directly from the File Explorer program. That's because most programs consist of several files, so you need to delete all files that make up that single program.

The simple way to uninstall a program is to right-click that program name in the Start menu. However, there are often other programs installed on your computer that do not appear on the Start menu. For a more comprehensive way to uninstall programs, follow these steps:

1. Right-click the Windows icon. A menu appears.

2. Click Programs and Features. The Program and Features window appears, as shown in Figure 28-6.

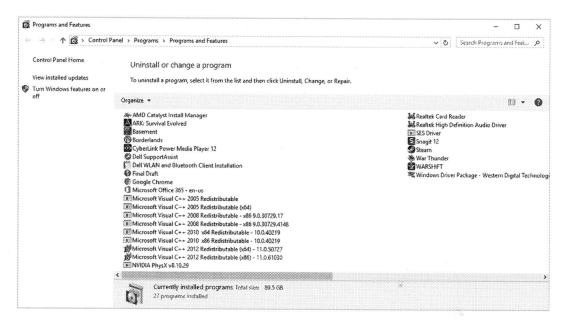

Figure 28-6. *Program and Features window lists all programs installed on your computer*

3. Click the program you want to uninstall.

4. Click the Uninstall button.

▒ **Note**   If you click the Repair button, you can restore a program back to its original default settings. The Repair option can be handy in case a program suddenly stops working correctly.

Summary

Most people don't do basic maintenance on their car because it's easier to just pay someone else to do that work instead. Likewise, it's often easier to let a computer technician worry about maintaining your computer. However, if you just perform simple maintenance tasks periodically, you'll greatly improve the chances of your computer working properly the next time you need it.

Windows 10 includes several basic maintenance tools, but you may want to buy third-party maintenance tools for more comprehensive features such as recovering deleted files that have been erased long ago or cleaning up the Windows registry file that contains information about every program installed on your computer. Over time, the Windows registry can get scrambled, which means your computer will run slower. By buying third-party software, you can often improve the performance of your computer in ways that the standard Windows 10 maintenance tools can't match.

Maintaining a computer isn't difficult. Just set aside some time on a regular basis, such as once every two weeks, and you'll be rewarded with a reliable computer. The more often you maintain your computer, the more likely your computer will run properly over time.

Index

© Wallace Wang 2016
W. Wang, *Absolute Beginners Guide to Computing*, DOI 10.1007/978-1-4842-2289-8

Get the eBook for only $4.99!

Why limit yourself?

Now you can take the weightless companion with you wherever you go and access your content on your PC, phone, tablet, or reader.

Since you've purchased this print book, we are happy to offer you the eBook for just $4.99.

Convenient and fully searchable, the PDF version enables you to easily find and copy code—or perform examples by quickly toggling between instructions and applications.

To learn more, go to http://www.apress.com/us/shop/companion or contact support@apress.com.